The Giant Buddhas of Bamiyan
Safeguarding the Remains

INTERNATIONAL COUNCIL ON MONUMENTS AND SITES
CONSEIL INTERNATIONAL DES MONUMENTS ET DES SITES
CONSEJO INTERNACIONAL DE MONUMENTOS Y SITIOS
МЕЖДУНАРОДНЫЙ СОВЕТ ПО ВОПРОСАМ ПАМЯТНИКОВ И ДОСТОПРИМЕЧАТЕЛЬНЫХ МЕСТ

THE GIANT BUDDHAS OF BAMIYAN

SAFEGUARDING THE REMAINS

edited by Michael Petzet

in cooperation with RWTH Aachen (Michael Jansen) and TU München (Erwin Emmerling)

with contributions from Catharina Blänsdorf, Ilaria Bonaduce, Maria Perla Colombini, Ulrich J. Dahlhaus, Erwin Emmerling, Edwin Fecker, H. Albert Gilg, Pieter M. Grootes, Jan-Eric Grunwald, Michael Jansen, Christian Manhart, Claudio Margottini, Edmund Melzl, Sekander Ozad-Seradj, Michael Petzet, Stephanie Pfeffer, Bert Praxenthaler, Pierre Smars, Laura Thiemann, Georgios Toubekis, Florian Unold, Michael Urbat, Fritz Wenzel, Yazhou Zou and others

MONUMENTS AND SITES
MONUMENTS ET SITES
MONUMENTOS Y SITIOS

XIX

Monuments and Sites / Monuments et Sites / Monumentos y Sitios
edited by ICOMOS
Office: International Secretariat of ICOMOS, 49-51 rue de la Fédération, F-75015 Paris

Funded by the Federal Government Commissioner for Culture and the Media upon a Decision of the German Bundestag

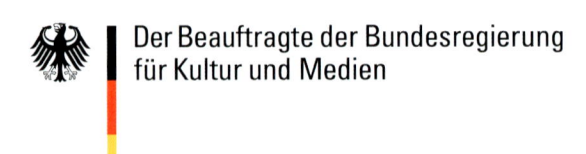

Der Beauftragte der Bundesregierung für Kultur und Medien

Front Cover: The feet of the Western Buddha seen from above [Photo: B. Praxenthaler 2009]
Back Cover: The cliff with the niche of the Eastern Buddha, [Photo: E. Emmerling 2009]
Inside Front Cover: Niche of the Western Buddha, [Photo: Y. Zou 2002]
Inside Back Cover: Niche of the Eastern Buddha with scaffolding, [Photo: E. Emmerling 2008]

Editorial Staff: Catharina Blänsdorf, Nora Eibisch, Melanie Eibl, Erwin Emmerling, Cristina Thieme, John Ziesemer

Picture Credits
ICOMOS would like to thank all authors for generously providing illustrations to this publication. Most photos were taken by members of the ICOMOS teams working in Bamiyan since 2002 (Jörg Fassbinder: p. 49; Edwin Fecker: pp. 103–105, 108, 110–115 top, 116 top, 145, 148–150, 152, 153, 171–173; Edmund Melzl: pp. 25–27, 84, 85; Michael Petzet: pp. 39, 42, 43, 65, 66, 75, 76, 88 bottom, 159 top, 161, 195; Bert Praxenthaler: pp. 67–72, 77–80, 86–88 top, 126–129, 138–144, 159 bottom, 163–169; Georgios Toubekis: pp. 117–121; Michael Urbat: pp. 57 left, 89–93, 96, 98–102, 130–133; Yazhou Zou: pp. 48, 50, 52–54), including the results of the cooperation with RWTH Aachen/Prof. Michael Jansen (pp. 44, 45, 51, 55, 57 right, 122, 123, 146, 151, 154–158; A. Fahim and Mario Santana: pp. 56, 58, 59; Pierre Smars and Ulrich J. Dahlhaus: pp. 60–63; Irmengard Mayer/TU Wien: pp. 115 bottom, 116 bottom), and the results of the cooperation with TU München/Prof. Erwin Emmerling (contributions by TUM: pp. 196–280, with illustrations by Catharina Blänsdorf, Edmund Melzl, and other authors). The illustrations on pp. 175–193 were kindly provided by Claudio Margottini. Further photo credits can be found in the captions.

ISBN: 978-3-930388-55-4   © 2009 ICOMOS – published by hendrik Bäßler verlag · berlin

Contents

Greeting by *Dr. S.M. Raheen*, Minister of Information and Culture 9
Greeting by *Habiba Sarabi*, Governor of Bamiyan. 11
Preface (*Michael Petzet*) 13

I THE GIANT BUDDHA STATUES IN BAMIYAN 17

Catharina Blaensdorf, Michael Petzet
Description, History and State of Conservation before the Destruction in 2001 17

II AFGHANISTAN – HERITAGE AT RISK 36

Christian Manhart
The Destruction of the Buddha Statues in March 2001 and the First UNESCO Activities 37

III ICOMOS ACTIVITIES 2002–2009 41

Report 2002 41

Michael Petzet
The first ICOMOS mission to Kabul and Bamiyan (12–21 July 2002) 43

Michael Petzet
Anastylosis or Reconstruction – Considerations on a Conservation Concept for the Remains
of the Buddhas of Bamiyan (2002) 46

Yazhou Zou, Florian Unold
First Considerations on the Stability of the Buddha Niches and their Stone Material 52

Recommendations of the First Expert Working Group on the Preservation of the Bamiyan Site,
Munich, 21–22 November 2002 54

Report 2003 55

Pierre Smars, Ulrich J. Dahlhaus
Mission to Bamiyan, October to December 2003 60

Recommendations of the Second UNESCO/ICOMOS Expert Working Group on the Preservation
of the Bamiyan Site, Munich, 18–20 December 2003 64

Report 2004 65

Bert Praxenthaler
Report on Salvaging Rock Fragments, 2004 66

Recommendations of the Third Expert Working Group on the Preservation of the Bamiyan Site,
Tokyo, 18–20 December 2004 74

Report 2005 75

Bert Praxenthaler
Report on Salvaging Rock Fragments, 2005 77

Fritz Wenzel
Options for an Anastylosis of the Buddha Statues in Bamiyan, 2005 81

Recommendations of the Fourth Expert Working Group on the Preservation of the Bamiyan Site, Kabul,
7–10 December 2005 82

Report 2006 84

Bert Praxenthaler
Report on Salvaging Rock Fragments, 2006 86

Michael Urbat, Jens Aubel
A Combined Geological and Paleomagnetic Approach towards the Repositioning of Fragments from the
Buddha Statues, 2006 89

Edwin Fecker
Report on Rock Mechanical Aspects Concerning the Eastern Buddha Niche, 2006 103

Georgios Toubekis
3D Laser Scanning and Post-Processing of the Niche of the Eastern Buddha, 2006 117

Michael Jansen
Presentation of the Cultural Master Plan Bamiyan (Kabul, 31 July / Bamiyan, 2 August 2006) 123

Recommendations of the Fifth Expert Working Group on the Preservation of the Bamiyan Site, Aachen,
14–16 December 2006 125

Report 2007 126

Bert Praxenthaler
Report on Salvaging Rock Fragments, 2007 127

Michael Urbat
Combined Geological and Paleomagnetic Analyses of the Back Plane of the Eastern Buddha Niche, 2007 130

Report 2008 134

Recommendations of the Sixth Expert Working Group on the Preservation of the Cultural Landscape
and Archaeological Remains of the Bamiyan Valley, NRICPT, Tokyo, 20–21 January 2008 134

Recommendations of the Seventh Expert Working Group on the Preservation of the Cultural Landscape
and Archaeological Remains of the Bamiyan Valley, Munich, 12–13 June 2008 135

Bert Praxenthaler
Report on Safeguarding the Remains of the Buddha Statues, 2008 137

Edwin Fecker
Report on Preservation Measures in the Eastern Buddha Niche, 2008 145

Report 2009 159

Erwin Emmerling
Conservation Concept for the Relief of the Eastern Giant Buddha and the Back Wall 160

Michael Petzet
Six Additional Tasks for 2009/2010. 160

Bert Praxenthaler
Report on Safeguarding the Remains of the Buddha Statues, 2009 163

Edwin Fecker
Report on Stabilisation Measures in the Eastern Buddha Niche, 2009 170

Claudio Margottini
**IV THE CONSOLIDATION AND STABILIZATION OF THE BUDDHA NICHES AND THE
    CLIFF IN BAMIYAN (2003/04; 2006)** **175**

**V THE MUNICH RESEARCH PROJECT ON FRAGMENTS OF THE GIANT BUDDHAS
    OF BAMIYAN (2007-2009)** **197**

Introduction (*Catharina Blaensdorf*) 197

Catharina Blänsdorf, Edmund Melzl
Technique of Modelling the Buddha Statues 201

Catharina Blänsdorf, Stephanie Pfeffer, Edmund Melzl
Identification of Wood Species 215

Stephanie Pfeffer, Catharina Blänsdorf
Materials Made of Plant Fibres: Ropes and Textile Fragment. 217

H. Albert Gilg, Catharina Blänsdorf, Eva Höfle, Laura Thiemann
Mineralogical Investigations on Loam Plaster Fragments of the Destroyed Buddha
Statues at Bāmiyān, Afghanistan. 219

Stephanie Pfeffer, Catharina Blänsdorf
Organic Additives of the Clay Layers: Plant Materials 227

Jan-Eric Grunwald
Organic Additives of the Clay Layers: Hair Identification 229

*Catharina Blänsdorf, Marie-Josée Nadeau, Pieter. M. Grootes, C. Matthias Hüls,
Stephanie Pfeffer, Laura Thiemann*
Dating of the Buddha Statues – AMS 14C Dating of Organic Materials 231

Catharina Blänsdorf, Stephanie Pfeffer, Edmund Melzl
The Polychromy of the Giant Buddha Statues in Bāmiyān. 237

Ilaria Bonaduce, Marcello Cito, Maria Perla Colombini, Anna Lluveras
The Characterisation of the Organic Binders 265

Niche of the Western Buddha, view from above
△ Photo: 13 October 2004

▽ Photo: 7 September 2005

△ Photo: 19 June 2007

▽ Photo: 25 October 2008

▽ Photo: 3 July 2006

▽ Photo: 7 July 2009

Islamic Republic of Afghanistan
Ministry of Information and Culture

The magnificent symbols of Ghandara art, the Great Statues of Buddha in Bamiyan, are not only symbols of pride for Afghans but indeed they belong to all humanity.

Unfortunately, these great heritage monuments were destroyed by enemies of our great history and rich culture.

With commendable support since 2002 from our international partners including ICOMOS, UNESCO, Japan and Germany, effective efforts were made to study and research the possibility of the restoration and reconstruction of the statues.

This publication provides details of all the efforts made including the research actvities, scientific studies and recommendations of the Expert Group Meetings initiated by ICOMOS and UNESCO.

I keenly look forward to this publication opening new chapters and helping us all in finding scientific ways towards the restoration of these great sites.

I thank Michael Petzet, President of ICOMOS, for his commendable efforts in safeguarding the remains of the Bamiyan Buddhas and wish him further success.

Dr. S.M. Raheen

Minister of Information and Culture
Islamic Republic of Afghanistan

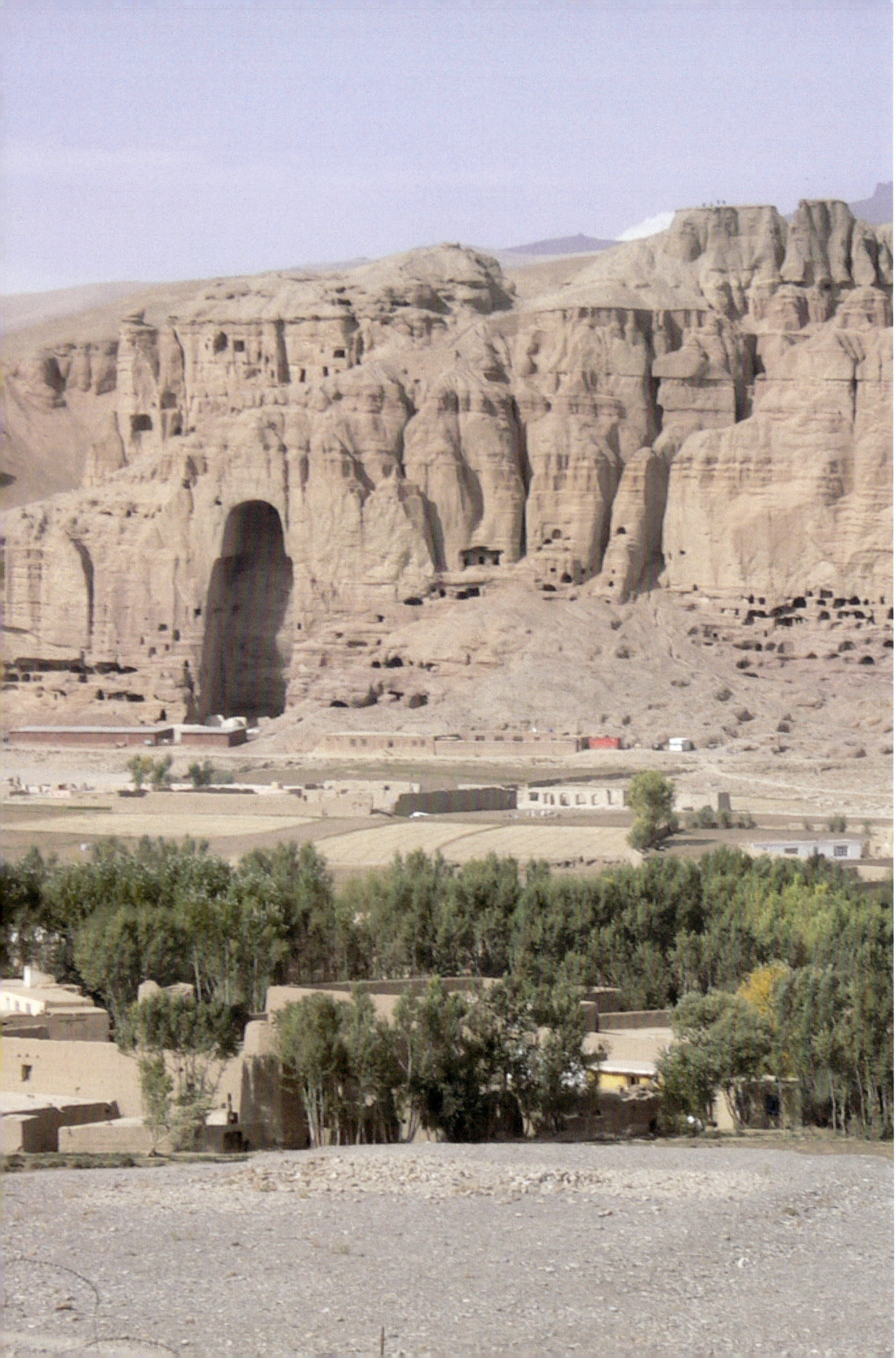

Islamic Republic of Afghanistan
Independent Directorate of Local Governance
Bamyan Province

It's a matter of pleasure that ICOMOS is publishing its volume XIX of the ICOMOS publication series "Monuments and Sites": Report on Safeguarding the Bamiyan Buddha Statues. At this juncture, firstly, I would like to take this opportunity to express my deepest gratitude and appreciation for the great work that ICOMOS has been doing from 2002 till now in safeguarding the remains of the Bamiyan Buddha sites. Bamyan is not only important for the people of Afghanistan but a window to look into the historic past of the evolution of civilizations across the Silk Route.

Appreciation and credit go to ICOMOS for their untiring work and valuable contribution towards restoring and safeguarding the world heritage site by providing the most experienced technical professionals and committed people. We acknowledge and appreciate all the efforts made by ICOMOS and individuals to safeguard the Buddha site even when the security situation was not so conducive in the country.

Secondly, one of the key achievements of ICOMOS has been in terms of raising hope among Afghans for rebuilding the Buddhas, at least one of the statues, by using the original remaining pieces and with external materials to exhibit it as one of the memorial monuments of the historic past and as witness to the cultural journey of glory and of painful suffering, including the destruction of the Buddhas. I strongly support the idea and initiatives to restore this rich cultural heritage.

I would also like to take this opportunity to thank and express my appreciation to the governments of Germany and Japan and to UNESCO for their continued support of ICOMOS for safeguarding the Buddha site.

It is worth mentioning that in addition to the Buddha site all historical monuments in Bamyan are in danger and need immediate attention and support from the International Community for safeguarding and preservation, for instance Shahr-e-Zuhak, GhulGhula City, Forty Tower, Kakarak Buddha Site, Gowhar Geen and Shahr-e-Sarkhoshak. I hope we will receive more support and assistance for safeguarding and restoring the rich cultural and natural heritage of Bamyan from friends and colleagues internationally, both individually and institutionally. I believe ICOMOS will serve as a forum to forge this partnership and initiative towards this cause.

As Governor of Bamyan and on behalf of the Provincial Government we wish to announce our full support towards safeguarding and restoring the rich cultural heritage of Bamyan, including restoration and preservation of the Budhha site.

I wish ICOMOS all the very best in their future endeavors and look forward to working together on our shared purposes.

Best Wishes,

Habiba Sarabi
Governor of Bamyan
09/12/2009

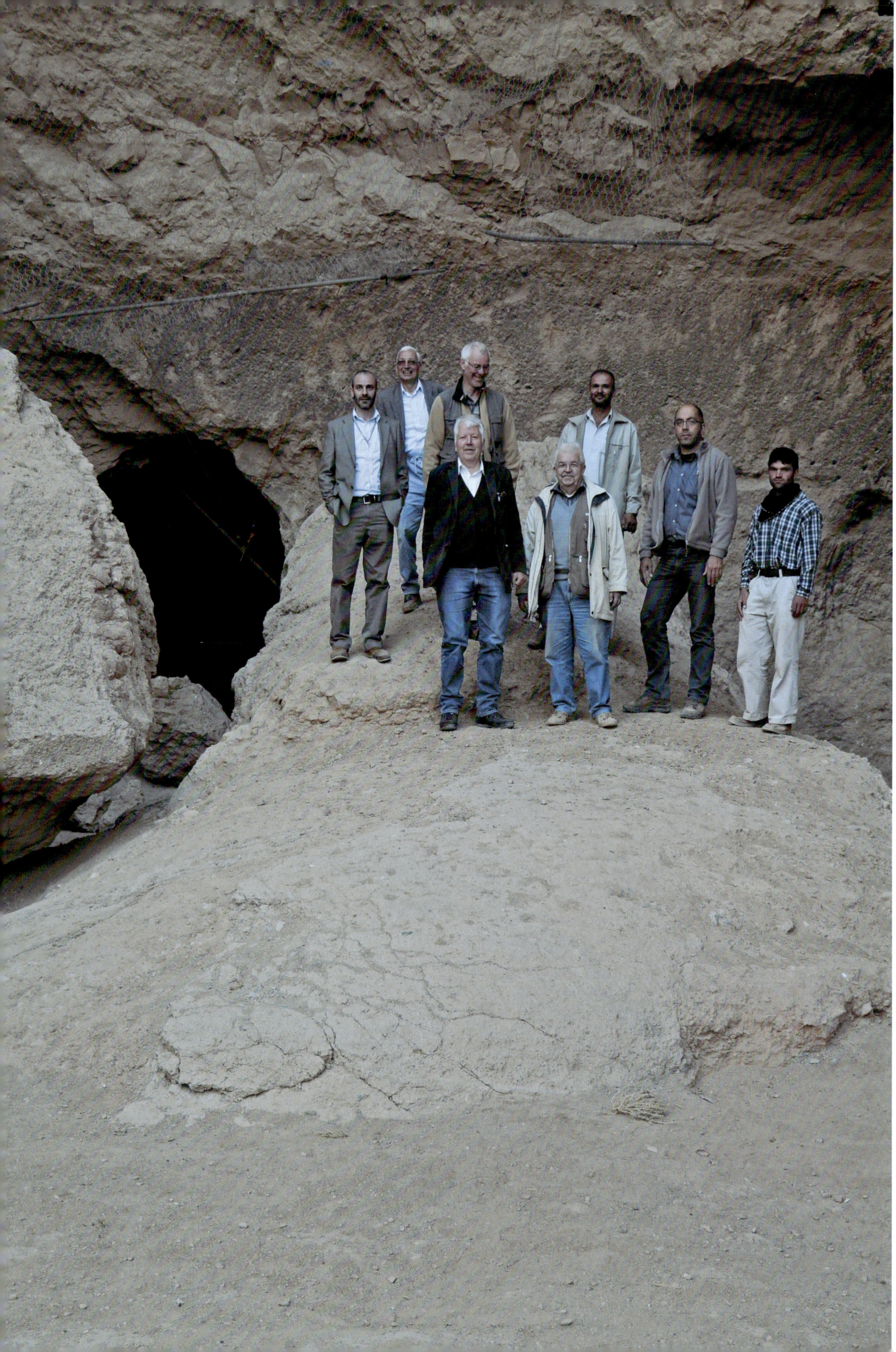

Preface

Thanks to funds provided by the German Foreign Office for rescuing cultural properties in Afghanistan our ICOMOS team, starting its first mission to Bamiyan and its work in Kabul (Babur Gardens) in 2002, has in the meantime made considerable progress in preventing further decay of the remains of the Bamiyan Buddhas, which were blown up by the Taliban in March 2001. Since 2004 when the back walls were secured against rock fall by means of wire nets approximately 2000 cubic metres of fragments have been recovered; not only sand and hopelessly deteriorated stone fragments, as was assumed immediately after the disaster, but identifiable small and large fragments weighing up to 60 tons. In the meantime, most of the fragments are stored in specially erected shelters to protect them against weathering. Now, the giant feet of the 55-metre Great Buddha (Western Buddha), originally hidden under a rubble heap, are once again visible, and the blocked caves in the backward part of the niche are again accessible. The back wall of the completely scaffolded niche of the 38-metre Small Buddha (Eastern Buddha) with original remains in situ is largely stabilised. In autumn 2010, this niche and the associated galleries could be presented to the public together with an exhibition of fragments in the partly reconstructed lower caves as a first important step of the safeguarding measure. Apart from two sensational finds of Buddhist relics thousands of plaster fragments from the surfaces of both statues were recovered and from the scientific investigation of these and other remains a wealth of scientific insights was gained, helping to date the statues in the period between the mid-6th to the early 7th centuries AD. As under the present circumstances the work of the ICOMOS team cannot be completed yet, this volume XIX of the ICOMOS series Monuments and Sites is not to be considered a final conservation report on the safeguarding of the two Buddha statues. Instead it is meant as a first work report, to which a great number of authors kindly made contributions.

As the safeguarding of the remains of the Bamiyan Buddhas is a project that receives worldwide attention, speculations have occurred time and again about a possible "reconstruction" of the Buddha statues and there have also been discussions to which the public media and some artists have contributed with their ideas. After every loss ideas of reconstructing the state before the destruction suggest themselves. For all reflections of ICOMOS on this matter the international principles of conservation linked to the famous Venice Charter are fundamental. During the restoration between 1969 and 1976 the team of the Archaeological Survey of India (ASI) already worked in accordance with these principles and achieved good results. And of course, these results, if they were not destroyed during the blowing up in 2001, had to be included in the ICOMOS conservation concept. R. Sengupta wrote: It may be mentioned that in carrying out the restorations on the above-mentioned images and all the units at Bamiyan, the internationally accepted policy laid out in the 'Venice Charter' by the International Council on Monuments and Sites (as practised in India for many years) was strictly followed. In archaeological restorations, the mutilated images are not renewed, nor the missing paintings replaced with new ones. Our goal was to preserve the great works of art in their present forms by such measures that would stop further deterioration. Our intention was to respect the original artistic creation, as well as to preserve the whole gamut of its history as it is written across the monument. The various mutilations reflect both the material environment and the long period of history to which the sculptures have born witness (R. Sengupta, Restoration of the Bamiyan Buddhas, in: Klimburg-Salter (ed.): The Kingdom of Bamiyan, Buddhist Art and Culture of the Hindu Kush, Naples 1989, p. 205).

One of the criteria for the inscription of cultural properties in UNESCO's World Heritage List according to the 1972 Convention is that reconstruction is only acceptable if it is carried out on the basis of complete and detailed documentation on the original and to no extent to the conjecture (Operational Guidelines, 2005, paragraph 86). But independently of the scepticism of many colleagues concerning the various suggestions for a reconstruction of the Buddha statues the ICOMOS team since the first mission in 2002 focussed for the time being only on practical and technical solutions in order to secure with limited funds the existing remains threatened by final decay and to consolidate the rock structures and especially the traces of the Buddha statues still visible on the back walls of the niches.

Besides, the remains in situ and the piles of fragments were pointing at a conservation concept called anastylosis, which is common practice at many archaeological sites worldwide (for this and for the following remarks see my paper 'Anastylosis or Reconstruction – Considerations on a Conservation Concept for the Remains of the Buddhas of Bamiyan', pp. 46–51). The method of anastylosis, developed in the field of classical archaeology but also applicable for partially destroyed monuments of later epochs, is referred to in article 15 of the Venice Charter: Only anastylosis, that is to say, the reassembling of existing but dismembered parts can be permitted. The material used for integration should always be recognisable and its use should be the least that will ensure the conservation of a monument and the reinstatement of its form. This means in order to be able to show original fragments on their original location and in their original context as part of an anastylosis, there is of course a need for more or less extensive provisional structures. The limits of anastylosis are reached when the original fragments are too sparse and would appear on the provisional structure as a sort of 'decoration'. Anastylosis, an approach which can indeed help to protect original material in certain circumstances, also illustrates the special role of the fragment in archaeological heritage preservation.

In the case of the Bamiyan Buddhas an anastylosis seems the most obvious solution, because before the destruction by the Taliban the statues had only been partly preserved due to losses in previous centuries. Consequently, a complete reconstruction of the 'original' state which is unknown in important details (faces, arms, etc) is totally out of the question. Besides, the remains of the Buddhas as important witnesses to Afghan history could play an important role for future tourism, even in their fragmentary condition. In this sense the conservation concept for the Buddha statues has continuously been discussed with representatives of the Afghan government and with UNESCO since the first meeting of the Expert Working Group on the Preservation of the Bamiyan Site (Munich, 21–22 November 2002), for instance in 2005: *The experts welcome that the Afghan authorities acknowledge the possibility of an anastylosis as one well-established method of proper relocation of the rock fragments to their original position.* And in 2008 *the participants recommend for the long-term preservation of all fragments, a reversible step-by-step strategy reflecting the different location and the mass of existing material: the 'Big Buddha' has a large amount of massive fragments (up to 70 t), the 'Small Buddha' has original plaster surfaces and rock fragments in situ (right arm with robe, fragments of shoulders and head). The completed identification of all fragments can be considered as a first step. A second step would be the adequate semi-permanent storage of the documented material close to the Buddha niches, considering the possibilities of reassembling.* Moreover: *Consider further proposals for the technical possibilities of an anastylosis (refer to Article 15 of the Venice Charter) as a method of reassembling the fragments of the Buddha sculptures based on a re-evaluation of the specific, 'concrete' conditions. Different possibilities of reassembling individual fragments should be considered and be discussed by the Advisory Board at the appropriate time.*

Under these circumstances the concept of an anastylosis in fact remains in my opinion the only appropriate solution, not least because the alternative of a museum presentation does not seem to make much sense, given the gigantic masses of material. The flexible approach followed in the discussions of the Bamiyan Working Group opens up the possibility of a different treatment of both statues and their very fragile stone material. In addition, there is the step-by-step method and the chance for future generations to continue working on certain parts in the sense of a partial reconstruction. From case to case such step-by-step measures could open up different chances. The ICOMOS team for example only recently developed and tested a new conservation method for the fragile conglomerate stone of the cliff, – finally there is a chance to consolidate individual fragments permanently (see report Emmerling, p. 160).

In any case, it is of course the responsibility of the Afghan government, in coordination with UNESCO, to decide upon the overall concept for the World Cultural Heritage Bamiyan Valley and its monuments. In addition, in the surroundings of the monuments there remains the question how to preserve the authentic spirit of the place in the sense of the Nara Document (1994). This means it is also a matter of the so-called intangible (immaterial) values increasingly discussed in recent years in connection with the World Cultural Heritage. In the case of Bamiyan these values are fortunately guaranteed by a strong genius loci in a spectacular cultural landscape with witnesses of Buddhist and Muslim traditions contributing to the cultural wealth of present-day Afghanistan.

Of fundamental importance for the results of the work in Bamiyan, presented in vol. XIX of the Monuments and Sites series, was the good cooperation with RWTH Aachen and Prof. Michael Jansen and his team. Apart from the documentation of the Buddha niches they contributed to a databank of all monuments and sites in Afghanistan (see pp. 45 f.) and to an inventory of the cultural heritage of the Bamiyan Valley. They also worked out a cultural master plan for Bamiyan (pp. 122–124). Since 2007 ICOMOS has also been working closely with TU München and Prof. Erwin Emmerling and his team. Their research project on fragments, coordinated by Catharina Blänsdorf, is published here in chapter V (see pp. 197 ff.). Besides, I would like to point out our restorers Edmund Melzl and Bert Praxenthaler, who have been working successfully in Bamiyan for years, as well as Prof. Dr.-Ing. Edwin Fecker, Dr. Michael Urbat and Dipl.-Ing. Georgios Toubekis, who committed himself untiringly to this project in the first years, and since 2008 the Afghan architect Dipl.-Ing. Sekandar Ozod-Seradj with his engineer Nomohiyadin Zeada and the stonemason Mujtabah Mirzai (Atelier Prof. Dr. Michael Pfanner, ARGE Pfanner, Scheffau/Allgäu). For all geotechnical problems we could also rely on Prof. Claudio Margottini, who planned and supervised the emergency consolidation of the Buddha niches in the years 2003/04 and 2006 funded by UNESCO. I would also like to thank our Japanese colleagues Prof. Kosaku Maeda and Mr Kazuya Yamauchi, Japan Center for International Cooperation in Conservation (NRICPT), as well as restorer Yoko Taniguchi for the good cooperation we have had for years. Among the Afghan colleagues who have helped a lot with their advice I would like to name Mr Abdul Ahad Abassy (Director, Department of Historic Monuments), A. Wasay Feroozi (Director, Preservation of Cultural Heritage) and Mohammad N. Rasuli (Director, Institute of Archaeology).

H. E. Dr. S. Makhdoum Raheen, Minister of Information and Culture, selected me as member of the Council on the Rehabilitation and Preservation of Afghanistan's Cultural Heritage (letter of 10 December 2002) and I would like to emphasise the good cooperation with the different Afghan representatives at the meetings of the Bamiyan Working Group in the years 2002–2008: Mr Ghulam R. Yusufzai, Vice Minister of Information and Culture, Mr Omar Sultan, Deputy Minister for Culture, Mr Quiamuddin Djallalzada, Deputy Minister for Urban Development, and lately Deputy Minister Mohammad Zia. My special thanks for her exceptional commitment in preserving the cultural and natural heritage goes to Ms Habiba Sarabi, Governor of Bamiyan.

As advisory body of UNESCO and the World Heritage Committee ICOMOS has been working under the guidance of UNESCO in Afghanistan since the first International Seminar on the Rehabilitation of Afghanistan's Cultural Heritage (Kabul 2002, see p. 39). The then-Assistant Director-General for Culture, Mounir Bouchenaki, requested me to become UNESCO's scientific advisor for Bamiyan (letter of 22 August 2003). I also wish to thank Prof. Francesco Bandarin, Director of the World Heritage Center, and Mr Giovanni Boccardi, Chief of Unit, Asia and Pacific. In the first years Christian Manhart, supported by Ms Sarah Finke, then Ms Junko Okahashi and more recently Ms Junhi Han and Dr. Roland Lin have been important partners at UNESCO. Furthermore, at the UNESCO Kabul Office we have received support from Mr Masanori Nagaoka and Mr Brendan Cassar. In recent years the latter has helped a lot in managing our projects: Fortunately, in 2009/2010 ICOMOS is able to carry out further measures thanks to funds provided within the framework of phase III of the Japan-Fund-in-Trust project 'Safeguarding the Cultural Landscape and Archaeological Remains of the Bamiyan Valley, Afghanistan'.

I would like to thank all colleagues, members of staff and helpers who have been involved in safeguarding the remains of the Bamiyan Buddhas, especially the excellent team of workers from the Bamiyan region; sometimes up to 50 workers who took greatest care in tackling the difficult task of salvaging the fragments from the rubble. My thanks also include the local craftsmen and the teams of de-miners as well as the local representatives of MOIC. Time and again, the salvage work was interrupted by finds of ammunition (my special thanks to the PRT New Zealand for their help in removing the Russian aircraft bombs from the Western Buddha niche, see p. 84).

Finally, I wish to thank once again all sponsors, first and foremost the German Foreign Office for its long-standing financial support, the German Embassy in Kabul for frequent assistance and the German Federal Government Commissioner for Cultural Affairs and the Media for the generous support of this publication. I am also grateful to UNESCO, which has not only supported our project, but has actually coordinated it within the framework of international cooperation. This has also become evident through the very useful recommendations of the Bamiyan Working Group, the meetings of which ICOMOS has been able to host in Munich three times so far, in 2002, 2003 and 2008. We are also very indebted to the Messerschmitt Foundation and to its chairman, Dr. Hans-Heinrich von Srbik, for providing us with the big scaffold that has been put up in the Eastern Buddha niche (see figs. p. 159, 161).

Last but not least I would like to thank all authors of this publication, some of whom have also given us extensive picture material, as well as Ioana Cisek and John Ziesemer from the ICOMOS Germany office for their indispensable help. Nora Eibisch and Melanie Eibl together with Cristina Thieme were responsible for the layout of the lavishly illustrated publication, printed by Bäßler Verlag Berlin.

Munich, 1 December 2009
Prof. Dr. Michael Petzet
President of ICOMOS Germany

Eastern Buddha before the destruction [T. Higuchi 1983/84] ▷

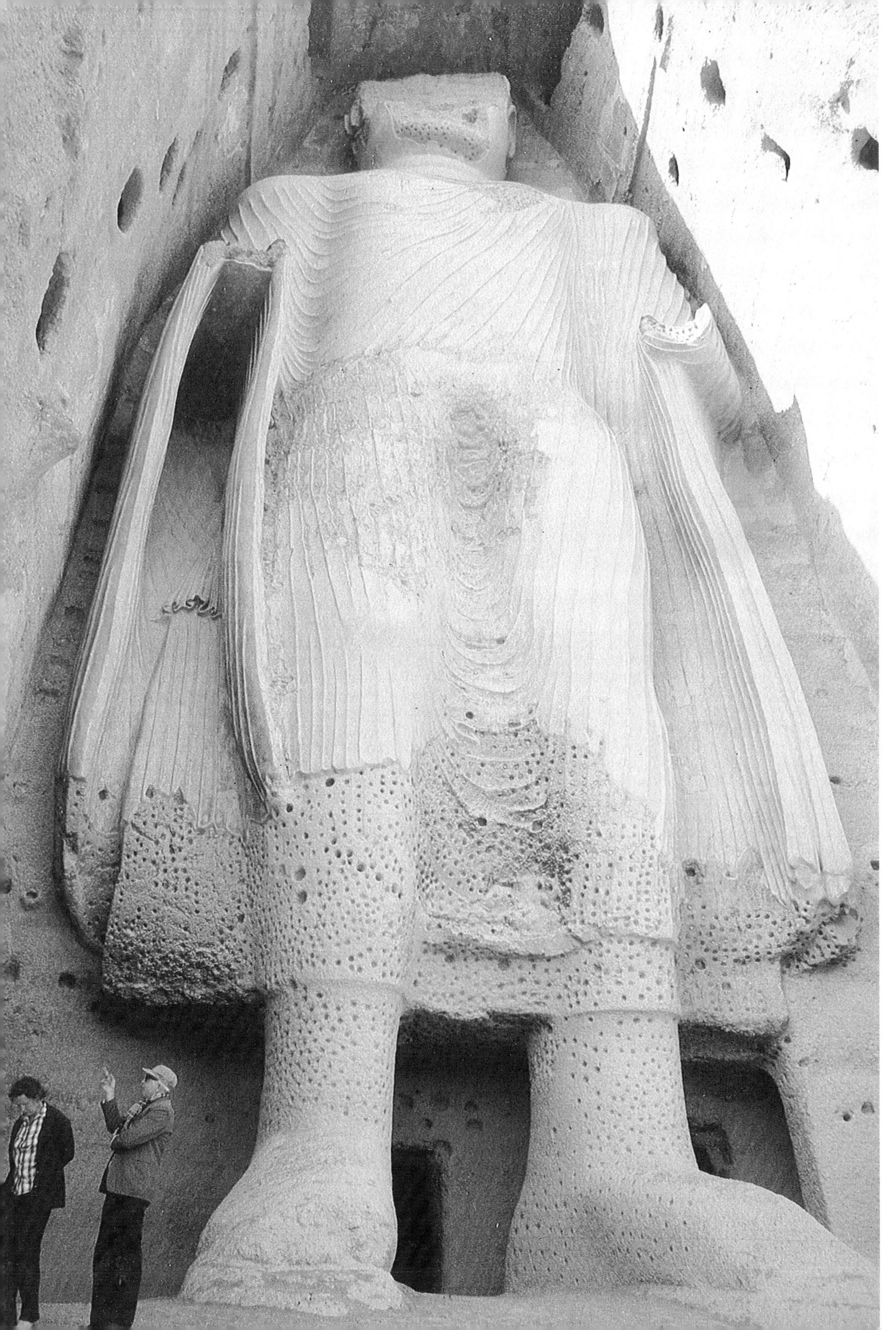

I THE GIANT BUDDHA STATUES IN BAMIYAN

Catharina Blänsdorf, Michael Petzet

Description, History and State of Conservation before the Destruction in 2001

The Bamiyan valley, 230 km northwest of Kabul and 2500 m above sea-level, separates the Hindu Kush from the Koh-i-Baba mountains. The city of Bamiyan is the centre of the valley and the largest settlement of the Hazarajat. From West to East, the Bamiyan river runs through the valley. The Cultural Landscape and Archaeological Remains of the Bamiyan Valley were inscribed on the World Heritage List in July 2003 and at the same time placed on the List of World Heritage in Danger:

The World Heritage Committee,

1. Inscribes the **Cultural Landscape and Archaeological Remains of the Bamiyan Valley, Afghanistan**, on the World Heritage List on the basis of cultural criteria (i), (ii), (iii), (iv) and (vi):

    Criterion (i): *The Buddha statues and the cave art in Bamiyan Valley are an outstanding representation of the Gandharan School in Buddhist art in the Central Asian region.*

    Criterion (ii): *The artistic and architectural remains of Bamiyan Valley, and an important Buddhist centre on the Silk Road, are an exceptional testimony to the interchange of Indian, Hellenistic, Roman and Sassanian influences as the basis for the development of a particular artistic expression in the Gandharan School. To this can be added the Islamic influence in a later period.*

    Criterion (iii): *The Bamiyan Valley bears an exceptional testimony to a cultural tradition in the Central Asian region, which has disappeared.*

    Criterion (iv): *The Bamiyan Valley is an outstanding example of a cultural landscape which illustrates a significant period in Buddhism.*

    Criterion (vi): *The Bamiyan Valley is the most monumental expression of the western Buddhism. It was an important centre of pilgrimage over many centuries. Due to their symbolic values, the monuments have suffered at different times of their existence, including the deliberate destruction in 2001, which shook the whole world.*

    The serial property contains the following elements: Bamiyan Cliff including niches of the 38 meter Buddha, seated Buddhas, 55 meter Buddha and surrounding caves, Kakrak Valley caves including the niche of the standing Buddha, Qoul-I Akram Caves in the Fuladi Valley, Kalai Ghamai Caves in the Fuladi Valley, Shahr-i-Zuhak, Qallay Kaphari A, Qallay Kaphari B, Shahr-i-Ghulghulah.

2. *Recommends that the State Party make every effort to guarantee an adequate legal framework for the protection and conservation of the Bamiyan Valley;*

3. *Further urges the international community and various organizations active in the field of heritage protection in the Bamiyan Valley to continue its co-operation and assistance to the Afghan authorities to enhance the conservation and protection of the property;*

4. *Recognizing the significant and persisting danger posed by anti-personnel mines in various areas of the Bamiyan Valley and noting the request from the Afghan authorities that all cultural projects include funds for demining;*

5. *Strongly encourages Member States, IGOs, NGOs, and other institutions to take this request into consideration when planning cultural heritage activities in the Bamiyan Valley, and to this end, appeals for financial and technical assistance for de- mining activities in the Valley;*

6. *Requests the Director-General of UNESCO to continue his efforts to effectively co-ordinate the various initiatives and activities benefitting the conservation process in the Bamiyan Valley, and in particular, ensure that the work of the World Heritage Committee and the Advisory Bodies are fully taken into account at the International Co-ordination Committee sessions and associated Working Groups;*

7. *Requests the World Heritage Centre and the Advisory Bodies to assist the Afghan authorities, in close co-operation with the UNESCO Kabul Office and the Division of Cultural Heritage, to elaborate a comprehensive and effective management plan for the Bamiyan Valley;*

8. *Requests a report on the state of conservation of the Bamiyan Valley to be submitted by the State Party with assistance from the World Heritage Centre, UNESCO Kabul and the Division of Cultural Heritage by 1st February 2004 for examination at the 28th session of the World Heritage Committee in 2004.*

The World Heritage Committee <u>decides</u> to inscribe **the Cultural Landscape and Archaeological Remains of the Bamiyan Valley, Afghanistan***, on the List of World Heritage in Danger.*[1]

Description of the Buddha statues

The giant Buddha sculptures of Bamiyan, the smaller Buddha probably dating back to the mid-6th century AD, the bigger one to the early 7th century (cf. the results of the C[14] examinations, pp. 231–236) are cut into the same cliff face with a distance of about 800 m between them. They were part of a large Buddhist complex with about 700 caves serving as sanctuaries, pilgrim hostels, and storage rooms. The Buddha niches were cut deep into the rock and may always have been open to the front.[2] The caves and tunnels in the rock and the niches of the Buddha statues were painted. Although the statues were neglected after the conversion of the region to Islam and partly damaged, large segments of the decoration survived.

The sculptures both show a standing Buddha. As the forearms are missing, an identification by the *mudras* (hand gestures) is not possible any more.[3] Western literature distinguishes, according to position or size, between an Eastern or Small Buddha (38 m tall) and a Western or Big Buddha (55 m tall).[4] Afghans identify the Eastern Buddha as *khink-but* (grey or moon white Buddha) and the Western one as *surkh-but* (red Buddha). These attributes are already mentioned in an Arab description of 1218[5] and a Latin text of 1700.[6] In the 18th century, local people identified them as a *female* and a *male* statue, in connection with tales probably reaching back several centuries.[7] Seen from a distance, the most characteristic difference is the shape of the niches: While that of the Eastern Buddha is straight, that of the Western Buddha shows recesses at the height of the shoulders, resulting in a trilobate shape.

Both sculptures were standing upright and composed in a completely frontal perspective. Originally, the forearms were sticking out horizontally to the front.[8] The upper garment, the *sangati* (or maybe a *kasaya*)[9], covered both shoulders and fell down to the shins. The thin fabric formed fine and regular ridges, clinging so close to the body that the anatomy was still visible.[10] Below the right forearms, in the recession formed by the edges of the *sangati* hanging over the arms, the lining of the *sangati* and parts of the undergarment (*uttarasanga*) could be perceived. On the Eastern Buddha, the undergarment protruded below the lower hem of the *sangati*.[11] The feet were bare. They seem to stand on flat ground, but the Indian team of restorers who worked there from 1969 to 1978, interpreted remnants found during their excavations as pedestals.[12] The hair was arranged in wavy curls, some strands have been preserved near the ears. A bulge at the top of the head may have indicated the *usnisa* (protuberance of the crane).[13] Even on the earliest sketches, the hands and the faces are missing. The peculiar fact that both faces are cut out above the mouths has raised many speculations. Today, the prevailing opinion is that the faces were cut out from the beginning, and that the upper part may have been fashioned as a wooden mask.[14] This would be a very unusual procedure, but there is no evidence for the faces having been destroyed.[15]

History of the Buddha statues

Already in Antiquity, the Bamiyan valley was important because it was situated on the route connecting the Silk Road and the southern countries such as India. From Northern India, Buddhism spread to the region of Bamiyan, at first under Asoka (3rd century BC), later on during the reign of the Kushan (1st to 3rd century AD). The giant clay Buddha statues from Surch Kotal and in Tajikistan are ascribed to this period.[16] The foundation of a Buddhist monastery in the Bamiyan valley is said to date back to the 2nd century BC.[17] It became an important centre of pilgrimage.[18]

Near Bamiyan, there are other Buddhist places of high cultural importance such as the Kakrak valley with a Buddha sculpture, which is 10 m tall, and caves dating from the 6th to 13th century, or the caves of Qoul-i Akram and Kalai Ghamai in the Fuladi valley.

Though stories and occasional descriptions of the Buddha statues can be traced back over centuries, very little is known about Bamiyan's Buddhist time. The most important historical description is included in the travel report *xi you ji* ('The Journey to the West') by the Chinese monk Xuanzang. On his way from Xi'an to India he passed through Bamiyan (*Fan yen na*) about 630 AD. He describes three giant sculptures near the convent: *To the north-east of the royal city there is a mountain, on the declivity of which is placed a stone figure of Buddha, erect, in height 140 or 150 feet. Its golden hues sparkle on every side, and its precious ornaments dazzle the eyes by their brightness. To the east of this spot there is a convent, which was built by a former king of the country. To the east of the convent there is a standing figure of Sâkya Buddha, made of metallic stone (teou-shih) in height 100 feet. It has been cast in different parts and joined together, and thus placed in a complete form as it stands. To the east of the city 12 or 13 li there is a convent, in which there is a figure of Buddha lying in a sleeping position, as when he attained 'Nirvâna'. The figure is in length about 1000 feet or so.*[19] This description refers to a standing Buddha of 45–50 m height, cut into the rock cliff, another standing Sakyamuni of 33 m height, made of 'metal-stone' and assembled from several parts[20], and a large lying Buddha (Parinirvana) of about 333 m length.

In 770, the region of Bamiyan became Islamic. In 870, a second Buddhism phase started. In 977, Islam irrevocably became the dominating religion in Bamiyan.

In 1218, Yakut al Hamawi described Bamiyan briefly in his geographic dictionary: *Bamiyan. This is the name of a city and an important district between Balkh and Ghaznah, settled between mountains, with one fortress. This city is small, but it is the main town in an extensive territory. Ten days of march separate it from Balkh and eight from Ghaznah. There you can admire a building supported by big pillars and covered with paintings representing all the birds created by God. There are two statues carved in the stone cliff and high from the base of the mountain until its top. One is called Surkhbud, the red statue, and the other Khinkbud the white statue. Nothing can be compared with these statues in the entire world.*[21] This was the last mentioning of the giant sculptures for a long time. Shortly afterwards, in 1221, Bamiyan was destroyed during the invasion of the Mongols under Genghis Khan: *[Coming] from Enderab, Genghiz Khan besieged Bamiyan, where the inhabitants sheltered themselves in its walls and fought with great courage. A son of Djaghatai Khan [Mutugan] was killed from an arrow during the battle. Genghiz Khan, full of anger for the loss of this young and particularly appreciated prince, ordered a general attack. The city was stormed and all its inhabitants were massacred without distinction in age or sex. The fortress was razed to the ground. The Khan gave to this place the name of maw-Baligh, that is Yaman Qal'a. Evil Place.*[22]

The rediscovery of the forgotten Buddha sculptures started in the 18th century. In 1700, they were mentioned by Thomas Hyde, who was the first European to mention them at all, based on Arab literal sources.[23] In the early 19th century, descriptions still based on hearsay, not on expeditions or any personal experience, were published, such as those by Wilford (1798 or 1801)[24] and by Elphinstone (1814).[25] In the 1830s, Europeans started to travel to Afghanistan as adventurers or during military campaigns. The first to visit Bamiyan probably were William Moorcroft and George Trebeck, who arrived there in 1824: *The figures stand in niches or recesses cut out of the rock, the upper part of which is arched, so as to form an alcove or vaulted canopy over the head of the figure; the sides advance so as to form wings, in which are staircases ascending to a gallery behind the neck of the statue, whilst other galleries run off from their sides, right and left, into the rock. The flights of steps of the larger image were so much decayed as to be inaccessible but one of those on the side on the smaller was tolerably entire, and led to the head of the figure. Both the figures have been damaged by order, it is said, of Aurangzeb.*[26] Alexander Burnes and Dr. Gérard visited Bamiyan in May 1832. Burnes described the statues and made a sketch (figs. 1, 2).[27] A precise drawing of the cliff with the Eastern Buddha was made by Charles Masson in 1832 or 1833 (fig. 3).[28] Sir Vincent Eyre, at that time prisoner of war in Afghanistan, produced several watercolour sketches in 1842 (figs. 4, 5).[29]

At that time, the knowledge about what the statues represented seems to have been completely lost. Locals did not know that they were Buddhas, neither did Westerners identify them as Buddhist art. Elphinstone, Burnes, Masson, and Ritter give evidence of rather clueless speculations. Elphinstone reports about the '*worship of Boodh*' and the story of the female and the male statue without recognising the connection to Buddhism. Burnes calls the traditions regarding '*the idols of Bamiyan*' '*vague and unsatisfactory*'. He refers to locals asserting that they were made in the Christian period, to explanations by Hindus, comparison to Buddhists and Jain art and Alexander's expeditions. He tends to see them as '*caprice of some person of rank, residing in this cave-digging neighbourhood*'[30], without deciding what they could be or trying to date them. Carl Ritter has summarized the knowledge obtained by the early travels to Bamiyan and the discussions about the '*But idols*' (fig. 2).[31]

In the late 19th century, a scientific interest in the statues arose starting with the publication by Talbot and Simpson who visited Bamiyan in 1885. Captain P. J. Maitland contributed sketches of the two Buddha statues (figs. 6–10) and interesting notes on Bamiyan: *The Bamian valley is about half a mile broad and well cultivated, but there is no town or even central agglomeration of houses, only small villages scattered up and down the valley. To the north is a fairly continuous wall of cliffs averaging about 300 feet in height; to the south is a central plateau separated by the glens called Dahaneh-i-Tajik and Dahanehi-Saidabad from the cliffs limiting the western and eastern part of the valley. On the edge of the central plateau is a small, conical, clayey hill, covered with the ruins of Ghulgulah. This is probably the ancient Bamian. The cliffs are everywhere pierced with numerous caves, but the greatest number is found on the north side of the valley, and here are also the famous idols, The But-i-Bamian. The cliffs round these are literally honeycombed with caves, which are found even in the debris slope at the bottom. They are almost all inhabited by Tajiks, or used as store rooms, and the entrance is frequently protected by a low mud wall.*

Facing the cliff the larger of the two big idols is to the left, the other to the right. They are about a quarter of a mile apart and supposed to be male and female, and their heights are respectively 180 and 120 feet. Their names are, as reported by former travellers, Sal Sal for the male and Shah Mameh for the female figure.

The idols are standing figures, sculptured in very bold relief in deep niches. Between the two large idols are, or rather were, two smaller ones, also in niches. These are equidistant from the large idols and from each other, that is to say, there is about 150 yards between each of the niches, large and small. One of the smaller niches is about 60 to 70 feet high, and is now empty, though a close inspection shows fragments of the idol that once filled it. The second small niche is still occupied by a sitting figure, which is about 40 feet high and known as the Bacheh, or child. The general shape of the niches is the same in all cases, but that of the large female figure is evidently unfinished, and the shoulders are not marked, nor the edges smoothed off.

The depth of the niches of the two large idols is about twice the thickness of the figures standing in them: the latter are therefore fairly well protected from the weather, and this accounts for their preservation, nearly all the damage done to them being due to the hand of man.

The whole interior of the niches, and particularly the arches over the heads of the idols, have been painted with what appears to be allegorical designs. Although much damaged, in fact, obliterated, where they could be easily got at, enough remains to show the general style of the work, which is exceedingly well executed, and forcibly reminds one of what is generally understood to be Byzantine art.

The idols themselves are rather clumsy figures, roughly hewn in the tough conglomerate rock, and afterwards thickly overlaid with stucco, in which all the details are executed. The whole arrangement clearly shows that this was not done at a later period, but is part of the original design of the figures. The stucco appears to have been painted, or at least paint was used in some places. The features of the figures

◁ Fig. 1

◁ Fig. 2

◁ Fig. 3

Fig. 4 ▷

Fig. 5 ▷

Fig. 6 ▷

Fig. 1   Alexander Burnes, 'The Colossal Idols, or Buts, of Bamian', in: Journal of the Asiatic Society of Bengal, 1833

Fig. 2   'Die Kolosse zu Bamiyan n. Al-Burnes Zeichnung', in: Carl Ritter, Die Stupa's (Topes) oder die architectonischen Denkmale an der Indo-Baktrischen Königsstraße und die Colosse von Bamiyan. Berlin 1838

Fig. 3   Charles Masson, sketch of the cliff with the Eastern Buddha, in: Journal of the Asiatic Society of Bombay, vol. V, 1836

Fig. 4   Vincent Eyre, sketch of the cliff with the Western Buddha, 1842

Fig. 5   Vincent Eyre, sketch of the cliff with the Eastern Buddha, 1842

Fig. 6. The Western Buddha, engraving after P. J. Maitland, in: The Illustrated London News, Nov. 6, 1886, p. 491

△ Fig. 7. The Eastern Buddha, engraving after P. J. Maitland, in: The Illustrated London News, Nov. 13, 1886, p. 535

▽ Fig. 8. View of the cliff with Eastern Buddha. M. G. Talbot and P. J. Maitland, The Rock-Cut Caves and Statues of Bamian, in: Journal of the Royal Asiatic Society XVIII, 1886

△ Fig. 9. Sketch of the Western Buddha. M. G. Talbot and P. J. Maitland, The Rock-Cut Caves and Statues of Bamian, in: Journal of the Royal Asiatic Society XVIII, 1886

▽ Fig. 10. Sketch of the Eastern Buddha. M. G. Talbot and P. J. Maitland, The Rock-Cut Caves and Statues of Bamian, in: Journal of the Royal Asiatic Society XVIII, 1886

△ Fig. 11. Military parade in front of the Western Buddha, in: The Graphic, January 6, 1894

△ Fig. 12. View of the Western Buddha, in: H. H. Hayden, Notes on some monuments in Afghanistan, Memoirs of the Asiatic Society of Bengal II, 1910

Fig. 13. View of the Western Buddha, photo taken by members of the Citroën Trans-Asiatic Expedition, in: The Illustrated London News, vol. 179, October 10, 1931, p. 557 ▷

have been purposely destroyed, and the legs of the larger one have been partly knocked away, it is said by cannon-shot fired at it by Nadir Shah. Both idols are draped in garments reaching to below the knee. The limbs and contour of the body show through, and the general effect of Muslin is excellently imitated in the stucco. The arms of both are bent at the elbow, the forearms and the hands projecting but the latter are now broken off. The feet have also been battered out of shape. Narrow stairways hewn in the interior of the rock lead up from cave to cave to the heads of the idols, and even to the summit of the hill.[32]

In 1894 a London magazine, The Graphic, published a picture showing a military parade on horseback in front of the colossus of the Western Buddha (fig. 11), a typographical reproduction probably using photographic material[33] and in 1895, the first photograph, showing the Eastern Buddha, was published.[34] In 1910, the British geologist H. H. Hayden published an article with a first series of photographs of the Bamiyan valley (fig. 12) and in the following decades the state of conservation of the Buddha statues is sometimes documented by souvenir photos made by tourists, for example the participants of the Citroën Transasiatic Expedition Beirut – Beijing of 1931 (fig. 13).

△ Fig. 14. M. Hackin, A. Godard and Y. Godard, view of the Western Buddha, in: Mémoires de la délégation archéologique française en Afghanistan, 1928

△ Fig. 16. M. Hackin, J. Carl, view of the cliff with the Eastern Buddha, in: Mémoires de la délégation archéologique française en Afghanistan, 1933

▽ Fig. 15. M. Hackin, A. Godard and Y. Godard, view of the Eastern Buddha, in: Mémoires de la délégation archéologique française en Afghanistan, 1928

▽ Fig. 17. M. Hackin, J. Carl, lower part of the Eastern Buddha, in: Mémoires de la délégation archéologique française en Afghanistan, 1933

Fig. 18. E. Melzl, Western Buddha, 1958 ▷

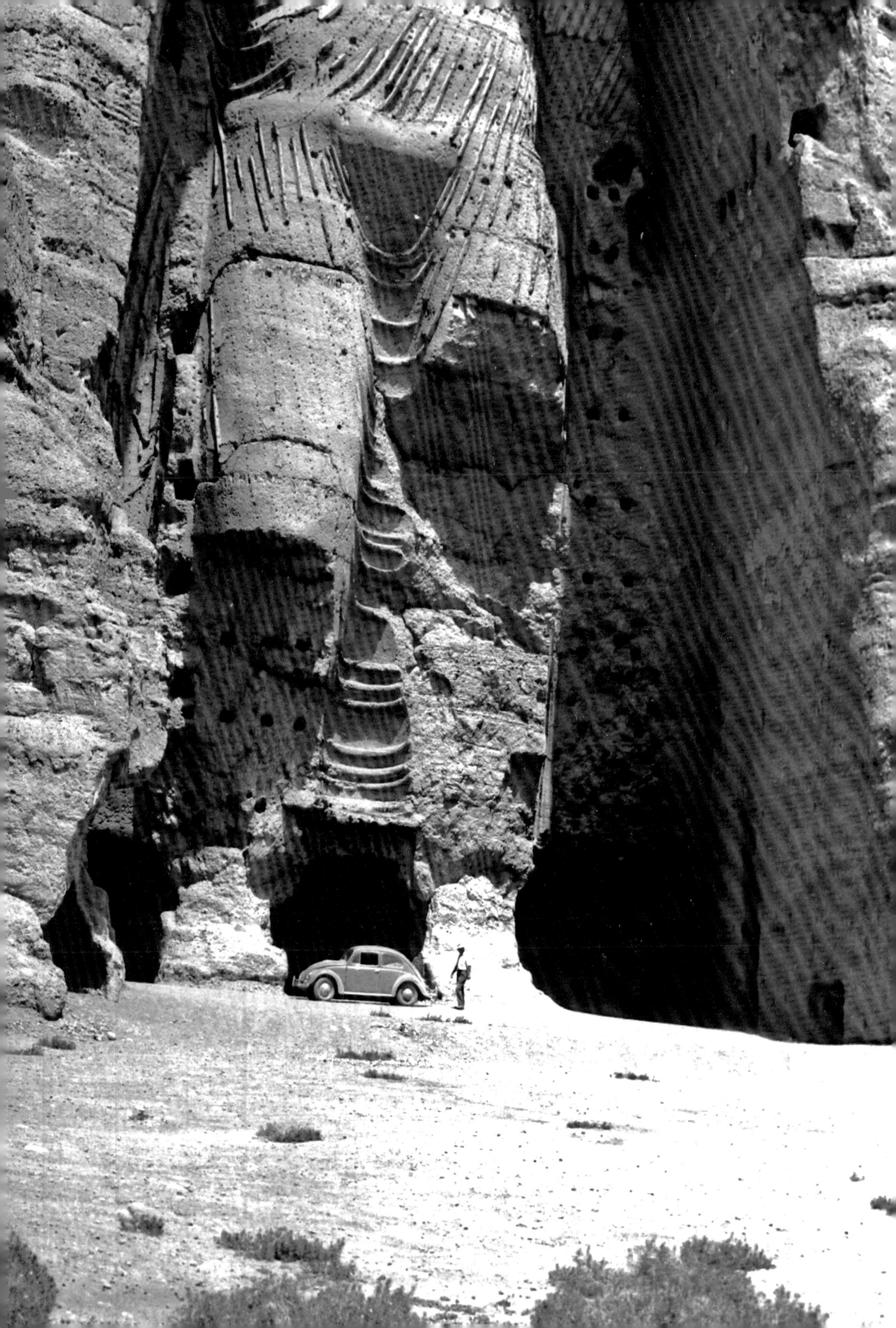

△ Fig. 19. E. Melzl, Western Buddha, 1958

▽ Fig. 20. E. Melzl, Eastern Buddha with brick-faced buttress, 1958

Structural Interventions and Conservation Measures by DAFA and ASI

In 1922, the Délégation Archéologique Française en Afghanistan (DAFA) was created under the protection of King Amanullah Khan. Its members carried out a comprehensive archaeological survey in Bamiyan with photographic documentation of the Buddha statues (figs. 14–17).[35] In this context, also structural interventions were made to stabilise the niche of the Eastern Buddha by means of an enormous brick-faced buttress on the west side (compare figs. 20, 21).[36] In the following years, the first analysis of samples of the murals of the caves was executed.[37]

In 1958, a young German restorer, Edmund Melzl, who lived in Afghanistan between 1956 and 1963 and in 2003 became member of the ICOMOS team in Bamiyan after more than 30 years of working in the restoration department of the Bavarian State Monument Service, stayed for some days in Bamiyan. We owe him a series of black and white photographs of the Buddha statues (figs. 18–24) documenting the state of conservation before the start of a general restoration undertaken by the Archaeological Survey of India (ASI).

In the framework of an Indo-Afghan joint project a team of experts from ASI restored from 1969 to 1978 the Eastern and Western Buddha: *The remedial measures they adopted included, inter alia a drainage system on the rock-roof of the niche to discharge snow-water, the buttress wall (buttress to the right of the Small Buddha, constructed by DAFA, see above) trimmed and treated to match the profile of the rock surface, to reduce natural wear and tear and the restoration of the stairs. As for the images, the emphasis was on preventing their further disintegration and not on reproducing the missing portions, although damaged legs were stabilized and broken edges filleted. The preservation of paintings necessitated elaborate physical and chemical cleaning, plastering and consolidation of the surface. In carrying out the conservation of the giant statues, the internationally accepted policy laid out in the 'Venice Charter' of the International Council on Monuments and Sites was strictly adhered to. At the end of the long restoration operation, Bamiyan retrieved much of its former glory.*[38] Apart from the publications and the rich photographic documentation (figs. 25–41) the conservation policy and the technical steps followed by ASI in Bamiyan can be assessed with regard to the famous 'Conservation Manual' by Sir John Marshall, Director General of Archaeology in India, for example paragraphs 88–91: *The joints of the new masonry are to be as inconspicuous as possible, so as to avoid unnecessary contrast with the jointless face of the original rock... Especial care must be taken to ensure that the new masonry is carried flash up to the rock above, and that the joint between is well sealed with grout... If the original rock face is weather-stained, an artificial stain (see para. 238) may be used for the new work etc.*[39] The very solid and conscientious work of ASI in the 1970s has certainly contributed much to the survival of the rather fragile Small Buddha niche during the disastrous attacks of 2001. At the same time as ASI, between

1970 and 1978, also Prof. Takayasu Higuchi carried out studies on the Bamiyan caves during the Kyoto University Archaeological Mission.[40]

△ Fig. 22. E. Melzl, view of the cliff between the Western and Eastern Buddha niche, 1958

△ Fig. 21. E. Melzl, view of the cliff with Western Buddha niche, 1958

Fig. 23. E. Melzl, view of the Bamiyan Valley with mausoleum and Eastern Buddha niche, 1958 ▷

Fig. 24. E. Melzl, view of the Eastern Buddha with new buttress, 1958

Notes

1 Decisions at the 27th session of the World Heritage Committee, Paris July 2003, 27 COM 8C.43 and 27 COM 8C.44.
2 The original appearance of the cliff cannot be reconstructed anymore. Examinations of the murals inside the Buddha niches showed that the sensitive stone had lost one meter by weathering since the niches were painted. SENGUPTA 1989.
3 According to Godard, the right hand of the Western Buddha can be conjectured as being raised in the *abhaya-mudra*, while the left hand was hanging down at the side of the body. GODARD et al. 1928, p. 12.
4 The English terms referring to the directions vary slightly: The 'Eastern Buddha' is also called 'East Giant Buddha', 'East Grand Buddha' or 'East Buddha'. The same applies to the 'Western Buddha'.
5 Geographic Dictionary of Yakut al Hamawi, translation of the Arab text in: BARBIER DE MEYNARD 1861, p. 80.
6 HYDE 1760, p.129–130, in: GODARD et al. 1928, p. 84: *Talia prope urbem Bamiyân (quae posteà Balch, seu Bactra) erant immania et prodigiosa illa persicè dicta Surćh-Bùt, id est Idolum rubrum, et C'hingh-Bùt, id es Idolum griseum seu cinereum.* According to Beal, Hyde is quoting Masâlik Mamâlik and the *Farhang-i-Jahângiri* of Ibn-Fakred-dîn Angju in this description, also saying that the smaller one is 'in formae vetulae' and called *Nesr*. BEAL 1884, p. 51, note 175.
7 Wilford 1798 reports that "*the Musulmans insist that they are the statues of Key-Umursh and his consort, that is to say, Adam and Eve.*" WILFORD 1798, p. 464, cited in: GODARD et al. 1928, p. 85. Wilford repeats information from Hyde on a large scale. Burnes writes that they are called *Silsal* and *Shahmama*, representing king Silsal and his wife. BURNES 1834, p. 185 and 187. Burnes also reports that he found a description in the history of Timourlane (= Tamerlane, 1336–1405), written by Tamerlane's historian Sherif o deen where the statues were called *Lat* and *Munat*. BURNES 1834, p. 188. – The smaller sculpture (Eastern Buddha) is normally identified as the 'female', but Vincent Eyre 1843 describes the Eastern as the male one. EYRE 1843, in: GODARD et al. 1928, p. 87–88. Talbot and Simpson identify the smaller one as the female. TALBOT/SIMPSON 1886, p. 332.
8 BAUER-BORNEMANN et al 2003, p. 9.
9 The *sangati* is part of the Buddhist monastic garment consisting of three elements (*tricivara*): Undergarment (*antaravasaka*), upper robe (*uttarasanga*), and outer robe (*sangati*). Additional parts are a waist cloth (*kushalaka*) and a buckled belt (*samakaksika*). – A *kasaya* is a rectangular piece of cloth, often showing small pieces of textile sewn together in patchwork style. The *kasaya* is wrapped round the body covering either one or both shoulders and worn over a skirt or an undergarment. The imitation of single square pieces of fabric sewn together refers to the tradition of mendicants who made their clothes from rags. The squares are often depicted even if the *kasaya* is characterised as a valuable fabric with embroidery and brocade.
10 Stylistically the Bamiyan Buddha statues are linked to the art of Gandhara and the Greco-Buddhist art characteristic of the schools of Gandhara and Mathura.
11 On the left arm of the Eastern Buddha, both edges of the *sangati* are draped on the inner side of the arm, so that the inside is not visible. On the Western Buddha, the part below the right arm has been missing for a long time. The drapery above the feet was destroyed, but probably the undergarment was not visible here.
12 SENGUPTA 1989, p. 205: '*A trial trench dug behind the right foot [of the Western Buddha] revealed the bottom of the feet, each rested on a lotus-like raised pedestal. With the bottom portion added, the image measured 55 meters, i. e. taller by 2 meters.*'
13 BURNES 1834 writes about the Western Buddha that '*there seems to have been a tiara on his head*'. BURNES 1834, p. 185.
14 The idea that the faces were cut out from the beginning for the reception of wooden masks was the result of the Indian examination: SENGUPTA 1989, p. 205. Sengupta describes the cuts made for inserting a wooden rack and traces of charcoal discovered during the restoration of the 1970's. – The cut-out faces are already clearly visible on the sketches made by Maitland in 1885 (cf. note 31 below).
15 Damages on the statues were already mentioned by Burnes: The Western Buddha '*is mutilated; both legs having been fractured by cannon; and the countenance above the mouth is destroyed.*' '*The hands [...] were both broken*'. BURNES 1834, p. 185. – Vincent Eyre 1843 describes the face of the Western Buddha as '*entirely destroyed*'. He also reports that the Eastern Buddha '*is greatly mutilated by cannon shot for which act of religious zeal credit is given to Nadir Shah*'. Godard 1928 explains the missing faces as a result of systematic mutilation. GODARD et al. 1928, p. 11 (Godard) and p. 88 (Eyre).
16 HAMBLY 1966, p. 46.
17 Date not ascertained, information referring to Hackin in: NATIONAL RESEARCH INSTITUTE FOR CULTURAL PROPERTIES JAPAN 2006, p. 133.
18 ARCHAEOLOGICAL SURVEY OF INDIA 2002, p. 3.
19 BEAL 1884, vol. 1, p. 50–51. – One *li* was equivalent to about 300 m in the Tang Dynasty; the measure *foot* is not a traditional Chinese measure, but perhaps the translation for chi which is 1/3 m.
20 The interpretation of *teou-shi* or *tu shi* (with *shi* meaning stone) is difficult as it is not a Chinese word, but seems to be phonetic translation which Xuanzang might have picked up during his journey. He mentions *teou-shi* nine times in the *xi you ji* (BEAL 1884, vol. 1, p. 51, 89, 166, 177, 197, 198; vol. 2, p. 45, 46). Three times it is mentioned as material of rather large images of deities: besides Bamiyan, there are the Deva Mahesvara in Varanasi, 100 feet long, and a life-size Buddha statue in Banaras (BEAL 1884, vol. 2, p. 45 and 46). The other mentions are found in lists of commercial transactions and products of Indian and Central Asian countries, where *teou-shi* is listed among gold, silver, copper, iron, crystals and precious vases, what gives the impression that *teou-shi* is material that is sold and transported.

Beal translates *teou-shi* as 'native copper' and refers to interpretations of JULIEN *in loc, n. 2.* (without explanation as BEAL 1884 contains no reference list) and the dictionary of Medhurst (Medhurst, Walter Henry, *A Dictionary of the Hok-këèn Dialect of the Chinese Language: According to the Reading and Colloquial Idioms: Containing about 12,000 Characters,* Macao 1832) interpreting it as a stone with equal parts of copper and calamine (silicate of zinc) (BEAL 1884, vol. 1, p. 166, note 3). In vol. 1, p. 51, note 176, on Bamiyan he refers to Medhurst (*sub voc.*) who explains that *teou-shi* is '*a kind of stone resembling metal. The Chinese call it the finest kind of native copper. It is found in Po-sze country (Persia) and resembles gold.*' Beal also points out that the statement that the parts of the statue are *cast* separately makes it plain that the statue was made of metal. WATTERS 1996, p. 118 suggests that *teou-shi* might be a phonetic translation from a Turkish word *tu*j (bronze) or connected to the Sankrit *rīti* (bell-metal, bronze) which is translated into Chinese as *tu shi* or *tu si*. He refers to JULIEN 1857 who translated the term *tu shi* as *laiton* or *cuivre jaune*.

21 Ibn Abdallah El Roumi El Hamawi Yaqout (1179–1229 AD), *Du Mo'Djem El-Bouldan – Dictionnaire géographique, historique et littéraire de la Perse et des contrées adjacentes*, Casimir Barbier De Meynard (trad.), Amsterdam 1970, p. 80.

22 Aboul Ghazi Behadour, *Histoire des Mogols et des Tartares, trad. Desmaisons, St. Petersbourg 1871.*

23 HYDE 1760, p. 129–130. In : GODARD et al. 1928, p. 3, reference (1).

24 WILFORD 1798, WILFORD 1801.

25 ELPHINSTONE 1814, p. 487, passage about the Hazaureh [= Hazara] in: GODARD et al 1928, p. 87.

26 Both died during the journey in 1825. Their travelogue was published *post mortem*. MOORCROFT/ TREBECK 1841, vol. II, pp. 388.

27 Excerpts of the letters of Dr. Gérard and the sketch by Alexander Burnes (1805–1841) were published in 1833 in the *Journal of the Asiatic Society of Bengal*, Vol. II. See also: BURNES 1834. In 1841, Burnes was assassinated at Kabul.

28 Charles Masson (1800–1853), reproduction of the drawing in: POSSEHL 1982, p. 407 u. pl. 39.1; POSSEHL 1990, p. 119, fig. 7. Most of Masson's pictures from Bamiyan are not published. They are deposited in the India Office Library in London. A list of the pictures in: Archer, Mildred: *British drawings in the India Office Library*. 2 vols., London 1969, vol. I, pp. 252–253 (MSS. Eur. G. 42 = 13 folios). Literature cited after: Mode, M., 'Ein vergessener Anfang: Carl Ritter und die „Kolosse von Bamiyan" ©, Zum 220. Geburtstag des großen deutschen Geographen.' *www.orientarch.uni-halle.de/ca/bam/bamiyanx.htm*.

29 Lieutenant Vincent Eyre, in 1842 British prisoner of war in Afghan hands, contrived to explore the Bamiyan caves. His short and incomplete notes were embodied in his book: EYRE 1843.

30 BURNES 1834, pp. 187–188. It is not clear which 'Christian period' he refers to.

31 RITTER 1838.

32 Talbot, Maitland and Simpson surveyed the Buddha statues and the caves B, D and E. Descriptions with sketches of the Bamiyan statues by Maitland were published in: TALBOT/ SIMPSON 1886, pp. 303–350.

33 The Graphic, Jan. 6th 1894, p. 6, col. 1.

34 Gray, J. A., *My residence at the court of the Amir*. see: GODARD et al. 1928, p. 10.

35 GODARD et. al. 1928; HACKIN/CARL 1933.

36 The Délégation Archéologique Française en Afghanistan (DAFA) was created in 1922 to carry out archaeological investigations in Afghanistan. Their work was interrupted during World War II. Starting again in 1947, research continued until 1982. In 2002, the activities were taken up again. Internet page of the DAFA: http://www.dafa.org.af. In November 1922, Alfred Foucher paid a first visit to Bamiyan: GODARD et al. 1928, p. 3. In the 1920s and 1930s, Alfred Foucher, André and Yedda Godard, Jean Carl, Joseph and Ria Hackin were members of the delegation. They investigated the murals and the architecture in Bamiyan and built the buttress on the west side (= left side) of the niche of the Eastern Buddha. Publications on Bamiyan: HACKIN/CARL 1933 ; HACKIN/CARL 1934.

37 Examination of painting technique and identification of materials from murals of different caves by Gettens and Johnson. GETTENS 1937/1938, p. 186.

38 Archaeological Survey of India 2002, pp. 13–14. – Several articles on the restoration carried out between 1969 and 1977 were published by the Archaeological Survey of India (ASI), see: LAL 1970; ARCHAEOLOGICAL SURVEY OF INDIA 1973; INDIAN-AFGHAN COOPERATION 1977. – SENGUPTA 1984, SENGUPTA 1989.

39 John Marshall, Conservation Manual, a handbook for the use of Archaeological Officers and others entrusted with the care of ancient monuments, Calcutta 1923, p. 27.

40 HIGUCHI 1984.

Fig. 26. The Western Buddha during restoration (photo: ASI)

Fig. 25. The Western Buddha before 1969 (photo: ASI)

Fig. 27. The Eastern Buddha at the beginning of the restoration (photo: ASI)

Fig. 28. The Eastern Buddha after the completion of the restoration (photo: ASI)

Fig. 29. West side of the Eastern Buddha niche before the restoration (photo: ASI)

Fig. 30. West side of the Eastern Buddha niche after restoration (photo: ASI)

Fig. 31. Wall of the corridor behind the feet of the Eastern Buddha during restoration (photo: ASI)

Fig. 32. Wall of the corridor behind the feet of the Eastern Buddha after the restoration (photo: ASI)

Fig. 33. Feet of the Eastern Buddha before the restoration (photo: ASI)

Fig. 34. Feet of the Eastern Buddha after the restoration (photo: ASI)

△ 29  △ 30

△ 31 ▽ 33 △ 32 ▽ 34

△ 35 ▽ 36 △ 38 ▽ 40 △ 39 ▽ 41

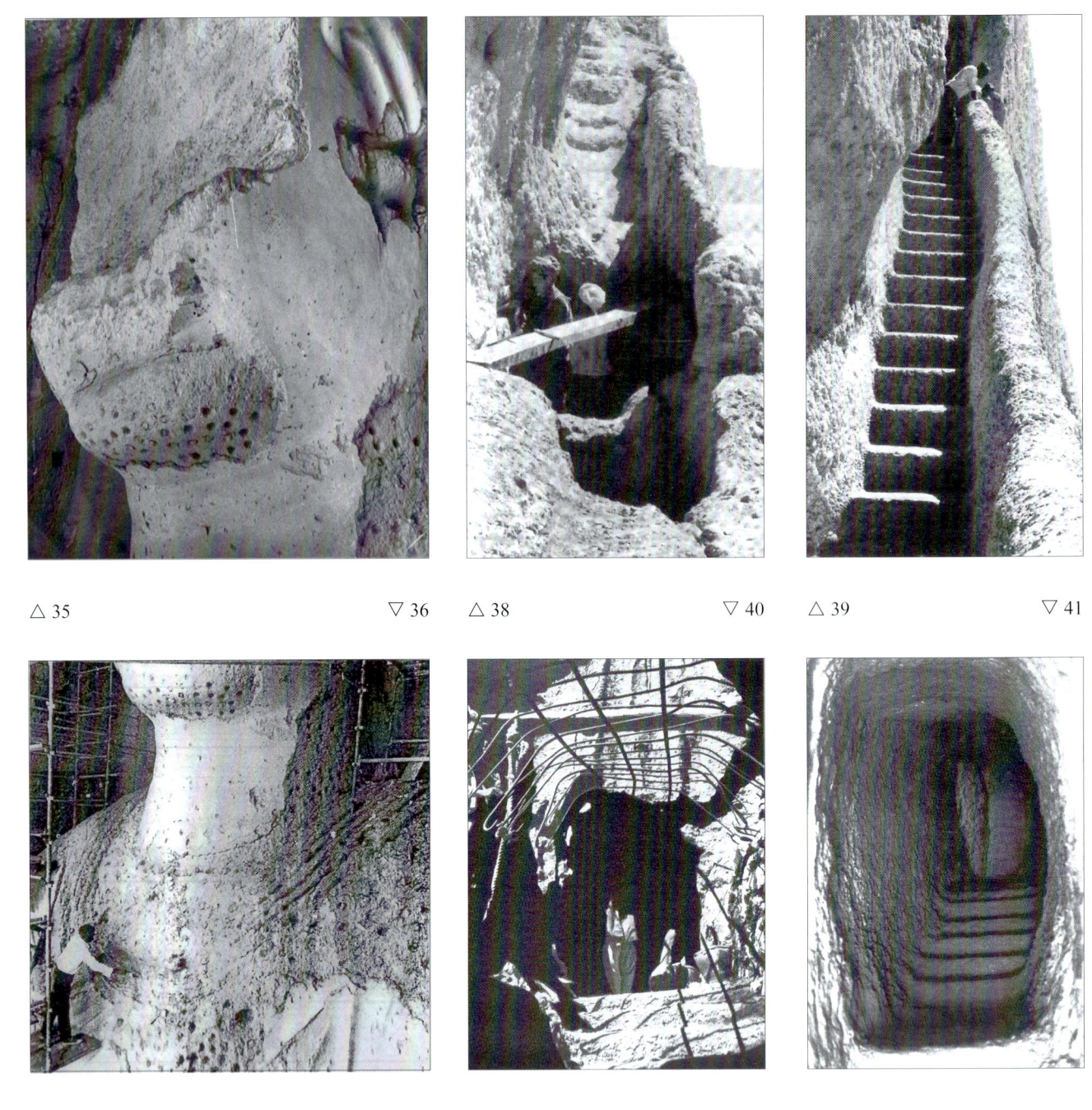

▽ 37

Fig. 35. Head of the Eastern Buddha, 1956 (photo: ASI)

Fig. 36. Chest of the Eastern Buddha before restoration (photo: ASI)

Fig. 37. Chest of the Eastern Buddha after the restoration (photo: ASI)

Fig. 38. Eastern Buddha, stairs before restoration (photo: ASI)

Fig. 39. Eastern Buddha, stairs after restoration (photo: ASI)

Fig. 40. Western Buddha, stairs during restoration (photo: ASI)

Fig. 41. Western Buddha, stairs after restoration (photo: ASI)

Fig. 42. Upper part of the Western Buddha with remains of murals on the vault (photo: Keith Worsley-Brown, June 1972)

Fig. 43. View of the Bamiyan valley and the Hindukush from the top of the head of the Western Buddha (photo: Keith Worsley-Brown, June 1972)

References

Archaeological Survey of India, ASI (ed.): *Restoration of the Buddha colossi at Bamiyan: 1969–1973*, New Delhi, 1973, pp. 1–23

Archaeological Survey of India, ASI (ed.): *INDO–AFGHAN Cooperation: Restoration of Bamiyan*. Government of India 1977, pp. 1–31

Archaeological Survey of India, ASI (ed.): *Bamiyan – Challenge to World Heritage*, Janpath, New Delhi 2002

Barbier de Meynard, Charles: *Dictionnaire Géographique, Historique et Littéraire de la Perse et des contrées adjacentes: Extrait du Mu´ğam al-Buldān de Yāqūt.* Paris 1861. Reprint: Sezegin, Fuat (ed.), Publications of the Institute for the History of Arabic–Islamic Science, Islamic Geography, Vol. 221. First Part Ābağ – Sirkān. Frankfurt am Main 1994

Bauer-Bornemann, U.; Melzl, E.; Romstedt, H.; Scherbaum, M.: *Überlegungen zum Umgang mit den Fragmenten der zerstörten Buddha-Statuen im Auftrag des deutschen Nationalkomitees von ICOMOS*, Dezember 2003 (unpublished report on the work in Bamiyan 23.10. – 3.11. 2003)

Beal, Samuel: *SI-YU-KI, Buddhist Records of the Western World, translated from the Chinese of Hsiuen-Tsiang*, London 1884

Burnes, Sir Alexander: *Travels into Bokhara, together with a narrative of A voyage on the Indus*. London 1834. Reprint Oxford University Press 1973

Elphinstone, Mountstuart: *An account of the Kingdom of Caubul, and its dependencies in Persia, Tartary, and India. Comprising a view of the Afghaun nation, and a history of the Dooraunee monarchy*. London 1814

Eyre, Vincent: *The Military Operations at Cabul (...): with a journal of imprisonment in Afghanistan*, London 1843

Gettens, Rutherford: *The materials in the wall paintings of Bamiyan, Afghanistan*, in: Technical Studies in the field of the Fine Arts, Volume VI, 1937–1938

Godard, A. Godard, Y., Hackin, J.: *Les Antiquités Bouddhiques de Bāmiyān, Mémoires de la délégation archéologique Française en Afghanistan*, vol. II. Paris, Brussels 1928

Hackin, Joseph and Carl, Jean: *Nouvelles Recherches Archéologiques à Bāmiyān. Mémoires de la délégation archéologique Française en Afghanistan*, vol. III, Paris 1933

Hackin, J. avec la collaboration de J. Carl: *Nouvelles recherches archéologiques à Bâmiyân*. Les Mémoires de la DAFA, vol. III, 1933

Hackin, J. & R.: *Le site archéologique de Bâmiyân. Guide du visiteur*. Paris 1934

Hackin, Joseph and Hackin, Ria: *Bamian. Führer zu den buddhistischen Höhlenklöstern und Kolossalstatuen. Alleinberechtigte deutsche Ausgabe.* Paris. Les éditions d'art et d'histoire 1939. (Translation of the French edition: Hackin, J. & R.: *Le site archéologique de Bâmiyân. Guide du visiteur*. Paris 1934)

Hambly, Gavin (ed.): *Fischer Weltgeschichte. Zentralasien*, Frankfurt a. Main 1966

Higuchi, Takayasu: *Bamiyan – Art and archaeological Researches on the Buddhist cave temples in Afghanistan 1970–1978*, Dohosha 1984. Reprint 2001

Hyde, Thomas: *Veterum Persarum et Parthorum et Medorum religionis historia, autor est Thomas Hyde, s. t. d. linguae hebraicae in Universitate Oxon., professor regius et linguae arabicae professor laudianus. Editio secunda, Oxonii, typographeo Clarendoniano, MDCCLX* (1760). The first edition was published in 1700.

Julien, M. Stanislas: *Mémoires sur les Contrees occidentals traduits du Sanskrit en Chinois, en l'an 648, par Hiouen-Thsang, et du Chinois en Français,* 1857

Klimburg-Salter, Deborah (ed.): *The Kingdom of Bamiyan. Buddhist art and culture of the Hindu Kush*, Naples 1989

Kossolapov, A.J.; Marshak, B. I.: *Murals along the Silk Road, Formika*, St. Petersburg 1999

Lal, B. B.: *Conservation of murals in the Bamiyan valley, Afghanistan*, in: Agrawal, O. P. (ed.): *Conservation of cultural properties in India* 5. Archaeological Survey of India (ASI), Proceedings of the 5th seminar: December 2–4, 1970, pp. 83–95

Moorcroft, William & Trebeck, George: *Travels in the Himalayan provinces of Hindustan and the Panjab*, in Ladakh and Kashmir; in Peshawar, Kabul, Kunduz and Bokhara from 1819 to 1825. Prepared for the press (...) by H. H. Wilson. London 1841

National Research Institute for Cultural Properties Japan (ed.): *Radiocarbon Dating of the Bamiyan Mural Paintings*, in: *Recent Cultural Heritage Issues in Afghanistan*, vol. 2, Tokyo 2006

Possehl, G. L.: *Discovering ancient India's earliest cities: The first phase of research*, in: Possehl, G. L. (ed.): *Harappan Civilization. A contemporary perspective*, New Delhi, Bombay, Calcutta 1982, pp. 405–413

Possehl, G. L.: *An archaeological adventurer in Afghanistan: Charles Masson*, in: South Asian Studies, vol. 6, London 1990, pp. 111–124

Ritter, Carl: *Die Stupa's (Topes) oder die architectonischen Denkmale an der königlich Indo-Baktrischen Köngisstraße und die Colosse von Bamiyan. Eine Abhandlung zur Althertumskunde des Orients, vorgetragen in der königl. Akademie der Wissenschaften, am 6. Februar 1837. Mit einer Karte und 8 lithographirten Tafeln*. Berlin, Nicolaische Buchhandlung, 1838

Sengupta, R.: *Restoration of the Bamiyan Buddhas*, in: Klimburg-Salter, Deborah (ed.): *The Kingdom of Bamiyan. Buddhist art and culture of the Hindu Kush*, Naples 1989

Sengupta, R.: *The restoration of the small Buddha at Bamiyan*. ICOMOS, York 1984 (Momentum 27.1), pp. 31–46

Talbot, M. G. and Simpson, W.: *The rockcut caves and statues of Bamian*, in: *Journal of the Royal Asiatic Society*, Vol. XVIII, London 1886, pp. 303–350

Tarzi, Zemaryalai: *L'architecture et le décor rupestre des grottes de Bamiyan*, Paris 1977, 2 vols (vol. 1: Texts, vol. 2: Sketches, photographs)

Watters, Thomas: *On Yuan Chwang's Travels in India AD 629-645*. Munishiram Manoharial Publishers, New Delhi 1996

Wilford, Captain Francis: *On mount Caucasus*, in: *Asiatick Researches*, vol. VI, 1798, pp. 462–468

Wilford, Captain Francis (ed.): *Asiatick Researches, Or Transaction of the Society Instituted in Bengal*, vol. 6, XII (On Mount Caucasus), London 1801

۲۰ ذی الحجۃ ۱۴۲۱ھ
بامیان میں بت شکنی کا تاریخی منظر
۱۲۵۰ من بارود نے دوہزار سالہ بتوں کے پرخچے اڑادیے
بت شکن کیلنڈر
۱۴۲۲ھ
بامیان کا ایک منظر
اسلامی صحافت میں ایک انقلابی قدم
اسلام
ضرب مؤمن
۱۴۲۲
2001
2002

II AFGHANISTAN – HERITAGE AT RISK

In the first volumes of its Heritage at Risk series, started in 2000, ICOMOS already pointed out the dramatic threats to the Afghan cultural heritage.[1] After more than two decades of warfare, the entire cultural heritage of Afghanistan was endangered by arbitrary acts of destruction. Heritage at risk were not only the world-famous Buddhas of Bamiyan, those giant statues cut into high cliff-faces and severely damaged by grenade attacks. Such destruction in the context of fundamentalist 'iconoclastic ideology' also favoured the reckless exploitation of the country's cultural heritage for the sake of the art market. Many archaeological sites were sacked. Also the outstanding collections of the Kabul Museum, hit by a rocket in 1993 during a battle between rival Mujaheddin groups, were pillaged, and the objects finally showed up on the international art market.

Considering the desperate situation in Afghanistan, UNESCO has tried to react with emergency plans, also involving the International Committee of the Blue Shield. The special commitment of the Society for the Protection of Afghanistan's Cultural Heritage (SPACH) regarding the rescue of the historic sites and cultural properties of Afghanistan needs to be pointed out. SPACH has also published more detailed information in its regular Newsletter.[2]

Before the final decision to blow up the Buddhas of Bamiyan in March 2001 ICOMOS and ICOM had protested in vain against the disastrous consequences of the edict of the Islamic Emirate issued on 26 February 2001:

SAVE THE CULTURAL HERITAGE OF AFGHANISTAN APPEAL BY ICOMOS AND ICOM

ICOMOS (International Council on Monuments and Sites) and ICOM (International Council of Museums) learned with great shock of the new decree issued by the Taliban leadership of Mullah Mohammad Omar ordering the systematic destruction of all statues in the country. This decision breaks the commitment made by the Taliban leadership in 1999 to protect all cultural heritage in Afghanistan and in particular the giant Buddha figures at Bamiyan.

Adding to the dishonour of breaking a commitment to preserve the ancient and diverse heritage of Afghanistan as part of that of the whole of mankind, such an act of destruction would be a total cultural catastrophe. It would remain written in the pages of history next to the most infamous acts of barbarity.

For many years, ICOM has alerted the world on illicit trade in cultural objects from Afghanistan. ICOMOS, in its 2000 World Report on monuments and sites in danger (see http:// www.international.icomos.org/risk/afgha_2000.htm), pointed out in detail the dangers to cultural heritage in Afghanistan, in particular the pre-islamic figures of the Buddha in Bamiyan. This decree of Mollah Mohammad Omar confirms the imminence of this danger.

As world-wide non-governmental organisations, ICOMOS and ICOM call on all people, governments, International Organisations and associations to take immediate action to prevent this cultural catastrophe from happening. A dialogue should be established with the Taliban leaders to ensure adequate protection of all Afghan heritage, whether pre-islamic or islamic. This is a matter of the highest importance and the greatest emergency.

Blowing-up of the Western Buddha, March 2001

Christian Manhart
UNESCO's Activities for the Safeguarding of Bamiyan

On 26 February 2001, the Islamic Emirate of Afghanistan issued the following edict from the City of Kandahar: *On the basis of consultations between the religious leaders of the Islamic Emirate of Afghanistan, the religious judgments of the Ulema and the rulings of the Supreme Court of the Islamic Emirate of Afghanistan, all statues and non-Islamic shrines located in the different parts of the Islamic Emirate of Afghanistan must be destroyed. These statues have been and remain shrines of infidels and these infidels continue to worship and respect these shrines. Allah almighty is the only real shrine and all false shrines should be smashed. Therefore, the Supreme Leader of the Islamic Emirate of Afghanistan has ordered all the representatives of the Ministry of the Promotion of Virtue and Suppression of Vice and of the Ministry of Information and Culture to destroy all the statues. As ordered, by the Ulema and the Supreme Court of the Islamic Emirate of Afghanistan, all statues must be annihilated so that no one can worship or respect them in the future.*

As soon as this order was made public, UNESCO issued appeals to the Taliban leaders, exhorting them to preserve the Afghan cultural heritage. These appeals were widely carried by the international press. The Director-General Koïchiro Matsuura addressed a personal letter to the Taliban leader, Mollah Omar, on 28 February. The Director-General also obtained the full support of the Islamic countries for UNESCO's activities to save the Afghan cultural heritage. On 1st March, Mr. Pierre Lafrance, Special Representative of the Director-General, left for Islamabad, Kandahar, Kabul, the United Arab Emirates, Qatar and Saudi Arabia. A number of Moslem religious leaders from Egypt, Iraq and Pakistan intervened at the request of UNESCO, issuing *fatwas* against the Taliban's order. The Director-General personally contacted the Presidents of Egypt and of Pakistan, as well as of the Organization of the Islamic Conference, all of whom tried to use their influence to persuade the Taliban to cancel the order. Following these interventions, a delegation of 11 international Moslem leaders went to Kandahar in order to try to convince Mollah Omar that the Koran does not prescribe the destruction of statues.

UNESCO launched an international petition for the safeguarding of the Afghan cultural heritage on its web site, and a special Funds-in-Trust account has been created for this purpose. The crisis gained a great deal of international media attention and UNESCO also received many letters of support for its actions in this matter from heads of state, ministers, other international organizations and individuals. Nevertheless, all these political and religious interventions proved to be in vain, and the Taliban destroyed not only the Buddhas at Bamyan, but also a large number of statues throughout Afghanistan.

After the destruction, in December 2001, an international conference of *Ulema*, Islamic religious leaders, was jointly organized with the OIC, ISESCO and ALECSO, to examine the position of the Moslem world towards the preservation of Islamic and non-Islamic heritage. This conference resulted in a clear declaration of principles in favour of the protection of cultural heritage, including statues that can be appealed to in the future…

In May 2002, UNESCO organized, in cooperation with the Afghan Ministry of Information and Culture, the first International Seminar on the Rehabilitation of Afghanistan's Cultural Heritage, held in Kabul, which gathered 107 specialists in Afghan cultural heritage, as well as representatives of donor countries and institutions. Under the chairmanship of H. E. Dr. Makhdoum Raheen, Minister of Information and Culture of the Afghan Government, the participants gave presentations on the state of conservation of cultural sites across the country and discussed programmes and co-ordination for the first conservation measures to be taken. This Seminar resulted in more than US$ 7 million being pledged for priority projects, allocated through bilateral agreements and UNESCO Funds-in-Trust projects. An eleven-page document containing concrete recommendations for future action was adopted, in which the need to ensure effective cooperation was emphasized.

To this end and following the Afghan authorities' request to UNESCO to play a coordinating role in all international activities aimed at the safeguarding of Afghanistan's cultural heritage, UNESCO has established an International Coordination Committee. The statutes of this Committee were approved by the 165th session of the Organization's Executive Board in October 2002. The Committee consists of Afghan experts and leading international specialists belonging to the most important donor countries and organizations providing funds or scientific assistance for the safeguarding of Afghanistan's cultural heritage. It meets on a regular basis to review on-going and future efforts to rehabilitate Afghanistan's cultural heritage. From 16 to 18 June 2003, the First Plenary Session of this Committee was organized at UNESCO Headquarters. The meeting was chaired by H. E. Dr. Makhdoum Raheen, Minister of Information and Culture, in the presence of His Highness Prince Mirwais, seven representatives of the Afghan Ministry of Information and Culture, and of more than 60 international experts, participating as Members of the Committee or as Observers.

The meeting resulted in concrete recommendations, which allowed the efficient coordination of actions to safeguard Afghanistan's cultural heritage to the highest international conservation standards. These recommendations concern key areas, such as the development of a long-term strategy, capacity building, the implementation of the World Heritage Convention and the Convention on the Means of Prohibiting and Preventing the Illicit Import, Export and Transfer of Ownership of Cultural Property, national inventories and documentation, as well as the rehabilitation of the National Museum in Kabul, the safeguarding of the sites of Jam, Herat, and Bamiyan. Several donors pledged additional funding for cultural projects in Afghanistan during and following the meeting.

Immediately after the collapse of the Taliban regime in December 2001, UNESCO sent a mission to Bamiyan to assess the condition of the site and to cover the remaining large stone blocks with fibreglass sheets protecting them from harsh climatic conditions during winter. In July 2002, a second UNESCO mission jointly organized with the International Council on Monuments and Sites (ICOMOS)

First international seminar on the rehabilitation of Afghanistan's cultural heritage, 27–29 May 2002

Meeting in Kabul, May 2002. From left to right: Henrik Lilius, Michael Petzet, President Hamid Karzai, Mounir Bouchenaki

and directed by its president, Professor Michael Petzet, was undertaken in order to prepare conservation measures at the Bamiyan site.

A project preparation mission to Bamiyan composed of German, Italian and Japanese experts was then undertaken from 27 September to 6 October 2002. It was noted that over 80% of the mural paintings dating from the 6th to the 9th century AD in the Buddhist caves have disappeared, either through neglect or looting. In one cave, experts even found tools of the thieves and the remains of freshly removed paintings.

In response to this situation, a contract was concluded with the local commander, who immediately provided ten armed guards to be responsible for the permanent surveillance of the site, and no further thefts were noted since. It was also noted with concern that large cracks have appeared in and around the niches where the Buddha statues had previously been situated, which could lead to the collapse of parts of the niches and inner stair cases. In response to this situation, the experts carried out complementary measurements and advised on appropriate actions to consolidate the cliffs and the niches. As a result of this mission, the Japanese Foreign Ministry generously approved a UNESCO Funds-in-Trust for the Safeguarding of the Bamiyan site with a total budget of $1,815,967. ICOMOS financed the restoration of a Sunni mosque and another building, both of which are located in close proximity to the niche of the large Buddha. The fore-mentioned building is now used to accommodate the guards, and to store the project equipment.[3]

Destruction of the Eastern Buddha [Al-Jazeera]

Notes

1 The following text is an abstract of H@R 2000, pp. 39–41 and H@R 2001/2002, pp. 25f.

2 Issue 6, May 2000; see also the reports on Afghanistan in *Archaeologia*, No. 365, March 2000, pp. 14–29, and James Lewis: *Afghanistan: the wounds of war*, in: Sources, May 2000, No. 123, pp. 13f.

3 Taken from Christian Manhart: *UNESCO's activities for the safeguarding of Bamiyan*, in: Claudio Margottini (ed.): *The Destruction of the Giant Buddha Statues in Bamiyan*, Viterbo 2009, pp. 39–41.

III ICOMOS ACTIVITIES 2002–2009

2002

In the years of the war and under the Taliban regime the rich cultural heritage of Afghanistan met with tremendous losses. Many monuments and sites could only be saved from total decay if rescue operations were started immediately. For that reason UNESCO and the Ministry of Information and Culture of Afghanistan organised a first International Seminar on the Rehabilitation of Afghanistan's Cultural Heritage (Kabul, 27–29 May 2002), the conclusions and recommendations of which, among other things, dealt with the state of conservation of the monuments of the Bamiyan valley: *The eyes of the world have been on the Bamiyan Valley since early 2001 since the destruction of the great Buddhist statues, a dominant feature of that famous place. It was noted that much discussion has taken place in Afghanistan and around the world about the future of this great site. The Seminar participants clearly recognized that the first emergency priority is the stabilization of the cliff face and the niches and caves carved into it, which are in a serious state of conservation and a matter of grave immediate concern. The decision to engage in reconstruction of the Buddhist statues of Bamiyan is a matter to be settled by the Government and people in Afghanistan, a point clearly recognized by the Seminar participants. In any case, the Seminar participants underscored that such work could be undertaken only after major stabilization work on the cliffs at Bamiyan has been completed, a process which is an essential first step in any conservation process at the Bamiyan Valley site.**

Under the guidance of UNESCO and thanks to the funds of 500.000 euros provided by the German Foreign Office in 2002 for the safeguarding of endangered cultural properties in Afghanistan, ICOMOS was able to work successfully despite difficult circumstances and used these financial means for a number of projects.

The Babur Park project, which could only be realised together with the Aga Khan Trust for Culture (AKTC), was a very extensive restoration measure. The park is a much visited place of recreation for the people of Kabul, in a spectacular location and very suitable for providing a German contribution to the rehabilitation of this city so terribly affected by years of war. The most essential parts of the park's surrounding walls were restored in 2002, and the palace ruin (the former German embassy) was cleared of rubble and – in preparation of the restoration – newly measured by the ICOMOS team, using this work to train Afghan architectural students.

In Kabul, apart from the Babur Park some project funds were used to rehabilitate the quarter of Ashekan wa Arefan, a severely dilapidated quarter with four mosques and very interesting historic building structures spared by the war. This measure in a very densely populated town quarter, also carried out together with AKTC, may be considered a pilot project and possible example for similar historic quarters in other towns in Afghanistan. From the conservation point of view, it is of great importance that not only some outstanding monuments are saved, but that for the sake of the population this unique historic stock of buildings in Kabul is preserved, i.e. as an example of 'town repair' instead of the usual total renewal (see also p. 43).

In connection with the first ICOMOS mission to Kabul and Bamiyan from 12–21 July (see report, pp. 43) a new concept for securing the remains of the Buddhas of Bamiyan (anastylosis in the sense of article 15 of the Venice Charter) was developed (cf. pp. 46–51). During the second ICOMOS mission in October 2002 the ICOMOS funds were used for cleaning the drainage system on the hill above the Buddha niches, for hiring men to guard the historic sites and for repairing a group of buildings, including a small mosque, next to the Western Buddha as well as for covering the fragments of the giant statues, - all in preparation of further safeguarding measures, such as stabilising those parts of the rock that are threatened to fall off and securing fragments endangered by decay.

Furthermore, ICOMOS in cooperation with the Technical University of Aachen started a databank of all monuments and historic sites in Afghanistan (first presented to the Expert Working Group workshop in Munich at the end of November, see p. 54). The databank will be established on the basis of all available written sources. This material, crucial for all future conservation work in Afghanistan, is meant to be complemented on the spot by checking and documenting the present state of the sites (see also pp. 44/45).

M. Pz.

---

* International Seminar in Kabul, 27–29 May 2002, conclusions IV/14.

Fig. a–c Kabul, views of the Babur Park, 2002

Fig. d   Babur Park, restoration of the surrounding walls

Fig. e   Babur Park, ruins of the palace

Fig. f   Babur Park, magnetometer prospection carried out by Jörg Faßbinder

Fig. g   Kabul, historic quarter Ashekan wa Arefan

The first ICOMOS mission to Kabul and Bamiyan (12–21 July 2002)*

The participants of the first ICOMOS mission to Afghanistan were Dr. Jörg Faßbinder (geo-physicist, Bavarian State Conservation Office), Prof. Dr.-Ing. Michael Jansen (RWTH Aachen), Prof. Dr. Michael Petzet (President of ICOMOS International), Dipl.-Ing. Mario Santana Quintero (M.Sc. of Conservation, member of ICOMOS Venezuela), Dr.-Ing. Zou Yazou (geo-engineer, University of the German Armed Forces, Munich). The ICOMOS group was looked after by Mr Jim Williams, representative of UNESCO. The Swiss expert on Afghanistan, Paul Bucherer-Dietschi (Foundation Bibliotheca Afghanica, Switzerland), participating in the mission as an observer, arranged a dinner on 14 July with the Afghan Minister of Urban Development and other members of the cabinet. In Kabul, we were also taken care of by colleagues from the Aga Khan Trust for Culture (Leslie Julian, A. Hasib Latifi, Abdul Wassay Najimi), with whom ICOMOS also worked in the Babur Park. On the day of our arrival in Bamiyan (15 July) our delegation was given a warm welcome by the governor/mayor who informed us about the local situation and the urgent wish to 'reconstruct' the Buddha.

The Babur Park

The Babur Park, fortunately cleared of mines some time ago, has become a major attraction for the people of Kabul despite the considerable damages during the war and the strongly neglected state at present. After initial visits and talks at the end of May there was opportunity to investigate the progress of repair made in the meantime, particularly with regard to the surrounding walls with their towers. Further possible steps of restoration were discussed. The ruins of the palace, the former German embassy, were inspected with representatives of the AKTC. It was important that the presence of Ratish Nanda, member of ICOMOS India, could be coordinated with our visit. With Mr Nanda, in charge of a park in Delhi designed by the son of Babur, we could discuss the choice of plants for the Babur Park and the questions of the historic water system.

The conservation concept for the Babur Park should refer to the state around 1640 when the mosque was built and the gardens were remodelled. This state is documented in a contemporary description, and in some details is still recognisable. In this context a number of old photos showing the park before the alterations of the 20th century were also of importance. Nevertheless, the restoration concept had to accept certain later additions, such as the pavilion from the 19th century. A relevant prerequisite for the planned excavations was the magnetometer prospection made on five test surfaces by Jörg Faßbinder. In spite of iron remains spread all over the gardens, which made magnetic field measurements difficult to implement, interesting results were achieved. On the other hand, the three-dimensional survey of the entire gardens with a total station (Prof. Jansen and Mario Santana), provide an important basis for future planning.

First ICOMOS mission to Bamiyan in 2002

Repair of historic residential buildings

Although Kabul was badly destroyed during the war a historic quarter (Ashekan wa Arefan) has survived with an abundance of important building fabric threatened by decay. Here there was a chance to implement various pilot projects together with the AKTC in the necessary urban repair. The undersigned and Professor Jansen visited a number of buildings in that quarter together with the architect Abdul Wassay Najimi.

With the funds at our disposal it was originally intended not just to launch pilot projects to repair urban architecture, but also vernacular architecture in Bamiyan. Visits to villages and farmsteads in Bamiyan, some of the latter resembling fortifications, proved however that in many places reconstruction had already begun. This is mostly repair work with traditional materials and techniques, as modern materials are not available. From a conservation point of view it is good to know that vernacular architecture is preserved in that traditional way. Under these circumstances, some of the funds made available for vernacular buildings in Bamiyan could be used for initial stabilisation measures to save the remains of the Buddhas in Bamiyan.

The Buddha statues in Bamiyan

The condition of the rock surfaces after the blowing-up of the Buddhas by the Taliban in March 2001 needed to be investigated by experts so that methods to stabilise the historic remains could be developed. The ICOMOS team started comprehensive measurements and investigations during the first mission in July, which – in contrast to public speculation about the necessary steps to "reconstruct" the Buddhas – resulted in a reasonable conservation concept (cf. pp. 46–51). The geo-engineer Dr. Zou Yazou, with whom the undersigned already worked in the 1990s on a concept for the stabilisation of the Great Buddha of Dafosi (Der Große Buddha von Dafosi/The Great Buddha of Dafosi (ICOMOS – Journals of the German National Committee XVII), Munich 1996), made first analyses of the state of

CHAM QUL'A_14.2_BALL1982.tif

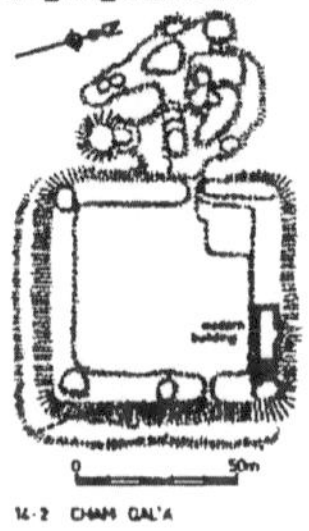

TIFF Bild

CHAQALAQ TEPE_15.1_BALL1982.tif

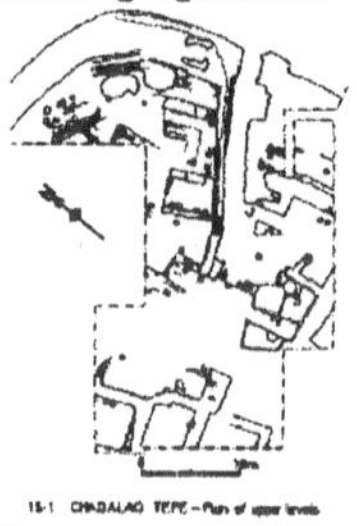

TIFF Bild

BAGH HINDU1982.tif

TIFF Bild

BAGH-I-NAZARGAH_10.1_BALL1982.tif

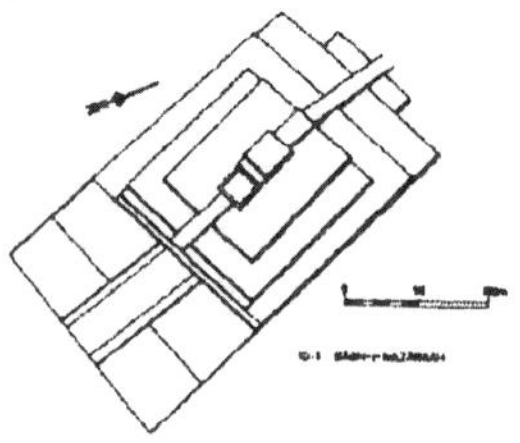

TIFF Bild

BALKH_6.1_BALL1982.tif

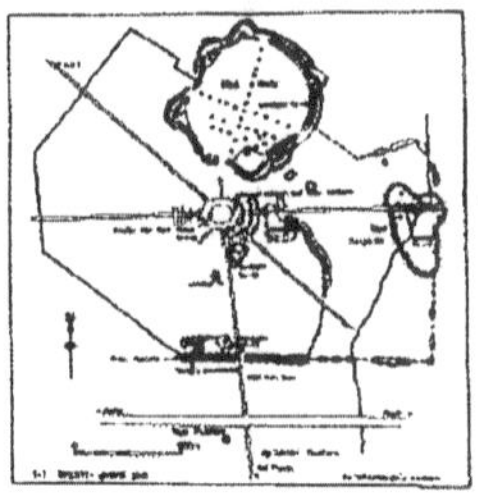

TIFF Bild

BALKH_6.2_BALL1982.tif

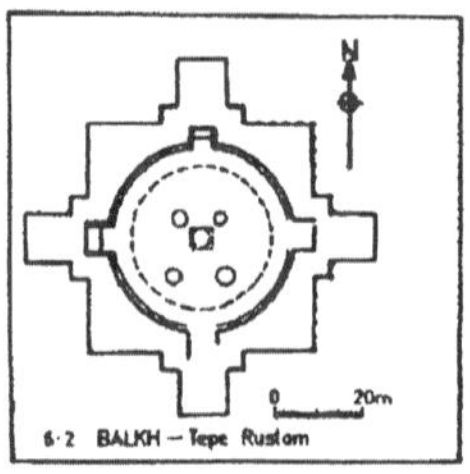

TIFF Bild

BALKH_6.3_BALL1982.tif

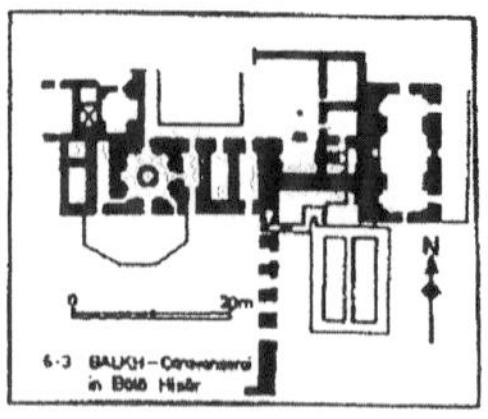

TIFF Bild

BALKH_7.1_BALL1982.tif

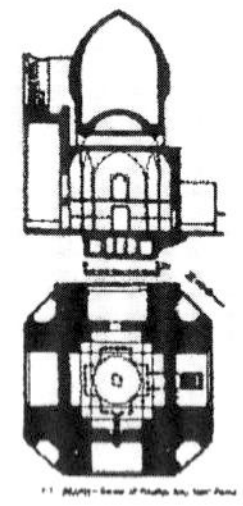

TIFF Bild

BAMIYAN_8.1_BALL1982.tif

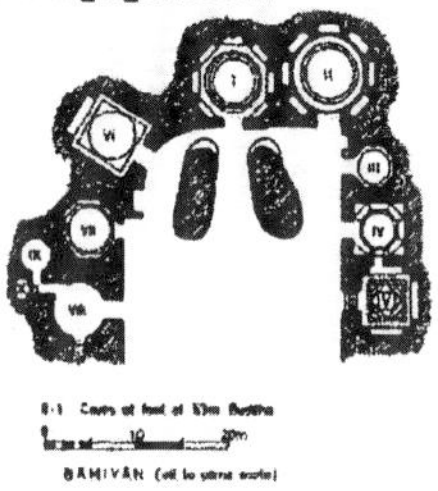

TIFF Bild

BAMIYAN_8.10_BALL1982.tif

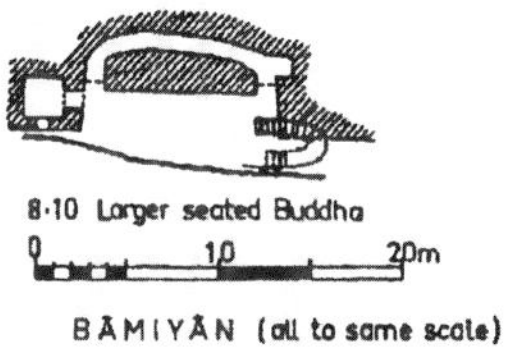

TIFF Bild

BAMIYAN_8.2_BALL1982.tif

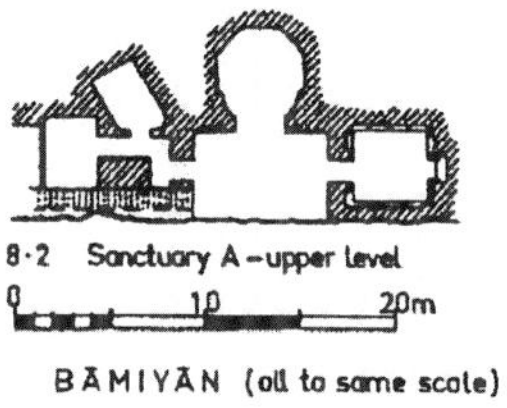

TIFF Bild

BAMIYAN_8.3_BALL1982.tif

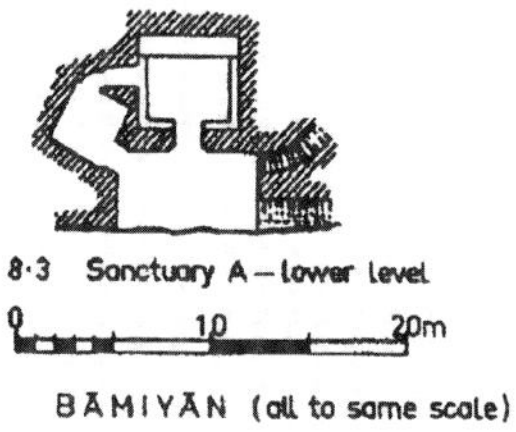

TIFF Bild

BAMIYAN_8.4_BALL1982.tif

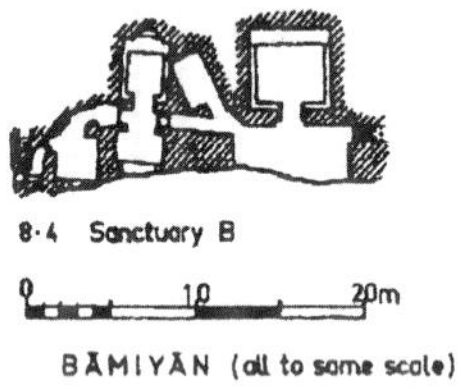

TIFF Bild

BAMIYAN_8.5_BALL1982.tif

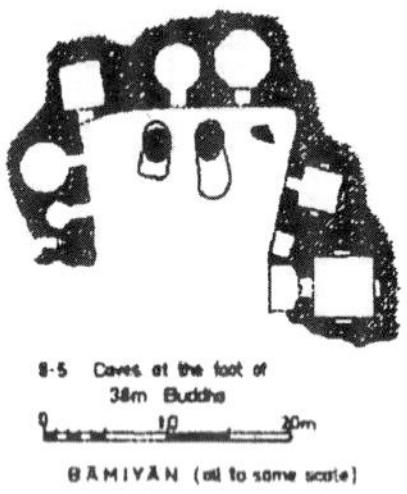

TIFF Bild

BAMIYAN_8.6_BALL1982.tif

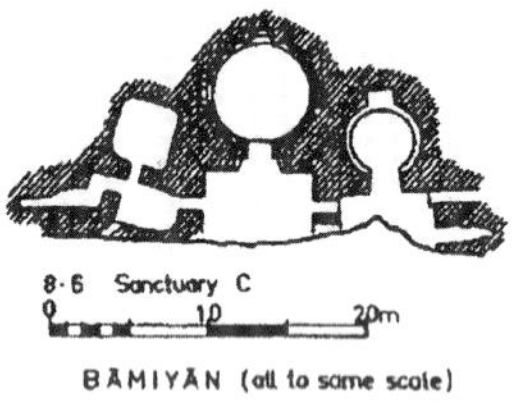

TIFF Bild

BAMIYAN_8.7_BALL1982.tif

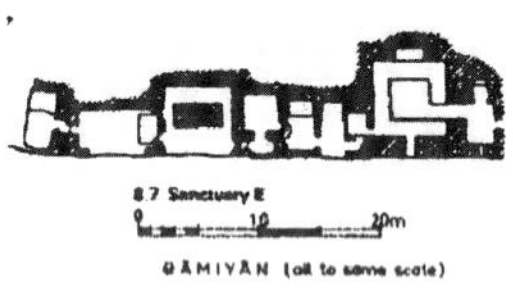

TIFF Bild

BAMIYAN_8.8_BALL1982.tif

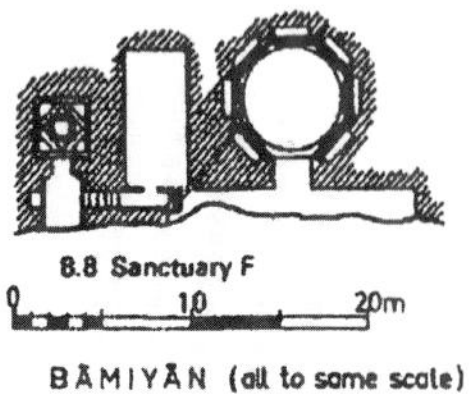

TIFF Bild

BAMIYAN_8.9_BALL1982.tif

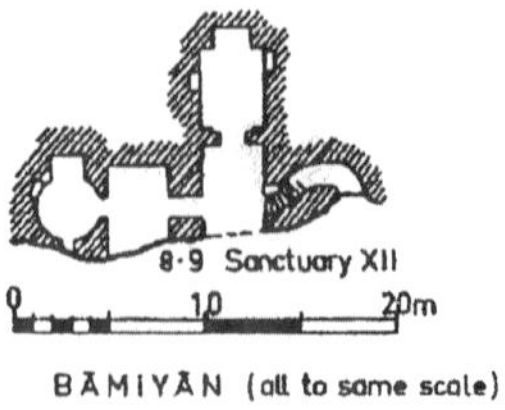

TIFF Bild

ABRAU_1.1_BALL1982.tif

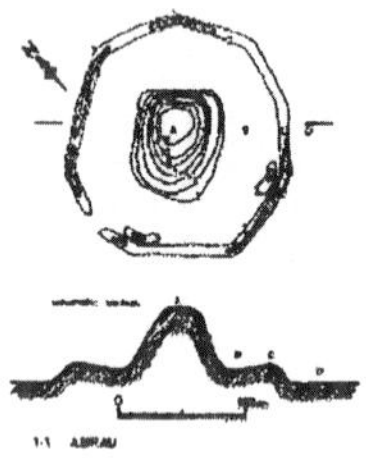

TIFF Bild

ABU HURAIRA_1.2_BALL1982.tif

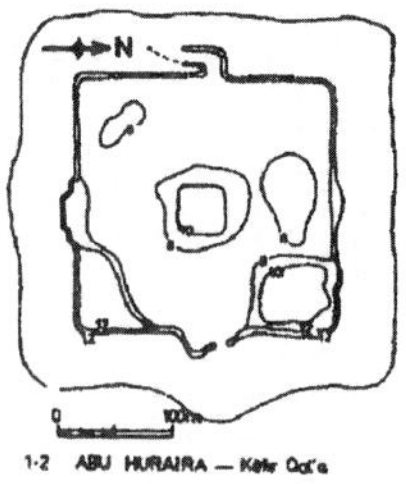

TIFF Bild

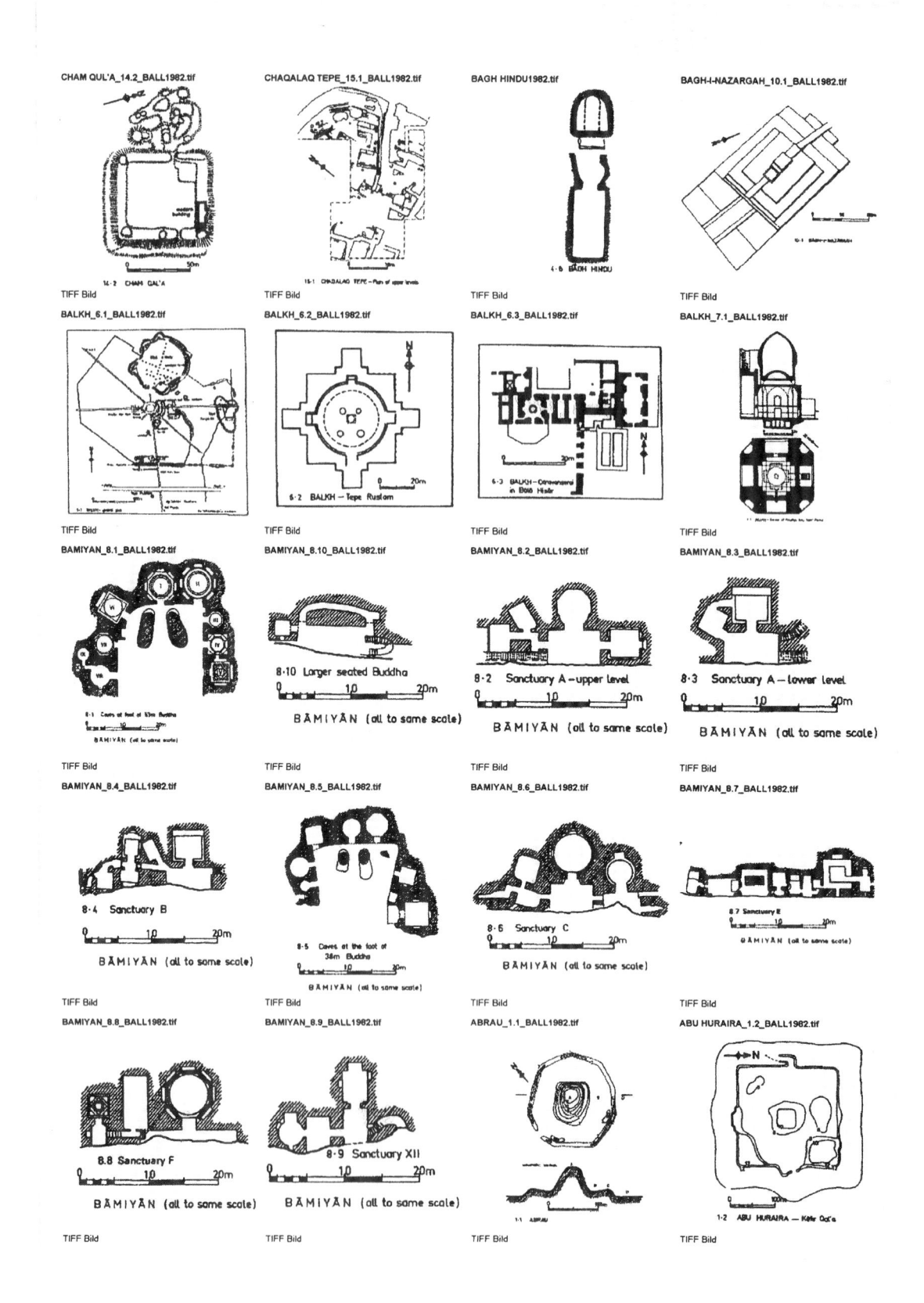

conservation of the fragments and the two Buddha niches (see p. 52 ff.). The main aim is to stabilise the rocks around the niches and the remains of the Buddha statues, being aware that not the whole cliff with its innumerable caves that have been in a process of weathering and decay for centuries can be consolidated, but instead only special areas and cracks which have become dangerous due to the explosions. The measurements with the total station (Mario Santana, see figs. pp. 51, 56–59) are a new basis for the future work. The magnetic field measurements by Jörg Faßbinder on a surface of c. one hectare in front of the Great Buddha have revealed architectural structures in the subsoil so far unknown. Although the ground was covered with iron scrap documenting the combat operations of the past years, the measuring surface could be cleared completely of this iron scrap. The result of this magnetometer prospection proves the existence of house ground plans as well as of building structures in the area of the Great Buddha. Clearly recognisable in the magnetic picture are also paths leading towards the statue as well as a boundary wall with entrance running along parallel to the rock. In a measuring campaign of a few days it would have been possible to measure the entire area between the two Buddhas – possibly the monastery area? – if this area had not been so contaminated by mines (Concerning magnetic prospection see Helmut Becker, Jörg W. E. Fassbinder, Magnetic Prospection in Archaeological Sites, Monuments and Sites VI, Munich 2001).

As far as the stabilisation of the most dangerous parts threatened to fall off and the safeguarding of details such as historic plasters on the Small Buddha are concerned, there is an urgent need to react quickly. The heaps of rubble reaching into the side caves of the niches would have to be fenced off to protect visitors and the clearing of material should only be done by experts and by no means as part of a general 'tidying up'. It was also observed that heavy helicopters of the American forces fly much too low over this region, thus causing dangerous vibrations.

M. Pz.

*Abridged version of a report by Michael Petzet, 29 July 2002.

DATA BANK CENTER Afghanistan

Aachen University of Technology RWTH
ICOMOS Germany 2002
Prof. Dr. M. Petzet
Prof. Dr. M. Jansen

Co-ordinator:
G. Toubekis

Gudrun Athing
Mayhar Azimi
Ricarda Bruns
Svenja Doepp
Karin Geiges

Karsten Ley
Isabelle Mehlhorn
Gustav Mossakowski
Astrid Sauerteig
Gero Velten

◁ Databank of monuments and historic sites in Afghanistan, established in cooperation with RWTH Aachen ▷

Michael Petzet

Anastylosis or Reconstruction – Considerations on a Conservation Concept for the Remains of the Buddhas of Bamiyan (2002)[1]

The blowing-up of the Buddhas of Bamiyan by the Taliban in March 2001, against which ICOMOS protested in vain together with ICOM (see p. 37),[2] was an incredible act of vandalism pointing like a beacon at the various risks and threats with which our cultural heritage is confronted. Without a thorough investigation of the condition one had to assume that of these sites in the middle of a spectacular cultural landscape only rubble and dust had remained after the explosion. Under these circumstances, considerations at the UNESCO seminar on the Preservation of Afghanistan's Cultural Heritage in Kabul in May 2002 still went into two directions: preserving the state after the destruction or reconstruction of the state before the destruction.

- Preserving the state after the destruction could be combined with the idea of refraining from any intervention, keeping this site unchanged as a kind of memorial to the act of vandalism by the Taliban, which upset the world.[3] However, it soon became clear that if only for the sake of the safety of future visitors those parts of the rock affected by the explosion need to be consolidated and that at least the existing remains of the sculptures should be preserved.
- After every loss ideas of reconstructing the state before the destruction suggest themselves; ideas which were considered by the Afghan government also in view of using this most famous historic site of the country for future tourism. In the public media the idea of reconstructing the Buddhas has come up time and again ever since:

– reconstruction of the state before the destruction in the sense of a 3 D-virtual computer reconstruction and physical models of the Great Buddha on the scale 1:200 and 1:25 (shown in the Swiss pavilion of the World Exhibition in Aichi, Japan) by Prof. Armin Grün, ETH Zurich, based on photogrammetric measurements made in 1970 by the Austrian professor Robert Kostka (Graz University)[4] or even of an 'original' state (e.g. a complete Buddha with a gold coating as mentioned in early sources?);

– reconstruction of one of the Buddhas in traditional techniques, i.e. hewn from the rock and coated with loam plaster, in which case the historic substance of the existing niche would suffer considerably – a project of the Afghan sculptor Amanullah Haidersad;[5]

– or reconstruction with modern materials (a brand-new Buddha made of concrete?) or at least its evocation with laser techniques in the context of a future sound-and-light show – a suggestion which after the disaster and under the present circumstances seems rather strange, for example, the laser project discussed in 2005 by the Japanese media artist Hiro Yamagata (see p. 83).

Some of these suggestions would in fact lead to a destruction of what was spared by the barbaric act of the Taliban. Also they point at the basic dangers of every process of reconstruction – a topic that was often discussed in the European conservation theory of the last century. In a preservation context reconstruction generally is related to the re-establishment of a state that has been lost (for whatever reason), based on pictorial, written or material sources; it can range from completion of elements or partial reconstruction to total reconstruction with or without incorporation of existing fragments. A necessary prerequisite for either a partial or a total reconstruction is always extensive source documentation on the state that is to be reconstructed; nonetheless, a reconstruction seldom proceeds without some hypothesis. One of the criteria for the inscription of cultural properties in UNESCO's World Heritage List according to the 1972 convention is that *reconstruction is only acceptable if it is carried out on the basis of complete and detailed documentation on the original and to no extent to the conjecture.*[6] Thus, reconstruction is possible in principle, but it requires a sound scientific basis. The comments in article 9 of the Venice Charter are in a sense also valid for reconstruction: *The process of restoration is a highly specialised operation. It is...based on respect for original material and authentic documents. It must stop at the point where conjecture begins* ... Besides, reconstruction is not expressly forbidden by the Venice Charter, as is often maintained. However, based on the Charter's highly restrictive overall attitude also in regard to replacements, we can conclude that the authors of the Charter were certainly very sceptical of all reconstruction work: Although reconstruction is not 'forbidden' the pros and cons must nonetheless be very carefully weighed. Just as a reconstructed completion that is based on insufficient evidence or questionable hypothesis in fact falsifies a monument, so an unverified 'creative reconstruction' cannot really restitute a lost monument, not even formally – and certainly not in its historical dimension. In addition, there is often confusion about the materials and the technical and artistic execution of the lost original.

Independently of the scepticism of many colleagues towards the various suggestions for a reconstruction of the Buddha statues the first ICOMOS mission to Bamiyan in July 2002 focussed for the time being only on practical and technical solutions to secure the existing remains with limited funds and thus to preserve these world-famous historic sites as places of memory for future generations. As part of the ICOMOS initiative to help save endangered cultural properties in Afghanistan, I was able to carry through with my colleagues a first investigation of the situation in Bamiyan. Putting questions of reconstruction aside, the first aim was to consolidate the rock structure of the two niches and especially the traces and remains of the Buddha statues which are still visible like silhouettes on the back walls of the niches. As historic monuments these traces are of utmost importance. Compared to my tasks in Dafosi/China (see p. 43), which in some respects were more difficult since a giant cave with three statues of up to 20 metres height had to be made earthquake-proof, in Bamiyan we were well aware right from the beginning that not the entire cliff – which for centuries has been affected by weathering and decay – and its innumerable caves could be secured, but only certain areas and dangerous cracks etc. which have widened since the explosions.

The biggest surprise for me was to see the heaps of rubble stretching as far as to the side rooms at the foot of the niches – not at all just 'dust' and indefinable debris, but at least some very big fragments of several tons and quite obviously still the entire material of which the Buddha statues consisted before they were blown up. Just as much as the still visible remains of the figures on the back walls of the niches this is historic material that should be protected, salvaged layer by layer and assigned to the various parts of the statues. Particularly these heaps of fragments, themselves depressing witnesses of the destructive frenzy of the Taliban, were the focus of the measurements and photographic documentation of our ICOMOS team.

In contrast to the ideas of a reconstruction, uttered without detailed knowledge of the situation and highly problematic for the reasons mentioned above, these fragments are pointing at a conservation concept called anastylosis which is common practice at many archaeological sites world-wide. This method developed in the field of classical archaeology but also applicable for partially destroyed monuments of later epochs, is referred to in article 15 of the Venice Charter. *All reconstruction work should however be ruled out a priori. Only anastylosis, that is to say, the reassembling of existing but dismembered parts can be permitted. The material used for integration should always be recognisable and its use should be the least that will ensure the conservation of a monument and the reinstatement of its form.* According to this method, the fragments of an ashlar stone building – for instance a Greek temple – found on or in the ground could be put together again; the original configuration is determined from the site and from traces of workmanship, from peg holes, etc. If extant, the original foundations are used in situ. Such a re-erection demands preliminary work in building research; an inventory of all the extant building components, which must be analysed and measured exactly, results in a reconstruction drawing with as few gaps as possible, so that mistakes with the anastylosis can be avoided. A technical plan must also be worked out to preclude damage during re-erection and to address all aspects of conservation, including the effect of weathering. Finally, the didactic plan for an anastylosis must be discussed, with concern also being given to future use by tourists. In order to be able to show original fragments – a capital, part of an entablature, a gable, etc. – on their original location and in their original context as part of an anastylosis, there is of course a need for more or less extensive provisional structures. The fragments in an anastylosis should only be conserved and presented as originals; they are not completed as in a restoration or embedded in a partial or complete reconstruction. The limits of anastylosis are reached when the original fragments are too sparse and would appear on the provisional structure as a sort of 'decoration'. Anastylosis, an approach which can indeed serve to protect original material in certain circumstances, also illustrates the special role of the fragment in archaeological heritage management as well as the particular significance of conservation work in this context. These are some general reflections on anastylosis in my *Principles of Monument Conservation*,[7] which can also be applied to the case of the Buddhas of Bamiyan.

Even if the task may seem unusual in view of the enormous dimensions of such giant statues of 55 m and 38 m height, anastylosis, quite common in conservation practice, in this special case seems urgent if one wants to save the entire historic substance still extant. As early as during the preliminary work for the anastylosis, which should go ahead at the same time as the consolidation of the rock to enable a sensible co-ordination of the steps of work, a whole range of technical details would have to be solved. It starts with the installation of a construction site, for which instead of a modern crane that could probably only be transported to the site with the greatest difficulties one could perhaps fall back upon wooden constructions or a properly anchored hanging scaffold with a movable platform. In front of the Western Buddha there is enough space for the construction site, where all layers of fragments could be spread out. In front of the Eastern Buddha where the terrain drops very steeply such a plane surface could be created provisionally. Assigning the stones to the various parts of the giant statues will be made easier by a comparison with the different stone layers. On the other hand the necessary works for fixing and stabilising cracks as well as for reassembling the fragments, all of which require very special methods, are made more difficult by the partly crumbling rock that resembles *nagelfluh*. Besides, as with every anastylosis special considerations are necessary for an inconspicuous load-bearing frame in the background, which in this case for obvious reasons should be of steel. Whereas every imaginable kind of reconstruction could interfere with the walls of the niches more or less drastically, only simple anchors would be necessary to hold the load-bearing frame for the anastylosis. The frame could stand free

Western Buddha, general view of the niche, 2002 ▷
Western Buddha, general view of the niche and view of the fragments from the top, 2002 ▷▷

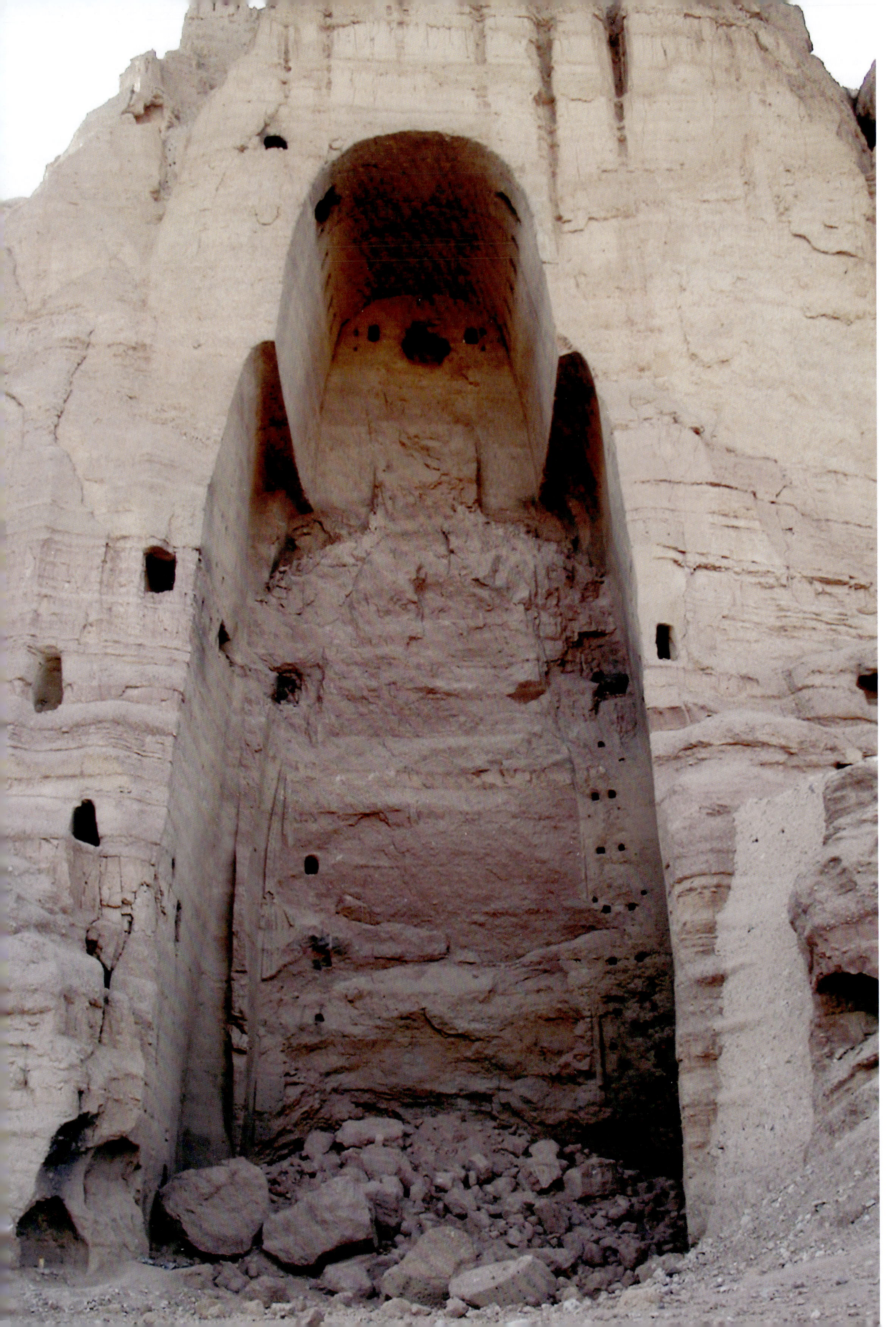

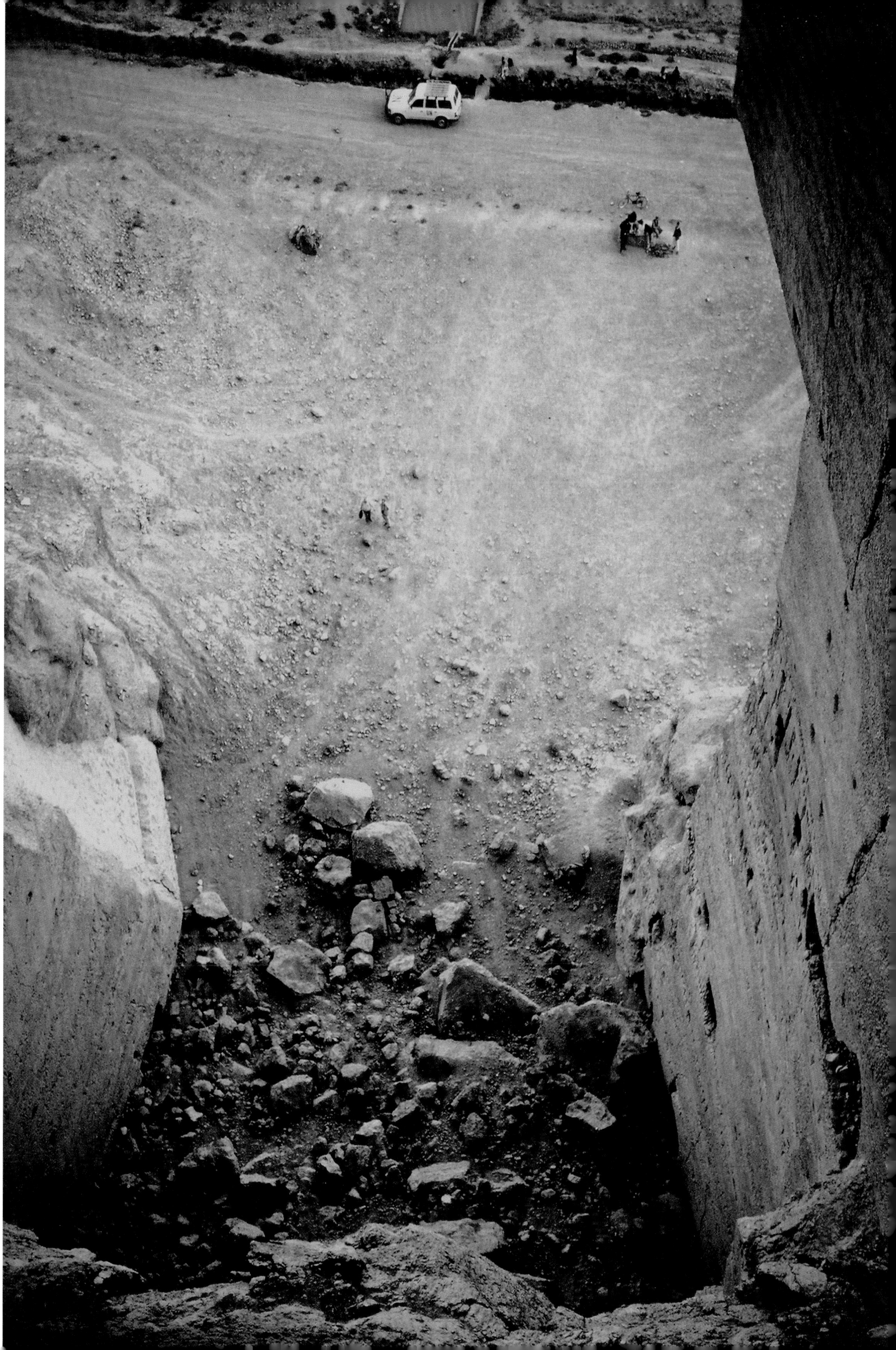

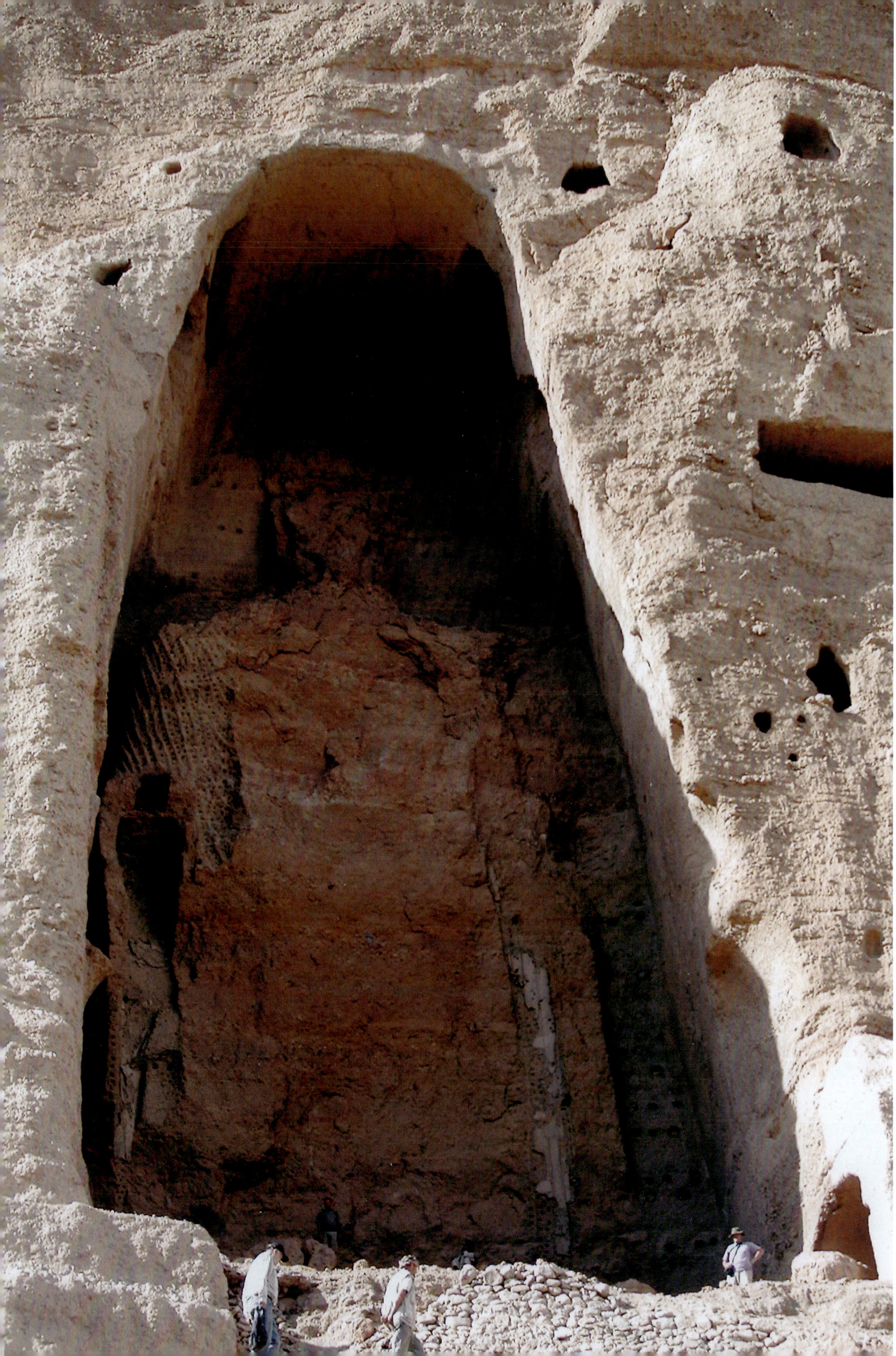

in front of the back wall, the latter preserved in its condition after the destruction and therefore showing the traces of the destroyed figures like a silhouette so that the memory of the disaster would be kept alive.

During our technical investigations in Bamiyan in July 2002 this conservation concept of securing the existing remains in conjunction with an anastylosis preserving all traces of history, including the memory of the destruction in 2001, seemed almost self-evident. From my point of view this is the only appropriate solution for this unique place. Any imaginable type of 'brand new' Buddhas would only harm the authentic spirit. In the meantime, such considerations seem to have found the consent of UNESCO, but of course we have to wait for further decisions of the Afghan government. So I can only hope that under the guidance of UNESCO this cooperation started in 2002 between an international ICOMOS team, Afghan colleagues and a regional workforce will continue.

It would be highly desirable if colleagues from India could also contribute, especially since the last comprehensive restoration work was executed by the Archaeological Survey of India (ASI). Considering the extraordinary importance of this world-famous historic site the safeguarding of the Bamiyan Buddhas should be a joint effort of many implemented step by step. However, as far as securing the most dangerous parts threatened to fall off and the consolidation of details such as historic plasters on the remains of the Small Buddha are concerned, there is a great urgency to start as soon as possible. Furthermore, the stone fragments filling even some of the side caves need to be blocked off by a fence in front of the niches to avoid visitors being injured but also to ensure that none of that material is removed, especially not during any uncontrolled 'clearing work'. Instead, the removal of every layer of the stone piles must always be under the control of experts.

Naturally, our first considerations on a conservation concept presented here in a very sketchy manner need to be further elaborated. Besides, this concept touches many principles of our profession and questions that are not only being dealt with in the Venice Charter, the foundation document of ICOMOS, but also in several Charters and Guidelines; e.g. the aspect of authentic material, which in the case of an anastylosis using only original fragments will even satisfy the strictest 'substance fetishist'. There is also the question of reversibility, which should at least be kept as a possible option, and finally the question of intangible values, which have become increasingly important in the past years. The latter are being guaranteed by a strong *genius loci* in a spectacular cultural landscape with all the witnesses of Buddhist and Muslim traditions, also constituting the cultural wealth of present-day Afghanistan. Taking this great tradition into consideration the Afghan government's wish to reconstruct to a certain degree what has been lost is quite understandable. Because in conjunction with the deep-felt human concern that arises over rebuilding after catastrophes, there is always the additional issue of the perceptible presence of the past at the monument site, an issue that involves more than extant or lost historic fabric.

◁ Eastern Buddha niche with remains of the statue, 2002

Notes

1 Revised version of Michael Petzet, *Anastylosis or Reconstruction – the Conservation Concept for the Remains of the Buddhas of Bamiyan*, in: ICOMOS 13th General Assembly, Madrid 2002, pp. 189–192; abridged version in: *Heritage at Risk 2002/2003*, pp. 16–19. – See also M. Petzet, *ICOMOS's Concept and Measures to Safeguard the Remains of the Bamiyan Buddhas*, in: Preserving Bamiyan, Proceedings of the International Symposium 'Protecting the World Heritage Site of Bamiyan', Tokyo, 21 December 2004, Tokyo 2005, pp. 93–99.

2 For the text see also *Heritage at Risk 2000*, p. 39.

3 In particular Prof. Ikuo Hirayama, UNESCO Goodwill Ambassador, pleaded at the International Seminar in Kabul (27–29 May 2002, cf. p. 39) for leaving the site as it is and for investing the money in humanitarian aid for refugees rather than in a reconstruction, *There are other world cultural heritages that memorialize atrocities (Auschwitz ... the Atomic Bomb Dome in Hiroshima). I suggest that the Bamiyan caves be preserved as a symbolic reminder of the barbaric destruction of culture by human beings.*

4 Cf. Grün, A.; Remondino, F.; Zhang, L., *The Reconstruction of the Great Buddha of Bamiyan, Afghanistan*, in: ICOMOS 13th General Assembly, Madrid 2002, pp. 49–55.

5 *Die Rückkehr des Buddhas von Bamian*, in: Süddeutsche Zeitung, 17 April 2002.

6 Operational Guidelines for the Implementation of the World Heritage Convention, 2005, paragraph 86.

7 Michael Petzet: *Principles of Monument Conservation/ Principes de la Conservation des Monuments Historiques*, ICOMOS-Hefte des Deutschen Nationalkomitees, vol. XXX, Munich 1999, pp. 43/44. – Michael Petzet, *Principles of Preservation/An Introduction to the International Charters for Conservation and Restoration 40 Years after the Venice Charter*, in: *International Charters for Conservation and Restoration* (Monuments and Sites I), 2nd edition, Munich 2004, pp. 7–29.

▽ Western Buddha niche, measurements with total station carried out by Mario Santana

Yazhou Zou, Florian Unold

First Considerations on the Stability of the Buddha Niches and their Stone Material, 2002[*]

The rock niches as well as the two Buddha statues were carved out of the rock faces (figs. 1 and 2). These rock faces are mainly composed of two types of rock that are present in alternating series of strata. The principal part (ca. 70 % of the statue) is a typical loosely deposited conglomerate. That conglomerate is interspersed with sandstone that, however, only makes up ca. 20 % of the volume of the statue; the remaining 10 % are surface material.

The compressive and tensile strength of the materials is very low, even the influence of small forces leads to destruction.

The conglomerate is highly susceptible to water. Under water, a specimen of the material disintegrated into a pile of sandy pebble stone after only a few seconds (see fig. 3).

Examinations have shown that the binding agent between sand and pebble granules mainly consists of sodium chloride salt, which also explains the cause of the high susceptibility to water. The crystals of the salt are clearly visible under the microscope.

The surfaces of the statues as well as of the other formations appear to be more resistant to water and mechanical influences. It remains to be examined whether this was caused by an artificial treatment of the surfaces in the past or by the many years of climatic strain on the areas near the surface and the chemical reaction connected with it.

The cracks in the niches can be subdivided into three groups - cracks that existed prior to the blasting, cracks widened by the blasting and new cracks caused by the

Fig. 1. The Western Buddha, 2002

Fig. 2. The Eastern Buddha, 2002

Fig. 3. Testing the conglomerate: dry specimen (left), after a few seconds under water (centre), after sedimentation (right)

blasting. The cracks that already existed prior to the blasting are mainly located in the vault area above the head and on the side walls of the niches and run downward in straight lines. The blasts caused new cracks especially in the area of the back wall of the niche (viewing area). Figures 4 and 5 (view from the bottom) show the location and extension of the various forms of cracks.

The areas at risk can be classified into three risk groups:

Risk Group gF-1: *Highly endangered areas*
  Areas often cut through by new cracks, a falling-down of major fragments is to be immediately expected, i.e. these areas are just in a state of limit equilibrium. These highly endangered areas are mostly located in the upper part of the back wall of the niche. The average weight of fragments that are at the risk of falling down is ca. 1 metric ton.

Risk Group gF-2: *Area with a locally endangered stability*
  These are areas that are not yet in a state of limit equilibrium with regard to their static stability. But concussions/vibrations or further weathering may lead to a falling-off of fragments, which, however, currently does not affect adjacent areas or the overall formation (static stability of the niche as a whole). In these areas already existing old cracks intersect with new cracks caused by the blasting. If, however, these cracks should further widen due to concussions/vibrations or weathering, the entire cave will lose its stability.

Risk Group gF-3: *Areas that, in case of failure, directly endanger the entire formation*
  With regard to their static stability, these areas (just like gF-2) are not yet in a state of limit equilibrium. That, however, may occur as a consequence of concussions/vibrations or further weathering. Here, the particular risk is caused by the cracks widened by the blasts.

At the Western Buddha, the stability of the niche is endangered on three spots (gSt-1 to 3, see Fig. 1). On the spots gSt-1 and gSt-2, the local stability is at risk. If the local stability is lost on several spots, the overall stability will be endangered by further weathering. On the spot gSt-3, the rock is cut through by cracks widened by the blasts. Inside the staircase, the widened cracks are clearly visible at that place behind the wall. The stability on this spot influences the entire stability of the cave.

At the Eastern Buddha, the overall stability of the niche is highly endangered on the two spots gSt-1 and gSt-2 (see Fig. 2). The cracks newly caused as well as the cracks widened as a consequence of the blasts are clearly visible here. The stability on both spots has a direct influence on the overall stability of the niche.

Proposals for the protection and identification of the fallen-off pieces of rock

The rocks are highly susceptible to water so that rain or melt water might cause the fallen-off pieces of rock to disintegrate into a pile of sandy pebble stone within a very short time. Therefore, the pieces of rock must urgently be protected against water and further weathering. A coating might provide a long-term protection if this is not in conflict with aspects of the preservation of historical monuments and other solutions are not possible. A suitable material would have to be found by specific examinations. Before that, the fallen-off pieces of rock should be identified for the reconstruction. The identification could be carried out together with measures for the protection of the fragments. For that purpose, the fragments must be transported. In order to avoid damage caused by transport and storage as well as in view of the assessment of possible reconstruction measures, it is necessary to determine the mechanical properties of the different rocks and adapt the transport measures to the strength properties.

Proposals for the stabilization

The endangered areas in the viewing walls of both niches (back walls of the niches) are so much at risk with regard to their stability that, prior to the performance of any possible reconstruction measures, it will be necessary to take measures for their stabilization (including the removal of areas that were damaged to a particularly large extent).
  Areas that cause a danger to the overall stability must be secured, since otherwise even slight concussions/vibrations in connection with weathering processes might cause the niches to collapse.
In order to guarantee the stability of the rock niches as well

as safety on site in the long term, it is necessary to secure also those areas that only constitute a danger to the local stability.

The rock and the conglomerate are so loose that it must be expected that they will disintegrate as a consequence of drilling work that may be necessary. This fact is to be taken into consideration in particular with regard to the cave systems (staircase) located behind the endangered areas where the classical system of stabilization by means of anchors cannot be used. The local stability of the endangered rocks and thus the overall stability of both niches with the caves located behind them (staircase) should be thoroughly examined prior to stabilization. A promising stabilization method can only be determined by means of tests.

* Abridged version of the report *Situation of the Buddha Statues in the Valley of Bamiyan, Afghanistan* by Dr.-Ing. Y. Zou and Dipl.-Ing. F. Unold, 5 November 2002. – See also Yazhou Zou and Florian Unold, *Die großen Buddha-Statuen von Bamiyan/Zustand, Stabilität und Möglichkeiten der Rekonstruktion*, in: Bautechnik 80 (2003), Heft 7, pp. 417–422.

Fig. 4. Upper part of the Western Buddha

Fig. 5. Upper part of the Eastern Buddha

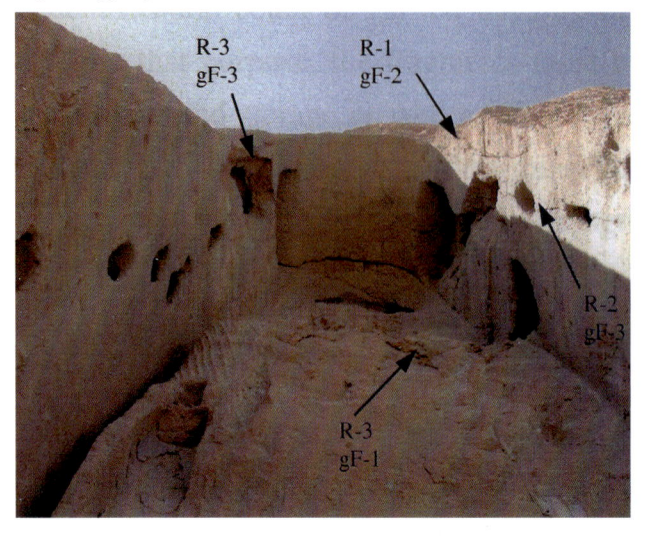

At the end of 2002 ICOMOS Germany organised the first meeting of a UNESCO/ICOMOS Working Group on the Preservation of the Bamiyan Site:

Recommendations of the First Expert Working Group on the Preservation of the Bamiyan Site, Munich, 21–22 November 2002*

Recommendations for Consolidation and Preservation

Recognizing the results of the expert groups that worked at the site of Bamiyan in July and September 2002, the participants at the international 'Expert Working Group on the Preservation of the Bamiyan Site' which was held in Munich on 21 and 22 November 2002, recommend that:

a) *The Bamiyan site, consisting of the Northern cliff of the Bamiyan Valley, with its caves, especially the niches of the monumental Buddhas, the remains of the blown-up Buddhas themselves, and the area in front of the cliff for, at least, 100 meters, should be consolidated and preserved. Further cultural area within the main Valley, including Foladi and Kakrak, should be identified and protected after adequate archaeological research;*
b) *an appropriate infrastructure be established for the conservation and preservation of the monuments;*
c) *the entire site be fully documented;*
d) *monitoring of the cliff and the existing fractures be performed;*
e) *emergency actions be executed immediately, according to priorities;*
f) *an execution plan be drawn up according to available data, together with new information, as necessary;*
g) *training of local people and their involvement in the activities be carried out;*
h) *the treatment and conservation of the loose fragments of the monumental Buddhas should include:*
   - *documentation,*
   - *geological investigations,*
   - *the professional placement of the remaining fragments of the Buddha statues according to stratigraphic identification,*
   - *protection of remains/fragments in a protected lapidarium.*

Activities should be carried out simultaneously, if possible, in order to optimise the time work schedule. Safety, especially in the niches, should have priority.

* Abridged version without recommendations on wall paintings and archaeological projects. For the full text see Heritage at Risk 2002/2003, pp. 19f.

Cliff with Western Buddha niche

2003

Thanks to funds for safeguarding cultural goods in Afghanistan provided by the German Foreign Office in 2003 ICOMOS was able to continue the work begun in 2002. A decisive factor for this successful work was the cooperation with UNESCO, which in agreement with the Afghan Ministry of Information and Culture (the most important contact persons being the heads of the departments of historic monuments and archaeology, Abdul Ahad Abbasi and Abdul Wasey Feroozi) coordinated the measures to save monuments and sites. However, the main focus of the ICOMOS activities in 2003 was no longer Kabul, where in 2002 and in cooperation with the Aga Khan Trust for Culture (AKTC) the restoration of the Babur Park and the historic quarter Ashekan wa Arefan were looked after. Instead, ICOMOS concentrated on the cultural landscape of the Bamiyan Valley, newly inscribed on the World Heritage List in Danger (see p. 17).

As Marcus Schadl, the contractor of ICOMOS for the tasks in Kabul, was taken over by the AKTC at the beginning of that year and additional funds for continuing this work were handled by the German Embassy, the work of ICOMOS in Kabul concentrated on occasional consultations. The group of stone restorers working in Bamiyan was able to give advice on how to conserve the stone of the She Jehan Mosque and the Babur Grave (consequences of failed restoration measures of past decades, completion of marble elements, etc). For these two objects in the Babur Park the AKTC was given a grant of 25,000 euros.

The start of the work of ICOMOS in the Bamiyan Valley was delayed due to the insecure situation in Afghanistan. Faced with the war in Iraq UNESCO cancelled a conference of the International Coordination Committee for the Safeguarding of Afghanistan's Cultural Heritage, planned to be held in Kabul in May. This first meeting then took place from 16–18 June in Paris. At this meeting the undersigned presented the conservation concept of ICOMOS for the Buddha statues developed since 2002 (see pp. 46–51) and a proposal by Professor Fritz Wenzel for stabilising the threatened rock parts. The stabilisation of the rocks was then started in September/October by the Italian company RODIO, which – following the concept of Professor Claudio Margottini – focussed at first on the most fragile rock section on the upper east side of the Small Buddha niche (see report by Margottini, pp. 175 ff.). These stabilisation measures of UNESCO on the rocks funded by the Japan Fund in Trust were a precondition for the safeguarding of

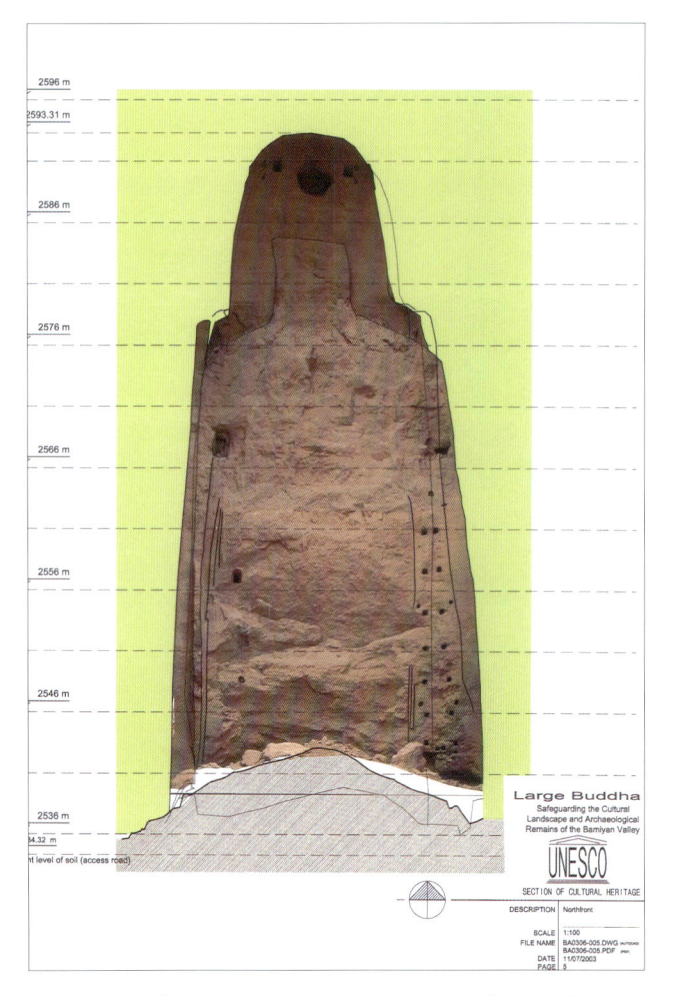

Western Buddha, measurements of the back wall (A. Fahim, M. Santana)

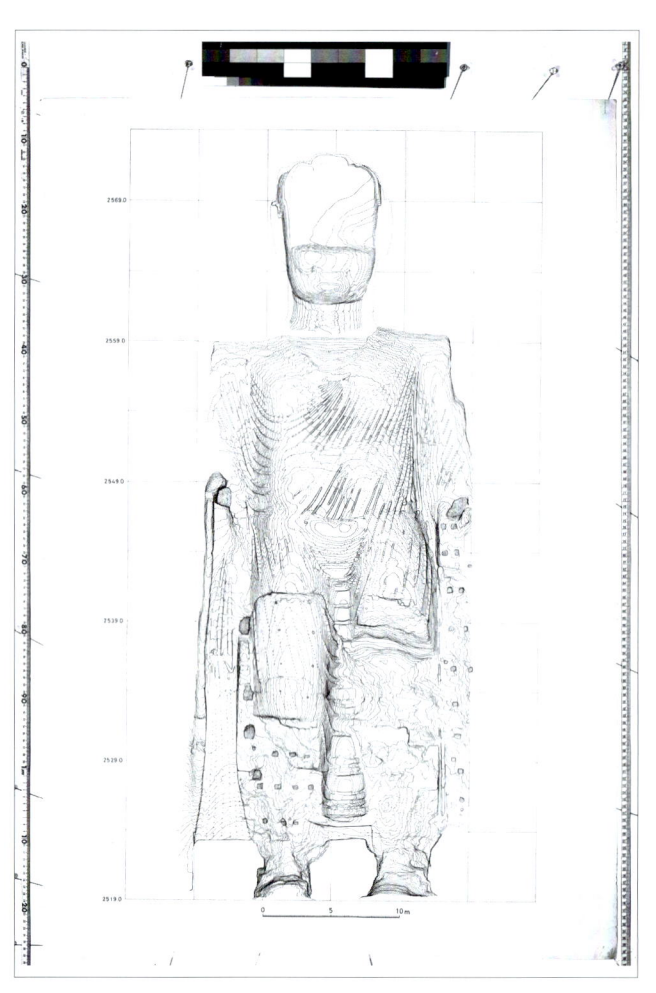

Western Buddha, photogrammetric measurement of the Western Buddha (R. Kostka 1974)

the Buddha fragments and all other conservation measures recommended by ICOMOS and its specialists in saving the existing historic fabric. Within the framework of the UNESCO/ICOMOS mission to Bamiyan (10–17 September 2003), in which Prof. Michael Jansen and the undersigned took part, the works of RODIO were harmonised with conservation aspects, such as protecting the remains of the Buddha statues on the back walls of the niches (especially the plaster remains of the Eastern Buddha).

New results were achieved by the ICOMOS mission of a group of German stone restorers to Bamiyan from 23 October to 3 November 2003 (See the report *Überlegungen zum Umgang mit den Fragmenten der zerstörten Buddha-Statuen* by Ulrich Bauer-Bornemann, Edmund Melzl, Henrick Romstedt and Michael Scherbaum.). This mission was carried out together with the geologist Dr Michael Urbat from the University of Cologne (see his report 2006, p. 89 f.). Thanks to his findings it will be possible to better identify the original position of the fragments.

For all these activities in the Bamiyan Valley it was helpful that in 2002 thanks to the funds from the German Foreign Office a group of mudbrick buildings, including a mosque, right next to the Great Buddha niche had already been renovated to serve as very useful 'headquarters' for the custodians and for storing findings and machines. In particular, it was also used to store the special scaffold provided to ICOMOS by the Messerschmitt Foundation and transported to Bamiyan with the help of the German armed forces.

Parallel to the preparatory work for saving the remains

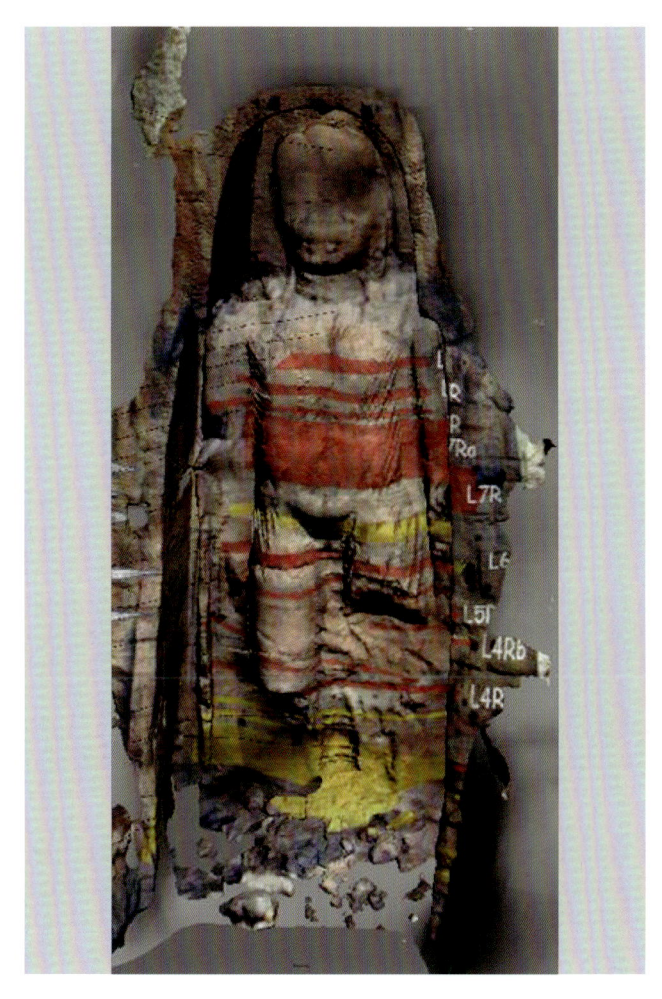

Western Buddha, tentative geological reference profile (M. Urbat)   Western Buddha, tentative sections of the original structure

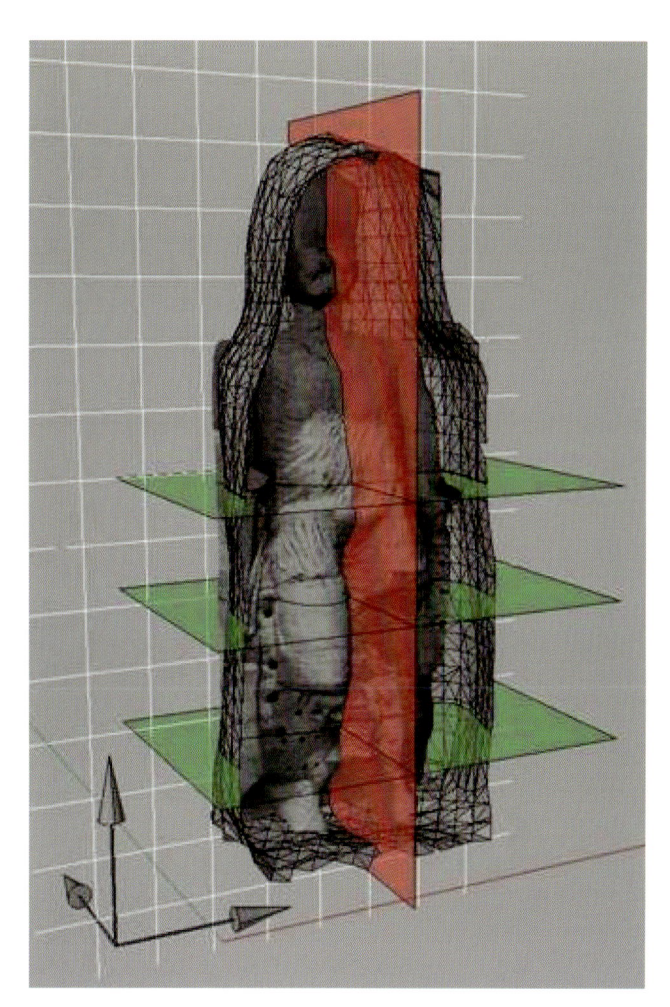

of the Buddha statues funds from the German Foreign Office enabled ICOMOS also to support the preservation of traditional earthen architecture in the Bamiyan Valley. In cooperation with the RWTH Aachen (see also pp. 61–63) the repair of historic mudbrick buildings was combined with investigations on the topology of earthen residential buildings and the traditional building techniques: Preserving the tradition of earthen architecture is particularly important for this quite unique cultural landscape inscribed in the World Heritage List, and ICOMOS's efforts to document and preserve the historic stock of mudbrick buildings add to the work of the Japanese colleagues within the framework of an overall inventory of the cultural heritage.

Finally, it needs to be pointed out that the data bank of all monuments and historic sites in Afghanistan made good progress in 2003. This work begun by ICOMOS in cooperation with the RWTH Aachen provides the fundamentals for the protection and conservation of monuments in the whole country, and as a sort of monument list it could become an indispensable basis in the future for a new Afghan monument protection law. While in 2002 the available literature was added, it was now a question of evaluating the present condition. This is being done in cooperation with the Society for the Protection of Afghanistan's Cultural Heritage (SPACH) and, whenever possible, with local personnel to investigate the historic sites.

M. Pz.

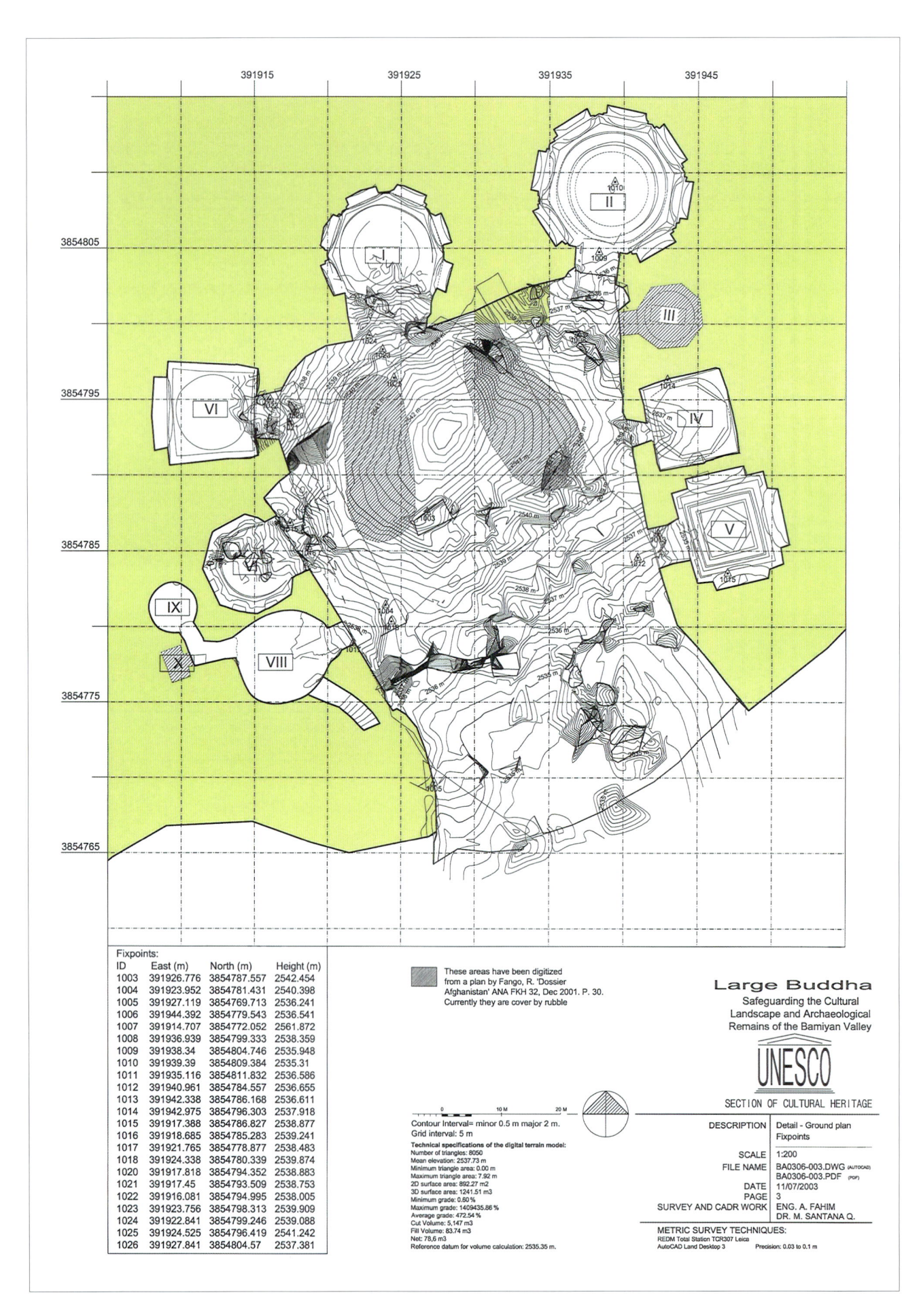

Western Buddha niche, ground plan with fix points (A. Fahim, M. Santana)

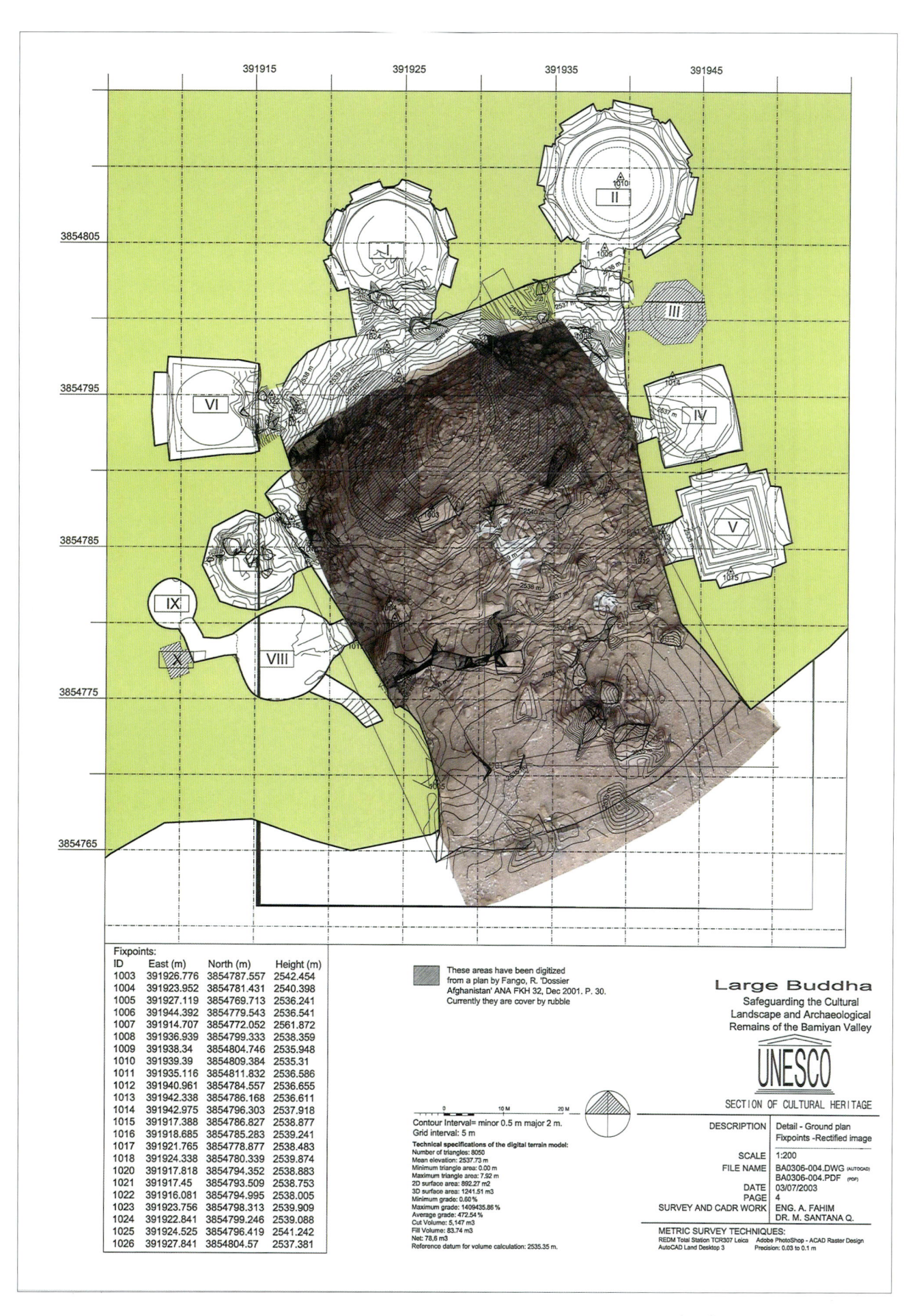

Western Buddha niche, ground plan with fix points, rectified image (A. Fahim, M. Santana)

Pierre Smars, Ulrich J. Dahlhaus
Mission to Bamiyan, October to December 2003

This short version of the report presents some of the works done during the mission of ICOMOS Germany and the University of Aachen (RWTH Aachen, Lehrgebiet Stadtbaugeschichte), in October–December 2003, and the cooperation with the Italian team working on the consolidation of the Eastern Buddha niche (compare report by Margottini, pp. 175 ff.).

Geological investigations at the Western Buddha
One of the recommendations made during the expert meeting held in Munich in November 2002 was to place the remaining fragments of the Buddha statues according to stratigraphic identification. In order to proceed to this identification, an accurate geological survey is necessary. In Bamiyan, this work was done jointly with Dr Urbat from the University of Cologne. Climbers from the Italian firm RODIO did the measurements in the niche.

Two types of measurements were done successively, each of them identifying a particular characteristic of the stone (colour and magnetic susceptibility). A rope was fixed at the centre of the niche, at the top. Then a climber went down taking measurements at regular intervals with handheld scanners. The exact position of each of the measurements was recorded with the total station from the area in front of the niche. It was not possible to continue the measurements down to the bottom as the wall is not vertical and it was impossible to stay in contact with the surface.

Detailed photographs of the Western Buddha
A set of 17 targets was fixed on the surface of the back wall of the niche to serve as reference points to orient high resolution photographs. This was done by a climber of the firm RODIO. The targets are made of small aluminium squares (8 cm x 8 cm) fixed using stainless steel screws and plugs. The operation was difficult: Many stones are unstable, particularly at the level of what remains of the shoulder of the Buddha, and the surface of the wall being very irregular, it is often difficult to stay in contact with it or to access the points where the targets had to be placed.

Survey of the caves in the upper-eastern part of the Small Buddha
While the Italian team was working on the reinforcement of the cliffs their first priority was to work on the upper-right part of the niche of the Eastern Buddha, which is especially unstable. The critical blocks are secured by long anchors.

Geological investigation at the Western Buddha

One of the difficulties of the operation resulted from the fact that the niche is surrounded by caves. To prevent the risk to perforate them, an accurate survey of their geometry was needed. We surveyed the caves in the upper right part of the Buddha. The operation was difficult because of the irregular geometry. On the other hand, it was not necessary to survey a lot of details as only an envelope of the volumes was needed.

Preparation of mortar samples
In the framework of the consolidation works done by the Italian team, many cracks were filled with cement mortar. The colour of this mortar is significantly different from the colour of the stone. One of the questions is therefore to decide which kind of mortar has to be used for the pointing. It has to be decided whether the intervention has to be clearly, slightly or possibly not visible. The mortar has also to resist the weather variations. A set of samples was prepared using different proportions of earth, sand and cement.

Documentation of the traditional architecture
Tolvara is a settlement of about 50 houses, lying in the plain in front of the site of the Buddhas, between Foladi and Bamiyan river (about 15 ha). Most of the houses are of the qala type (qala = fortress): squares of about 30 m of side, formed by walls protecting a variable number of units of living. This kind of architecture is very common in Afghanistan. To some extent and as already mentioned by Meunié (1962) it can also be compared to the architecture in pre-Saharan Morocco.

In general terms, the documentation of traditional earthen architecture is particularly important. Earth is often misunderstood and is still regarded by many as a second-grade material. Studies of particular situations can help to recognise its technical and cultural values. This huge heritage still requires many studies.

On the plan of the Valley of Bamiyan drawn in 1936 by Jacques Meunié, there is not yet a village but just a few separate qalas. The plan does not have very accurate dimensions, but the old qalas can still be identified in the village of today. The situation is rather simple: with the exception of house 39, all the houses with towers at the corners already existed in 1936. This is partly confirmed by photographs taken in 1934 by an English traveller, Robert Byron. Two mills drawn on the plan are still there but completely ruined. More recent photographs (probably taken in the 1960s, as some photographs of the set illustrate the works of reinforcement on the Small Buddha) show the village in apparently the same extension as today.

Qalas usually contain a number of living units, each of them sheltering a family. Most of them are organised around a central courtyard. Some bigger qalas have more than one courtyard. The units occupy from one up to four sides of the qalas. Often, they just have one floor, but there are exceptions. The external walls are built in cob, the internal ones in adobe.

Photo documentation of the Western Buddha with a set of 17 targets ▷

Documentation of the village and its buildings
A photographic inventory of (nearly) all the buildings of the village was prepared. Once again, the digital photographs are stored on files and organised using HTML files. Those photographs show the different typology, but they also show the very poor state of the village. Most of the houses are destroyed and only a few of them inhabited. The entire vision given by the photographic inventory was completed by more detailed surveys. A set of representative houses was chosen so that they would give a good image of the typological variety. Architect L. Hochscherff surveyed the houses, helped sometimes by U. Dahlhaus and our translator. As a typical piece of local 'industry', a mill was also surveyed.

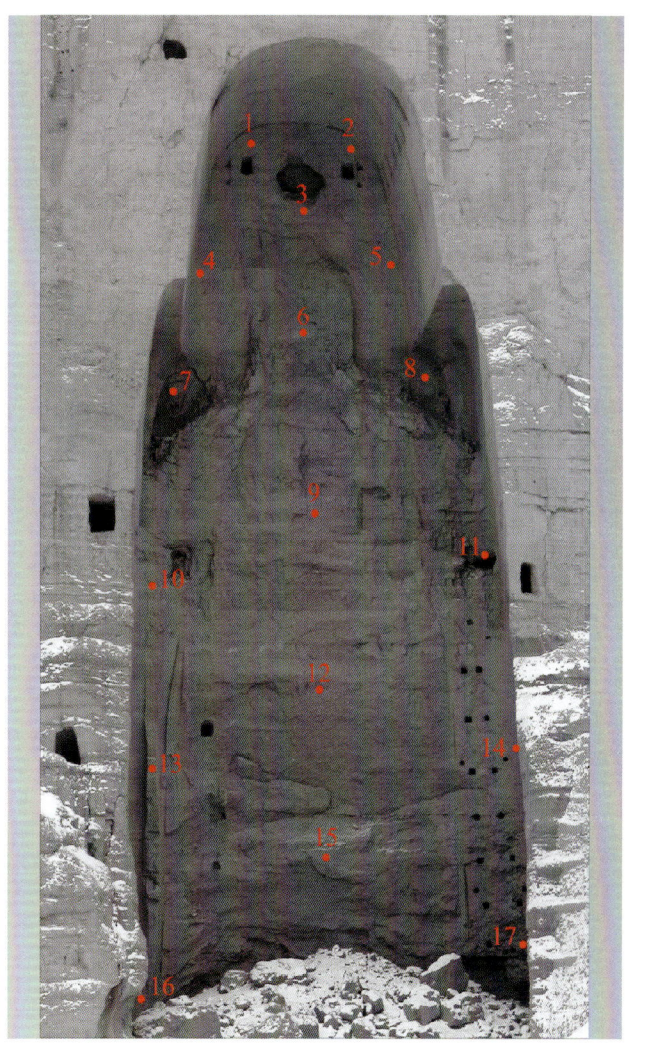

View of the Bamiyan valley (photo: Mario Santana)

Satellite image of the village of Tolvara (reproduction of the original by Pasco)

△▽   Tolvara in 1934 and 2003 (photos of 1934: Robert Byron)

Recommendations of the Second UNESCO/ICOMOS Expert Working Group on the Preservation of the Bamiyan Site

Munich, 18–20 December 2003[*]

Consolidation of the cliffs and niches

<u>1. General</u>

In view of the presence of anti-personnel mines at the Bamiyan site, further demining should be an integral part of all consolidation efforts and be included in future budgets;

a) *Information now available on the destructive effects of seismic hazards at the Bamiyan site should be included in future consolidation plans;*
b) *Investigations should be completed in areas that are not yet accessible, in particular in the lower eastern part of the Small Buddha, and in the lower western part of the Large Buddha. In addition, isostatic maps should be developed and tests on the effectiveness of grouting and anchoring, as well as on the compatibility of old and new materials and further rock mechanic laboratory tests, should be carried out;*
c) *A long-term monitoring system of the cliffs and weather conditions should be installed in 2004. It is essential to include capacity building programmes for the local community in the installation and maintenance of this monitoring system. It would also be desirable to install a basic earthquake monitoring unit and to carry out a study on the effect of the 1956 earthquake;*
d) *The Archaeological Survey of India will be consulted in order to obtain information on consolidation work carried out in Bamiyan in the 1970s.*

<u>2. Small Buddha niche</u>

a) *Plans for the preservation of the Buddha silhouette should be developed and emergency conservation measures started;*
b) *The final consolidation of the Small Buddha niche should be carried out, notably through stabilizing the remaining upper eastern part of the niche;*
c) *It is recommended that consolidation work start on the upper western part.*

<u>3. Large Buddha niche</u>

a) *Plans for the preservation of the Buddha silhouette should be developed and emergency conservation measures started;*
b) *Water infiltration should be limited.*

Conservation of the fragments of the statues of the Buddha

1. *The fragments of the statues should be covered during winter 2003/2004 in order to protect them from deterioration. ICOMOS will provide funds for this purpose to the Afghan Ministry of Information and Culture;*
2. *The safeguarding and conservation of the fragments will be a priority in 2004. Appropriate techniques for moving the fragments out of the niches should be studied, taking into account their fragility and their weight. The fragments should be protected by a temporary roof;*
3. *The fragments should be placed outside the niches under shelter. At the Small Buddha site, an appropriate location (possibly below the slope) will be determined in which to place them;*
4. *Detailed geological analysis of the back of the niches and the fragments should be carried out in order to determine the original position of the fragments. For this purpose, the 3-D documentation successfully carried out by the Japanese firm PASCO should be complemented by studies by ICOMOS in cooperation with the Universities of Aachen and Cologne. The Geological Department of the University of Kabul will be invited to cooperate. Training and capacity building for Afghan students should be included;*
5. *The appropriate conservation, notably the stabilization of this particular kind of rock, should be further studied by ICOMOS stone restorers;*
6. *Further studies of the presentation of the fragments in situ should be initiated.*

---

[*] Abridged version without recommendations on preservation of wall paintings and archaeological activities, for full text see H@R 2004/2005, p. 30f.

2004

Only after the work of the Italian company RODIO, which had started in 2003, had been finished (see report Margottini, p. 175 ff.) and the rear walls of the niches had been secured by steel nets in June 2004 to avoid the risk of falling stones, the salvage of the decaying fragments of both statues could begin. Thanks to funds provided by the German Foreign Office the ICOMOS team in co-operation with the Afghan authorities and the UNESCO office in Kabul made considerable progress between end-June and end-October 2004. At first it was most appropriate to safeguard those fragments of the Buddha Statues which show signs of original surface and to store them in a place protected from rain and snow. The restorers, Edmund Melzl and Engelbert Praxenthaler, as well as engineer Georgios Toubekis (Technical University Aachen) made the site ready and carried out various tasks. Shelters were built in a suitable location in front of the Buddha niche to store the stone material, whilst finds of original plaster had to be secured and stored in boxes inside the mudbrick buildings near the Western Buddha, which had already been restored by ICOMOS in 2002. Parts of these buildings are now used as local office of the Department of Historical Monuments.

The new shelter structures consist of two rooms of 11 m x 9 m and 35 m x 9 m, both 3.80 m high and open to the front of the Western Buddha niche. The area has been secured by a surrounding fence with an entrance gate between the two buildings, so as not to obstruct the view towards the Buddha niche. To harmonise with the reddish appearance of the overall cliff-face and the general traditional architecture of the valley the construction was done in mudbrick with stone foundations and plastered with red mud. Care was taken not to disturb any archaeological sub-surface deposits. The lightweight roof construction was designed in such a way that it can be easily removed to give full access to the individual compartments. The work was executed entirely by a local Bamiyan company. Two employees of the national Monuments Department assisted in the entire process of the project. They supervised the local workers and were acquainted with international standards in documentation and conservation.

The niche of the Western Buddha measures approximately 300 cubic metres and the pile of rubble rises to 8 m above ground level so that about 1600 cubic metres are to be moved. Sand and crumbling pieces of rock have been moved by hand and shovel and placed near the Buddha niche. A layer was laid down separating original ground surface and the niche material so as to be able to distinguish these materials from each other in the future. All pieces were checked for signs of original surface.

Security aspects determined all activity as it was known that the area of the niches served as ammunition stockpile in the years before the destruction. Throughout the progress of the works finds of battle as well as exploded and unexploded ordnance came to light. A de-mining expert assisted the works daily to remove dangerous artefacts and to check the

The Western Buddha niche in 2004

metal finds.

All the debris was examined shovel by shovel by the workers in search of remains of mud plaster and then carried by wheelbarrows to the western side of the fenced area. Pieces of stone showing signs of original surface were transferred to the shelters and stored on wooden pallets. Heavy fragments of rock were moved by a fork lifter or by a 30-ton crane to the shelters. The transport and movement of stone pieces had to be carried out very carefully because of the generally delicate condition of this material. Wooden boards placed between the steel rope and the boulders successfully prevented damage to the rock surface during movement. By using a fork lifter in combination with wooden boards, medium-sized fragments of up to about eight tons could be lifted and carried without damage.

These fragments have been documented describing size, find location, surface condition, signs of carving and physical characteristics. Any original surface on smaller pieces could be identified by a change in colour whereas bigger fragments show holes of almost identical conical shape which used to hold wooden spikes anchoring the surface mud plaster.
The analysis of some mud plaster remains, carried out at

the Leibniz Laboratory, Kiel University under Prof. Grootes, revealed the composition of the original plaster surface of the Buddhas: *The six ^{14}C ages for the Great Buddha cluster between 1440 and 1460 years BP with a simple average of 1452 ± 7 and those for the Small Buddha between 1495 and 1540 years BP with an average of 1513 ± 23. The age difference of 60 ± 24 is statistically significant (2.4 σ). The sample from the niche wall of the Great Buddha shows with 1505 ± 15 years BP an age similar to that of the Small Buddha. The ^{14}C ages fall, unfortunately, in two ^{14}C age plateaus of the radiocarbon dendro-calibration curve, namely AD 540–600 for the Small Buddha and AD 600–640 for the Great Buddha, which results in calibrated age ranges of AD 60–640 and AD 535–600 (2 σ, 95 % probability) for the Great and Small Buddha respectively. Thus the Small Buddha was constructed before the Great Buddha* (cf. also pp. 231–235).

Besides, the larger plaster fragments from the clothing of the Small Buddha, which are still *in situ* on the rear wall of the niche, have been provisionally consolidated by Engelbert Praxenthaler, a safeguarding action at the last minute, because the precious plaster fragments were severely threatened. In 2004 only about a third of the fragments could be saved from the niche of the Great Buddha. The consolidation of the rear walls, so far only provisionally secured with the help of steel nets, is also extremely urgent.

M. Pz.

Report on Salvaging Rock Fragments, 2004

At the Western Buddha the rubble heap resulting from the explosion of the Buddha had a maximum height of eight metres, an average width of 22 metres and a depth of 16 metres. This equalled a volume of c. 1400 m³, which – if one reckons that one wheel barrow can take 50 l – would amount to 28,000 wheel barrow loads. The entire original substance of the Western Buddha, from sand to fist-size stones up to rocks weighing between 80 and 100 tons, had to be recovered from the niche, then documented and protected against the weather. Fastening a protective net of wire cloth on the niche's back wall protected to a certain extent against rockfall during the work in the niche.

Only the surface of the rubble heap had been cleared of landmines. More unexploded ammunition, such as anti-tank mines and aircraft bombs, had to be expected in the rubble. The search for mines in the Buddha rubble, which was necessary every day, was carried out by professional de-mining experts of UNMACA. The de-miners instructed the Afghan workers how to handle metallic finds properly and took care of the appropriate removal of live ammunition. This careful handling with metal and mine detection sometimes led to considerable delays in the excavation work.

Afghan and international experts at the Bamiyan site, 2004

Niche of the Western Buddha with rubble heap before beginning of the salvage work in July 2004

The construction of the shelters begins.

Salvage and classification of rock fragments

After on-site inspection the stone material was divided into two main categories. Conglomerates with mostly red colouring and of differing grain size (from sand to gravel graining) alternate with reddish sandstone-like layers (silt). The silt stone appears very stable, but just like the coarser conglomerate it is extremely moisture-sensitive and erodes very quickly into salty, brittle clay layers.

All fragments were photographed both at the find spot and in the depot and then described on a data sheet. For the salvaging of the rock fragments at the Great Buddha we differentiated between fragments with visible traces of the statue and fragments without traces of the original stone surface. For the first category there were different identifying features. First of all, on the whole we could recognise a yellow-ochre (Indian?) coating; secondly, there were traces of hewing by means of pick hammers. Another unmistakable feature were the typical conical reinforcement holes of 4–5 cm diameter for the wooden pegs that gave the clay plaster a better adhesion and supported the modelled course of the folds. Additional features were the blackened spots. This blackening could be the result of the explosions or of smoke and soot, if the pieces originate from somewhere near the caves.

The fragments were salvaged by hand (shovel and wheelbarrow) and with the aid of machines (forklift, heavy-duty crane). During the process of loading the wheelbarrows every shovel of rubble from the niche was checked for fragments of clay plaster, wooden pieces and other distinctive features. Larger stone fragments could be transported by means of a Volvo forklift (up to six tons) and a heavy-duty crane (Nissan-Kato, maximum capacity 30 tons). For the crane transport the rock fragments were equipped with

△ a ▽ b △ c

Fig. a. Rock fragment weighing tons with typical rows of reinforcement holes

Fig. b. Heavy-duty crane salvaging fragments

Fig. c. Salvaging fragments with a crane

Fig. d – Fig. f. De-miners at work

Fragments being lifted into the shelter through the open roof ▷

▽ d ▽ e ▽ f

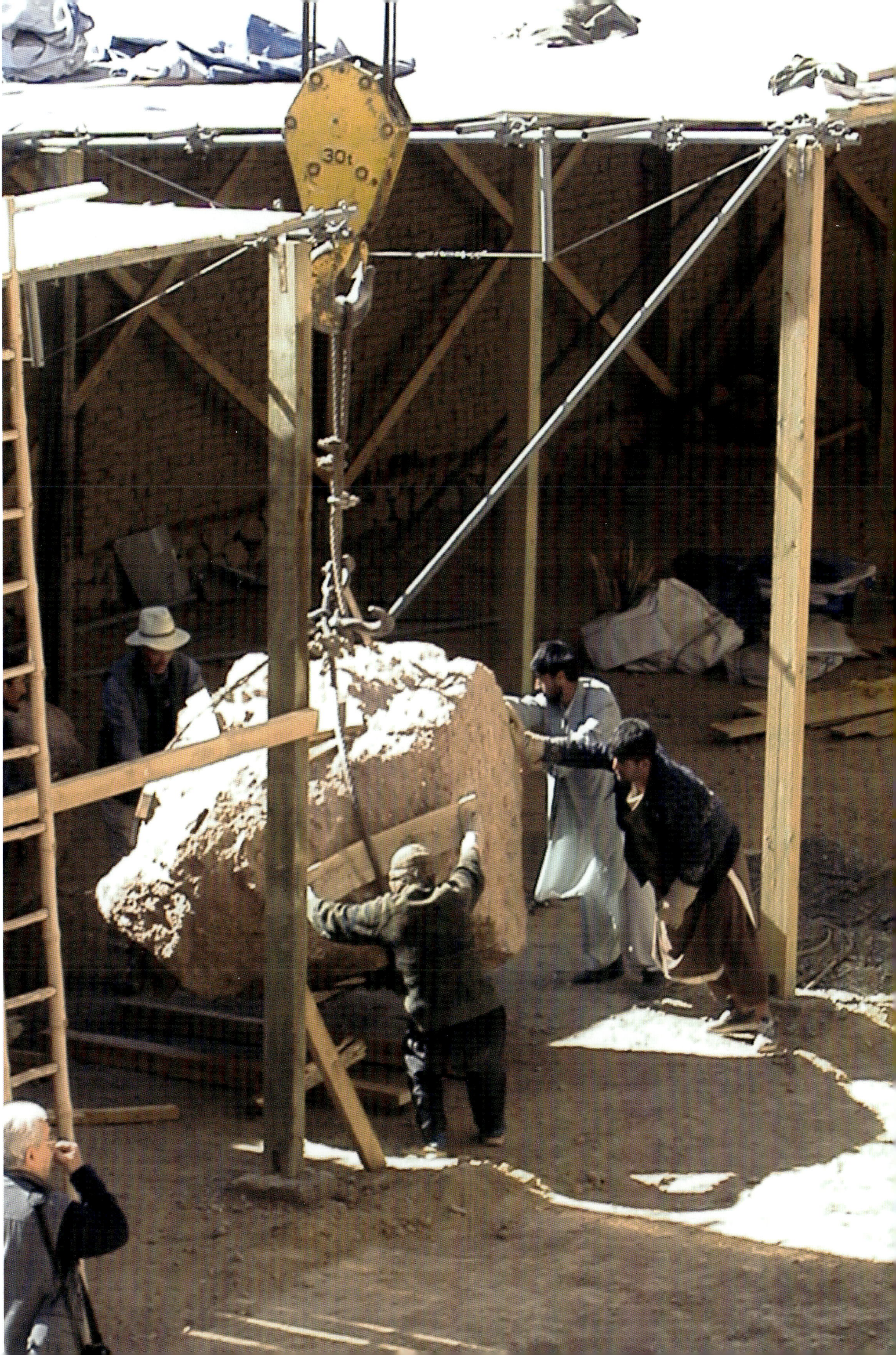
30t

△ ▽　Afghan workers removing the rubble with shovels and wheel barrows

△ Clay plaster fragments in situ at the Eastern Buddha: loosened after the explosions, partly detached from the rock surface and in danger of falling off

△ △ Emergency measure, alpine style, spot-bonding of clay plaster fragments in situ

▽ ▽ Clay plaster fragments in situ at the Eastern Buddha, spot-bonding with clay-gypsum mixture

ICOMOS Mission, Afghanistan, Bamiyan: Gr. Buddha

تشریح پارچه ها / Description of rock fragments / Beschreibung der Felsfragmente

001	نمبر پارچه ها/fragment-/Felsfragment-Nr.: GBF-053
002	موقعیت اصلی پارچه/location of find/Fundlage: Nische of Gr. Buddha, Mitte
003	موقعیت در دیپو/locatin of storage/Lagerort:
004	اندازه روی پارچه measure/Maße (in cm ca.): 205 x 160 x 170
005	وزن/weight/Gewicht (in t ca.): 8
006	سطح/surface/Oberfläche ca. m²: 190 x 130 = 2,47 m²
007	نوعیت سنگ/stone/Gestein: Conglomerate (red) + few SILT
008	تشریح/description/Beschreibung: Oberfläche mit ockerf. Beschichtung, einige Steine ausgebrochen, 18 Löcher / surface with ocre coating, some stones broke out 18 wholes
009	علامت روی سنگ/marks of working/Bearbeitungsspuren: 18 holes, ocre coating
010	مخصوص/special/Besonderheiten: 3 Holzpflöcke, einer abgebrochen / 3 wooden pegs, one is broken
011	گرفتن نمونه/taking of sample/Probenentnahme:

editor/ Bearbeiter: [signature]

Location, date/ Ort, Datum: Bamiyan, 16.8.05

Form in three languages for describing the rock fragments at the Western Buddha

wire-ropes. To avoid damages to the unstable material and to distribute the pressure wooden boards and square timbers were placed between wire-rope and rock.

Very large fragments (two tons and more) were lifted through the unroofed roof and deposited on square timbers in the eastern section of the great hall. Smaller fragments were put on pallets and transported with a forklift to the western section of the hall. On the whole, the fragments had to be stored temporarily in the eastern area of the terrain. For the time being, to be able to identify the individual fragments they were labelled with a black felt tip pen. Later on, the fragments were numbered with small tin-plate signs. (Fragments at the Western Buddha were numbered GBF_001 etc; at the Eastern Buddha KBF_001 etc.)

Fragments of clay plaster

During the safeguarding of the rock fragments and the removal of rubble and sand pieces of clay plaster and appendant material, such as string and wooden pegs, were regularly found. These pieces were deposited in zinc-plated tin boxes, taken to the office for examination, where they were documented and stored.

Stabilisation of plaster remains on the Eastern Buddha

Some areas of the original clay coating were not destroyed by the explosion. However, they were acutely in danger of falling off as in some parts they had become detached 2–5 cm from the stone surface. Moreover, into the crevice between the clay plaster and the rock small pieces of rubble had fallen that threatened to further detach the clay plaster pieces from the surface.

This rubble was removed. To prevent these original pieces from falling-off, putty links were applied between rock surface and clay plaster. Beforehand, the composition of the putty was experimentally tested and adapted to the fragment materials that needed to be stabilised. A mixture of 3:1 clay powder and gypsum was found suitable. The mass was sufficiently stable and adhesive, but was also elastic and soft enough not to damage the original clay plaster fragments.

This emergency stabilisation was carried out by abseiling from the back wall of the niche. It seems the danger of plaster fragments falling off through vibrations (rockfall, minor earthquakes) has been prevented for the time being. (Only in 2007 after the clearing of the niche scaffolds could be erected and the complete consolidation of the clay plaster sections could be carried out.)

Documentation

For the documentation of the operations the find spot was denoted, the object was described in writing and the storage location recorded. Furthermore, all objects were digitally photographed. For the image files the jpeg format with a low compression level was chosen. Clearly identifiable file names were assigned: the name of the object allows inferences of the type of object.

Example: clay plaster fragment no. 001 of the Small Buddha, image 01: 'KBL_001_01.jpg' (KB stands for 'Kleiner Buddha' [= Small Buddha], L for 'Lehmfassungsfragment' [= clay plaster fragment]).

In addition, in the IPTC boxes of the jpeg files basic information about the objects was noted down. Consequently, just by consulting the image file and without any additional text relevant information can be obtained about the object, the name of the mission, the photographer, the type of object, the find spot, the storage location, plus short descriptions and catchwords.

Rock fragments

The rock fragments of the Great Buddha were classified into fragments with original surface and fragments without any traces of treatment. Larger fragments were photographed at the find spot and in the depot and then described on an inventory sheet.

Area

At intervals of several days the area of the Great Buddha niche was photographically documented from above and from the front, depending on the state of the salvaging. This enabled us to document both the progress of salvage and the find spot of the larger fragments. As position for photographing the ground plan one of the upper lateral openings of the Buddha niche was chosen. To be able to document the entire floor surface of the niche with as little distortion as possible the camera was attached to a tripod arm (*c.* 1.7 m long), which was then held out of the niche opening. The picture detail could be controlled with the fold-out display of the camera. For the referencing of the niche photos four levelling boards (of tin, 15 x 15 cm, white surface) were attached to the side walls of the Buddha niche. The height of these boards was geared to measuring point 17 of the mission of October to December 2003 (see report Mission to Bamiyan, Afghanistan, ICOMOS Gemany, P. Smars, U. Dahlhaus, p. 11 ff.). To level the points a barometric level was used, and a tape measure to measure the distance. By means of a metal straddling dowel the measuring points were anchored in the walls of the niche (made by a blacksmith in the Bamiyan bazaar). The height of measuring point 17 roughly corresponds to the height of the rubble heap (from the ground level of the niche 840 cm). The position for taking the frontal pictures was the northeast corner of the big storage building.

A systematic salvage of the Buddha fragments, including storage in an interim depot, could only start in early August as the buildings were not finished before the beginning of October. In the period between mid-September and end of October about 300–400 m^3 of material could be cleared from the Great Buddha niche, two thirds of which were sand or small pebbles.

Bert Praxenthaler

Recommendations of the Third Expert Working Group on the Preservation of the Bamiyan Site

Tokyo, 18–20 December 2004*

Activities regarding the safeguarding of the fragments of the Buddha statues

1. In 2005, the securing of fragments by the ICOMOS team should be continued at both niches. As soon as all the fragments are identified, documented and stored accordingly, the next steps should be decided by the Afghan authorities, assisted by international experts.

2. The ICOMOS conservation concept, in accordance with the relevant international guidelines (Charter of Venice etc), should be implemented. All fragments, sculptured and non-sculptured, should be preserved.

3. ICOMOS is encouraged to propose appropriate ways to conserve and to present the fragments. The technical possibilities of an anastylosis should be considered.

4. The Ministry of Information and Culture should reinforce cooperation with ICOMOS in the implementation of the conservation measures, also with regards to the facilitation of local administrative procedures.

5. ICOMOS should continue the important ^{14}C analysis to date the plaster surface of the statues. The collaboration with the ^{14}C dating analysis for mural paintings by NRICP/Nagoya University is recommended for the further development of the study on the chronology of the Bamiyan site.

Consolidation of the cliffs and niches

Priorities in 2005, as part of a more general stabilisation plan of niches and cliffs, should be:

Small Buddha

1. The emergency consolidation measures on the western part of the niche of the Small Buddha should be completed, notably:
a) A monitoring system of the most relevant discontinuities has to be installed and should be working in real time;
b) A temporary support of iron/wood beams able to support any lateral deformation of the pillar-shaped instable fragment should be installed;
c) Temporary steel ropes binding the pillar-shaped instable fragment and fixing it in a stable place of the cliff should be installed;
d) Passive anchors located below and above this critical fragment should be installed, as well as a set of passive nails to connect the pillar-shaped fragment internally;
e) At the top external part of the niche of the Small Buddha, long passive anchors should be installed and grouted.

Large Buddha

2a) Complete identification and stabilisation of minor but unstable areas of the Large Buddha niches is required;

Prevention of water infiltration
b) At the Western Great Buddha site, water infiltration should be prevented and cracks should be grouted and filled.

Back of both niches
3. The fragile areas of the back of both niches should be safeguarded in cooperation with the ICOMOS team as soon as possible. Passive anchors and nails should be installed at the bottom of these areas.

* Abridged version without conservation of mural painting, archaeological projects, preparation of management plan and master plan, restoration of traditional architecture/creation of a site museum. For full text see http://whc.unesco.org/uploads/activities/documents/activity-343-1.doc.

Third Bamiyan Working Group, Tokyo, December 2004

Western Buddha niche with shelters constructed in 2004 and a group of buildings, including the ICOMOS office and a mosque (right), repaired in 2002

2005

In 2005, the salvaging and safeguarding of fragments, which had begun in June 2004, were taken up again thanks to funds provided by the German Foreign Office. After the winter break, which the provisional shelter erected the previous year had survived in good condition, the team had to focus on organising the work, receiving active support from representatives of the Afghan Central Government and the Governor of Bamiyan. The works, continued until October 2005 and involving up to 50 workers from Bamiyan and its surroundings, were managed and supervised by the small ICOMOS team, consisting of Dipl.-Ing. Georgios Toubekis (RWTH Aachen) and restorers Edmund Melzl and Bert Praxenthaler (supported in September by restorer Ernst Blöchinger). For without permanent control an adequate handling of the fragments would not be guaranteed despite the support from our Afghan colleagues. Under these circumstances, in 2005 it was possible to salvage almost two thirds of the fragments of the Western Buddha and also to make considerable progress at the site of the Eastern Buddha.

Works in the area of the Buddha niches, accompanied by a de-mining team, were delayed time and again by ammunition findings. In order to move large rock fragments a crane as well as a fork lifter were hired. At the site of the Western Buddha more than 100 fragments with sculpted surface could be salvaged. These rocks weighing up to 30 tons were deposited in the new shelters. The salvaging situation is much more difficult at the site of the Eastern Buddha, because the slope drops quite steeply there, thus only allowing a small platform of little depth immediately in front of the Buddha niche. However, by means of a crane placed further down the access road about 160 rock fragments could be salvaged here as well. For depositing these fragments further shelters were laid out inside the encircling wall to the left and right of the gateway.

View of the Bamiyan valley with the former bazaar in the foreground

Special attention was given by the restorers to the small salvaged fragments originating from the surfaces of the two giant statues: several layers of clay plaster, wooden pegs and ropes used for forming the folds of the Buddhas' robes, also plaster fragments with polychrome remains. Countless fragments were documented and deposited in the shelves of the ICOMOS office. Not only can these remains, made up of organic material, be dated by means of the carbon 14 method (see the summary on carbon dating, p. 235); they can also answer questions concerning the original colouring of the Buddhas and the different treatment of the two giant statues' surfaces. Dr. Michael Urbat (Palaeomagnetic Laboratory at the Geological Institute of the University of Cologne) accompanied the mission in September to evaluate the possibilities of assigning the rock fragments by geological methods (cf. report p. 90). The geological methods allow a precise indication of the original position of the stone fragments, which can then be integrated into 3D models of the niches developed by the RWTH Aachen (see report Toubekis, pp. 117–121) – a crucial prerequisite for future measures in accordance with an anastylosis, for which Prof. Dr.-Ing. Fritz Wenzel (Büro für Baukonstruktionen, Karlsruhe) developed suggestions (see figs. p. 81).

The Fourth Expert Working Group on the Preservation of the Bamiyan Site (Kabul, 7–10 December 2005, see below) discussed, among other things, a laser beam project "for the projection of the artist's images of Buddha in Bamiyan", apparently costing more than 60 million dollars, – a gigantic light-show with no less than 13 Buddhas by the Japanese media artist Hiro Yamagata who lives in California. The Working Group showed some interest in a future development of tourism and in the equipment for generating power. However, the group noted that 'the solar panels and cables should not interfere with the Bamiyan landscape'.

M. Pz.

Report on Salvaging Rock Fragments, 2005

Western Buddha

So far, at the Western Buddha more than 100 rock fragments with clearly recognizable sculpted surface have been recovered. These stones weighing up to 30 tons were deposited in the shelters. The large pieces were put on scantlings, the smaller ones on wooden pallets made by carpenters in the Bamiyan bazaar. The smaller stones without any recognizable surface as well as the sand are deposited at an acclivity in the north-western area of the fenced-off terrain, to the left of the Buddha niche. After the recovery the rock fragments are numbered, documented photographically and in writing and – if appropriate – stored in one of the shelters. Depending on the weight of the rocks polyester heavy-duty belts and steel ropes with wooden interlayers are used for the transport with a crane. The Afghan workers exposed the rock fragments layer by layer by putting one shovel of sand after the other into a wheelbarrow. In this process the material was always checked for finds, such as parts of the clay surface, wooden pieces, etc. These special finds were collected and stored in the shelves of the ICOMOS office.

Recovery of rocks by means of a 35 t heavy-duty-crane at the Western Buddha

The shelters at the Western Buddha from above. The roof is partly open to lift Buddha fragments into the shelter by means of a crane.

Shelves in the ICOMOS office for the storage of finds

△ ▽ Progress made in salvaging the fragments of the Western Buddha in 2005

△ The crane lifting fragments from the upper platform of the Eastern Buddha niche ▷

▽ The Eastern Buddha niche from above

Eastern Buddha

In 2005, the salvage of fragments also began at the Eastern Buddha. The situation at the Eastern Buddha is much more difficult as the slope drops relatively steeply, only leaving a small bricked-up platform of three metres depth in front of the Buddha niche. A wheel loader can only just drive on that platform. The access road is narrow and unpaved. In the niche manual work was therefore predominant.

It was not possible to position the crane in the centre immediately in front of the niche. West of the platform the base for the crane was enlarged and levelled. Half beams put under the crane arms improved the stability of the crane. Thus, the crane could almost reach the entire platform surface in front of the Buddha niche.

So far, up to 160 rock fragments have been recovered from the Eastern Buddha niche. Another problem at the Eastern Buddha was the lack of shelter space. For the storage of the sand drain fleece was laid out six metres beneath the path on a terrace, and with the gravel material of the surrounding area an enclosing wall on the valley side was erected. Using a chute the recovered sand could be stored here. In the west, inside the enclosing wall and to the left and right of the gateway additional storage space was laid out. As an interim depot a widening of the path to the west and beneath the platform and the niche was chosen. These areas were fenced off, walled in and roofed.

Support of the geological investigation

Dr Michael Urbat from the Palaeomagnetic Laboratory of the Geological Institute at the University of Cologne joined the mission for several days (in Bamiyan from 31 August to 7 September) to evaluate the possibilities of spatialising the rock fragments with geological methodologies. At the Western Buddha measurements of a relatively high resolution were carried out from a ladder in the lower area of the back wall. In a vertical distance of 10 cm a Kappameter was used to define the susceptibility of the back wall and analogously the values of the rock fragments. At the Eastern Buddha comparable measurements could be carried out at a height of about 30 metres in the area of the left shoulder by using the means of abseiling.

Bert Praxenthaler

State of the Eastern Buddha niche on 6 September 2005: more and more rock fragments appear in the rubble

Fritz Wenzel
Options for an Anastylosis of the Buddha Statues in Bamiyan, 2005

The question is whether and how the remaining fragments of the Buddhas should be reinserted into the rock niches – as an anastylosis – at their original location. Since so far only a small portion of the fragments has been measured and documented, at present only general suggestions for a solution can be made. Decisions about the number, location and the surface treatment of the fragments to be inserted can be postponed to a later planning phase.

The structure of a steel solution with inserted fragments resembles a wire model, the external rods of which represent the Buddha's contours. This solution has the advantage that the back wall of the niche is visible in between the fragments and that the remaining broken-off parts of the Buddha, which have meanwhile been attached to the wall, also remain visible.

After the different studies of variations, we would like to recommend the proposal with the recessed masonry-work representing the Buddhas, with fragments inserted and protruding by the thickness of a rock. This solution allows the unambiguous distinction between original parts and reconstruction, and manufacturing the reconstructed parts from local brick and suitable lime mortar.

◁▽ Proposals by Prof. Fritz Wenzel for an anastylosis of the Western Buddha (Büro für Baukonstruktionen, Karlsruhe)

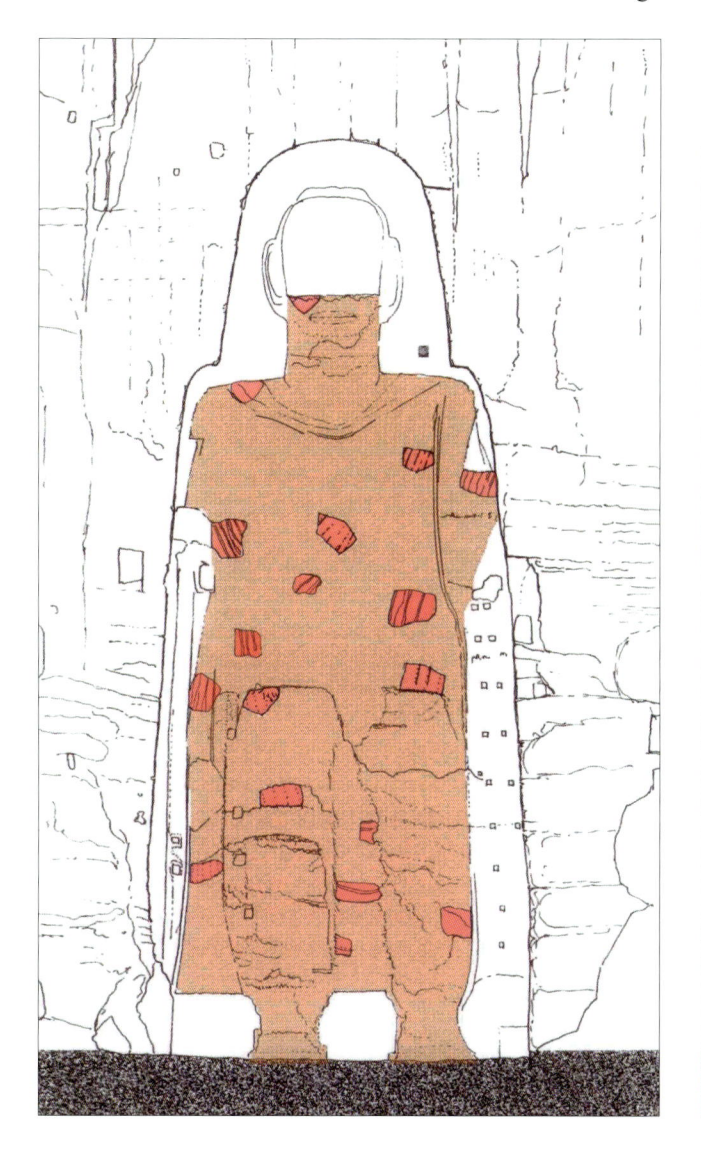

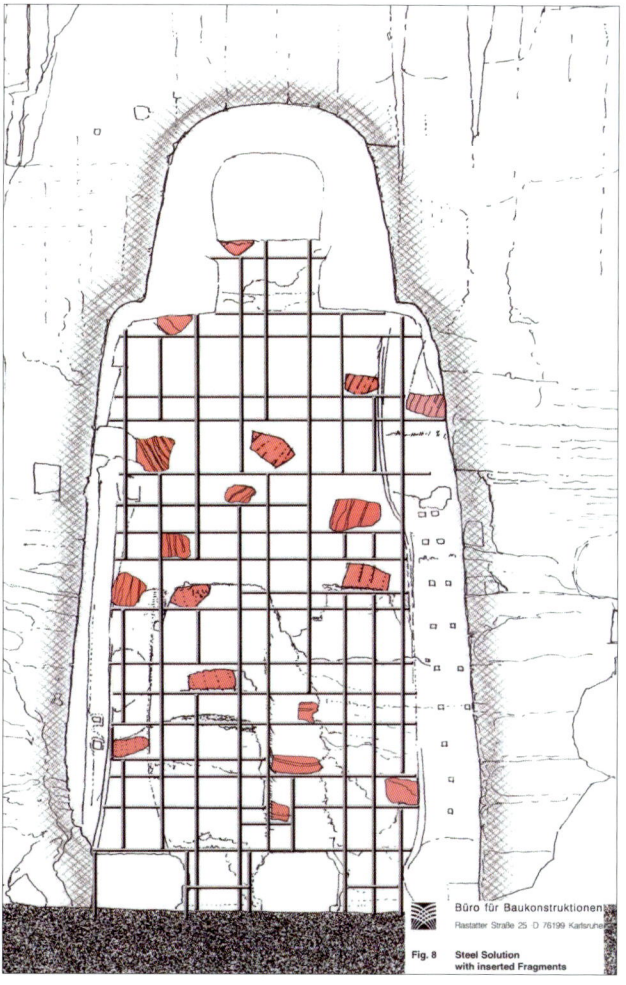

Recommendations of the Fourth Expert Working Group on the Preservation of the Bamiyan Site

Kabul, 7–10 December 2005*

Conservation of the Buddhas, documentation and relocation of the fragments

The Experts,
1. Acknowledge the extraordinary efforts of the ICOMOS team for their progress in recovering fragments form both Buddha niches and storing them safely, especially the preservation of remaining original plaster in situ by fixing it provisionally to the back wall of the niche;
2. Acknowledge the results of the analysis on the surface material of the Buddha figures and their contribution to the understanding of the history including the original colouring of the figures;
3. Acknowledge the results of the combined geological and paleomagnetic approach towards the identification of the original position of rock material executed by the University of Cologne;
4. Acknowledge the presentation of the 3D model and visualization of both Buddha figures by Aachen University and encourage to further develop this model for future documentation as well as ideal planning instrument to ensure accuracy and estimation of costs;
5. Welcome that the Afghan authorities acknowledge the possibility of an anastylosis as one well established method of proper relocation of the rock fragments to their original position;
6. Encourage the finalization of the ICOMOS activity in safeguarding and documenting all remains of the Buddhas in both niches in combination with the geological and paleomagnetic analysis;
7. Encourage the installation of scaffoldings as an essential basis for further geological documentation of the back walls for a successful identification of the rock fragments to be relocated and to ensure the accessibility for necessary consolidation and monitoring activities;
8. The possibilities for anastylosis (material used for integration and stabilization) should be further investigated (see Article 15 of the Venice Charter);
9. Underline that for the above mentioned activities the assistance of the Mine Action Programme for Afghanistan is essential to guarantee safety and security from unexploded devices on site;
10. Recommend that the proposed general stabilization plan for cliffs and niches takes into account the necessity of stabilization of the vaults at the bottom of both Buddha niches especially the endangered caves surrounding the feet of the Eastern Buddha and is coordinated with the ICOMOS activities to ensure the safety and success of the ongoing work.

General stabilisation plan for the consolidation of niches and cliffs

1. The programme should include the investigation of structural conditions of the caves and the Great Cliff. Within this strategy, priorities can be identified as follows, in part already sanctioned in 2004;

A. Eastern Giant Buddha

2. The emergency consolidation measures on the western part of the niche should be completed and enlarged to the external top part of the niche;
3. The East Giant Buddha niche is now in less risky condition and scaffolding should be planned within the niche and outer surface, just after the completion of on going consolidation work on western side and top and after cleaning the niche;

B. Western Giant Buddha

4. Complete identification and stabilisation of minor but unstable areas of the West Giant Buddha niche is required;
5. At the Western Great Buddha site, water infiltration should be prevented and cracks should be grouted and filled;

C. Back side of both niches

6. The fragile areas of the back of both niches should be safeguarded in cooperation with the ICOMOS team as soon as possible. There is the need to understand distribution, depth and intensity of failures in the back side of both niches, also affecting the stability of underneath caves. Any stabilization plan should be properly studied, before execution. Possible techniques might include seismic noise, fragility test on stones, engineering geology tests, Ground Penetration Radar, etc;

---

* Abridged version without sections on conservation of mural paintings, capacity building, Bamiyan museum, Bamyian master plan and World Heritage management plan, General stabilisation plan for the consolidation of niches and cliffs, and laser beam project for the projection of the artist's images of Buddha in Bamiyan.

Laser beam project with 13 Buddhas by the Japanese media artist Hiro Yamagata

2006

In 2006, the ICOMOS activities in safeguarding the Bamiyan Buddha statues continued from mid-June to end of October thanks to funds provided by the German Foreign Office. In the same year the Trevi Company used funds from the Japan Fund in Trust to carry out the most urgent emergency interventions in the upper corridor on the rear side of the Western Buddha niche and in some minor lateral parts, based on a concept developed by Claudio Margottini. By stabilising the rock above the niche and on the upper west side Trevi also completed the stabilisation of the Eastern Buddha niche, where the company had already secured the most dangerous part on the upper eastern side in 2003/2004 (see report Margottini, pp. 175 ff.). Three Russian aircraft bombs found under the rubble on the floor of the east side of the Western Buddha niche delayed the salvaging work considerably. The first bomb, containing 2/3 TNT and 1/3 Napalm, was blown up on 8 September thanks to the help of the New Zealand garrison. The ICOMOS team recovered all material from the Eastern Buddha niche and once the niche had been cleared work started on putting up the scaffold made available by the Messerschmitt Foundation. Supervised by Georgios Toubekis and in cooperation with the building research department of the Technical University of Vienna the cleared niche was completely examined in preparation for a CAD model. The aim was to carry out a documentation by means of a 3D laser image scanner: a three-dimensional recording of the Eastern Buddha niche (see also report Toubekis, pp. 117–121) serving as a basis for future consolidation measures and also for a virtual reconstruction. In addition, in October 2006 Prof. Fecker made in-depth investigations of the rock mechanic aspects in the Eastern Buddha niche. Also, the geologist Dr. Michael Urbat (institute of geology and mineralogy at the University of Cologne), after his short missions in October 2003 and September 2005, used the results of his third geological mission for a comprehensive analysis (see report, pp. 89–102). A highlight of this salvaging work was the sensational find of a relic in the rubble next to the right foot of the Eastern Buddha on 20 July 2006. The ICOMOS activities were also presented at UNESCO/ICOMOS workshops in the Afghan Foreign Ministry in Kabul on 31 July and in Bamiyan on 2 August 2006.

Restorer E. Melzl and the bomb

Blowing-up of an aircraft bomb on September 8, 2006

Relic with manuscript on birch bark found in the rubble near the Eastern Buddha's feet

A sensational find in the rubble of the Bamiyan Buddhas on 20 July 2006

During the work to save the remains the giant statues revealed one of their secrets: Quite miraculously a relic that can be linked to the creation of the Eastern Buddha had been preserved in the sand under the stone rubble. In the summer of 2006 the floor level of the Eastern Buddha was reached, the cave rooms badly damaged by the explosions were exposed and most of the fragments were salvaged. In the course of this work Edmund Melzl and his Afghan team made a completely unexpected find on 20 July 2006. Under the rubble, between the remains of the Eastern Buddha's feet, fragments of writing on birch bark were found wrapped in a plain textile pouch. Two copper sheets, one of them gilt and with a floral decoration and a copper ring, could come from a wooden receptacle. The seal on the textile wrapping probably shows the bird Garuda and the snake Naga. In addition, two clay pellets, thought to contain ashes from the cremation of Buddha, were found.

The manuscript written on birch bark is supposed to be a canonical Buddhist text, which as the quintessence of the Buddhist teachings was used in reliquaries and in connection with consecration rituals. One may therefore assume that the find, which under the given circumstances is quite sensational, is part of a votive offering hidden inside the giant statue since its consecration and that it may originally have included more pieces. In any case, the writing seems to match a possible date of creation for the statue in the 6th century AD. Fragments of a leaf turned out to come from a *ficus religiosa* or Bodhi tree. According to the legend, Buddha achieved enlightenment under a Bodhi tree in Bodh Gaya. The original Bodhi tree was destroyed in 600 AD by King Sesanka. The event was recorded by Xuanzang, along with the planting of a new Bodhi tree sapling by King Purnavarma in 620 AD. The leaf thus could have come from the original Bodhi tree. Furthermore, in one of the rear caves a number of so far unidentified fragments of writing were discovered. The relics were handed over to the Governor, Dr. Habiba Surabi.

M. Pz.

Handing over the relic to the Governor, Dr. Habiba Surabi

Report on Salvaging Rock Fragments, 2006

By beginning of July 2006 around 150 rocks with recognisable sculpted surface had been recovered at the Western Buddha. Around 70 square metres of original hewn stone surface had been salvaged and documented at the Western Buddha; most of them were stored in the two shelters. Typical for the stone surface here are the rows of smaller reinforcement holes (conical, c. 4 x 6 cm). West of the niche the depot for sand, small boulders and rocks without sculpted surface was enlarged.

The salvage work at the Eastern Buddha was carried out by means of a small wheel loader, steel rope chain hoists and leverage force. The Buddha fragments were pulled to the exit of the niche by using pulleys. Leverage force and manpower were also used for this action. The pulled-down fragments could then be transported to the depot with a wheel loader. As in the year before, sand and small boulders were piled up southeast beneath the niche's platform, using separating foils and a wall as barrier. A large part of the recovered rocks were temporarily stored west of the niche's platform. By autumn, the storage sites for this material had been enlarged and roofed. About 200 rock fragments were salvaged.

Bert Praxenthaler

△ Depot for sand, small boulders and rocks without sculpted surface

▽ Depot for rocks with sculpted surface

▽ Storage site for remains of exploded bombs, grenades and mines in the shelves of the office building

△ a

△ b

△ c

△ d

△ e

△ f ▽ g

a) Sand and small boulders piled up southeast beneath the niche's platform

b) Construction of new provisional shelters west of the Buddha niche

c) Niche of the Eastern Buddha from above with excavated platform and stairs

d) Moving of large fragments of the Eastern Buddha

e) Moving of large fragments of the Eastern Buddha

f) Transporting the pulled-down fragments with a wheel loader

g) Fragment of the Eastern Buddha with typical sculpted surface

△ Eastern Buddha niche, the ground level with the destroyed caves in the background has been reached
▽ Parts of the niche's back wall had to be supported as stone slabs kept on falling down

Michael Urbat, Jens Aubel

A Combined Geological and Paleomagnetic Approach towards the Repositioning of Fragments from the Buddha Statues, 2006

1 Introduction
1.1 Concept and previous missions in 2003 and 2005

The rationale behind the geological work in the Bamiyan valley presented here is to identify the original position and spatial relationship of the remains of the destroyed, Eastern and Western Buddha. Our approach adopts the fact, that the majority of fragments are characterized by nothing but the, however distinct, geological details of the formerly monument hosting rock (hereafter called sediment). Only a few fragments feature archaeological modifications, such as sculptured surface, which could alternatively be used in any restoration process. In addition, none of the fragments allows for reassembly based on shape or size of the fragments. Crucially, the size of even the largest remains is small compared to any part, e.g. the head, of the former Buddha figures (fig. 1)[1].

The general idea of using geological methodology as to identify the original position of the Buddha fragments is comfortably described by the term 'pattern matching'. Pattern, accordingly, is defined as an array of distinct geological and mineral magnetic information or features which characterize the sediment on a cm-scale. The cliff, i.e., the vertical sedimentary succession of the entire back plane of the Buddha niches, represents such a unique pattern (hereafter referred to as reference pattern). The fragments will contain a distinct part of the entire reference pattern and the minimum size of any fragment to be matched will depend on the minimum amount of recognized pattern features (fig. 2). One vertical line (reference pattern) down the back plane of the niches would be sufficient, if the sedimentary layers were strictly horizontally bedded and have no lateral variation.

There are two mutually beneficial ways to establish the desired patterns. One approach is based on mainly sedimentological information (see 2.2.1) and the other one adds paleo- and rock- magnetic characteristics of the sediment layers (see 2.2.2). Both ways of characterizing

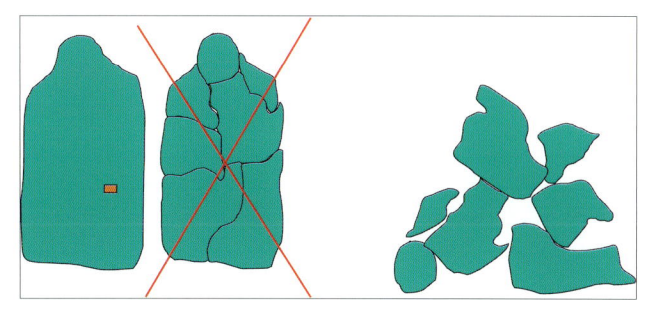

△ Fig. 1. The Buddha fragments cannot be re-positioned in analogy to a broken vase, for example. Potsherd characteristics like shape or ornament need to be replaced by an array of geological and magnetic, sometimes archaeological properties of the Buddha fragments referred as pattern in this report. Small orange rectangle approximates the size of the largest fragments relative to the original height of the standing Buddha figures.

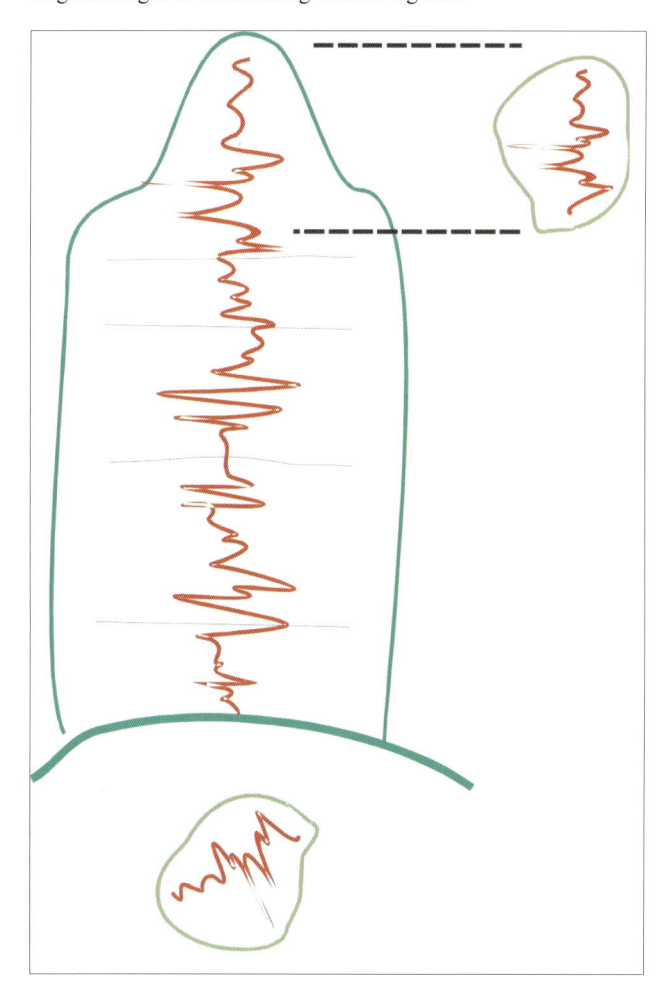

Fig. 2. The fragments originally were part of the sedimentary composing the cliff which hosted the Buddha figures. The term reference pattern used in this report is illustrated by the wiggly red line down the back plane of the Buddha Niche. A displaced fragment contains a distinct part of the reference pattern and is re-positioned vertically by matching the fragment pattern to the reference pattern. Schematic not to scale. ▷

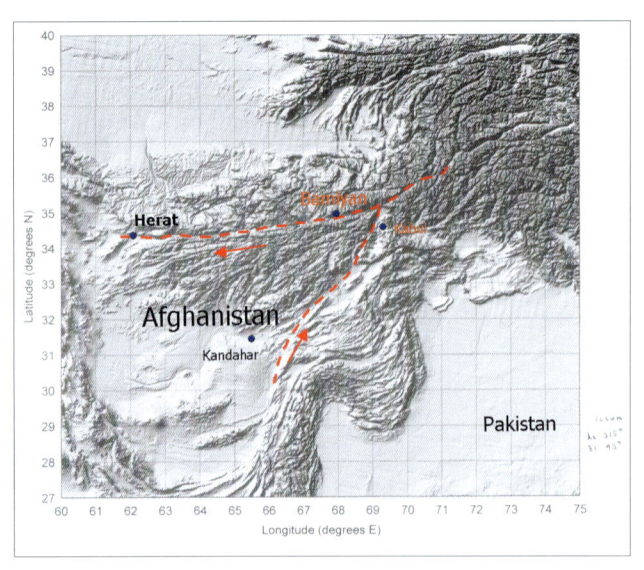

Fig. 3. Tectonic evolution of the Bamiyan Valley along the major east-west trending Herat fault (upper stippled line)

the Buddha material are designed to be (mostly) applicable on-site and, due to practicability, avoid, but not exclude, more sophisticated laboratory methods. Wherever possible, non-geological information such as sculptured surface of the Buddha figures or remains (cement, cavities) from pre-destruction restoration activities (altogether hereafter referred to as archaeological details) will be integrated in the establishment of a characteristic pattern.

Ultimately, the results obtained will be integrated in a 3D computer model featuring both Buddha niches, which is presently developed in the group around Michael Jansen at the RWTH Aachen. Essentially, this latter step in the analysis of the Buddha remains can provide the essential (technical) basis, before any further preservation activities are considered.

Fig. 4. Example of thin section under the microscope from one of the reddish layers from the Western Buddha niche. Note that any natural cement that would support the stability of the rock fails to do so, because it only appears in nests. Matrix is mostly clay. Length of the long side is 7.3 mm.

A feasibility study of the theoretical approach (K. Krumsiek, M. Urbat, University of Cologne) including the set up of a tentative geological reference profile (see 3.1) was carried out in the frame of the first mission to Bamiyan in October 2003 (M. Urbat). Due to the short time on site and, more crucially, the inadequate accessibility of the vertical, several tens of meters high back plane of the niches work at this stage had to be limited to the measurement of two independent physical properties (magnetic susceptibility and colour variation) in order to approximate the sedimentary succession in the niche of the Western Buddha. These physical logs were supplemented by the visual description of rock fragments as well as some additional palaeo- and rockmagnetic measurements carried out at the Paleomagnetic Laboratory, University of Cologne. This first geological mission yielded promising results and confirmed the practicability of the theoretical approach, which however needed to be modulated with respect to the on-site conditions. Crucially, the final proof of the suggested method could not be given, because the established patterns from the back plane of the niches and the fragments could not be realized at the same scale (lack of resolution).

These initial geological results were considered in close cooperation with the ICOMOS organized experts on natural stone restoration Ulrich Bauer-Bornemann, Edmund Melzl, Hendrik Romstedt and Michael Scherbaum, who participated in the same October 2003 mission to Bamiyan. The more general discussion as well as recommendations on the preservation of the Buddha statues, based on such mutually beneficial, restorational/geological considerations is given in a further report to ICOMOS (Bauer-Bornemann et al., 2003).

The second geological mission in September 2005 succeeded the visit of the Bamiyan site in October 2003. At this time rescue and archaeological documentation of the fragments was underway, bringing more and more, so far covered, fragments to the surface. Moreover, after two winters of exposure the suspected weathering of the fragments needed closer inspection with respect to the validity of the previously envisaged geological approach. Under these premises the main purpose of the September 2005 mission was to proof the suggested method and establish a workable approach to implement the geological methodology into the present overall activities around the fragments from the Western Buddha. In fact, a first successful pattern match, hence the original position, of one of the fragments could be established (see 3.1). Potential and merits of integrating archaeological details were discussed and implemented with the results established by the archaeologist onsite Bert Praxenthaler (see respective ICOMOS report).

1.2 The 2006 mission (Eastern Buddha)

The third geological mission in late October 2006 (J. Aubel on-site, M. Urbat) targeted the Eastern Buddha niche and fragments, which had so far, due to the restricted access, been covered to only a minor extent. It was, however, clear from the previous visits to Bamiyan that the geology constituting the eastern niche differs from the western part of the cliff in that layers which might challenge the geological approach appeared more prominent. In the course of the overall activities around the Eastern Buddha all fragments had been cleared from the niche in October 2006 and scaffolding of the back plane of the niche was to be completed prior to the start of the geological investigations (potentially providing a first time unrestricted access to one of the back planes of the niches and, hence, a first time opportunity to establish the required vertical reference patterns essential for the suggested approach). Due to unforeseen time delays in the set up of the scaffold only the lowermost layers of the back plane could be inspected. These results, however, indicate that the geological method established for the Western Buddha is successfully transferable to the Eastern Buddha with only minor modifications (see 3.1.2).

2 Explanatory notes
2.1 Geological overview

Supposedly in Oligocene/Miocene times (i.e., around 24 million years ago) the Bamiyan Valley developed as an intramountain, west – east oriented, basin along the major Herat-Fault-System, hence, in the course of major tectonic movements in this area (Krumsiek 1980, fig. 3). The basin was subsequently filled with debris originating from the surrounding, elevated parts of the relief – mostly conglomerates of different composition and compaction, sometimes volcanics. Today these deposits constitute the succession of almost horizontally bedded layers the Buddha figures were sculptured in. Lang (1972) suggests at least four different formations during the Miocene, including the so-called Bouddha-Formation, which is laterally replaced by the Qal'ocah Formation of middle Miocene age (around 15 mio. years) in the Bamiyan Valley. The west-east trending, almost vertical wall that hosts the Buddha niches today, developed much later during Pliocene-Pleistocene times (< 2.4 mio. years) as a consequence of fluvio-glacial erosion. Although, in vicinity to, and within the western and eastern Buddha niches the Miocene sedimentary succession is almost horizontally bedded, strata cannot be correlated from one niche to the other, because the sediment layers are offset at a local NE-SW trending fault. Consequently, both the Buddhas were hewn out of different strata, with different lithologic/ static properties, respectively.

Geology on site

In a simplified view the sediment of the Bamiyan cliff is composed of horizontally bedded, centimeter to meter thick layers of various conglomerates interbedded with finer grained clay, silt and sand layers or mixtures thereof (also see Zou and Unold, 2002).

Importantly, the conglomerate as well as the interbedded layers are highly variable in composition, grain size, thickness and colour. From a visual inspection of the surrounding blocks the conglomeratic layers in the niche of the western Buddha vary in thickness between several dm and some few meters. The size (diameter) of the usually well rounded components ranges from a few to almost 20 cm within the respective layers. The composition per

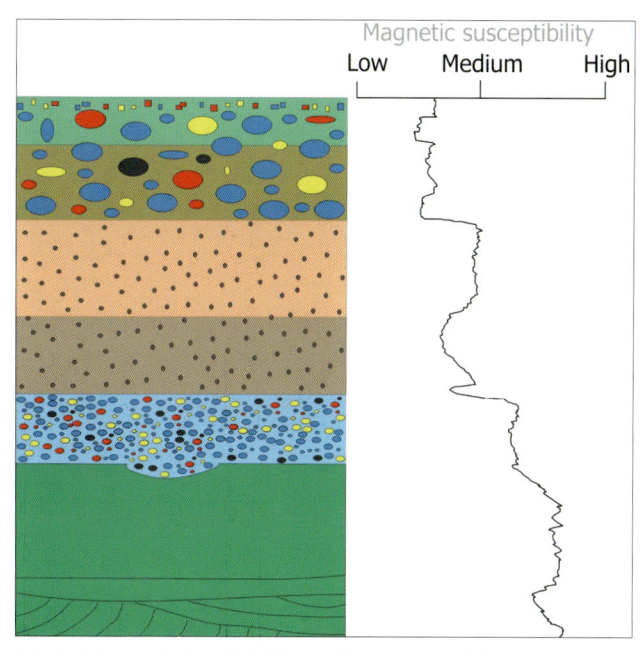

Fig. 5. Schematic drawing illustrating several of the above named sedimentological features – magnetic susceptibility (notional curve) is discussed in the following chapter.

layer is equally highly variable and reflects the Mesozoic and Paleozoic lithology in the vicinity of Bamiyan Valley including volcanic, intrusive and older sedimentary components. Most of the conglomerate layers appear to be relatively loosely packed, with no or only minor (natural) cement to support the stability of the components. Voids in between the pebbles are rather filled with clay or silt, which was likely deposited in the same process as the main components of the conglomerate.

The various conglomeratic layers are interbedded with, equally diverse, silty or sandy layers of reddish or minor yellowish colours. The thickness of these layers may vary between 1–2 cm up to 1–2 meters. These layers are important for several reasons, because first they can be used as marker beds within the reference profile, second they provide the only material that can be sampled for additional paleomagnetic NRM measurements (re-orientation in the horizontal plane), and third these layers reveal that the supposedly horizontal beds do have a rather high lateral variability (figs. 13, 15).

The material that the layers consist of can be considered matrix supported sand or silt, with no contact between the sand or silt size components (fig. 4). These are mostly poorly rounded, often even fractured quartz, and less often feldspar, pyrite or volcanic components in varying concentration. The matrix appears to be mostly clay, interspersed with varying amounts of carbonate cement. Unlike the clay matrix, the cement in all of the inspected thin sections only appears in little nests and never persists. The reddish or more yellowish colour of the layers originates from the red clay matrix with various amounts of carbonate (yellow).

Like the conglomerate, the interbedded layers are hence loosely packed clastic components, with no sufficient amount of cement which would result in a higher stability of the material. The above observation also easily explains the strong HCl reaction (carbonate) of all of the samples

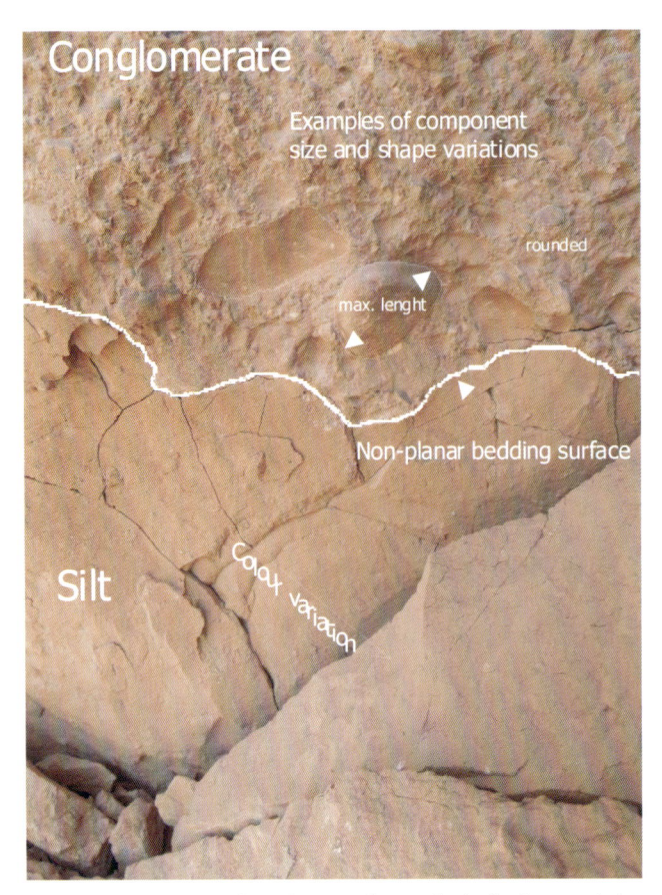

Fig. 6. Illustration of various sedimentological characteristics employed in the pattern matching approach.

Fig. 7. Schematized magnetic susceptibility variation to illustrate typical variations in between the various lithologies (detrital) and within lithologically homogenous layers (diagenetic). Both features are useful for the pattern matching approach.

investigated on site, as well as the fact that all of the material dissolves in water within seconds (this has been noted previously by Zou and Unold, 2002 – and was confirmed with various samples on site). Salt was not detected in any of our samples (which again confirms the high variability amongst the individual layers), and, hence, cannot account for the low stability of the material as was suggested by Zou and Unold (2002) in this case.

2.2 Methods
2.2.1 Geological criteria

The geological approach to discriminate the required reference pattern is based on a detailed visual description of the varying sedimentological and structural features of the respective layers (figs. 5 and 6). Such are:
- colour variations of the sediment matrix,
- type and composition of rock components of the conglomerate,
- shape of these components (rounded versus non-rounded or etched),
- sorted or unsorted with respect to shape or composition of components,
- grain size changes of non-conglomerate layers (i.e., clay, silt, sand or mixtures thereof),
- the former terms classify sediment according to grain size,
- mineral composition of non-conglomeratic layers,
- type of natural cement, if present at all,
- sedimentary structures (for example cross bedding, channels),
- bedding (dip, lateral variation),
- secondary alteration, if visible.

2.2.2 Paleomagnetic measurements

The main application of the magnetic methods uses the magnetic susceptibility κ, defined as $\kappa = M/H$, with $M = $ *magnetization* and $H = $ *applied field* of the sediment for the vertical positioning of the fragments with respect to the reference pattern. At its simplest, the magnetic susceptibility, as a measure of the magnetizability of the sediment, is a scalar property and will vary in direct response to the varying sediment composition of each sample. κ reflects a composite of magnetic properties including the diamagnetic, paramagnetic and the various ferromagnetic contributions from the respective minerals, rock fragments or matrix. Note, that the dominating contribution to κ is likely to originate from ferromagnetic minerals, like the iron oxide magnetite, although such account for < 1 vol % of the entire sediment and will have grain sizes of only a few microns (μm). These magnetic minerals can be detrital in origin or secondary, and, hence, uncorrelated to primary sedimentary features. Importantly, both the primary and secondary magnetic signals can be used for the identification of the Buddha remains, if κ of the fragments was not altered since the destruction of the Buddha figures. A possible scenario for the latter could be quicker weathering of the fragments over the past few years due to intensified exposure.

In general, κ will be measured, closely spaced, perpendicular to the bedding plane with a handheld, so-called, kappameter designed for field use. The measurements result in a continuous record of susceptibility values that mirror the distinct properties of the various sedimentary layers of both the back plane of the Buddha niches and the Buddha remains. Accordingly, κ can be viewed as an approximation of the above described sedimentary or secondary diagenetic alteration of the rock. Crucially, it does add important information, which is not easily accessible from a visual geological inspection alone (see results chapter). The respective measurements are quick (< 10 s), non destructive and cost free, however, like the geological documentation require direct contact with the rock surface while taken (crucial in terms of accessibility of the back plane of the niches). Note, that the susceptibility characteristics employed in the pattern matching approach rely on the relative changes of the intensities over a certain thickness of sediment rather than the absolute value of a single measurement (fig. 7).

Additional, more sophisticated analyses of the magnetic properties of the rock can be obtained using laboratory methods (Urbat 2003)[2]. The latter measurements cannot be achieved on-site and will require samples to be taken to the laboratory, and, hence, will only be employed in critical sections where on-site criteria do not provide sufficient details. Note, that these laboratory measurements will be required especially for (supposedly few) fragments whose up/down orientation or necessary amount of rotation in the horizontal plane can not be otherwise determined. Under such circumstances the vector properties of the remanent magnetic minerals contained in sediment (having stored the orientation and intensity of the former earth's magnetic field) will be used.

2.2.3 Archaeological details

Archaeological details such as parts of the sculptured robe, re-enforcement cavities or mud plaster (see respective archaeological reports, fig. 8) all in first place indicate that a fragment belongs to the front part of the former Buddha figures. Roughly estimated the amount of such fragments is less than 25 % of the total remains. All other fragments originate from the inner body of the figures and do, accordingly, not features anything but geological and magnetic information. Given the relatively small size of even the few largest fragments (which measure about 2 meters across) in relation to the 55 m and 35 m high standing Buddhas an unambiguous assignment of the remains to their original position – for example using high resolution photographs from pre-destruction times – based on archaeological details alone will only exceptionally be possible. Clearly, in combination with the geological and magnetic characteristics of a fragment such archaeological features (fig. 9) are of utmost importance for any successful re-positioning (i.e. the establishment of a characteristic pattern) as the front/back orientation of a fragment is clearly indicated (fig. 8).

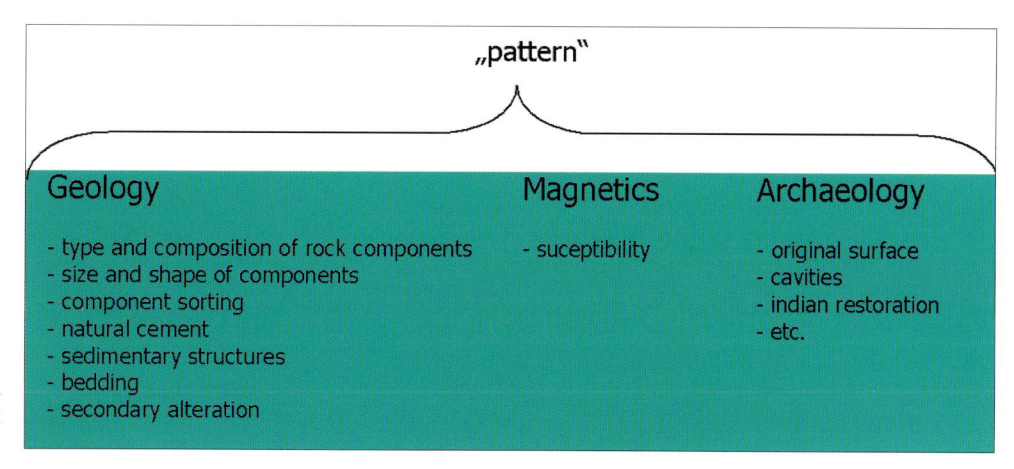

Fig. 9. Summary of criteria applicable on-site constituting a pattern

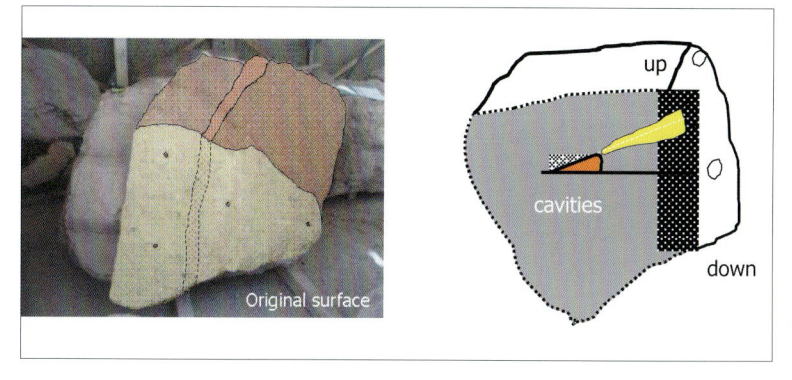

„pattern"

Geology	Magnetics	Archaeology
- type and composition of rock components - size and shape of components - component sorting - natural cement - sedimentary structures - bedding - secondary alteration	- suceptibility	- original surface - cavities - indian restoration - etc.

Fig. 8. Left photograph illustrates one of the larger fragments from the Western Buddha featuring original surface (highlighted in yellow, covered with mud plaster typically having a thickness of about 1–2 cm, small dots indicate location and size of re-enforcement cavities). Also shown and highlighted in brown and red colours is the 3-dimensional orientation of the sedimentary layers with respect to the surface. Right hand schematic illustrates how the re-enforcement cavities provide (additional) information on the up/down orientation of a fragment, given that these cavities were forced into the rock under the acute angle with respect to horizontal.

Note that measurements of magnetic susceptibility as well as a thorough geological description of the sediment (fragments, back plane of the niches) are not feasible for parts covered with mud plaster (i.e. original surface). These values, however, are easily obtained from the non-covered sides of the fragments (fig. 8).

2.3 Situation on site

Both the geological as well as the magnetic analyses require direct contact with the material to be investigated. Hence, unrestricted access to the back plane of the niches and the respective fragments is the essential prerequisite for the success of the suggested pattern matching approach. Recovery of fragments from the heap of remains at the bottom of the respective niches continued over the past few years (figs. 10–12) and was completed in October 2006 for the Eastern Buddha. The fragments from both niches were placed in storage next to the western and eastern sites and scaffolding of the eastern back plane was begun in late October 2006, providing access to the lowermost 10 meters above ground of the 38 m high wall. The upper part of the wall could, as of yet not be investigated adequately. As for the Western Buddha niche only one 4.5 m long section from the lower part of the 58 m high back plane could be geologically researched using an extension ladder (see 3.1).

The remainder of the wall awaits further inspection by the geologist in order to set up the essential reference profiles once direct access to the wall can be gained.

3 Results

3.1 Back plane (reference profiles)
3.1.1 Western Buddha niche

One of the most important prerequisites for any successful pattern matching approach will be the establishment of a thorough, high resolution reference pattern from the back walls of the respective niches. A first step towards such a reference profile for the Western Buddha was made during the 2003 mission based on successive measurements of magnetic susceptibility (fig. 13). It must be clearly stated that this recorded susceptibility profile cannot provide anything but a rough frame for the required reference pattern at high resolution, because it lacks the geological details and the spatial resolution of the susceptibility measurements is too low.

During the fieldwork in October 2003 both the 58 m high wall in the back of the Buddha niche would only be accessible with the aid of a professional climber (provided by RODIO, Inc.). Any attempts in the niche of the Eastern Buddha were cancelled in 2003, because engineering work by the Italian firm RODIO to consolidate the intensely fractured side walls of the niche was in full swing, and furthermore, the equally highly fragile wall appeared to be too high a risk (for the climber, but also to further damage the wall) without time consuming preparatory work. We therefore attempted to approximate the reference profile in the niche of the Western Buddha by way of scanning for magnetic susceptibility and colour variations. The lowermost approx. 10 m of the profile could not be accessed, because it was then hidden by the blasted rock fragments.

Magnetic susceptibility was measured using a handheld Kappameter KT-5c (AGICO, Brno, CZ) at a spacing of approximately every 20–30 cm (fig. 13), while the location in the wall was measured at the same time using a Total Station (Topcon GTS) with a local reference system, placed in front of the niche. The measured profile follows a sub-vertical line downwards from the window on top of the former head of the Buddha. Several additional susceptibility profiles at a spacing of about 10 cm were measured perpendicular to bedding of the larger blocks within the niche.

Relative colour variations (fig. 13) down the same reference profile were measured using a spectrophotometer Minolta CM-2002 (MINOLTA, Japan) at approx. every 80–100 cm. Again the position of each respective measurement was determined using the Total Station. A denser sampling rate could not be realized with the relatively fragile spectrophotometer, which proved less user-friendly under rock climbing conditions.

Despite the still restricted access to the back wall of the niches, the first real test of the pattern matching approach could be established during the September 2005 mission. One of the larger, as of yet not recovered fragments from the Western Buddha niche (fig. 14) was suspected to originate from the lower part of the back plane based on geological criteria (see previous paragraph). The 4.5 m long section from the back plane (in 2003 still hidden by fragments) was investigated using an extension ladder. The lithological succession is summarized in figure 14. Importantly, a several cm-thick red clay layer with unique primary bedding structures (dewatering streaks), which had been noted in the fragment as well, could be used as a marker bed (i.e., a tie point). Susceptibility profiles were measured for the back wall section and the targeted fragment. Both the susceptibility profiles were measured at high resolution, i.e., at about every 5–10 cm, and, hence, for the first time on the same scale of resolution. Confirmed by the position of the marker bed both the susceptibility profiles from the back wall and the fragment yield a perfect match (fig. 14), and, hence, validate the suspected original vertical position of the fragment. Minor deviations of the two susceptibility profiles reflect the slight lateral variability of the sedimentary layers.

3.1.2 Eastern Buddha niche

Before the 2006 mission the Eastern Buddha had been given less attention due to the situation on site. During the 2006 geological mission several short profiles from the lowermost part of the back plane could be geologically and magnetically investigated by Jens Aubel. In summary, while the sedimentary layers in this lower part of the wall are sufficiently distinct (fig. 15) to promote the success of the pattern matching approach in analogy to the results from the Western Buddha, the apparently more prominent coarse conglomerates in the upper part of the cliff (observation from the distance) will possibly require special attention.

Susceptibility measurements were taken at the highest possible resolution (i.e. at about every 5 cm) with the handheld KT-5c Kappameter from the sections indicated in figures m and ff, as well as from several fragments, which could be assessed (see 3.2.2). Magnetic susceptibilities are on the same order as was noted for the Western Buddha sedimentary succession and displays an equally distinct variation with the lithology (figs. 16, 17). Hence, these results are more than promising for the suggested pattern matching method to be used for the Eastern Buddha as well.

3.2 Fragments[3]
3.2.1 Western Buddha

The main purpose of investigating the fragments, in 2005 accessible in greater number and detail than was previously possible, was to establish whether they are in fact geologically distinct to a degree, that the idea of pattern matching is further supported. A second important goal was to check on any possible alteration (weathering) of the remains which might challenge the geological approach. In addition, the recovered fragments provided a good opportunity to look into useful combinations of geological criteria and archaeological details from the original (carved) Buddha figure surface.

The results can be summarized as follows:
As was previously suspected (Urbat 2003) a selection of 22 fragments confirms, that all of the sedimentary layers are geologically distinct amongst the individual fragments. Hence, the most important prerequisite for the pattern matching approach is satisfied. The following summary is based on fragments GBF 001, 002, 004, 006, 007, 047–049 and 052–0653 plus several observations from not yet registered fragments from the western and eastern Buddha niches:

- In all fragments the layering (bedding plane) was clearly visible, and, hence, allowed for the recognition of the sedimentary horizontal plane (basic re-orientation of the fragment).
- Since all of the investigated fragments had remains of the original surface, which in a first approximation indicates a vertical plane, the horizontal indicated by the layering could easily be confirmed. Note, that any acute angle between the bedding plane and the original surface may hint towards an original position of the fragment with a nonvertical carved surface (e.g. shoulder areas).
- All layers, which can be generally classified under a common term (e.g. conglomerate, silt, sand etc.) yield individual geological features allowing for a clear distinction among one another. Individual characteristics include colour, composition of components or mineral grains, size and shape, layer thickness and succession, type and amount of natural cement, HCl reaction and magnetic susceptibility (fig. 5).
- Magnetic susceptibility displays three typical ranges of values: low ($0.2 - 0.5 \cdot 10^{-3}$ SI), medium ($0.6 - 1.0 \cdot 10^{-3}$ SI) and high ($1.1 - 2.3 \cdot 10^{-3}$ SI). Lowest values are typically associated with the conglomerates. Importantly, visually homogenous non-conglomeratic layers typically display characteristic susceptibility variations in the medium and high ranges, even within the same layer (fig. 7).
- Several fragments have tectonic fractures on a small scale (hence unrelated to the detonation of the Buddha statues) or typical bedding structures (e.g. non-planar bedding surfaces) which will than be correlative with the respective tectonic or sedimentary features on the back wall of the niches as well (figs. 13, 14).
- Fragment GBF_049 (180 x 150 x 150 cm), which contains both conglomeratic and silty layers could be positively identified as one of the fragments which had been investigated during the first geological mission in 2003 (termed fragment 1531 at the time, fig. 18). Being one of the fragments on top of the heap of remains in 2003, hence only partly covered, three faces of the fragment experienced maximum exposures over the past two years. Importantly, no critical alteration or weathering of the material could be observed in 2005. This refers to the susceptibility measurements which were reproducible in 2005 as well as to any visible signs of material alteration (for example colour), apart from some minor mechanical damage due to the recovery of the fragment.

3.2.2 Eastern Buddha

Results from the Western Buddha fragments can be adopted for the eastern fragments. Absolute values are on average slightly lower as compared to the Western Buddha fragments due to an increased (less magnetic carbonate content), yet vary distinctly enough to identify a significant pattern to be used in the re-positioning approach (fig. 19).

4 Conclusions and recommendations

The geological details of the Buddha fragments combined with results from magnetic susceptibility measurements yield sufficient information to successfully solve the puzzle – at least for the larger sized remains of the Buddha statues (1 m across and up), even if only methods are used which can be easily applied directly on-site. The application of laboratory methods would allow for a re-positioning of even smaller fragments as has been described in Urbat (2003). Considering the rather small size of even the larger fragments (m-scale) as compared to the original height of the entire Buddha figures, it is suggested that the described pattern matching approach based on geological and magnetic criteria will be essential for any significant re-positioning of the remains, even if they do contain original Buddha surface (archaeological details). Importantly, any combination of archaeological details (for example, orientation of reinforcement cavities, fig. 8) with the suggested approach will significantly enhance the results. Further results of the 2003, 2005 and 2006 geological missions can be summarized as follows:
- A combination of geological and magnetic criteria satisfies the needs of the pattern matching approach. Geological, magnetic and archaeological criteria need to be combined as neither of them will provide sufficient detail in all cases.

△ Fig. 10a, ▽ Fig. 10b. Temporary storage of geologically investigated Western Buddha fragments in September 2005 (10a), situation at the foot of the Western Buddha niche at the same time.

▽ Fig. 11a, b. Temporary storage of Eastern Buddha fragments in October 2006 (larger sized fragments above, smaller sized fragments measuring less than 1 meter across below). Unfortunately, the tight storage of the fragments substantially restricts the required access for the geological analyses.

△ Fig. 12a, ▽ Fig. 12b. Eastern Buddha niche in October 2006 (above), maximum height of the scaffold attained by the end of the geological mission in November 2006 (below, upper level is about 10 meters above ground)

- Minor weathering of the fragments does not challenge the approach.
- A thorough geological description of both the fragments and the back plane of the niches by a trained geologist is essential for the success of the method.
- The respective reference profiles from the back walls still need to be established and therefore direct and unrestricted access to the walls is required. This can only be achieved with a scaffolding or a crane.
- Lateral variability of horizontal layers is high and requires more than one reference line per niche.
- Resolution and details of the preliminary frame for the pattern matching approach established by Urbat (2003, western niche) is not sufficient for a successful application of the suggested method and needs to be refined.
- It is not feasible to restore dust or, for example, loose sand.
- The fragments need to be cleaned from dust or rubble to improve the geological and magnetic recording – this will be best achieved using a vacuum cleaner or blower.
- Unrestricted access to each respective fragment is mandatory for a successful geological and magnetic analysis. The present storage of the recovered fragments does not match this requirement. The fragments will have to be pulled out for analysis.
- It is strongly recommended to implement a common reference system with respect to any position in the Buddha niches. Fixed reference points to be used by all involved parties need to be established.

References

Bauer-Bornemann, U.; Melzl, E.; Romstedt, H.; Scherbaum, M.; Urbat, M., *Steinrestauratorische Beratung zu den zerstörten Buddha-Statuen*, ICOMOS report 2003, unpublished, 10 pp.

Krumsiek, K., *Zur plattentektonischen Entwicklung des Indo-Iranischen Raumes*, Stuttgart 1980: Geotekt. Forsch., 60, 1–223.

Lang, J., *Bassins intramontagneux néogènes de l'Afghanistan central*, Paris 1972: Rev. Géogr. Phys. Géol. Dyn. (2), 14, 4, 415–426.

Urbat, M., *Buddha statues – Bamiyan Valley/Afghanistan: Geological criteria for conservation/reconstruction*, UNESCO/ICOMOS report 2003, 8 pp.

Urbat, M.; Krumsiek, K., *Paleo- and rockmagnetic criteria for the reconstruction of the giant Buddha Statues, Bamiyan/Afghanistan*, Nice, France 2004: Geophysical Research Abstracts, Volume 6, EGU General Assembly. ISSN 1029–7006.

Urbat, M., *Buddha statues – Bamiyan Valley/Afghanistan: Geological criteria for conservation/ reconstruction*, Part II. UNESCO/ICOMOS report 2005, 9 pp.

Zou, Y.; Unold, F., *Situation of the Buddha Statues in the Valley of Bamiyan, Afghanistan*, ICOMOS report 2002, unpublished.

Notes

[1] The term figure rather than statue is used here, because the Buddhas were not completed as freestanding sculptures and rather remained semi-detached to the geological strata (cliff) they were hewn out.

[2] The paleo- and rockmagnetic measurements in the laboratory confirm two important aspects with respect to a possible reconstruction of the original context of the rock fragments. First, a combined interpretation of the laboratory induced magnetizations IRM (flat acquisition curves and values of the remanent coercivity Bcr > 100mT) and ARM as well as the high-temperature susceptibility measurements confirms the high variability of the respective sedimentary layers with respect to their composition, i.e., the prerequisite for a meaningful positioning of rock fragment with respect to the reference profile. The dominant carrier of the remanent magnetization is a high coercivity phase (presumably hematite-like, Fe_2O_3), however, with differing grain size distribution and possibly varying relative concentration and oxidation state. Second, this hematite-phase carries a stable NRM direction, which is the prerequisite for a meaningful reorientation of a rock fragment in the horizontal plane. The hematite-phase (which has a maximum grain-size of only a few μm) resides in the clay matrix of the interbedded layers and likely in the matrix in between the conglomerate components, hence, could be used in the conglomerate layers as well. The reddish colour of the entire sediment succession likely originates from the hematite contribution.

[3] For any denotation of the fragments in this report the consecutive numbering introduced by the ICOMOS experts (B. Praxenthaler, E. Melzl) is adopted. GBF stands for Great Buddha fragment in conjunction with a 3-digit number starting from 001, which indicates the successive recovery of individual fragments from the niche irrespective of other fragment characteristics. In 2005, only those fragments with remains of the original surface have been included in the documentation. The fragments are temporarily stored under canopy next to the Buddha niche (fig. 10).

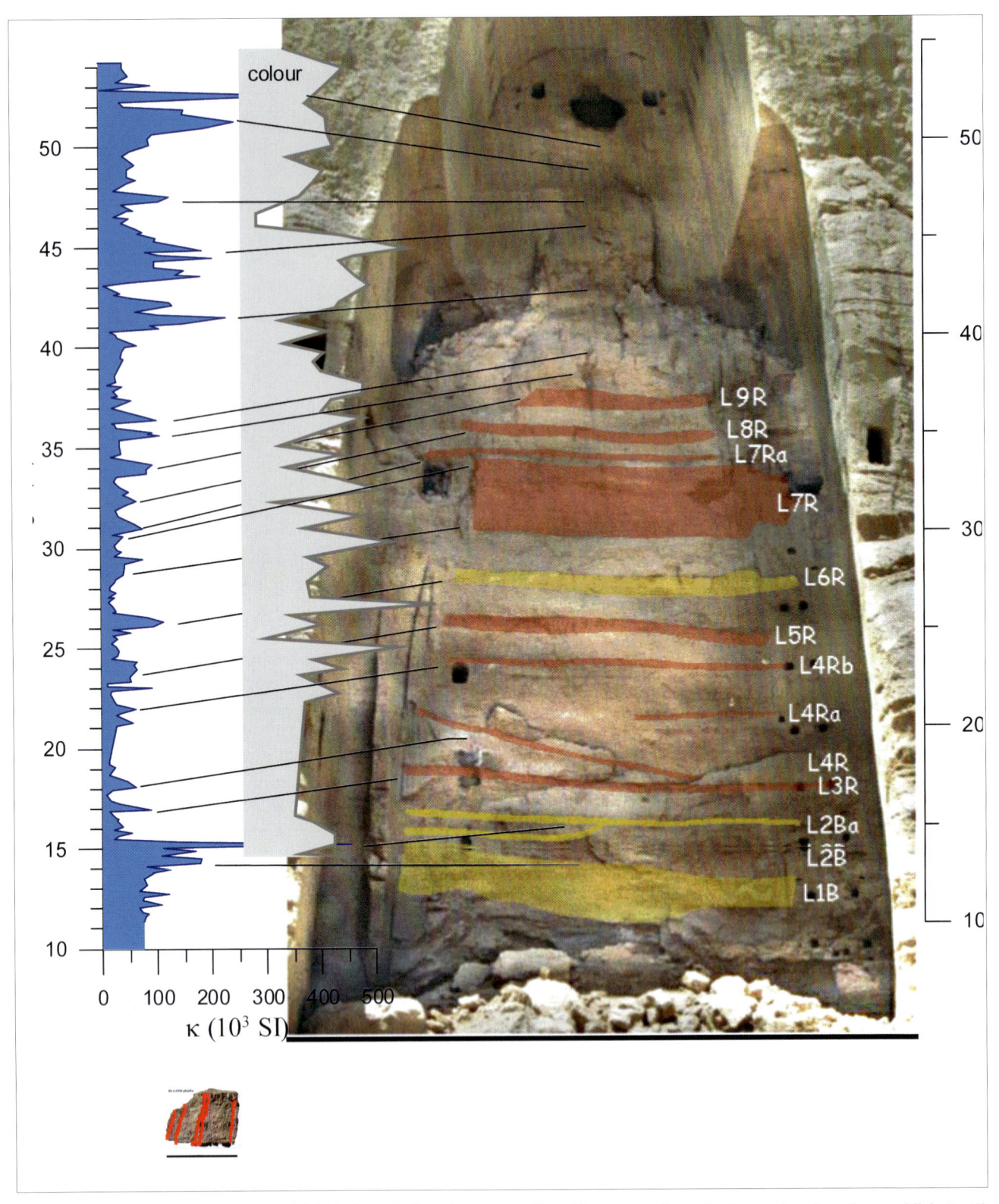

△ Fig. 13. Western Buddha niche. Initial 2003 geologic reference profile with suggested numbering system based on reddish (LxR) and light brownish (LxB) silt/sand layers interbedded with the conglomerates. Also shown is magnetic susceptibility κ and suggested correlation to the respective layers (thin black lines). Highest susceptibilities correlate with concrete remains on the wall which originate from a former Indian consolidation work in the 1970s. Shown in grey is the colour variation measured with the photospectrometer. Size of a 2 m size rock fragment is shown for comparison.

Fig. 14 ▷
First successful pattern match based on geological and susceptibility details of a fragment from the Great Buddha. The fragment originates from the lower part of the back wall just below Layer L1B (Urbat 2003). Inset (western Buddha niche, upper right indicates the location of the 4.5 m long profile investigated on the back wall of the niche as well as position and approximate size of the matched fragment in September 2005. Note that absolute susceptibility values as well as the shape of the two curves match nicely.

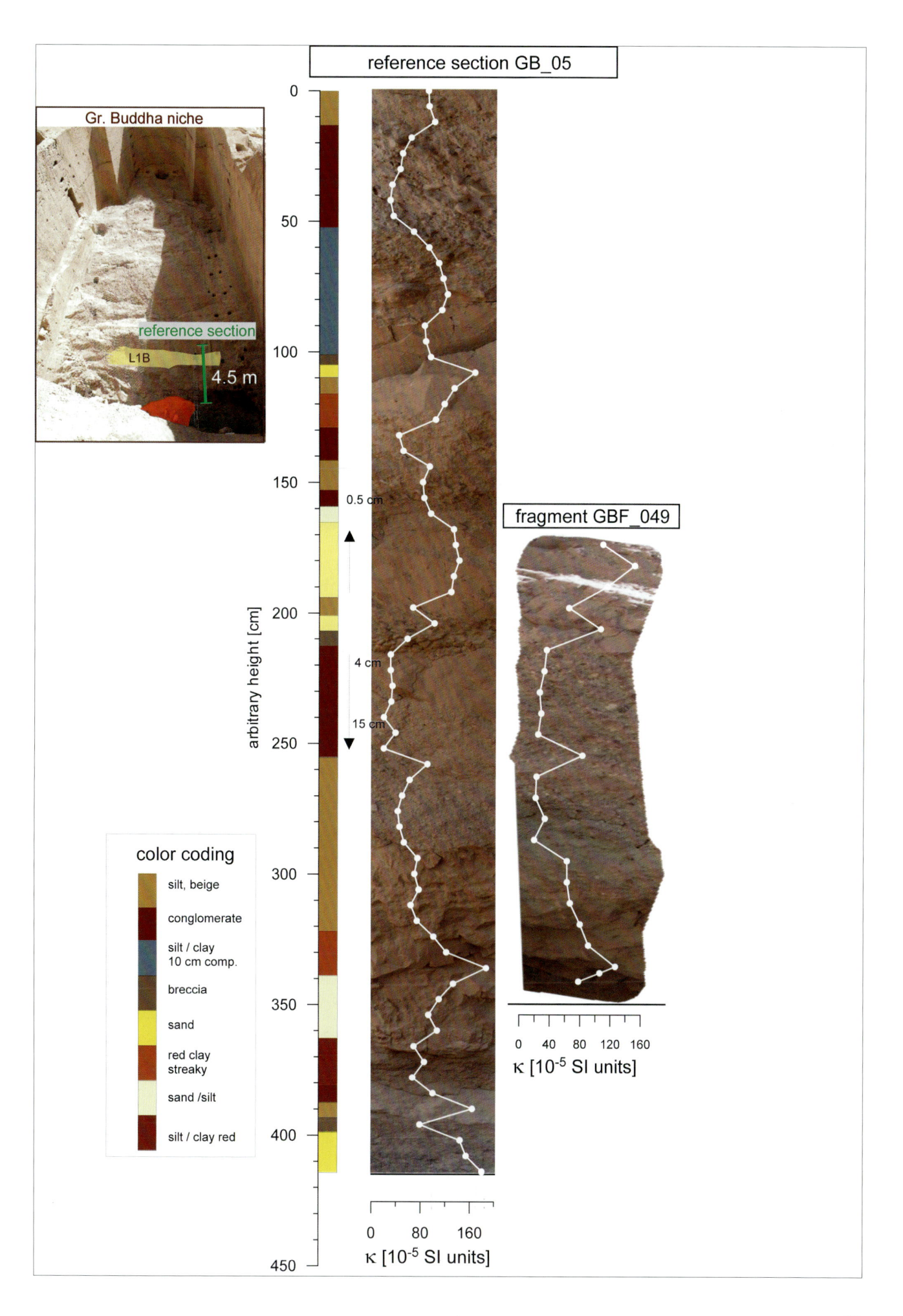

reference section GB_05

Gr. Buddha niche — reference section L1B, 4.5 m

color coding
- silt, beige
- conglomerate
- silt / clay 10 cm comp.
- breccia
- sand
- red clay streaky
- sand / silt
- silt / clay red

arbitrary height [cm]

0.5 cm
4 cm
15 cm

fragment GBF_049

κ [10^{-5} SI units]

κ [10^{-5} SI units]

Fig. 15. Eastern Buddha niche - lower part of the back plane including entrance to the central chamber. Solid black line indicates the position of the 4.2 m long reference section EB-RC1. Overlaid colours highlight the sub-horizontally bedded succession of conglomeratic and silty layers (with suggested numbering EB-RC1-1C through EB-RC1-6C) and indicate their notable lateral variation and deviations from horizontal, which calls for at least two more reference lines (indicated by stippled lines).

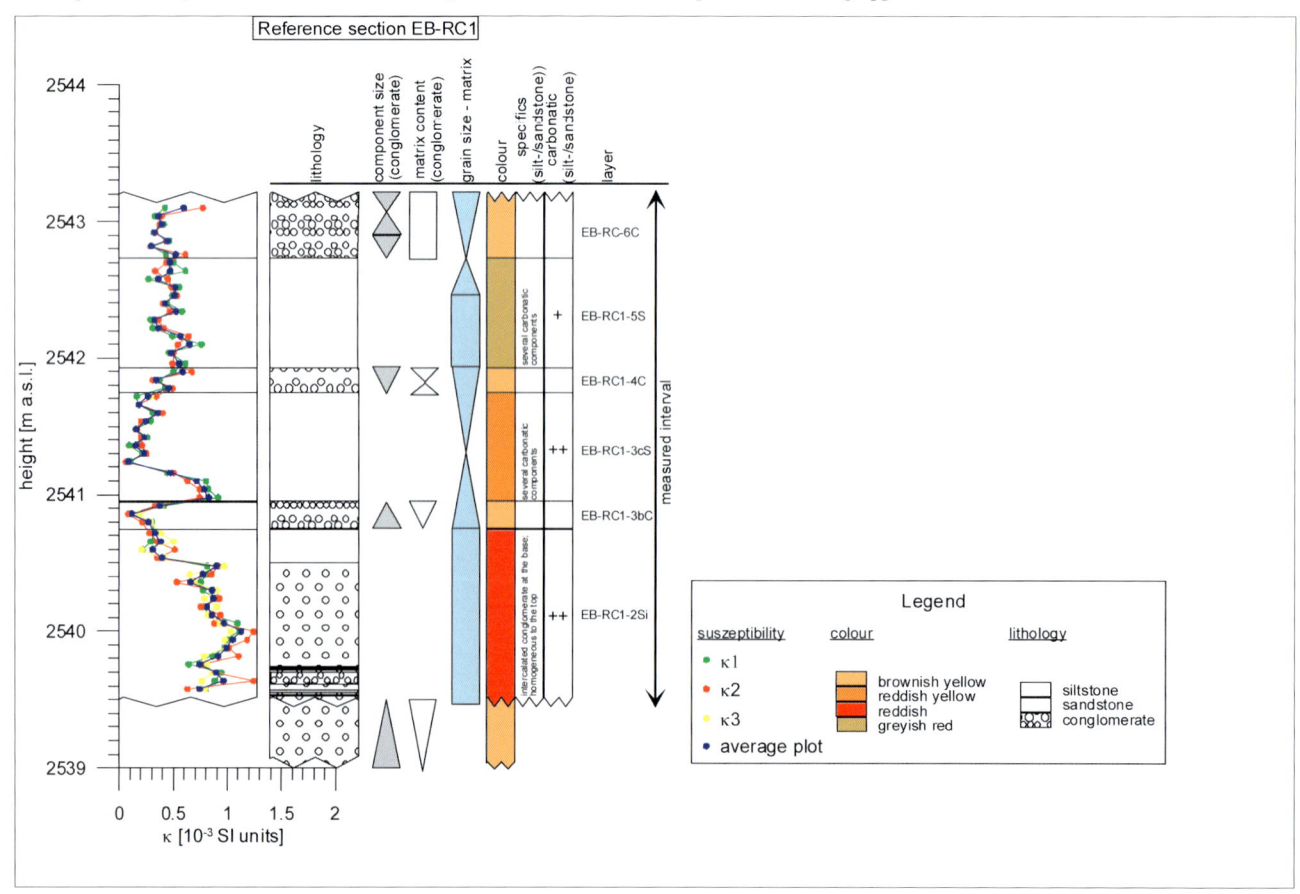

Fig. 16. Summary plot of geological and magnetic results from reference section EB-RC1, Eastern Buddha niche. Both the geological details as well as the susceptibility logs vary distinctly on a cm-scale down section. Susceptibility (κ1 through κ3) measurements were taken repeatedly within a lateral displacement range of about 1m, while keeping the vertical position (m.a.s.l.) of the respective measurements. The reproducibility of the measurements clearly satisfies the needs of the pattern matching approach.

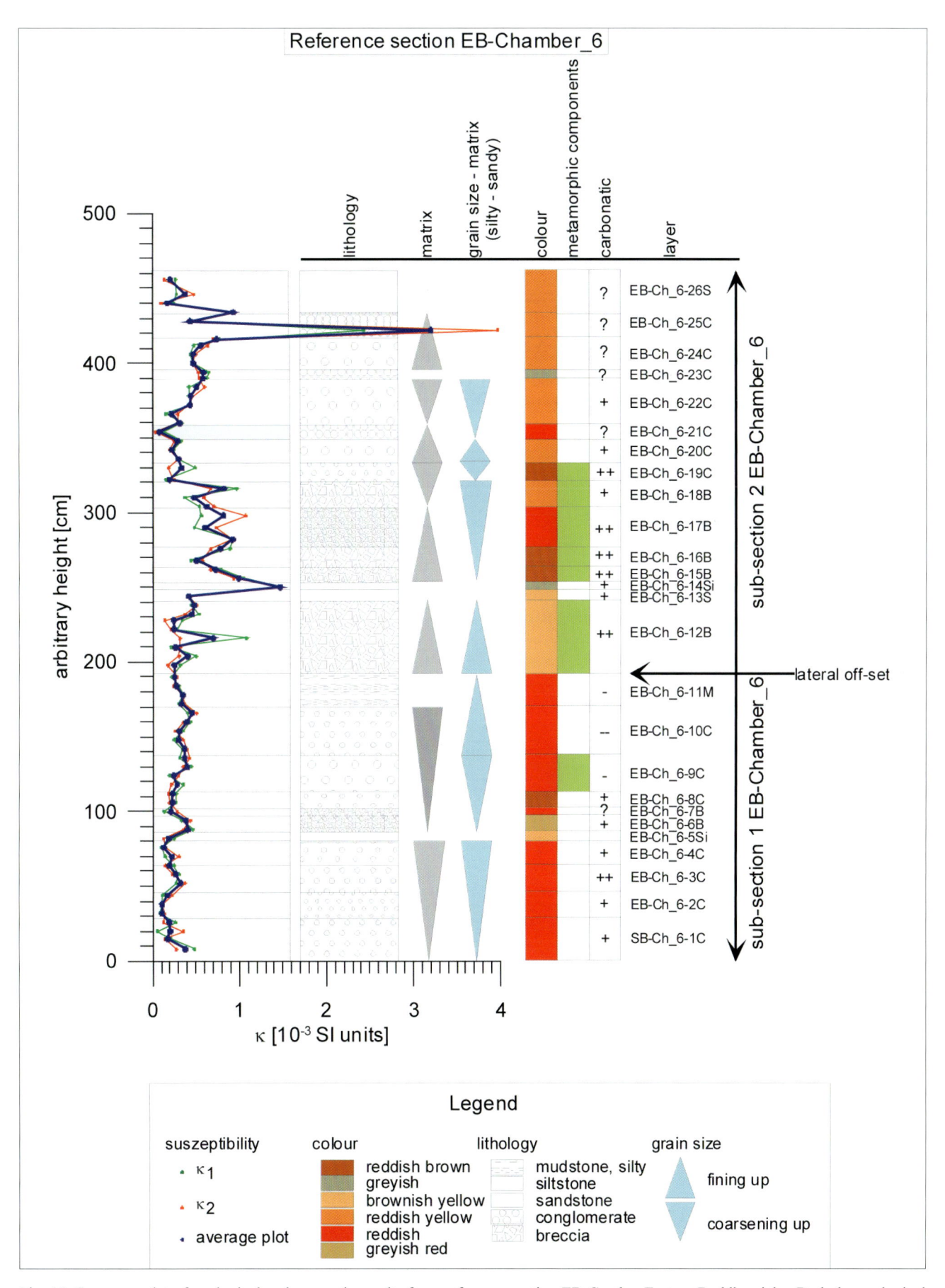

Fig. 17. Summary plot of geological and magnetic results from reference section EB-Camber Eastern Buddha niche. Both the geological details as well as the susceptibility logs vary distinctly cm-scale down section. Susceptibility (κ_1 through κ_2) measurements were taken repeatedly within lateral displacement range of about 1m, while keeping the vertical position (m.a.s.l.) of the respective measurements. The reproducibility of the measurements again clearly satisfies the needs of the pattern matching approach. Highest susceptibility peaks correspond with cements remaining from pre-destruction consolidation works.

Figs. 18a, b. Fragment GBF_049 under canopy in 2005 and in the niche in 2003 (right side). In the left-hand picture parts of the original Buddha surface including the typical reinforcement cavities are clearly visible.

Fig. 19. Susceptibility measurements taken from three selected Eastern Buddha fragments

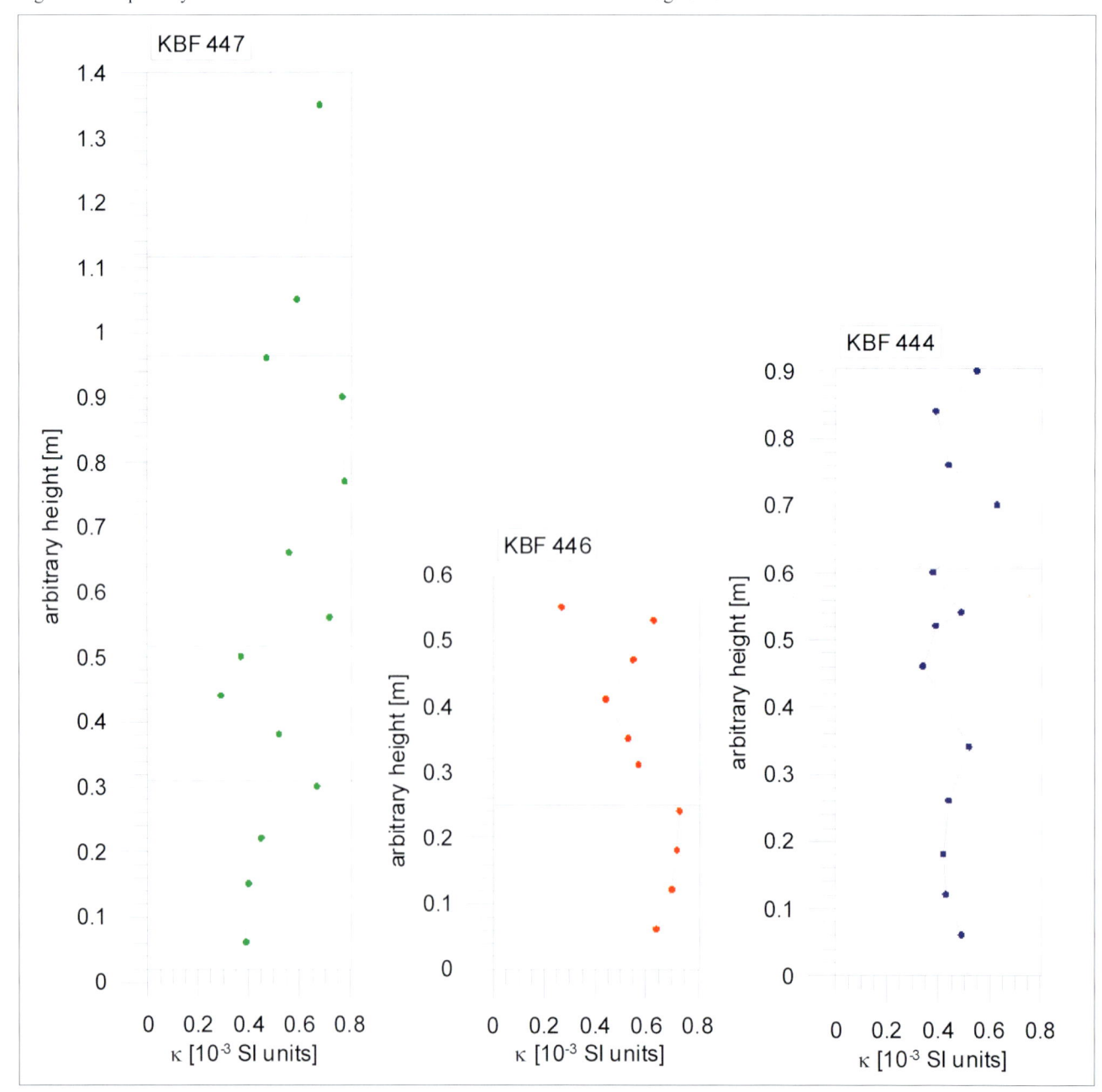

Edwin Fecker

Report on Rock Mechanical Aspects Concerning the Eastern Buddha Niche, 2006

When creating sculptures in stone the artist has generally the possibility to take a perfect block from a quarry, from which he can in his experience create the desired sculpture. This is not the case for sculptures which are built out of the in-situ rock. If so, the artist has to take the conditions of the different rock structure and the discontinuities for granted and he has to integrate them into his sculpture. This is especially valid for sculptures with the dimensions of the Buddhas of Bamiyan, where a permanent rock alternation is observed over the total height of 40 resp. 60 m and where the discontinuities are setting limits to the sculpture.

Furthermore geological processes, which take place in every valley more or less quickly, are naturally influencing the structures embedded in valley flanks, too. Today the geological processes have built a cliff which is rising nearly vertically between 100 and 150 m high from the Bamiyan Valley. Due to the gravity tension joints parallel to the slope, open on top, are created in such an oversteeped valley. The result is that 10 to 20 m thick slabs of the cliff wall are toppling or parallel to joints large parts of slabs are collapsing, e.g. due to earthquakes. At the cliff of the Eastern Buddha, being about 500 m long and 100 m high, a rock fall and

Eastern cliff of the Bamiyan valley with the niche of the Eastern Buddha. At the foot of the cliff several rock masses from slope movements can be recognised.

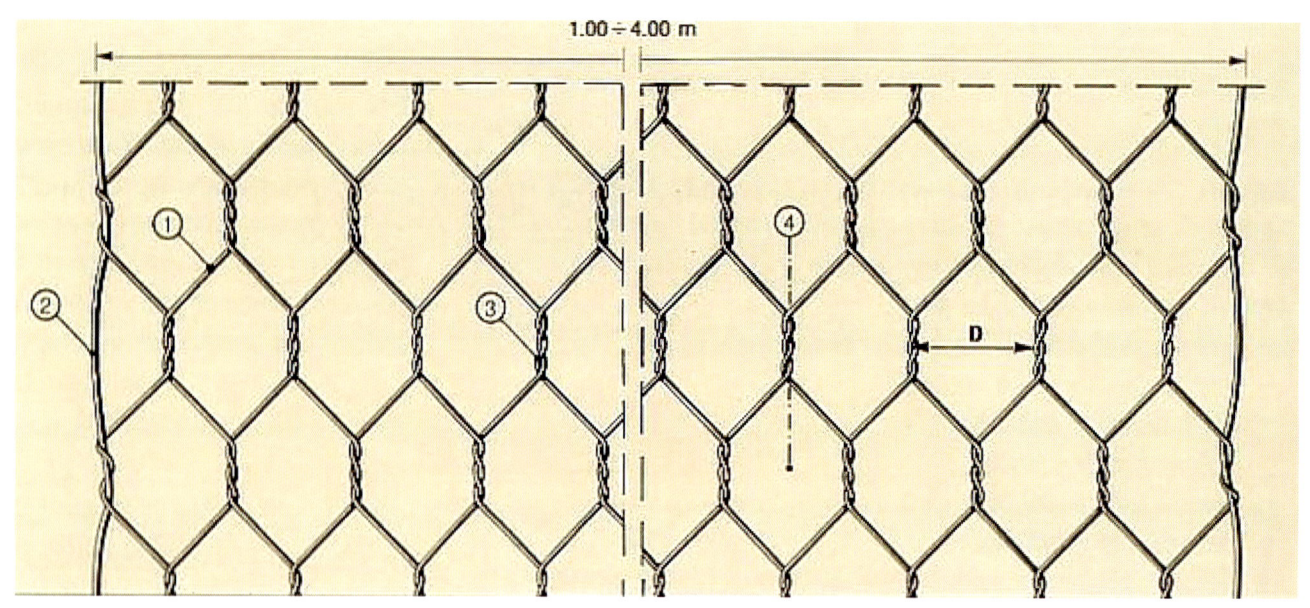

Double-twisted hexagonal 8 x 10 type steel wire mesh. 1 mesh wire, 2 lateral wire, 3 double twist, 4 twist axis (www.hydrogeo.net/rete_doppia_torsione.htm)

Site plan of the niche of the Eastern Buddha (from Hackin and Carl, 1933)

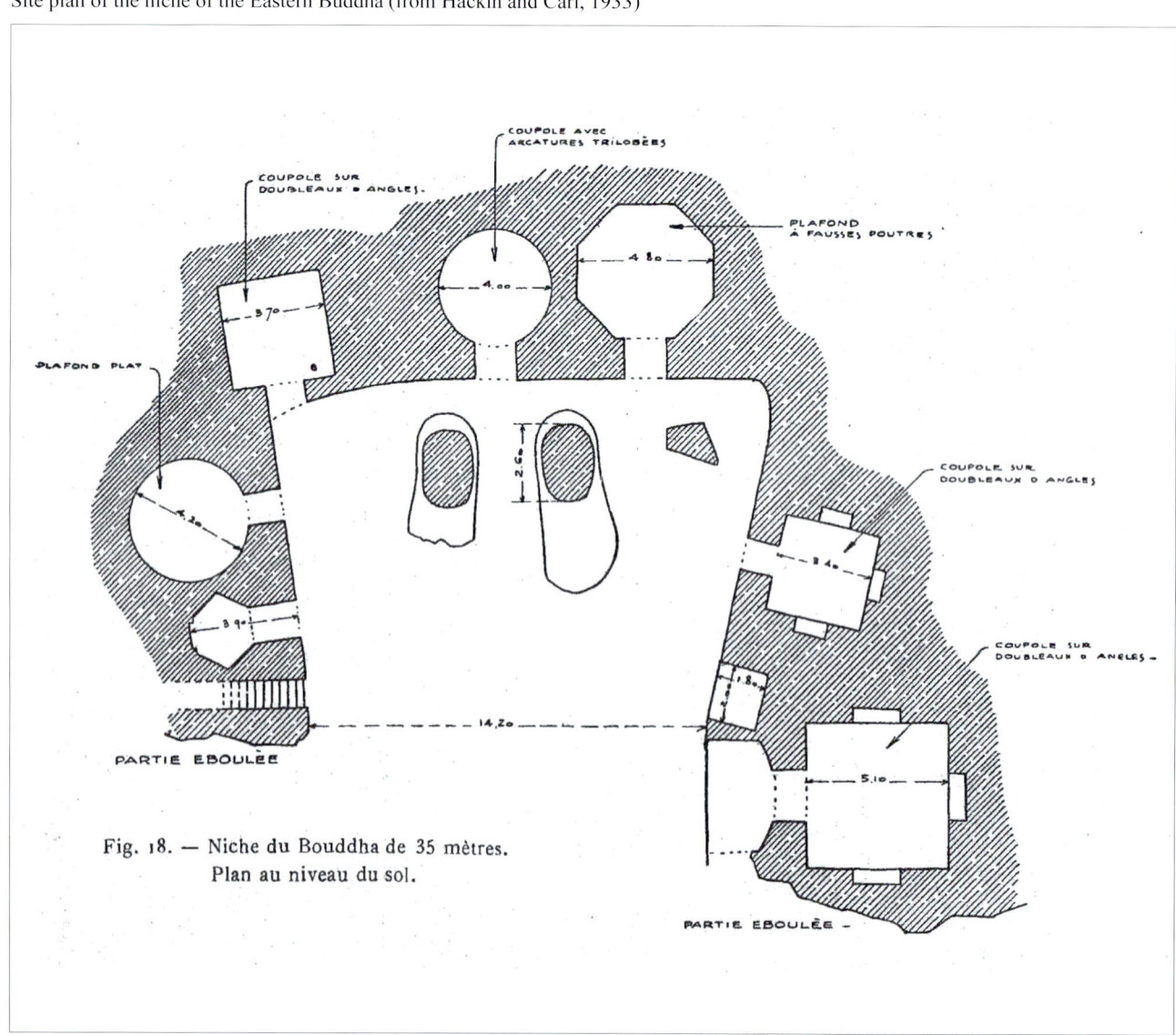

Fig. 18. — Niche du Bouddha de 35 mètres. Plan au niveau du sol.

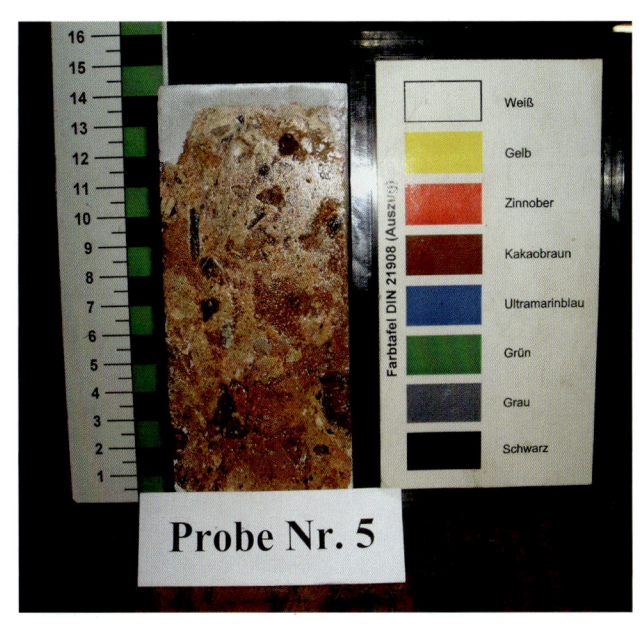

Example of a test specimen prepared for a uniaxial compression test. The sample is sawn from a rock sample. The upper end surface is completed with plaster.

several other mass movements are well-cognizable; if they took place in historic times it must be reserved to more exact examinations and is not the subject of this report. What can be said about it in any case is shown in a comparison of today's situation with the drawing of Charles Masson from the year 1832 (see fig. 3, p. 20). In that drawing the most west sliding mass had not yet come off, so it must be younger than this year.

If the tension joints of the cliff pass the niche of the Buddha itself they are an aspect of global stability of the niche and may not be disregarded.

Another geological process which could influence the stability of the niche is weathering caused by precipitation. As the in-situ sedimentary rocks, mainly coarse-, mid- and fine- grained conglomerates and siltstones, do not have a very solid grain-to grain bonding they are weathering strongly when water is penetrating into their pores. Of course this circumstance must have been known to the builders of the Buddhas of Bamiyan, that's why they worked the Buddhas out of the in-situ rock in a 40 m high niche, so that they have not been exposed to precipitation.

For me it seems even probable that the water loosening of the rock has been taken as a working support when excavating the niche, the galleries and the caves, because there are no traces of treatment with hammer and wedge at the surfaces of the preserved fragments of the Buddha.

A second advantage is that the annual precipitation in the Bamiyan Valley is very low (according to http://www.klimadiagramme.de/Asien/bamiyan.html at present in average 133 mm/year), which is opposed to a fast weathering.

As a third fact the roof of the cliff is superposed by a big weathering layer which avoids that large water quantities are penetrating into the niches through the joints, but will evaporate partially or concentrate on the surface in channels and smaller gullies and will drain off. However, the geological processes have impaired the structure in the course of the centuries. Especially the channels which have transported the water from the superposed weathering layer to the cliff wall are the reason for natural destructions close to the niche, what led to considerable conservation measurements by archaeologists, restorers and engineers of the Archaeological Survey of India from 1969–1977.

But the most important destructions have their reason in the species *Homo Sapiens*. In the last centuries such interventions are documented repeatedly. They are culminating in the destructions of beginning of March 2001, when a strong explosive charge has been initiated in the middle cave behind the Buddha, which blasted the largest part of the Buddha and left a lot of local instabilities, which are subject of this report.

Geological Characteristics of the Niche

Subsequently the geological characteristics in the niche of the Eastern Buddha are described to provide the basis for continuing consideration. Some of this knowledge is based on former publications, some is based on my own studies. Furthermore I would like to refer that this theme is subject of studies of the Geological Institute from the University in Cologne where it will be described much more detailed. I'm only concentrating here on the geological aspects which are important for rock mechanic purposes.

Type of Sedimentary Rocks

In the area of the niche of the Eastern Buddha mainly conglomerates with different sized pebbles (coarse-, mid- and fine-grained) are present. The conglomerate layers are interrupted from some siltstone layers. The layers are inclined few degrees towards East. In the examined area of the niche they can simplified be taken as horizontally bedded.

Figure 1 shows samples of the conglomerate which contains fine-grained pebbles (samples no. 1 and 2).

Alteration of samples no. 1 to 5 under water after 24 hours.

Figure 2 shows a sample of the siltstones (sample no. 3) and figure 3 a sample of the conglomerate with medium-sized pebbles (sample no. 5). The cementation of both rock types, conglomerates as well as siltstones, is not very strong and two of them (samples no. 3 and 4) do not contain cementing agents, that's why they totally decay in their individual grains in the case of water immersion. These rocks are only compacted by overburden, without a chemical cementation. The conglomerate of sample no. 5 seems to have at least a little cementation.

Grain Size

As we would not take rock samples from the back wall of the niche we collected the above mentioned samples underneath the niche (sample no. 1 to 5, figs. 1–3). It is not sure that they come from the niche of the Small Buddha, but I do not consider this to be essential, because for the conclusions that are drawn from the examination it is not relevant if the samples are from the niche or close-by. The grain size distribution of the samples is shown in figures 4–7. To determine the grain distribution the samples have been stored under water for 24 hours. After this the percentage of the different grains composing the samples has been determined by sieving and sedimentation analysis. At sample no. 5 this method could not be used, because the alteration under water was moderate and the sample did not decay in its individual grains.

Density

In the niche of the Eastern Buddha siltstones and conglomerates with highly variable composition of the matrix and the pebbles are present. That's why larger variations are likely to occur as regards the density. From literature (Margottini, 2004) a natural density of $\rho = 2.28$ g/cm³ and a dry density of $\rho = 2.23$ g/cm³ is known for the siltstone.

The few samples which we have examined should give a first indication and are not exhaustive. The results are sufficient for the purposes for which this parameter is needed in our context. We have determined a mean natural density of $\rho = 2.00$ g/cm³ for the siltstone (sample no. 3), which corresponds to a specific weight of $\gamma = 19.62$ kN/m³. For the conglomerates (samples no. 1, 2, 4 and 5) we have determined a mean natural density of $\rho = 2.15$ g/cm³, which corresponds to a specific weight of $\gamma = 21.09$ kN/m³ (see figs. 8 and 9). The water content w of the individual samples is shown in figure 10. The water content is very low, which is why the dry density differs only marginally from the natural density.

Jointing

The main joint system in the niche of the Eastern Buddha is parallel to the valley which runs at this point in near East-West direction. Due to the explosion of March 2001 the new formed discontinuities do not follow the rules for naturally created joints. Indeed the new formed back wall of the niche runs nearly parallel to the valley, but compared with a natural joint it is very irregular. That's why we cannot indicate a single value for the spatial position as usual.

From the back wall of the niche a topographic record has been made by a scanner in October 2006. For future support measurements this record is a much more exact basis than describing the back wall with a mean spatial position. This is also valid for the new smaller discontinuities which additionally separate the back wall of the niche and the caves at the base of the niche.

Earthquakes

Bamiyan is located on the Herat fault, a 1200 km long, east-west suture through central Afghanistan, that trends northward into the Hindu Kush mountains north of Kabul at its eastern end. The Bamiyan region is located in the transition zone between the intense seismic activity that characterises the Indo-Asian continental plate boundary in eastern Afghanistan, and the largely inactive central part of Afghanistan. Written records of historical earthquakes in Afghanistan are sparse. Even in the 19th and early 20th century communications remained poor due to the skeletal development of roads, phone lines and government infrastructures, resulting in few published notices about earthquake locations and damage. Historically, the western Herat fault has remained largely inactive; however, a significant earthquake occurred near Bamiyan on June 9th, 1956. The causal fault that slipped in this $M = 7.4$ earthquake is not known although it appears to have occurred in the region bounded by the Herat fault and the Andarabad fault, 80 km to the north of Bamiyan in the Sadat valley (see Ambraseys & Bilham).

According to Reineke (Bamiyan Masterplan Campaign 2005) an earthquake was registered located west of Bamiyan with a magnitude of $M = 4.9$ in May 28th 1997. As a result of these earthquakes the region belongs to the moderate dangerous places in Afghanistan. The danger of mass movements (rockfall, mudflow etc.) triggered by tectonic events is, compared with other regions in Afghanistan, low but evident (see fig. 11 taken from USGS). Comparing the seismicity of this region with Germany it becomes apparent that however we are concerned with a relatively active earthquake zone. There is no zone in Germany with earthquakes with a magnitude of 7.4. In Germany earthquakes with a magnitude 7 and more are not at all to be expected. If an anastylosis of the Small Buddha is provided, a ground acceleration of 1.6 to 2.4 m/sec² due to earthquakes must be taken into consideration.

Mechanical Rock Characteristics in the Niche

The mechanical properties of the rocks in the niche have not yet been explored in detail. Margottini (2004) has executed some Schmidt-hammer tests to estimate the uniaxial compressive strength of the rocks. From the tests he has derived 30 MPa for the conglomerates and 36 MPa for the siltstones. Such tests are only index tests which are used for a first orientation. That's why we have decided to analyse the rock material from the area of the Eastern Buddha in the laboratory.

Uniaxial Compressive Strength

From the rock samples which we collected underneath the niche of the Eastern Buddha the Institute for Soil and Rock Mechanics of the Technical University Karlsruhe sawed out specimens to execute uniaxial compression tests.

The mean value for the uniaxial compressive strength of the conglomerate (samples no. 1 and 2) results in 2.99 MPa (see figs. 12 and 13). The value for the uniaxial compressive strength of the siltstone (sample No. 3) is 6.91 MPa (see fig. 14).

Sample no. 5, which concerns also a conglomerate, has – in contrary to the conglomerate of samples no. 1 and 2 – some cementation. The uniaxial compressive strength of this sample is 6.73 MPa (see fig. 15).

Weathering Resistance

As we already pointed out, the rock in the area of the Small Buddha niche contains only little or no chemical cementation. The grain-to-grain bonding is mostly a result of a mechanic compaction. The desintegration of the rock due to water susceptibility can be characterised by the alteration test under water according to DIN4022, part 1 (see fig. 16).

For this test the samples are immersed into water for 24 hours and afterwards their alteration under water is determined or it can be demonstrated that they do not show any changes. This test is a characteristic for the content of chemical cementation.

The five samples that we have examined with this test show the following result: Samples no. 3 and 4 without cementation are intensely alterable during this test, samples no. 1 and 2 are alterable and sample no. 5 is moderately alterable.

Also noticeable in the test result is the high water susceptibility of sample no. 3.

Stability Observations

Due to the explosion in March 2001 rock sections which have been partially loosened and are now on the verge of falling can be observed at the back wall of the niche of the Small Buddha and in the caves at the base of the niche. In case of a normal rock slope these rock parts would have been broken away.

I am describing them to give a decision-making-aid to conservationists for future measurements. If the costs would be the decisive factor, breaking off the loosened rock parts would be the cheapest solution by far. But if conservation aspects play the overriding role, technical solutions may and will be found to secure the loosened rock parts, which of course will be involved with higher costs.

Back Wall of the Niche

The back wall of the Eastern Buddha is still showing in its highest part rests of the head of the Buddha. This is a large rock plate which is affected in joints parallel to the slope by new formed ones (see figs. 17 and 18). The joints are slightly open. The whole part must be secured. I am considering the danger of larger rock falls in the near future to be low.

The right shoulder is affected in many parts due to several new formed joints parallel to the wall and loosened from the back wall (see fig. 19). Some joints are open. In my opinion the danger that some parts may fall down and the total section may follow is high. Especially caused by an earthquake – even of low magnitude – the section may lose its hold and fall down.

The left shoulder is also affected in many parts due to several new formed joints parallel to the slope and loosened from the back wall (see figs. 20–22). Some joints are open up to about 10 cm. In these open joints decimetre large rock pieces can be seen which have been fallen into the open joint from the upper side of the shoulder. Only a rock gusset of about 1.5 m² avoids the falling of the section. The rock gusset is also showing disintegration. In my opinion the danger that the whole part will fall is very high. Although this shoulder part seems to have been in the condition of a possible fall since 2001 we suspect that this part may fall even without the effect of an earthquake.

Underneath the right hand of the Eastern Buddha a dress pleat partially in good condition continues downwards which is slightly loosened from the back wall at the east edge below by some joints parallel to the wall (see fig. 23). The joints are scarcely open and seem to end under the pleat. I consider the danger of falling of this section to be very low.

Caves at the Base of the Niche

It was in the middle cave behind the feet of the Eastern Buddha (cave no. 5) where the explosive charge has been initiated. Hereby the partition walls to caves no. 4 and no. 6 as well as the front wall of all three caves were completely blasted out. Caves no. 4, 5 and 6 have a common ceiling now which is crossed by a newly formed gaping vertical joint (see figs. 24 and 25). This joint parallel to the slope extends only partially into the cave no. 6, and is feathering in the west wall of cave no. 6. In the east wall of cave no. 4 it is still some centimetres open. How it continues in the rock could not be found out with the available means.

As this joint runs parallel to the back wall of the caves and thus also parallel to the back wall of the niche it is no imminent danger for the stability of the back wall of the niche. It impairs at most the stability of the ceiling in the cave no. 5. The way I see it, there is no danger of collapse of this ceiling.

But there are some smaller rock plates which could fall down from the ceiling of the three caves. These plates have been temporarily supported with wooden beams. Later a final support measurement must be provided for them.

The other caves which are arranged around the niche (caves no. 1 to 3 and no. 7 to 8) have new formed joints, too – mostly in the ceiling. But the joints have no adverse effect on the stability. Only in cave no. 7 the ceiling is crossed by a net of new joints which could lead to smaller block falls. A final support measurement must be provided.

Fig. 1. Samples no. 1 and 2: fine-grained conglomerates

Fig. 2. Sample no. 3: siltstone; Sample no. 4: fine-grained conglomerate

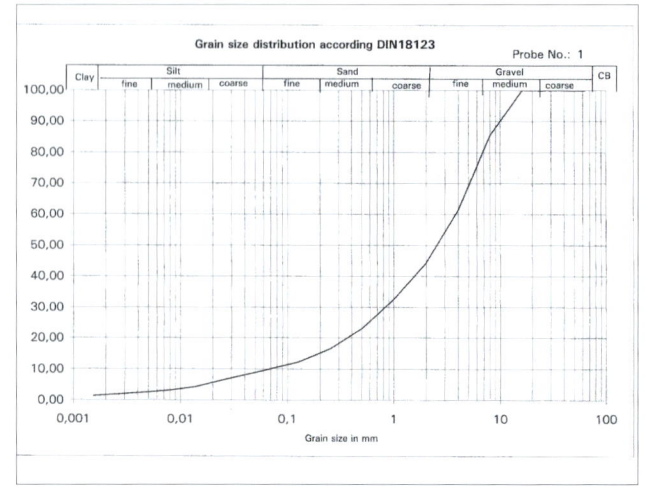

Fig. 3. Sample no. 5: medium-grained conglomerate

Fig. 4. Sample no. 1: grain-size distribution, according to DIN18123

Support Measurements

The support measurements for the back wall of the Eastern Buddha and for the caves at the base of the niche can be made in two steps. As first step the endangered rock parts must be supported at least in such a way that they are no danger for the persons who are entering the niche and the caves. The second step is to decide about a permanent support without or with the least interference with the historical substance.

Temporary Support Measurements

Since October 27, 2004, the back wall of the niche of the Eastern Buddha has been covered with a steel wire mesh to catch falling rock debris. It is a double-twisted hexagonal wire mesh with a mesh width of D = 84 x H = 121 mm, the diameter of the wire is 2.7 mm.

According to Muhunthan et al. (2005) this wire mesh is suitable to sustain rock impacts of 0.6 x 0.6 x 0.6 m pieces which are falling from the back wall. It will not be able to catch larger blocks. For double-twisted hexagonal wire mesh, impacts near the top of the installation should not exceed 10 kJ. Especially if the wire mesh does not sit snugly against the back wall larger blocks can fall free for several meters and get as much impact energy to break through the wire mesh (see fig. 26). Therefore, it is recommended to safeguard the wire mesh with steel wire ropes. Especially both shoulders should be crossed from several sides and the cross points should be connected with rope clips. The wire ropes (DIN3060, D = 11.0 mm) are to be well anchored on top and at bottom. How to do this without interfering in the historic substance can be decided on site.

The rock parts which are on the verge of falling from the ceiling of the caves no. 4 to 6 have been temporarily supported with wooden props in the meantime. When these props will be removed for a final support they have to be loosened with extreme attention. Removing the props is always much more dangerous than putting them up, because wedges are driven in when putting up the props. Hereby the supported plate may be moved and existing rock bridges may possibly be broken. When removing the props the rock part falls down.

Permanent Support Measurements

As I do not consider an interference in the historic substance desirable, e.g. by an anchorage of the dangerous rock zones in the back wall, I would like to propose a support measurement which would not influence the historic substance. The fundamental idea of this support is a steel girder construction which leans against the back wall and supports the dangerous rock zones by the retaining force applied to the back wall.

It would be self-evident to erect two vertical H steel beams at the point where the rests of both feet of the Eastern Buddha are located. The steel beams should have load distribution plates as contact surface which could be adapted to the feet surfaces. In the height of the beginning back wall, about 3.5 m above the bottom of the niche, a first crosslink between the vertical beams could be made where a support for the ceiling above niches no. 4 to 6 will be connected.

From the back wall area up to the shoulders both inclined beams could be connected by steel framework, which could serve as holding device for blasted parts of the Buddha body. A first draft of the framework is shown in figures 27 and 28.

Conclusions

Before executing further works in the niche of the Eastern Buddha I urgently recommend to increase the carrying capacity of the wire mesh by additional steel wire ropes. As a permanent support of the loose rock formations a fastening by anchors is imaginable. Alternatively, without intervention of the historical substance, I take a steel framework for suitable which leans against the back wall and serves as a support for the rock formations in danger of falling. At the same time this steel framework could be used as a load carrying system for a partial anastylosis.

References

Ambraseys, N. & Bilham, R., *The tectonic setting of Bamiyan and seismicity in and near Afghanistan for the past 12 centuries.* http://cires.colorado.edu/~bilham/BamiyanAfghanistan.pdf

Godard, A. et al., *Les Antiquités Bouddhiques de Bamiyan. Mémoires de la délégation archéologique française en Afghanistan*, Tome II, Paris 1928

Margottini, C., *Instability and geotechnical problems of the Buddha niches and surrounding cliff in Bamiyan Valley, central Afghanistan, Landslides*, Vol. 1, pp. 41–51, 2004

Mode, M., *Ein vergessener Anfang: Carl Ritter und die "Kolosse von Bamiyan"*. http://www.orientarch.uni-halle.de/ca/bam/bamiyanx.htm

Muhunthan, B. et al., *Design guidelines for wire mesh/cable net slope protection.* Prepared for Washington State Transportation Commission. In cooperation with U.S. Department of Transportation, April 2005 http://www.ce.wsu.edu/TRAC/Publications_Reports/WA-RD612.2WireMesh.pdf

Reineke, Th., Bamiyan Masterplan Campaign 2005. Environmental Assessment of the Bamiyan Valley in the Central Highlands of Afghanistan. Aachen Center for Documentation and Conservation, RWTH Aachen University

U. S. Geological Survey: Earthquake Hazards Program. Regional Information. http://earthquake.usgs.gov/regional/world/afghanistan/gshap.php

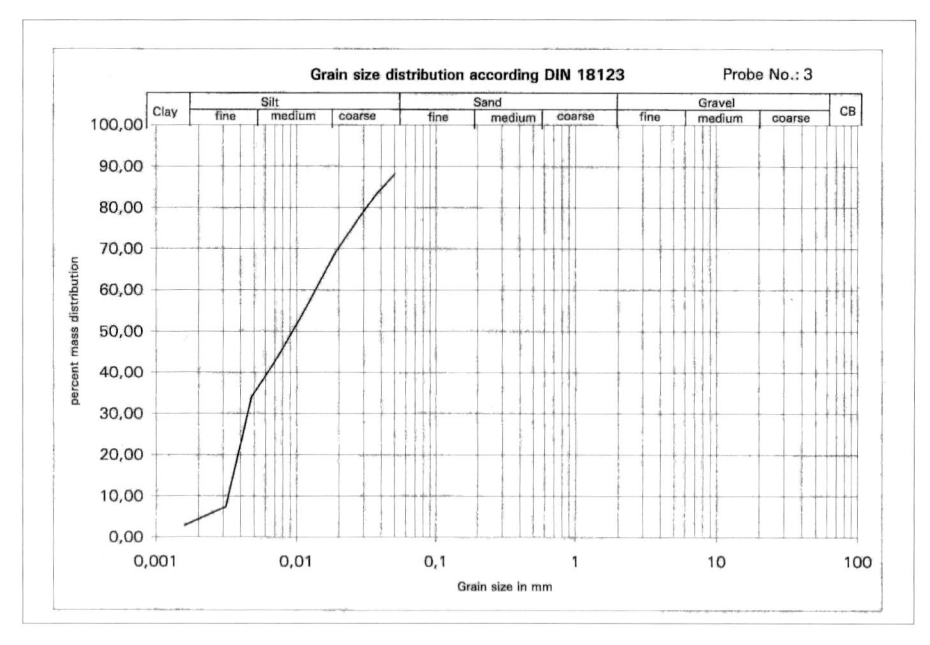

Fig. 5. Sample no. 2: grain-size distribution, according to DIN18123

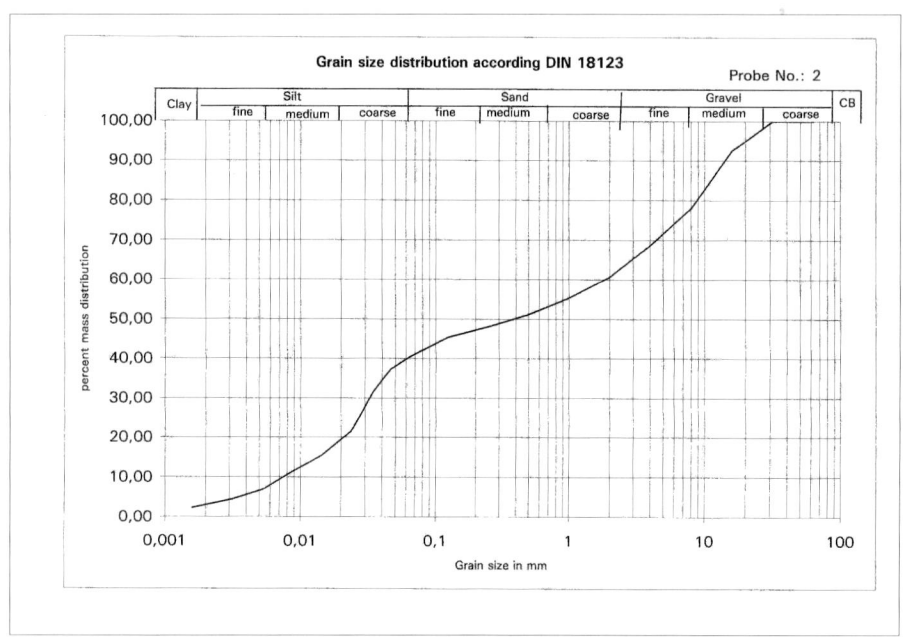

Fig. 6. Sample no. 3: grain-size distribution according to DIN18123

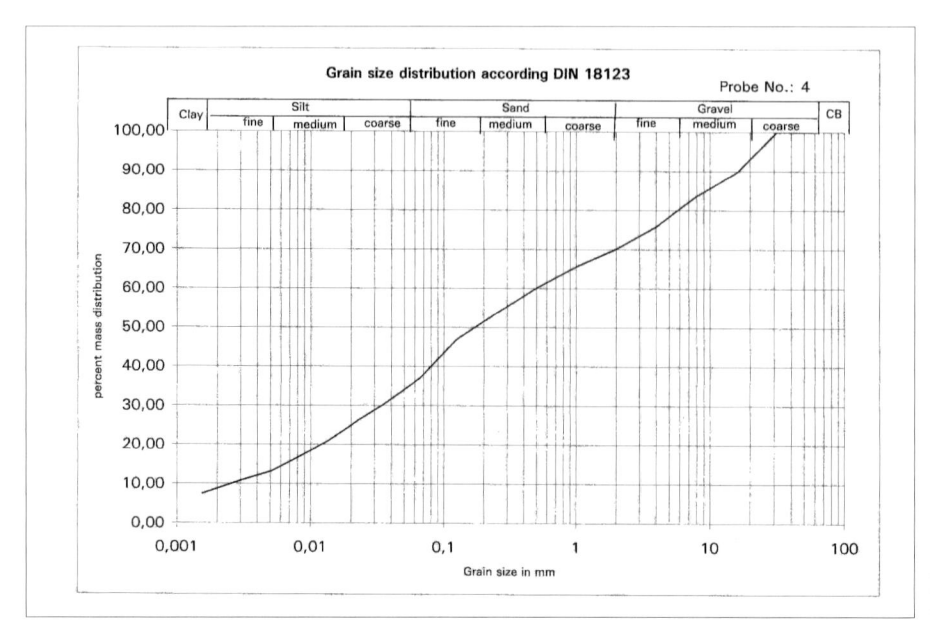

Fig. 7. Sample no. 4: grain-size distribution, according to DIN18123

Fig. 8. Density by dipping and weighing method, according to DIN18125

Lehrstuhl für Felsmechanik Institut für Bodenmechanik und Felsmechanik Universität (TH) Fridericiana zu Karlsruhe			**Density by Dipping and Weighing Method** according DIN 18125				
Project:	Bamiyan					Project No.:	e-2683
Probe number:			Nr. 4	Nr. 3	Nr. 3	Nr. 1	Nr. 1
Depth: [m]							
Mass of wet material	m	g	333,9	188,2	212,4	356,0	634,8
Mass below water	m_u	g	178,8	95,1	104,9	195,8	348,7
Temperature of water	T	°C	20,0	20,0	20,0	20,0	20,0
Density of water	ϱ_F	g/cm³	1,0	1,0	1,0	1,0	1,0
Volume of dipped probe	V	cm³	155,1	93,1	107,5	160,2	286,1
Tara Nr.							
Water content	w	%	1,6	3,6	3,6	0,7	0,7
Density	$\rho = \frac{m}{V}$	g/cm³	2,153	2,021	1,976	2,222	2,219
Dry density	$\rho_d = \frac{\rho}{1+\frac{w}{100}}$	g/cm³	2,119	1,951	1,907	2,207	2,203

Fig. 9. Density by dipping and weighing method, according to DIN18125

Lehrstuhl für Felsmechanik Institut für Bodenmechanik und Felsmechanik Universität (TH) Fridericiana zu Karlsruhe			**Density by Dipping and Weighing Method** according DIN 18125				
Project:	Bamiyan					Project No.:	e-2683
Probe number:			Nr. 2	Nr. 2	Nr. 5	Nr. 5	Nr. 4
Depth: [m]							
Mass of wet material	m	g	279,2	361,3	612,1	370,3	489,8
Mass below water	m_u	g	147,8	188,2	336,9	194,4	257,2
Temperature of water	T	°C	20,0	20,0	20,0	20,0	20,0
Density of water	ϱ_F	g/cm³	1,0	1,0	1,0	1,0	1,0
Volume of dipped probe	V	cm³	131,4	173,1	275,2	175,9	232,6
Tara Nr.							
Water content	w	%	1,3	1,3	1,4	1,4	1,6
Density	$\rho = \frac{m}{V}$	g/cm³	2,125	2,087	2,224	2,105	2,106
Dry density	$\rho_d = \frac{\rho}{1+\frac{w}{100}}$	g/cm³	2,098	2,060	2,193	2,077	2,073

Fig. 10. Water content w, according to DIN18121

Abteilung Felsmechanik Institut für Bodenmechanik und Felsmechanik Universität Karlsruhe (TH)						**Water content w** according DIN 18121				
Project:	Bamiyan								Project No.:	e-2683
Probe number:	No. 1		No. 2		No. 3		No. 4		No. 5	
Depth: [m]										
Probe type:	Conglomerate		Conglomerate		Siltstone		Conglomerate		Conglomerate	
Container No.:	16	35	25	39	08	31	14	11	12	02
$A = m + m_B$ [g]	1593,3	1259,7	878,6	770,9	571,9	994,1	1460,2	1165,3	984,4	1078,8
$B = m_d + m_B$ [g]	1584,1	1252,2	871,0	763,1	560,8	966,2	1440,2	1151,3	975,1	1065,4
$C = m_B$ [g]	232,0	237,5	228,6	224,4	235,4	224,2	225,5	226,1	235,9	225,9
$m_w = A - B$ [g]	9,2	7,5	7,6	7,8	11,1	27,9	20,0	14,0	9,3	13,4
$m_d = B - C$ [g]	1352,1	1014,7	642,4	538,7	325,4	742,0	1214,7	925,2	739,2	839,5
$w = 100 \cdot m_w / m_d$ [%]	0,7	0,7	1,2	1,4	3,4	3,8	1,6	1,5	1,3	1,6
Mean value: [%]	0,7		1,3		3,6		1,6		1,4	

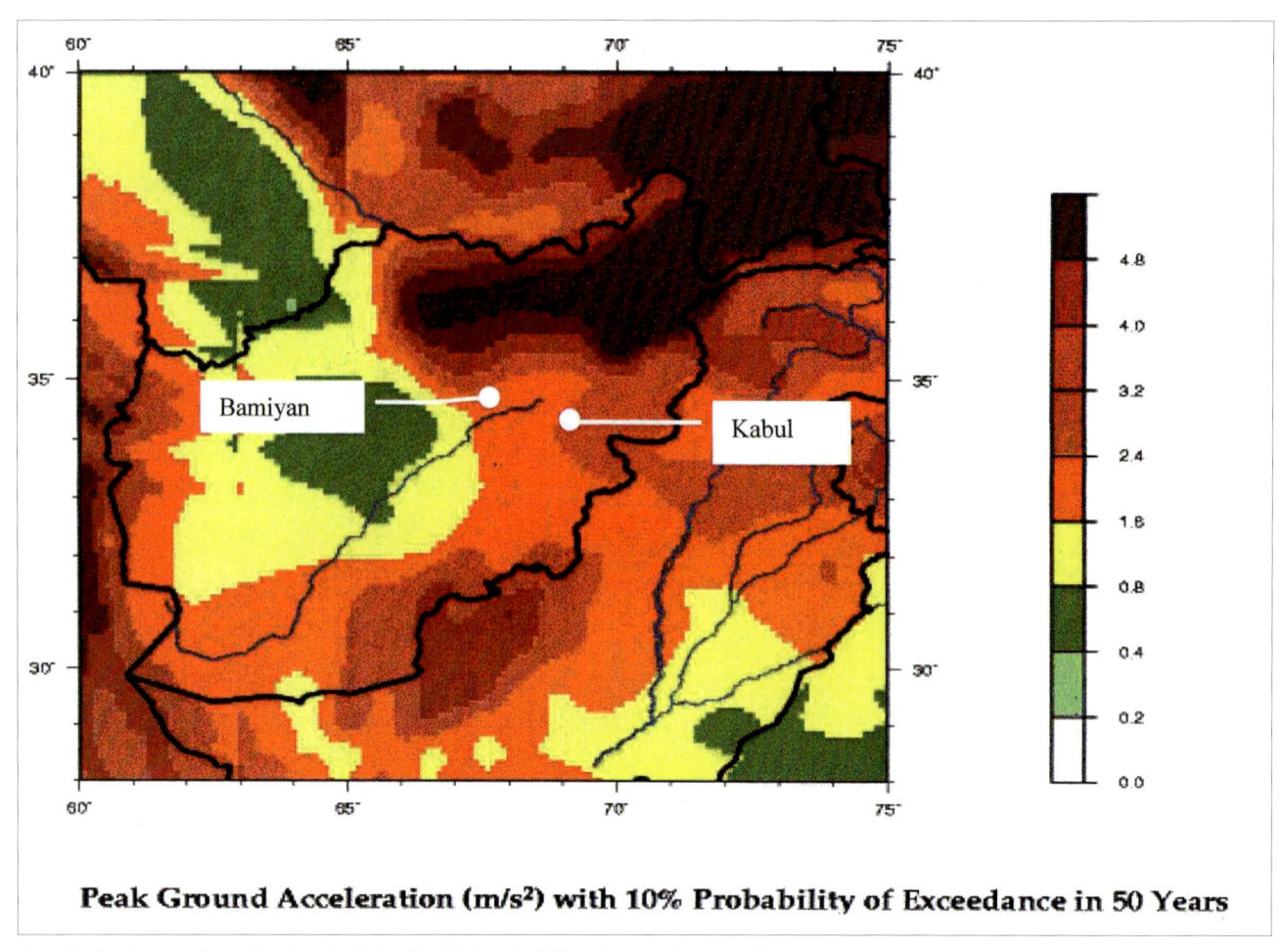

Fig. 11. Peak ground acceleration (m/s2) with 10% probability of exceedance in 50 years

Fig. 12. Uniaxial compression test sample no. 1 (conglomerate)

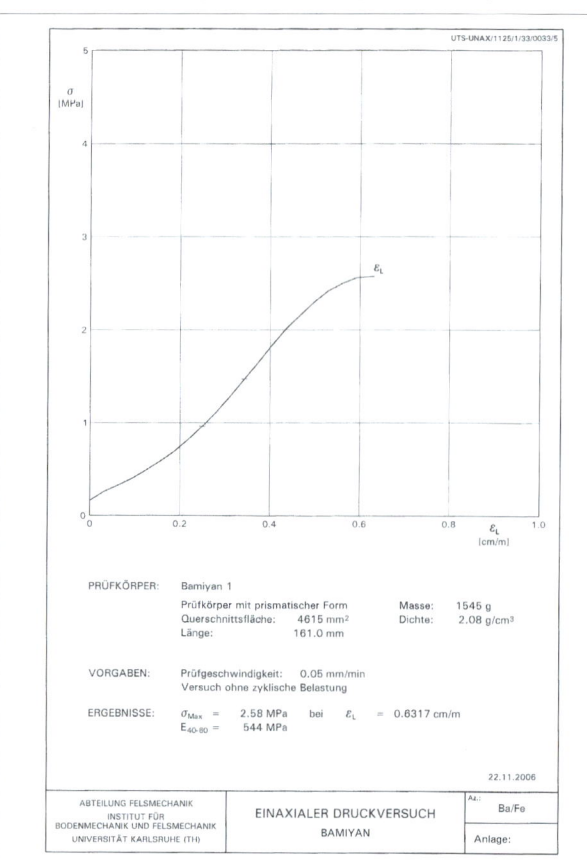

Fig. 13. Uniaxial compression test sample no. 2 (conglomerate)

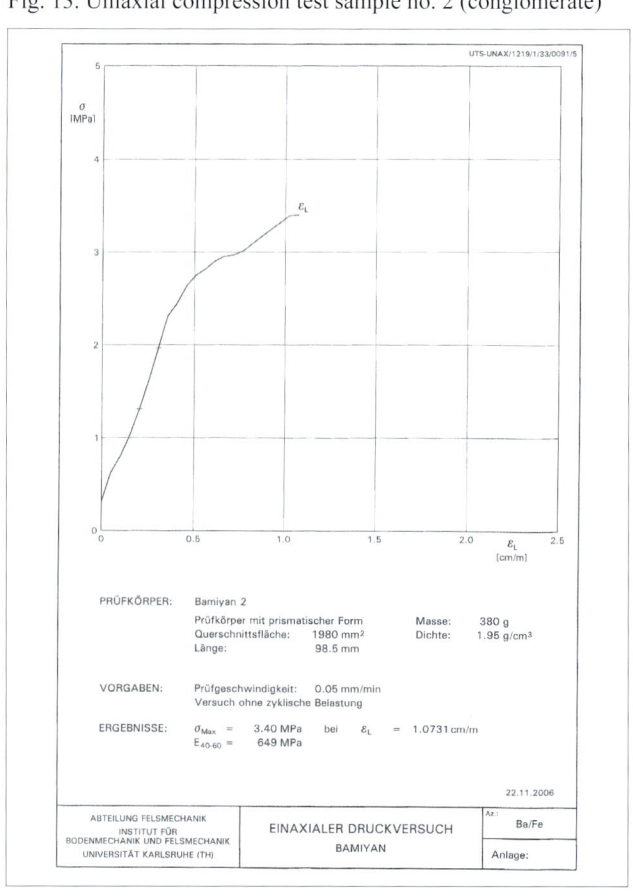

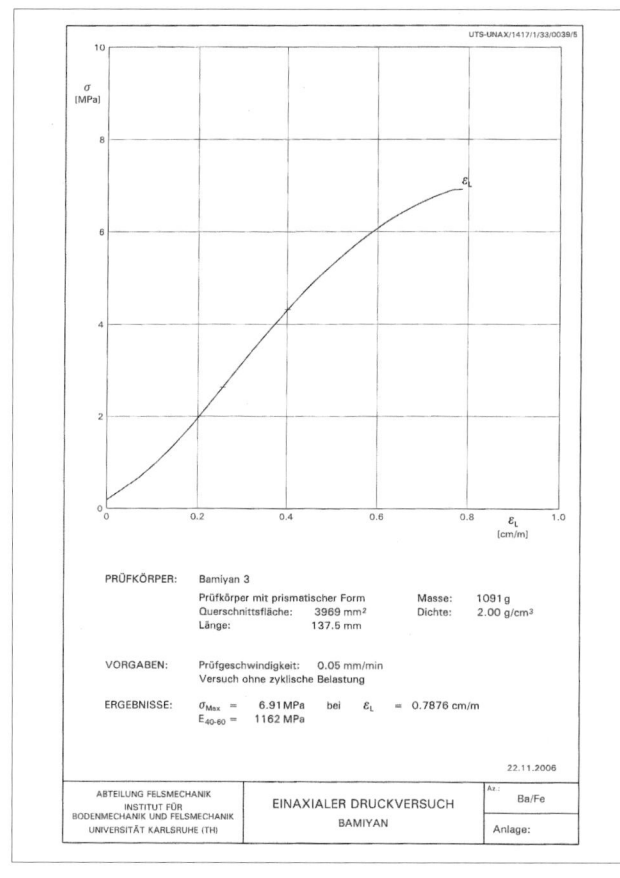

Fig. 14. Uniaxial compression test sample no. 3 (siltstone)

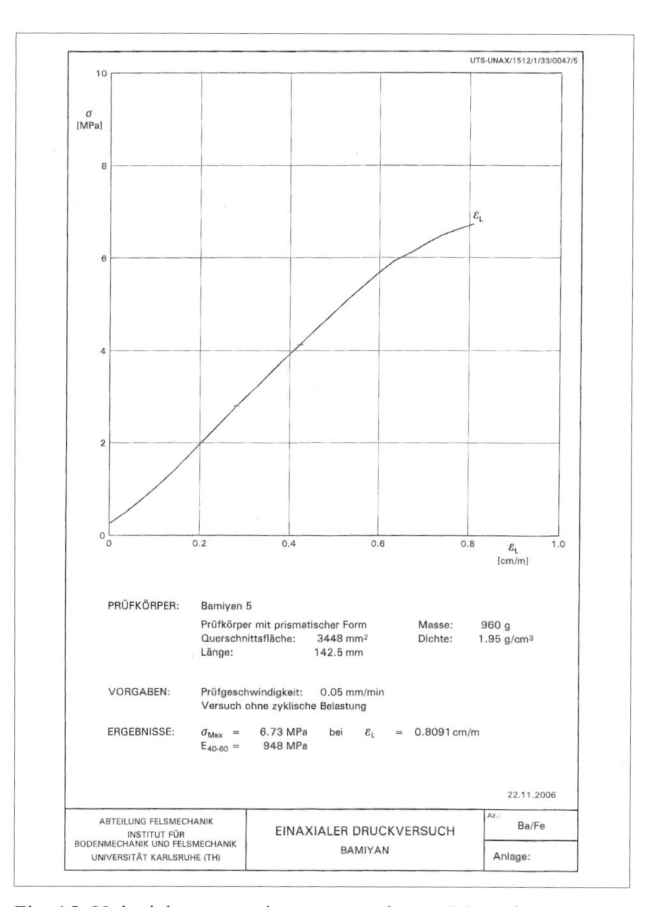

Fig. 15. Uniaxial compression test sample no. 5 (conglomerate)

Fig. 16. Alteration under water, according to DIN 4022 part 1

	Abteilung Felsmechanik Institut für Bodenmechanik und Felsmechanik Universität Karlsruhe (TH)				Alteration under water according DIN 4022, part 1			
Project:		Bamiyan					Project No.:	e-2683

Test No.	Probe number	Depth [m]	Before test W_1 [%]	After test W_2 [%]	Alteration under water after 24 h			
					not alterable	moderate alterable	alterable	intense alterable
1	Probe No. 1		0,7	15,2			X	
2	Probe No. 2		1,3	24,9			X	
3	Probe No. 3		3,6	71,6				X
4	Probe No. 4		1,6	36,3				X
5	Probe No. 5		1,4	9,5		X		
6								
7								
8								

Not alterable: No probe changes determinable

Moderate alterable: Probe surface softened or parts crumble away

Alterable: Probe decayed, but component parts still solid

Intense alterable: Probe totally decayed and muddy

Fig. 17. Remains of the head of the Eastern Buddha

Fig. 20. Left shoulder of the Eastern Buddha

Fig. 18. Remains of the head of the Eastern Buddha (detail with new discontinuities)

Fig. 21. Left shoulder of the Eastern Buddha (new discontinuities parallel to the back wall)

Fig. 19. Right shoulder of the Small Buddha (new discontinuities parallel to the back wall)

Fig. 22. Left shoulder of the Eastern Buddha (detail of an open joint containing rock debris)

Fig. 23. Discontinuities under the dress pleat

Fig. 24. Cave no. 5 after the explosion

Fig. 25. Caves no. 4 to 6 with new joint in the ceiling

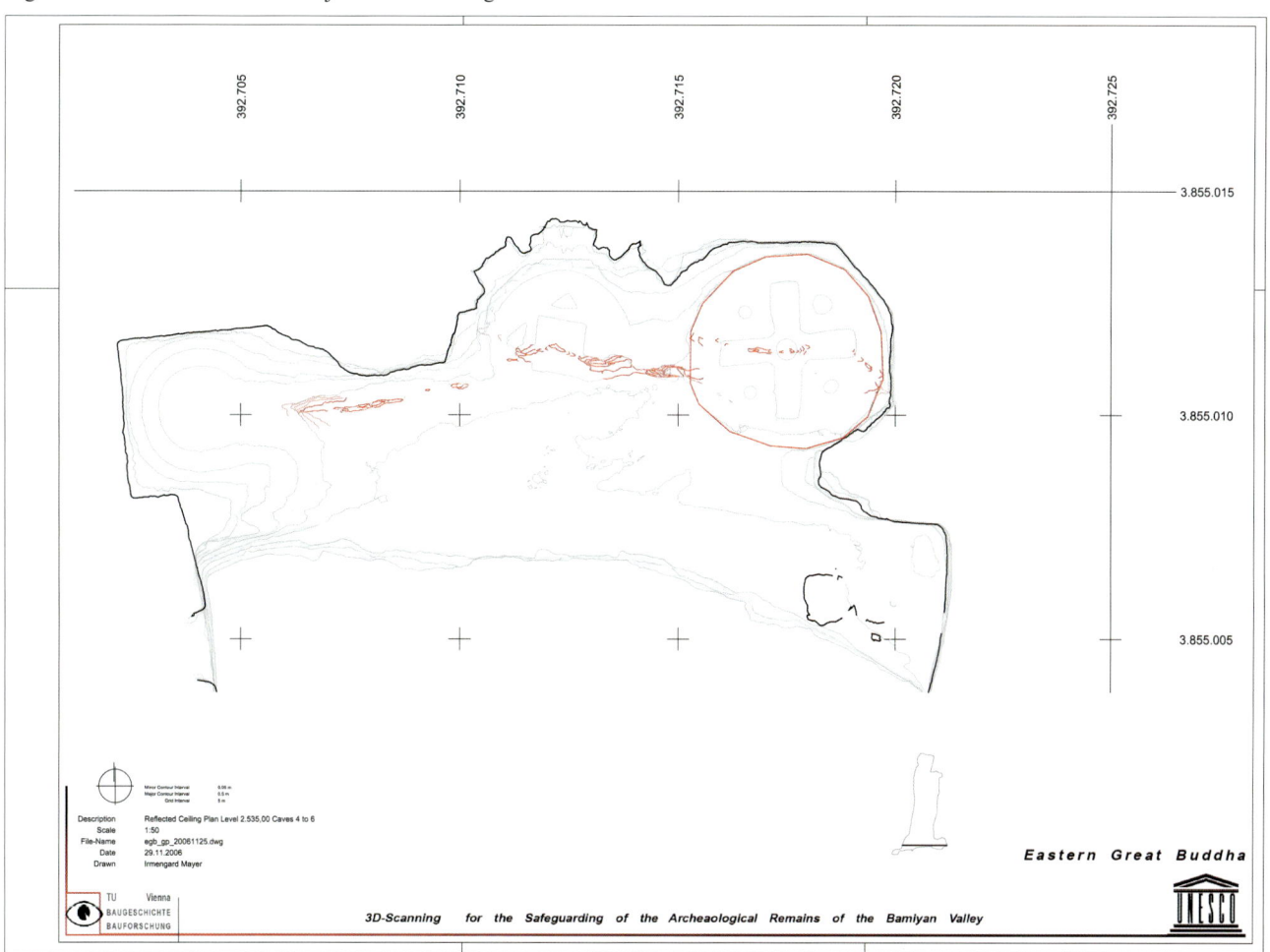

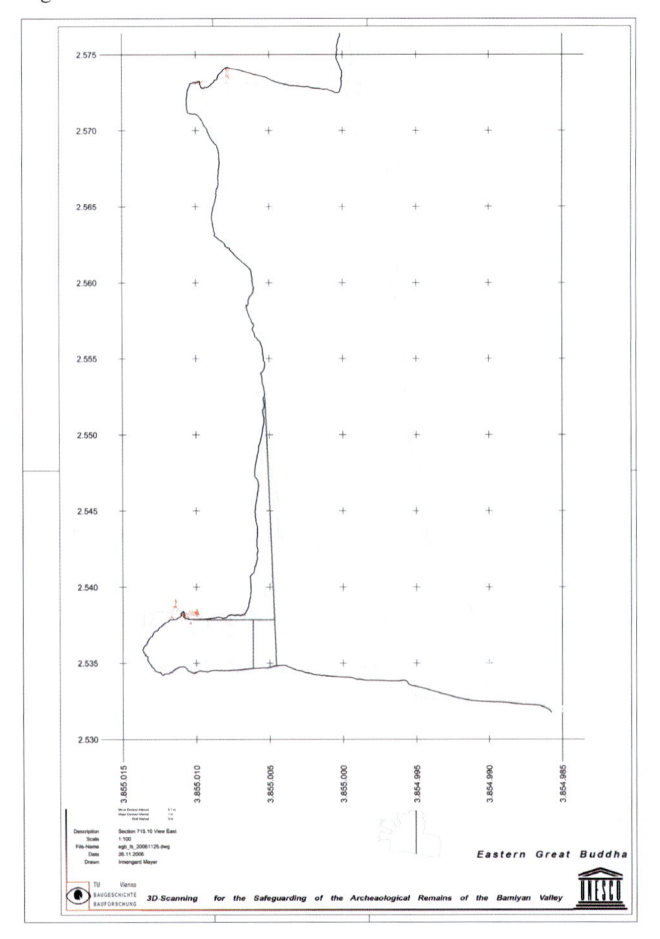

Fig. 26 Steel wire mesh covering the back wall

Fig. 27 Section view of framework

Fig. 28 Front view of framework

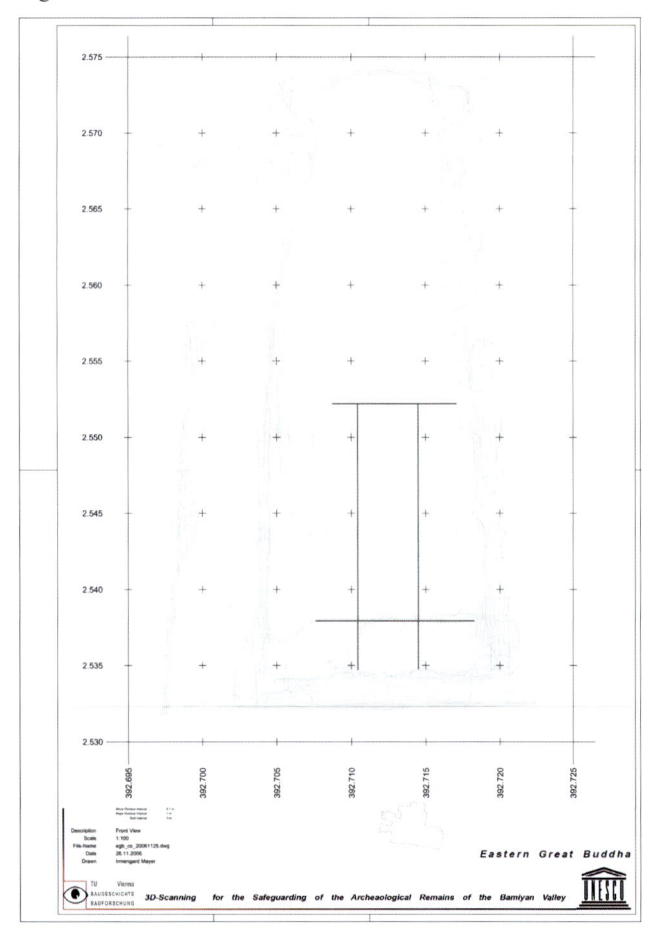

116

Georgios Toubekis

3D Laser Scanning and Post-Processing of the Niche of the Eastern Buddha, 2006

In 2006, the Institute of History of Art, Building Archaeology and Restoration (Prof. Marina Döring-Williams) of the Architectural Faculty in cooperation with the TUWIL-Competence-Centre of the Vienna Technical University (TU Wien) executed the 3D laser scan of the Eastern Buddha in Bamiyan within the documentation campaign of RWTH Aachen University.

A Riegl Laser Measurement System Z420i in combination with a Canon EOS 1Ds (f = 20 mm, 10 Megapixel) digital camera mounted on top of the scanner was used. The scanner works on a contactless and non-destructive principle with a range of 1.2 m to 800–1000m distance to the measured object.

The scanner allows a very flexible alignment of the resolution according to the scan size and the scan distance by adjusting the angle of the moving laser light (0.12–0.02 degree). The standard noise of the Riegl LMS Z420i is ± 8 mm. To obtain a full model of an object it is necessary to make several scans from different positions. The system is designed for direct communication with a separate digital camera and ensures the automatic adjustment of the pictures to the measurements of the individual scans. Every time the digital camera is mounted again on the scanner body a manual calibration (mounting calibration) has to be performed by manually assigning features visible in the scan to the digital pictures.

A LEICA Total Station TCR 1105 was used for measuring all scan positions exactly and for linking the newly obtained measurements with the UTM reference-system and the Site Control Points established by the Japanese survey team of NRICP Tokyo. In close range to the most eastern Ground Control Point B3 and complementary to other existing fix points of the site reference system a new fix point directly in front of the Eastern Buddha niche was measured and fixed into the ground (BP01). In order to cover the niche of the Eastern Buddha completely 23 separate scan-positions were required. The scan-positions unfortunately could not been chosen freely but were determined by accessibility and safety concerns which left some parts of the niche unreachable for the laser beams. To calculate the single scans into the overall reference-system approximately 40 reflectors were set up within the niche. Flat Circular Retro reflectors of 5 cm and 10 cm diameter were distributed equally to cover the scanned area. Biaxial Bireflex Flat Circular Retro reflectors (5 cm) were used on the adjunct sides and back wall of the niche in order to create the necessary tie points for the calculation and automatic processing of the different scan positions. The result of each scan is a point cloud of single surface measurements. To reach a sufficient precision of the final model the resolution was set to ensure a point distance equal 8 mm on the surface of the cliff stone. Additionally to the measured point cloud of the Riegl LMS Z420i a set of

The site of the Bamiyan Buddhas (view towards east)

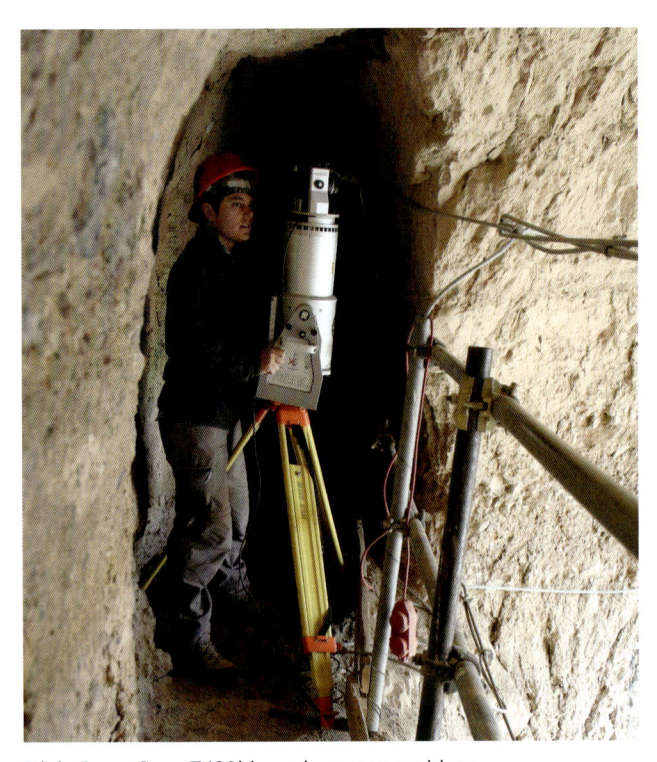

Rielg Laser Scan Z420i in various scan positions

pictures is taken automatically after each scan by the on top mounted digital camera Canon EOS 1Ds. Due to the internal calibration values of the system the color information of each pixel from the digital image is automatically assigned to the measured point cloud. This process allows the automatic mapping of the taken pictures on the final mesh at a later stage. The software RiScan Pro 1.2 used during the scan process is provided by the laser scanner manufacturer Riegl. For the meshing or triangulation of the measurement points in the post processing phase the Software QTSculptor v2.85 of Polygon Technology was used. The calculation of the 4 GB of Raw Data would have required more computational resources than provided by the used computer system (Pentium D CPU 3.2 GHz, 4 GB Ram, NVIDIA GeForce 7900 GT). In order to overcome this difficulty, the model was divided into three parts, which were calculated separately and merged at the end. The number of triangles should be chosen as low as possible to limit the file size, but as high as necessary to be able to recognize important details. When dividing the point-cloud it is important, that sufficiently large overlapping areas remain. In this case 1.2 million triangles were created by QTSculptor v2.85 out of the 77 million measurement points. The last step is the assignment of the digital images on the mesh. The images can be applied automatically using the mounting calibration which has been assigned on site. From the final 3D model further plans such as sections, views and orthophotos have been created from all viewpoints. Main purpose of these maps will be the precise orientation and localisation of further results that will be obtained from the ongoing geological analysis of the preserved fragments and especially the geological profile of the backside of the niche. First tests on site revealed that the geological features of each fragment allow a precise identification of the composition of the conglomerate suitable to identify its place of origin based on geological profile matching [Urbat et. al. 2004]. The maps obtained from the high-precision measurements are the basis for the documentation of the geological profile of this portion of the cliff.

Although the explosions destroyed large portions of the Buddha figure and all separation walls between the caves at the backside of the niche several distinctive edges endured the detonation and are clearly visible both at the site and within the 3D textured niche model obtained from the new measurements. The processed plans from the niche model revealed significant distinctions in the geometry of the niche in comparison to previous publications. Also the shapes of the caves slightly differ from the ideal form of hexagonal and octagonal cave typologies known from previous maps [Ball 1982, Klimburg-Salter 1989].

Reconstruction of destroyed structures

From the documentation of the site prepared by the Archaeological Mission to Central Asia at Kyoto University in the years 1972–1978 the team at RWTH Aachen obtained a high resolution scan (6800 x 10400 pixel) of the original 1/50 scale ink drawing of the contour line interpretation from the Small Buddha (38 m or Giant Eastern) sculpture. Unfortunately the original stereo pictures have not been found. In this drawing each of the 10 cm isohypse contour lines is clearly readable and was manually digitized. The 3D surface of the Eastern Buddha was generated with *Geomagic Studio v.10* Software.

In order to combine the results from the Riegl Laser Scan measurements with this 3D surface of the Buddha figure reconstructed from the contour line drawings both datasets were transferred to *Geomagic Studio v.10* for further processing. Based on characteristic features visible in the contour line drawings and still traceable at the site the surface model could be orientated within the 3D model of the niche generated from the laser scans by manual alignments.

The results reveal the amount of material that has been lost due to the detonation of the figures. It also becomes clear that the Small Buddha was more a relief structure, carved out of the soft conglomerate stone. The depth of the destruction can be measured from the actual rock surface to the surface of the reconstructed figure and range in between 10–170 cm.

The results where presented first time on the occasion of the 5th UNESCO Expert Working Group Meeting for the Preservation of the Bamiyan Site in December 2006 at RWTH Aachen University. The immersive virtual environment BARCO CAVE™ (Cave Automatic Virtual Environment) at the Virtual Reality Centre of RWTH Aachen University represents an advanced version of the system [Cruz-Neira 1993] and is used for research of multimodal and interactive 3D interactions and visualization of complex numerical and technical simulations in real time. The CAVE system is a cube of 3 m x 3 m that allows a five sided projection of stereo images onto the walls and ceiling. The resolution of images or videos projected is 1600 x 1200 pixels per plane using ten BARCO Sim6 Ultra projectors that project the stereo images.

The user of the CAVE wears a pair of polarized glasses

Textured 3D model of the niche of the Eastern Buddha

with attached reflectors so that his position in spaces is constantly measured by an optical tracking system based on six ARTtrack1 cameras. The viewpoint of the spectator is processed in real time and the stereo images are rendered accordingly by a PC Cluster of a total of ten Render Clients connected to the projectors. One Master Station controls the synchronisation of all calculations with a specially designed application programmed in *VISTA* a cross platform VR Toolkit under development at RWTH Aachen. The projected stereo images personalized to the eye distance of the user and the processing of the images according every movement of the spectator in real time create a complete immersive 3D for the user of the CAVE.

These maps are used in the ongoing geological analysis of the preserved fragments and the geological profiling of the backside of the niche conducted by ICOMOS. The plans obtained from the high-precision measurements are the basis for the documentation of the geological profile of this portion of the cliff. Tests on site revealed that the geological features of each fragment allow a precise identification of the composition of the conglomerate stone which is suitable to identify its place of origin based on geological profile matching [Urbat 2004]. The plans also serve as basis for further planning of necessary consolidation works conducted by ICOMOS. They give precise information on the existing geometry and the location and gradient of dangerous cracks.

Based on these plans restoration works are currently underway by ICOMOS to reconstruct the destroyed separation walls between the ceremony halls at the bottom backside of the niche of the Eastern Buddha.

Conclusion

The abundance of generated detail information by means of high precision measurement technologies poses the questions on how to incorporate all this information in sets of plans that have to describe the monument as a whole [Weferling 2006]. Since our work is aimed to support the practical preservation and restoration works on site primary aim was to generate a model serving as a means of communication that provides the general outline precise enough so that more specific observations and findings can be incorporated easily at a later stage.

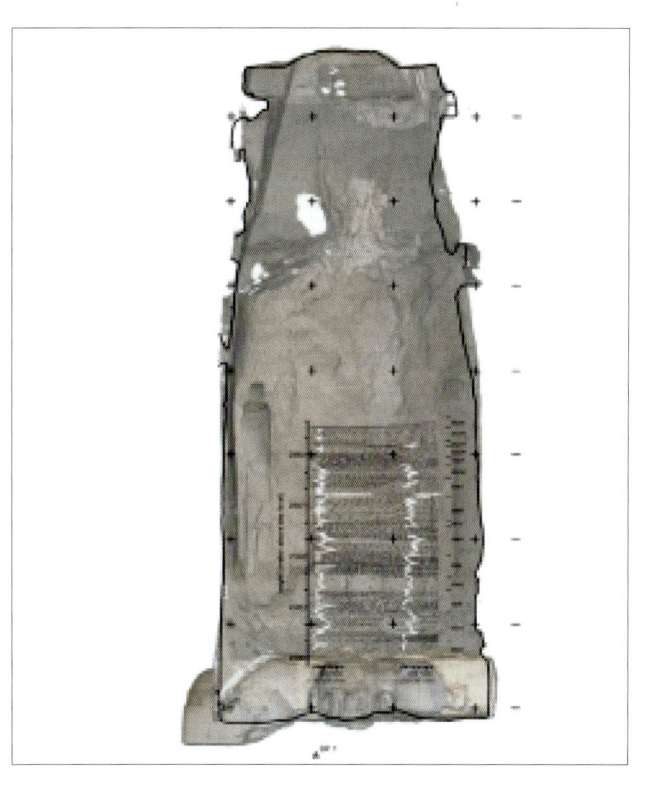

The precision and high density of the laser scan measurements capture delicate details (original clay plaster and carved cliff surface) and facilitate the production of detailed 2D plans of the geometry of the niche (section, views) in almost all directions. This allows the study of otherwise inaccessible head and shoulder portions of the remains of the destroyed figure. Though the creation of the initial contour line drawing of the Japanese researchers consequently entailed detail information losses that could not be retained in the reconstructed 3D surface of the figure the results are adequate to serve as a sound communication model that is able to integrate all ongoing research results from restorers and geologists and to serve as planning basis for future interventions on the site. Also it is precise enough to contribute to the discussion process on the future of the site in the sense of 'work in progress' without pre-assuming a final state that has to be achieved. Based on this virtual model it is possible to study and to compare concepts for technical measures in the future in detail prior to their execution.

Due to the enormous object size and the complexity of the niche it became clear that the original shape information of the destroyed Buddha figure is essential in order to make the spatial configuration readable and understandable again. In how far this shape has to be reconstructed in future interventions such as a full or partial anastylosis can now be evaluated comprehensively by making use of the CAVE at the Virtual Reality Centre Laboratory situated at RWTH Aachen University.

References

Ball, W., *Archaeological gazetteer of Afghanistan. Catalogue des sites archéologiques d'Afghanistan.* Avec la collaboration de J.-C. Gardin. Tome 1–2, Paris 1982

Cruz-Neira, C.; Sandin, D. J.; DeFanti, T. A., *Surround-Screen, Projection-Based Virtual Reality: The Design and Implementation of the CAVE*, Computer Graphics Vol. 27 (Proc. SIGGRAPH 93), 1993, pp. 135–142

Grün, A.; Remondino, F.; Zhang, L., *Reconstruction of the Great Buddha of Bamiyan, Afghanistan.* International Archives of Photogrammetry and Remote Sensing, Vol. 34 (5), pp. 363–368, Corfu (Greece) 2002

Grün, A.; Remondino, F.; Zhang, L., *Photogrammetric Reconstruction of the Great Buddha of Bamiyan, Afghanistan, The Photogrammetric Record.* An International Journal of Photogrammetry, Vol. 19 (107), pp. 177–199, United Kingdom 2004

Higuchi, T., *Bamiyan. Art and Archaeological researches on the Buddhist cave temples in Afghanistan 1970–78*, Publication of the Kyoto Archaeological Mission to Central Asia, Dohosha, 4 vols, 1983–1984

Klimburg-Salter, D., *The Kingdom of Bamiyan*, Istituto per il Medio ed Estremo Oriente (ISMEO), Naples 1989

Luhmann, T. (ed.), *Photogrammetrie und Laserscanning*, Heidelberg 2002

PASCO: *Final Report for the Preparation of Topographic Maps and 3-Dimensional Model of the Bamiyan and Foladi Cliffs.* UNESCO/Japan Funds-in-Trust Project for the Safeguarding of the Bamiyan Site, Pasco Corp., Tokyo 2003

Petzet, M., *Anastylosis or Reconstruction – the conservation concept for the Remains of the Buddhas of Bamiyan*, in: ICOMOS 13th General Assembly, Madrid 2002, (pp. 189–192)

Jansen, M.; Toubekis, G.; Walther, A.; Döring-Williams, M.; Mayer, I., *Laser scan measurement of the niche and virtual 3D representation of the Small Buddha in Bamiyan*, in: *Layers of perception: Proceedings of the 35th International Conference on Computer Applications and Quantitative Methods in Archaeology (CAA)*; Berlin, Germany, April 2–6, 2007/ed. by Axel Posluschny, Berlin 2008

Toubekis, G.; Petzet, M.; Jarke, M.; Jansen, M., *Preservation of the UNESCO World Heritage Site of Bamiyan: Laser Scan Documentation and Virtual Reconstruction of the destroyed Buddha Figures and the Archaeological Remains*, in: *Proceedings of the 22nd CIPA Symposium on Digital Documentation, Interpretation & Presentation of Cultural Heritage*, October 11–15, 2009, Kyoto (accepted)

Urbat, M.; Krumsiek, K., *Paleo- and rockmagnetic criteria for the reconstruction of the giant Buddha Statues, Bamiyan/Afghanistan.* Geophysical research abstracts, Volume 6, EGU 1st General Assembly, Nice, France, 2004

Weferling, U., *Geometrieerfassung in der Bauaufnahme: Wann, Wieviel, Womit?*, in: Riedel, A.; Heine, K.; Henze F. (eds.), *Vom Handaufmaß bis High-Tech II, Modellieren, Strukturieren, Präsentieren, Informationssysteme in der historischen Bauforschung*, Philipp von Zabern, Mainz 2006

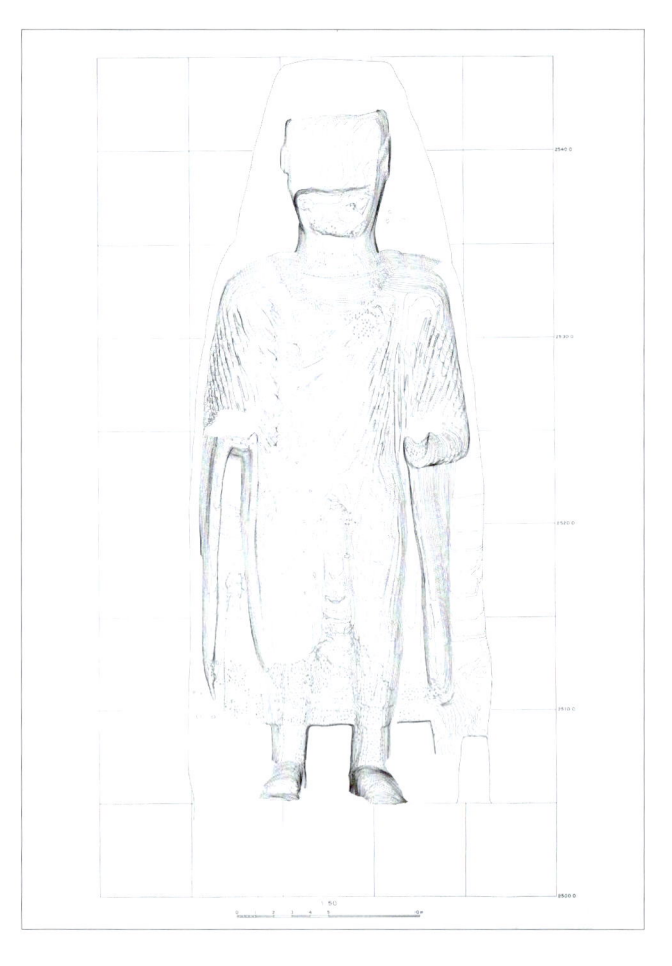

Model of the Eastern Buddha generated from isoline drawing of 1978

Virtual reconstruction of the Eastern Buddha with texture information

Left: view within the virtual environment. Right: view of Eastern Buddha in 1978

121

Bamiyan Masterplan Campaign 2005

PREMISES FOR THE DEVELOPMENT OF A UNESCO PROPOSAL FOR A DRAFT MASTER PLAN FOR THE BAMIYAN VALLEY

PRESSURES AND INFLUENCES ON THE CULTURAL HERITAGE OF BAMIYAN

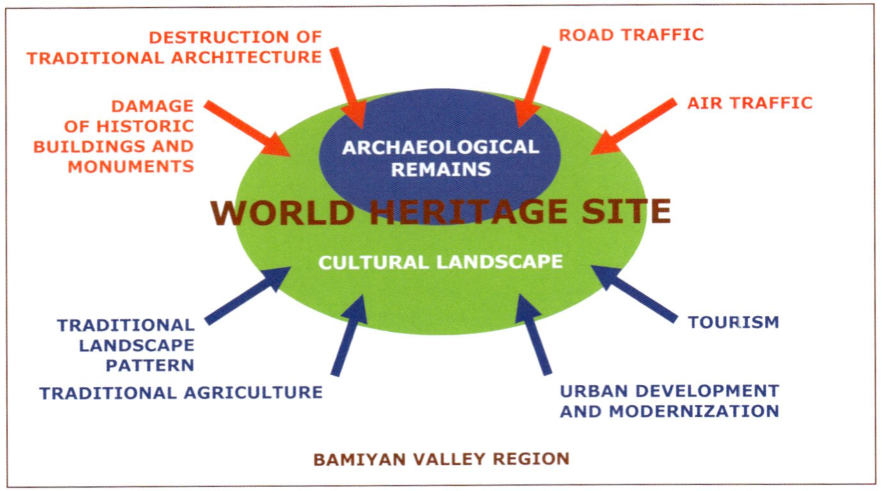

Pressures on the World Heritage Site (Archaeological Remains and Cultural Landscape):
- DESTRUCTION OF TRADITIONAL ARCHITECTURE
- ROAD TRAFFIC
- AIR TRAFFIC
- DAMAGE OF HISTORIC BUILDINGS AND MONUMENTS
- TOURISM
- URBAN DEVELOPMENT AND MODERNIZATION
- TRADITIONAL AGRICULTURE
- TRADITIONAL LANDSCAPE PATTERN

BAMIYAN VALLEY REGION

ZONING OF THE WORLD HERITAGE SITE AND CULTURAL LANDSCAPE OF BAMIYAN VALLEY, AFGHANISTAN

ZONE	PROTECTION	ELEMENTS
World Heritage Property as of 2003	- Protection by International Law	8 clearly identified World Heritage Sites - Archaeological and Architectural sites
Historic and Archaeological Sites and Zones	- Protection by National Law, especially the 1980 "Law on the Preservation of the Historical and Cultural Heritage"	- Caves - Old Cemeteries - Historical Architectural Monuments - Traditional Settlements
Traditional Settlements and Historical Monuments		
Natural and Agricultural Setting	- not Object to legal protection yet	- Irrigated Agricultural Landscape - Natural Setting of Hill Slopes
Regulated Development Zones — Disturbance and Development	- Object to detailed strict Planning	- Proliferation of Settlements in the North slopes of the valley - Designated Planning areas for Urban Development

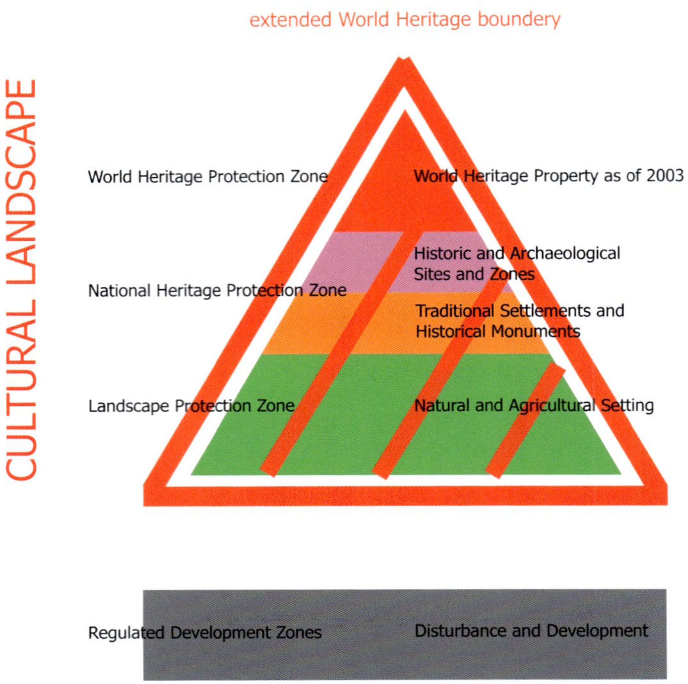

extended World Heritage boundary

CULTURAL LANDSCAPE

- World Heritage Property as of 2003 / World Heritage Protection Zone
- Historic and Archaeological Sites and Zones
- National Heritage Protection Zone
- Traditional Settlements and Historical Monuments
- Landscape Protection Zone
- Natural and Agricultural Setting
- Regulated Development Zones — Disturbance and Development

The Bamiyan Valley with its Monuments and Landscape inscribed in the World Heritage List represents a fragile equilibrium of uses and demands.
The master plan to be developed has to reflect these coactions and the stresses and demands put on the valley.
Thus, we encounter five main premises for the planning and controlling of the future development of the valley:

1) Prevent any further damage of historic buildings and monuments
2) Prevent any destruction or damage of historic architecture
3) Avoid stresses produced by road traffic in immediate vicinity of the World Heritage Site
4) Avoid stresses produced by presumably increasing air traffic in the valley
5) Respecting the boundaries of the World Heritage Site and its setting

These premises lead to five predominant actions:

1) Relocation of the main road through the Bamiyan Valley away from the World Heritage Site
2) Relocation of the air field outside the valley
3) Registration and monitoring of traditional architecture possible subsidizing of repair measures through the authorities
4) Proposals for a new urban development zone outside the cultural landscape
5) Avoidance and/or relocation of disturbing uses and structures

Introduction

Michael Jansen

Presentation of the Cultural Master Plan Bamiyan (Kabul, 31 July / Bamiyan, 2 August 2006)

The Bamiyan Valley in Afghanistan is located within the Hindu Kush mountain range at a height of around 2500 m above sea level. The previous Buddhist monastic sanctuaries, caves and several fortified settlements from the Islamic Ghaznavid and Ghurid period extend for several kilometres on the north side of the valley facing south and leaving the fertile plane open for agriculture. The valley follows the Bamiyan river which is a tributary to the Kunduz river and part of the large Amudarya Water Basin System. During many centuries these valleys served as passageway for the intercontinental trade along the Silk Road.

From the first written records by the travelling monk Xuanzang who visited Bamiyan in about 630 AD the ensemble of the Giant Buddha figures of Bamiyan has been known as the world largest depiction of a standing Buddha figure; the Big Buddha (Western Buddha) measured 55 m and the so-called Small Buddha (Eastern Buddha) 38 m. Situated within the Silk Road on the crossroads of the civilizations of the East and the West Bamiyan is regarded as an exceptional testimony and outstanding representation of Buddhist art in the Central Asia region. International intervention and protest could not prevent the complete destruction of the Giant Buddha Figures executed by the Taliban leadership in March 2001. Very early after the fall of the Taliban regime in 2002 a joint UNESCO/ICOMOS expert fact finding mission took place to Bamiyan and examined the situation. In 2003 *The Cultural Landscape and Archaeological Remains of the Bamiyan Valley* were inscribed in the UNESCO World Heritage List as a nomination of eight different areas representing historic and religious developments from the 1st to the 13th centuries AD.

Environmental Factors

The cliff of the Bamiyan Valley has been formed at the confluence of two large River beds approximately 20 million years ago. Typical for such a comparatively young basin the valley is characterized by a mountain desert relief with huge peneplains, alluvial fans and vast debris deposits. Glacial activity has washed the landscape smooth and the vast hills composed out of debris of conglomerate stone are easily affected by weathering processes and highly susceptible to water. The Bamiyan Valley exhibits a continental climate which is prone to episodically heavy rain events alternating with extremely long drought periods. Braided river and torrential rivers rise rapidly after rainfalls; they mobilize and

Presentation of the Bamiyan cultural master plan by Prof. Michael Jansen on August 2, 2006

transport big amounts of physically weathered debris. Most of this material in motion is deposited on alluvial fans in the main valley or transported to the main drain of the Bamiyan valley in the direction of the Kunduz river basin. Therefore alternating fluvial erosion and fluvial accumulation takes place leading to constant change of the landform due to the meandering river sections.

Extreme weather condition could be observed during the years of field survey (2005–2007) leading to extraordinary flood events. These events are a major threat for settlements and infrastructure (especially bridges) as well as for the people and their livestock. The irrigated and cultivated land is mainly found at the bottom of the valley while the area outside of cultivated fields is almost completely used for animal grazing and harvesting plants for fodder and fuel. The field survey (Reinecke 2005) has revealed disturbances and degradation of the vegetation cover of the soil due to intensive harvesting. Irrigated areas entirely depend on the availability of surface water for irrigation coming from the nearby mountains as snowmelt water. A sophisticated network of water distribution forms the precondition of the irrigation agriculture. Occasionally sources of spring water exist which is used for drinking water.

The re-study of the existing zoning plan for the World Heritage Programme which was submitted on an emergency basis upon the nomination of the site also had to include the documentation of other not yet registered cultural components like further archaeological areas, monuments and traditional architecture of national importance, components of historic landscape.

In addition, the identification of future expansion areas for modern building construction activities had to be made. The Bamiyan Valley with its monuments and landscape inscribed in the World Heritage List represents a fragile equilibrium of uses and demands. The master plan to be developed has to reflect these coactions and the stresses and demands put on the valley. Thus, we encountered five main premises for the planning and controlling of the future development of the valley:

1. Prevent any further damage of historic buildings and monuments;
2. Prevent any destruction or damage of historic architecture;
3. Avoid stresses produced by road traffic in immediate vicinity of the World Heritage Site;
4. Avoid stresses produced by presumably increasing air traffic in the valley;
5. Respecting the boundaries of the World Heritage Site and its setting.

These premises lead to five predominant actions:
1. Relocation of the main road through the Bamiyan Valley away from the archaeological sites;
2. Relocation of the air field outside the valley;
3. Registration and monitoring of traditional architecture possible subsidizing of repair measures through the authorities;
4. Proposals for a new urban development zone outside the cultural landscape;
5. Avoidance and/or relocation of disturbing uses and structures.

Preserving Bamiyan – Integrated Development Cultural Masterplan

As a result RWTH Aachen University elaborated a set of plans using detailed high-resolution satellite imagery analyzing the development of the Bamiyan Valley and presenting a zoning proposal for future planning purposes in Bamiyan (*Bamiyan Cultural Master Plan*) to be implemented by the Afghan authorities involved. For that purpose a series of public presentations in the capital Kabul and the provincial centre of Bamiyan were realized leading to the adoption of the plan by the Ministry of Urban Development in March 2006.

It was noted that the actual definition of the boundaries of the World Heritage Site as stated in the inscription dossier are imprecise and to some extent incomplete. The overall extension of the World Heritage Site is described in vague terms when referring to the Cultural Landscape whereas eight archaeological areas are named and described precisely as Word Heritage properties.

A general aim of the authors of the RWTH Aachen report is to stress the fact that the extension of the World Heritage sites Bamiyan reaches far beyond those areas described by name and location in the annex of the inscription dossier. As one result of the field campaign in summer 2005 more information could be collected concerning the overall extension of the World Heritage Site. This information was summed up in a zoning model as indicated below. It is to stress that this model intends to emphasise the unity of the different entities intended to be protected, namely the *Cultural Landscape and the Archaeological Remains of the Bamiyan Valley.*

References

NRICP 2004, Protecting the World Heritage Site of Bamiyan, Key issues for the Establishment of a comprehensive Management Plan, National Research Institute for Cultural Properties (NRICP), Tokyo

NRICP 2005, Preserving Bamiyan, Proceedings of the International Symposium "Protecting the World Heritage Site of Bamiyan", Tokyo, 21.12.2004, Recent Cultural Heritage Issues in Afghanistan, Volume 1, National Research Institute for Cultural Properties (NRICP), Tokyo

NRICP 2006, Protecting the Word Heritage Site of Bamiyan, Management Plan 2006, Part 3 (Management and Planning issues for the Protection of the Site), Part 4 (Programme for Action: Action plan for 2006-2011), National Research Institute for Cultural Properties (NRICP), Tokyo

Recommendations of the Fifth Expert Working Group on the Preservation of the Bamiyan Site

Aachen, 14–16 December 2006[*]

Emergency consolidation of the Giant Buddha niches and cliffs

The Participants of the Working Group

1. Acknowledge the accomplishment of emergency operations over the last four years in consolidating the two Giant Buddha niches and cliffs;
2. Recommend implementation of a permanent manual system for regular monitoring of the stability of the niches by local professionals;
3. Agree on the priority for the consolidation of the back walls of both niches, and note the preliminary proposal to be implemented upon scaffolding, then grouting and anchoring as necessary, but with a minimum of impact on the heritage values;
4. Note the persistence of large cracks, and that a damage assessment of the back walls of the niches should be conducted for future planning on the use of appropriate techniques for necessary intervention;
5. Note the importance of the use of material compatible with the original material of the statues on the back walls of the niches;
6. Endorse a proper testing by a joint team composed, at least, of an engineer/geologist and a conservator/restorer, in order to choose the appropriate material before implementation of further major interventions such as grouting of the back walls;
(...)
10. Recommend continued cleaning of the existing drainage network on top of the cliffs and the establishment of a map of the drainage network.

Conservation of the Giant Buddha statues

The participants of the Working Group

1. Acknowledge the substantial progress made by ICOMOS experts in the salvaging and storage of the fragments of the two Giant Buddha statues, where all works in the Eastern Giant Buddha niche have completed, and recommend continuation in 2007 for the Western Giant Buddha niche;
2. Encourage the finalization of the scaffold tower in the Eastern Giant Buddha niche which started in 2006 to make the back walls accessible to restorers, engineers and geologists, and foresee a similar scaffold in the Western Giant Buddha niche after successful completion of the salvaging works;
3. Note the necessity to increase the carrying capacity of the wire mesh at the back wall of the Eastern Giant Buddha niche by additional steal wire ropes, in order to ensure safety of all individuals executing the works;
4. Acknowledge the efforts of the Afghan authorities for the enhanced site-security, and stress the necessity of establishing a sustainable site-security plan.
5. Acknowledge the salvaging of plaster pieces with wooden pegs and strings from the surface of the Buddha statues (more than 3000 pieces), and appreciate the proposal of the Afghanistan authorities to safely store them in 2007 at the Bamiyan Training Centre for further analysis;
6. Note the extraordinary findings including birch fragments of manuscripts in July 2006 in the ground next to the right foot of the Eastern Giant Buddha, and recommend conservation of these highly fragile pieces of different materials in cooperation with relevant specialists. Establishment of a specialised laboratory at the Bamiyan Training Centre is encouraged for necessary studies;
7. Underline the priority in 2007 to develop a strategy for the consolidation of the back walls of both niches in cooperation of restorers and engineers;
8. Note the importance of reconstructing the partition walls between the small niches at the base of the Eastern Giant Buddha niche, destroyed by the explosion in 2001, as a necessary first step in 2007 in order to support the cliff structure above;
9. Acknowledge the latest results of the geological mapping in identifying the original position of the rock material, and encourage the finalization of documentation of all preserved/salvaged fragments in both niches upon geological and paleomagnetic analysis and 3D recording. The creation of a 3D model, already progressed for the Eastern Giant Buddha statue, contributes to the virtual positioning of the fragments;
10. Consider continued investigations for the technical possibility of an anastylosis (refer to Article 15 of the Venice Charter) as a method of reassembling the fragments of the Buddha statues.
11. Suggest the Ministry of Information and Culture to establish an Advisory Board on its future decisions on the possibilities of an anastylosis of the Giant Buddha statues.

---

[*] Abridged version without archaeological investigations, implementation of the cultural master plan, and training.

2007

Thanks to funds provided by the German Foreign Office the activities of the ICOMOS team, supervised by Dipl.-Ing. Georgios Toubekis, Edmund Melzl and Bert Praxenthaler could continue (as from June 2007). A clearly visible sign of the progress made in safeguarding the remains of the Buddha statues was the erection of tubular steel scaffolding made available by the Messerschmitt Foundation in the niche of the Eastern Buddha. After the work of putting up this scaffold had already started the year before, in 2007 it was erected up to the height of the statue's shoulder (planning: Dipl.-Ing. Thomas Strauch, Ingenieurgemeinschaft Pesch & Strauch, Cologne). This made it possible to inspect the fragile back wall closely. Apart from the detailed geological investigation of the rock face (see report by Dr. Michael Urbat, pp. 130–133) for the purpose of allocating individual fragments, the scaffold helped to identify further threatened zones. These detailed inspections have shown that without additional consolidation measures on the back wall the original, in-situ surfaces of clay plaster belonging to the Buddha statue will be highly endangered. This threat also applies to the cave structures in the lower area of the niche, whose partition walls were completely destroyed by the enormous explosion of 2001 (see report by Prof. Edwin Fecker, pp. 145 ff.). Here, the original space geometries could be defined on site and initial space-defining "reconstructions" could be carried out on a trial basis (see fig. below).

At the site of the Western Buddha, progress was more complicated because due to the disastrous road conditions of parts of the road between Kabul and Bamiyan the necessary heavy crane could not be transported. Under these circumstances, the recovery of larger fragments was only carried out manually and with the aid of hoists. Naturally, this slowed down the work progress considerably. Still, it was a success that one foot of the Buddha statue became clearly recognisable where a huge rubble heap had been before, and that some of the caves in the lower area were once again made accessible. At the end of the campaign in early November the ICOMOS team could present the progress made on-site to the Afghan Minister of Information and Culture.

M. Pz.

Preparing the reconstruction of the partition walls in the niche of the Eastern Buddha

Report on Salvaging Rock Fragments, 2007

At the Western Buddha the salvage work was continued by using two wheel loaders. Rock fragments weighing up to four tons could be recovered. In order to be able to store the great number of recovered fragments additional storage sites were erected. For this purpose in parts of the western storage hall a second level was installed. Three sections were cleared out. The fragments affected were temporarily stored in the specially enlarged and levelled western area of the terrain. Afterwards, in the rear section of the hall about four-metre-long and one-metre-tall walls could be erected, onto which transverse steel beams with a length of four metres could be placed. On these beams – c. 50 m of additional space – we deposited smaller fragments on pallets. By 14 July the depot with its new storage space was completely full.

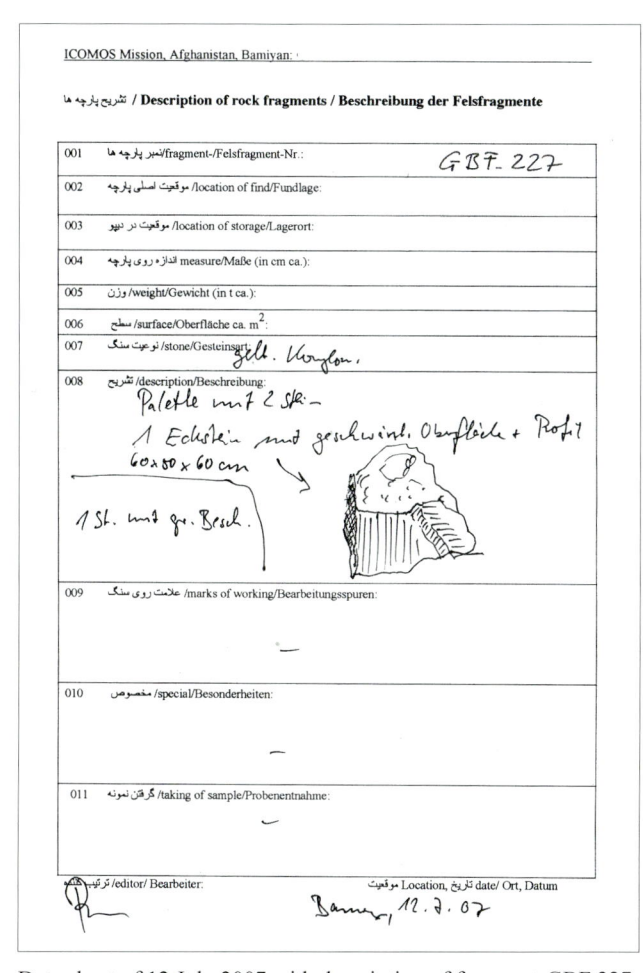

Data sheet of 12 July 2007 with description of fragment GBF 227

View from above into the niche of the Western Buddha

Storage of fragments from the Western Buddha

Storage of clay plaster fragments in zinc plate boxes.

New storage space for the fragments of the Eastern Buddha

Continuation of erecting a scaffold in the Eastern Buddha niche

View from the platform of the Eastern Buddha to the west, showing the two improved shelters ▷

In the course of this mission 110 new fragments were recovered and documented (out of a total of 230 fragments so far). Also several fragments, which had remained undocumented the year before, could now be inventoried. The documentation was done in the usual way. Every rock fragment was described on a data sheet and photographically documented with respective number so that they could be re-identified. The fragments salvaged so far (GBF_001 – GBF_230) have a visibly sculpted or coated surface with a total surface of 86 square metres. The result is that the feet of the Buddha have emerged quite clearly and that the two western caves have been cleared.

For the interim storage of the clay plaster fragments shelves were put up provisionally in the eastern cave at the entrance to the niche. There the zinc plate boxes containing the clay plaster fragments were stored. Besides, for a safe storage of the clay plaster fragments two depots were provided at the so-called Heritage Center.

At the Eastern Buddha the depots could be completed and the erection of the scaffold was continued. The storage space was slightly extended and secured by a retaining wall.

Bert Praxenthaler

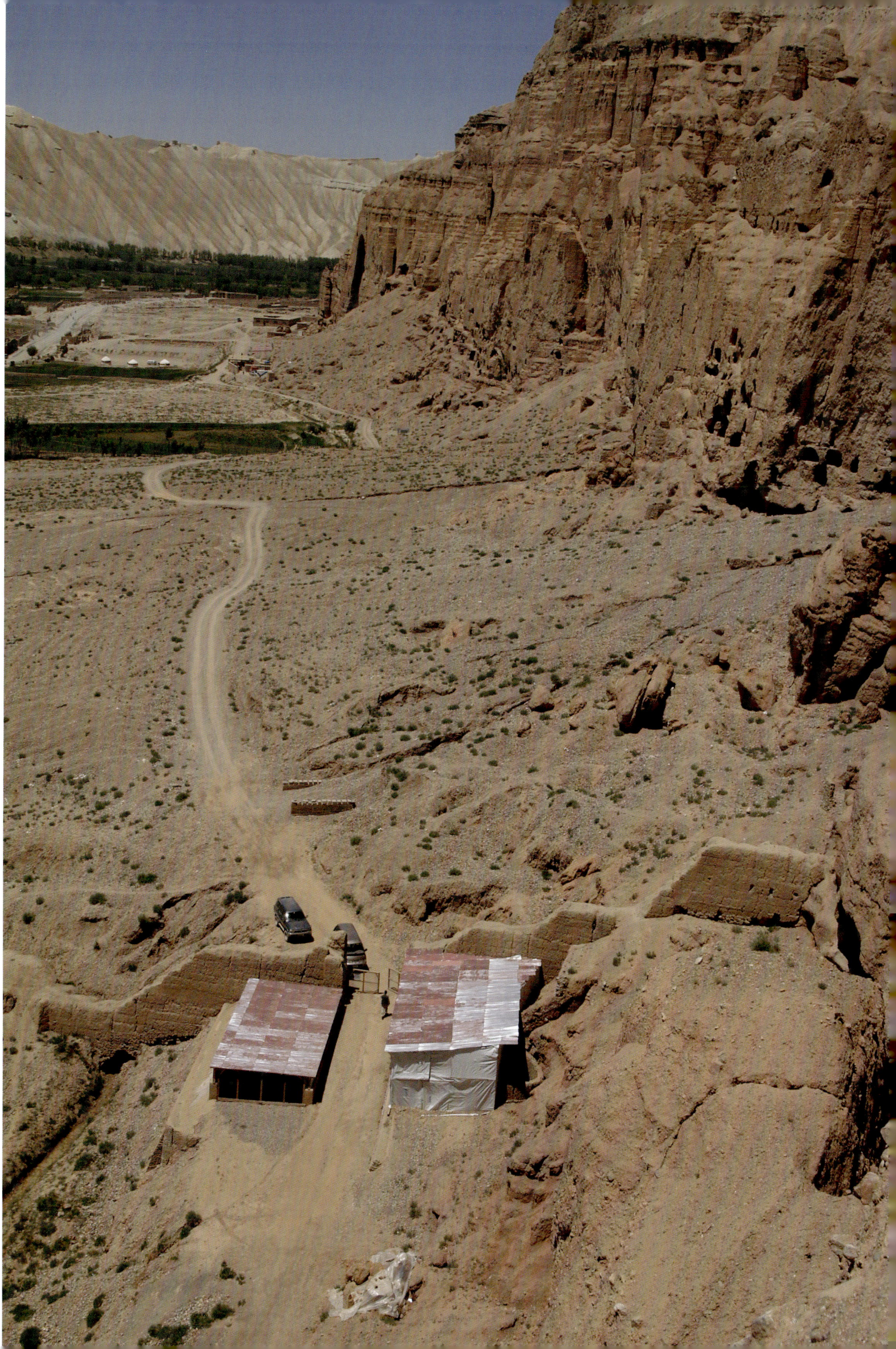

Michael Urbat

Combined Geological and Paleomagnetic Analyses of the Back Plane of the Eastern Buddha Niche, 2007

Geological criteria and paleomagnetic measurements

As mentioned before, the geological approach to discriminate the required reference pattern is based on a detailed survey of the varying sedimentological and structural features of the respective layers. A two profile design was chosen covering the right and left hand sides of the eastern back wall to account for the suspected lateral variability of the sediment layers (fig. 2).

Both profiles start immediately above the ceiling of the caves, i.e. at 2538.469 m.a.s.l. (profile 1, left or western side) and 2538.445 m.a.s.l. respectively. The respective starting points in meters above sea level (m.a.s.l.) were levelled using a laser aided air level using the reference point of 2535 m.a.s.l. near the floor of the niche also used in the recent ICOMOS related activities including the 3D laser scan of the eastern niche. Between the starting point of a profile and its respective end point a tape measure was than fixed to the back plane of the niche.

For the rock magnetic measurements we used the newly acquired (University of Cologne) handheld magnetic susceptibility meter SM-30 (ZH-Instruments, CZ) which has a sensitivity of 1×10^{-7} SI units and hence can measure rocks with very low susceptibilities or even diamagnetic substances. The sensitivity of the instrument is about one order of magnitude higher compared to the instrument (KT-5) we had been using during our previous missions (precursor instrument by the same manufacturer). Several tests on-site indicate that both instruments yield comparable results, albeit with a better resolution of weakly magnetized layers by the new instrument (figs. 2–4). Measurements were taken at about every 5 cm throughout both profiles, largely determined by the 50 mm pick up coil of the SM-30 (KT-5 was 6 cm).

Situation on site, Eastern Buddha

Both the geological as well as the magnetic analyses require direct contact with the material to be investigated. Hence, unrestricted access to the back plane of the niches and the respective fragments is the essential prerequisite for the success of the suggested pattern matching approach.

Due to the unknown material properties of the steel pipes used to construct the scaffold several tests needed to be performed as to understand any potential effects on the magnetic measurements. Critically, the metal scaffold would potentially influence the measurements of magnetic susceptibility both of the back plane of the niche as well as from the few larger fragments left within the niche which are closely encased by the foundation pillars of the scaffold (fig. 1).

Back plane (reference profiles), Eastern Buddha niche

A reference section of the back plane of the Eastern Buddha niche was successfully completed from 2538.4 m.a.s.l. to 2552 m.a.s.l. (figs. 2, 3 and 4). Both the lateral and vertical variability of rock layers is much higher than had previously been suspected and, hence, yielded very promising results for the pattern matching approach. A classification in terms of 15 lithological units is suggested which accommodate overall depositional facies of the sediment (fig. 3). Apart from prominent colour changes, component composition, size and shape variation of the prevailing silty, sandy and conglomeratic through breccious units variations in the amount and composition of the sediment matrix are dominant features of the geological succession. The amount of matrix ranges from almost 80 vol% (matrix supported fabrics) through absent in the clast supported fabrics. The amount and composition of matrix (natural cementation)

Fig. 1. Extensions made to the original scaffold consist of two grounded towers to a maximum height of about 20 meters above ground. Shown here is balcony type in the upper part. Any extensions to the scaffold reaching up higher were avoided in order to not interfere with the most unstable parts of the rock surface within and directly below the shoulder area.

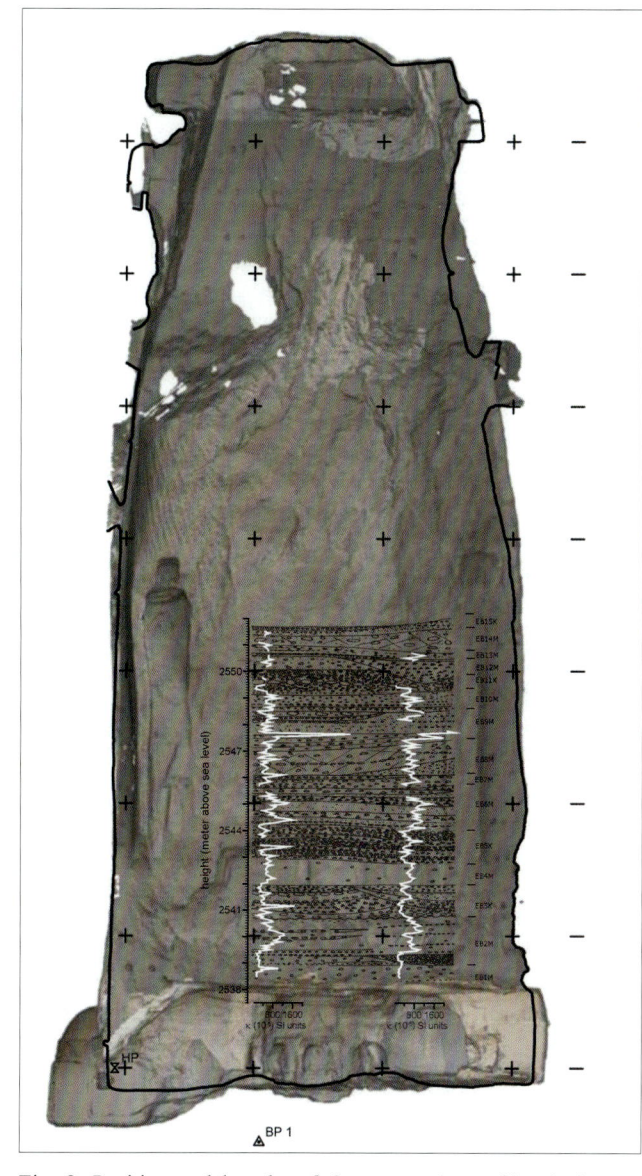

Fig. 2. Position and lengths of the two main profiles (reference sections) within the eastern Buddha niche. Profiles start at 2538.4 m.a.s.l. right above the chambers. Background 3D scan courtesy of RWTH Aachen group. Lithology as a result of the November 2007 geological survey is also shown as a detail in figure 4.

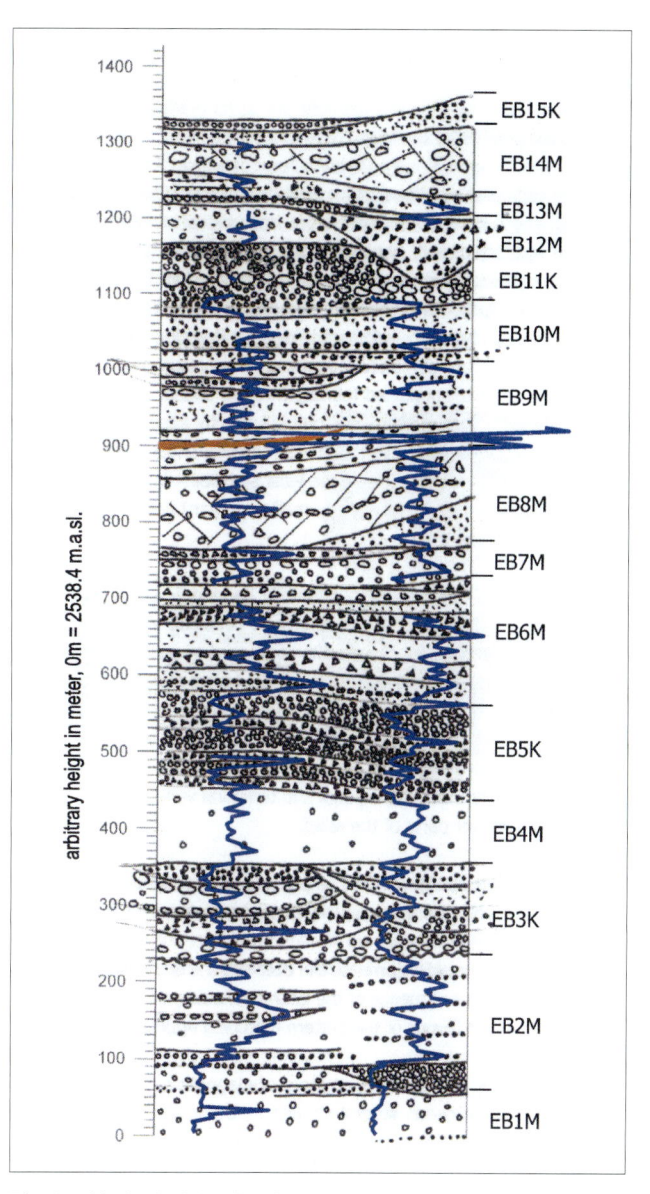

Fig. 3. Lithological details of the eastern back wall between 2538.4 and 2552 m.a.s.l. Scale on the left side is in meters arbitrary height. Colour coding approximates actual colour variations of the rock, signatures approximate lithological variations from silty through conglomeratic material. Note high lateral variability, for example in unit EB3K (channel fills), where EB3K denotes Eastern Buddha unit 3 clast supported fabric (M units indicate matrix supported fabrics). Blue curves = susceptibility κ. For details of respective lithological units see the next page.

will directly affect the stability of the respective rock units and can be used as a rough (relative) estimate of the uniaxial shear strength (see report Fecker 2006). As a rule-of-thumb clast supported fabrics will have the least stabilities. It is clear from the detailed geological survey that the stability of the rock face will vary on a small scale (cm) both laterally and vertically (and 'into' the wall when viewed two-dimensionally).

Generally, while the assumption of overall near horizontally bedded layers is confirmed, the internal lateral variation within the lithological units reflect a high energetic depositional environment with usually high to very high accumulation rates, especially for those units composed of unsorted, breccious material with clast sizes up to 25 cm across. As I stated in previous reports (see p. 89 ff.) all the layers appear to be erosion material from the surrounding elevated parts of the relief (i.e., the uprising Hindukush mountain chains in the Tertiary largely in the course of the ongoing Indian – Asian collision and the Himalayan orogeny) and as such were deposited in the developing intramountain Bamiyan basin as high energetic debris flows, or, for example material charged streams (channel fills reflecting a typically high spatial and temporal variability, hence, alternatively deposition and erosion) originating in the higher parts of the relief.

Magnetic susceptibilities (with κ around 50×10^{-5} SI units) are on the same order as was noted for the Western Buddha sedimentary succession and display an equally distinct variation with the lithology (figs. 3 and 4).

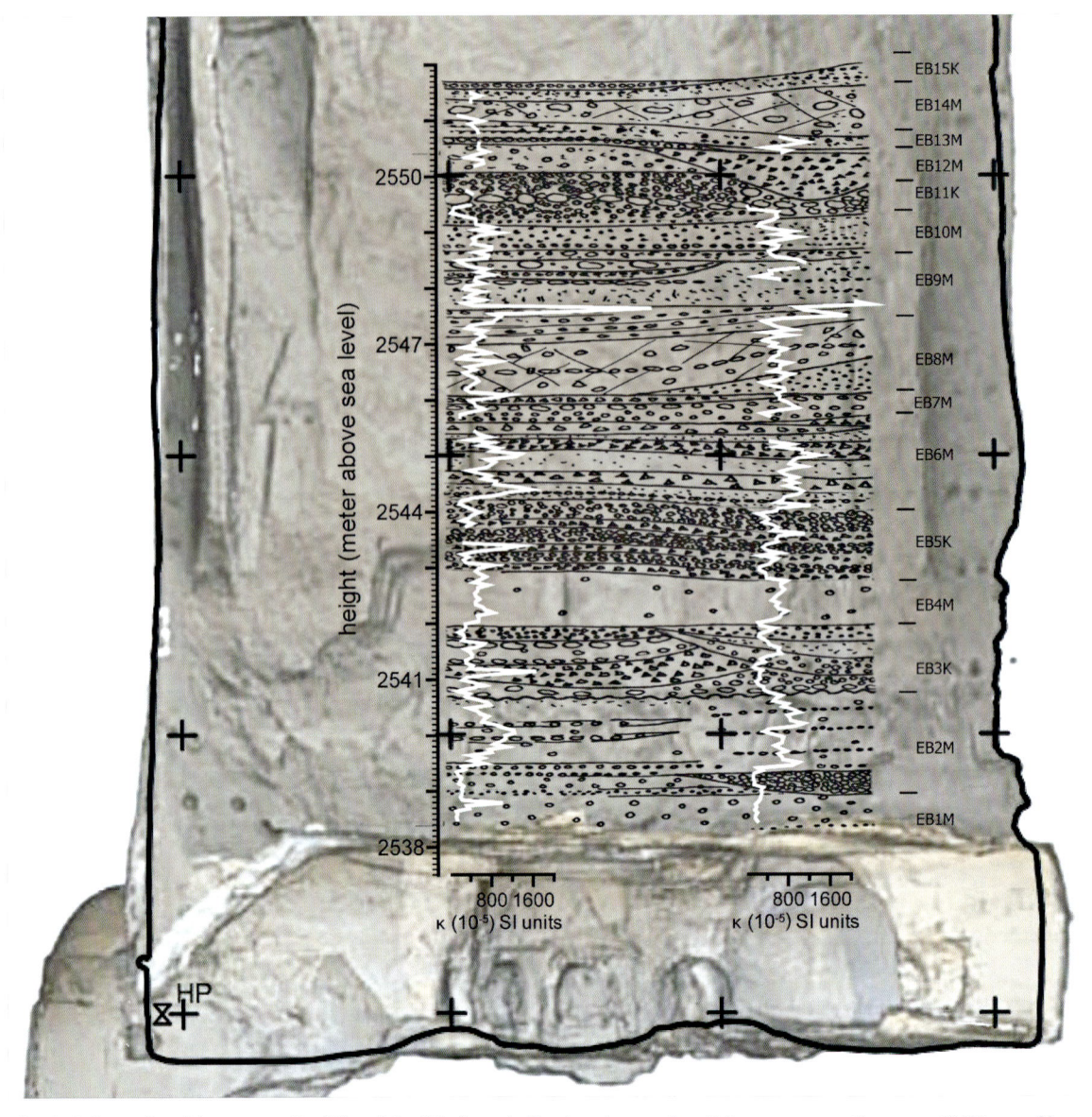

Fig. 4. Schematic of the eastern Buddha niche lithology indicating the results of the two magnetic susceptibility profiles. Major lithological units shown in more detail in figure 3. Height is in meters above sea level, profiles start at 2538.4 m.a.s.l. levelled from the reference point BP1 at 2535 m.a.s.l. Backgroung 3D scan is courtesy of RWTH Aachen group.

Clearly, while the general trends are readily correlative in between the two measured lines, within unit variation is high as would be expected as a consequence of the lateral variability of the units. Yet, individual lithological layers are always reflected by κ - in favour of the pattern matching approach.

Only few lithological units indicate that the measurement of magnetic susceptibility is not appropriate (fig. 4), because the size of the clasts exceeds several cm and matrix is absent or too minor. Given the random distribution of clasts, each of them having an individual magnetic susceptibility though, any attempt to match the equally randomly sampled signal in a fragment would obviously be in vain (sections where there are no κ values in fig. 3).

While the susceptibilities of the scaffolding poles in fact are high (around 20000×10^{-5} SI units for material bought in Kabul, around 8000×10^{-5} SI units for 'Messerschmitt' poles) as compared to the rock our tests on site indicate that neither the cage like construction of the scaffold surrounding the fragments left within the niche nor the measurements of the back plane will be affected if the SM-30 is operated about 40 cm away from the nearest pole. The same note of caution applies to the compensation step within each measurement where the sensor is removed from the rock face.

Fragments Eastern Buddha, additional

Two larger fragments which remained inside the niche were surveyed geologically and paleomagnetically (KBF_015, KBF_0XX). As was stated for the back plane of the niche, individual layers can clearly be described and susceptibilities vary distinctly with indivdual lithological layers. Fragment KBF_015 is tentatively placed at 2544 m.a.s.l. on the left hand side of the niche (fig. 5). KBF_0XX likely originates from a higher part of the succession for which the reference pattern has not been completed yet. A third fragment was not further considered, because the only side displaying geological information was not accessible.

Conclusions and recommendations

The detailed geological survey of the lower half of the eastern back plane yielded, together with the two susceptibility lines with measurements taken every 5 cm, a supposedly sufficient reference pattern for the pattern matching approach. A division into 15 major lithological units (EB1M through EB15M) is proposed. The notable lateral and vertical variability of the sediment also indicates that the stabilities of lithological layers will be highly individual with respect to any position on the back plane of the Eastern (or Western) Buddha niche. As a rule-of-thumb decreasing natural cementation (with clast supported fabrics as an end member) is correlative with decreasing shear strength of the rock (some absolute numbers for prominent rock types in Fecker 2006).

It is strongly recommended to complete the detailed geological survey of the back wall before any further consolidation work is being considered. Any consolidation works done to the back plane of the niche might directly influence any future geological/rock magnetic work within that respective area and should be discussed beforehand.

References

Bauer-Bornemann, U.; Melzl, E.; Romstedt, H.; Scherbaum, M.; Urbat, M., *Steinrestauratorische Beratung zu den zerstörten Buddha-Statuen*. ICOMOS report 2003, unpublished, 10 pp.

Fecker, E., *Report on Rock Mechanics Aspects concerning the Small Buddha Niche in Bamiyan, Afghanistan*. ICOMOS report 2006

Krumsiek, K., *Zur plattentektonischen Entwicklung des Indo-Iranischen Raumes*. Stuttgart 1980: Geotekt. Forsch., 60, 1–223.

Lang, J., *Bassins intramontagneux néogènes de l'Afghanistan central*. Paris 1972: Rev. Géogr. Phys. Géol. Dyn. (2), 14, 4, 415–426.

Strauch, T.; Toubekis, G., *Bericht zur Gerüsterstellung Small Buddha Niche in Bamiyan, Afghanistan*. ICOMOS report 2007

Urbat, M: *Buddha statues - Bamiyan Valley/Afghanistan: Geological criteria for conservation/reconstruction*. UNESCO/ICOMOS report 2003, 8 pp.

Urbat, M.; Krumsiek, K., *Paleo- and rockmagnetic criteria for the reconstruction of the giant Buddha Statues, Bamiyan/Afghanistan*. Nice, France 2004: Geophysical Research Abstracts, Volume 6, EGU General Assembly. ISSN 1029-7006.

Urbat, M., *Buddha statues - Bamiyan Valley/Afghanistan: Geological criteria for conservation/reconstruction*. Part II. UNESCO/ICOMOS report 2005, 9 pp.

Urbat, M.; Aubel, A., *Buddha statues - Bamiyan Valley/Afghanistan: A combined geological and paleomagnetic approach towards the repositioning of fragments*. ICOMOS report 2007, 22 pp.

Fig. 5. Fragment KBF_015 from within the niche. White lines approximate prominent lithological layers, yellow curve displays magnetic susceptibility kin 10–5 SI Units. Vertical dimension of the fragment is 1.2 meters.

2008

In the year 2008 the ICOMOS activities in Bamiyan, funded by the German Foreign Office, could not start before mid-August. Unfortunately, under these circumstances it was not possible to complete the upper part of the scaffold in the Small Buddha niche, since the necessary material was not available on site. Nonetheless, the scaffold has already proved its worth for the work of restorer Bert Praxenthaler on the remaining plaster fragments of the Small Buddha (in this context the sensational find of another relic from the time the Buddha statue was made, see also report Praxenthaler, p. 137). The team of local workmen was primarily employed to salvage stone fragments from the area of the Western Buddha. Two Afghan colleagues joined the ICOMOS team: architect Sekandar Ozod Seradj and Mujtabah Mirzai, a stonemason trained at the Dombauhütte Passau. Furthermore, as rock engineer we once again had Prof. Dr.-Ing. Edwin Fecker, and for the increasingly important matters of conservation/restoration the team was supported by Prof. Erwin Emmerling (chair of conservation sciences at the Technical University of Munich). A decisive progress was the reconstruction of the partition walls of the rearward caves, completely destroyed by the explosions of 2001; this was carried out jointly by the architect's office Seradj and the rock engineer (see report, pp. 145 ff.). Also for static reasons this work was a necessary precondition for stabilising the back wall with its remains of the Buddha statue.

In the meantime, by means of the 3D documentation developed in cooperation with the RWTH Aachen (see pp. 117–121) the condition of the Eastern Buddha niche has been recorded in an exemplary way. It must also be considered a success that the storage for more than 9,000 fragments of loam plaster, collected and documented by restorer Edmund Melzl since 2004, has been improved. Together with further relics from the two Buddha statues they were transferred from an interim storage inside the buildings near the Western Buddha, to two rooms in the Cultural Center (Heritage Center) erected by the Japanese colleagues. Thanks to the close collaboration with the Japanese colleagues under Prof. Kosaku Maeda the two work and storage rooms for ICOMOS in the Heritage Center are a crucial basis for future research on the Buddha statues. Samples of the various materials were analysed by the chair of conservation sciences at the Technical University of Munich and other institutions within the framework of an activity contract made with UNESCO (see reports of the Munich research project, pp. 197 ff.).

M. Pz.

The programme of the ICOMOS activities 2008 corresponds with the recommendations of the 6th and 7th Bamiyan Expert Working Groups:

Recommendations of the Sixth Expert Working Group on the Preservation of the Cultural Landscape and Archaeological Remains of the Bamiyan Valley

NRICPT, Tokyo, 20–21 January 2008*

*Abridged version without conservation of mural painting, archaeological investigations, implementation of the cultural master plan and preparation of the management plan, training.

Consolidation of the Giant Buddha niches:

The Participants of the Working Group

1. *Appreciate the work of all international experts on the Giant Buddha niches and acknowledge the successful completion of emergency operations in consolidating both niches. In order to ensure the stability of the niches in the future, regular supervision of the existing manual crack gauge system is necessary;*
2. *Recommend that the existing drainage network on top of the cliffs of both Buddha niches be monitored and cleaned regularly (maps of the drainage network needed);*
3. *Note the successful construction of the Messerschmitt scaffold in the niche of the Eastern Giant Buddha and recommend its completion in the top area of the niche as a priority for further documentation and conservation measures to be carried out;*
4. *Acknowledge the geological and geomagnetic documentation already applied on a test trench in the bottom part of the backside of the Western Giant Buddha niche and the almost completed documentation of the back wall of the Eastern Buddha niche as a result of the installation of the scaffold construction. We recommend the completion of this important work in both niches;*
5. *Recommend a detailed rock mechanical damage assessment be combined as a basis for further analysis of the back niche of the Small Buddha which began in 2007;*
6. *Recommend as a priority the conservation of the original surface fragments in-situ at the back wall of the East Buddha niche by a restorer. The appropriate conservation strategy for the endangered parts of the backside (e.g. shoulders, head) has to be defined jointly using all the necessary technical expertise (underlining the importance of the role of restorers);*
7. *Note that the monitoring results from the buttress of the Eastern Giant Buddha niche indicated no necessity of immediate action, however, monitoring should continue.*

Conservation of the Giant Buddha statues:

The participants of the Working Group

1. *Acknowledge the substantial progress made by ICOMOS experts in the salvaging of the fragments of the two Giant Buddha statues and endorse the finalization in 2008 for the Western Giant Buddha niche; for the remaining material additional temporary shelters are to be constructed;*
2. *Appreciate the successful installation of a 35 m scaffold construction in the Eastern Giant Buddha niche and recommend its finalization to make the back walls accessible to restorers, engineers and geologists, and foresee a similar scaffold in the Western Giant Buddha niche after successful completion of the salvaging works;*
3. *Note the necessity to increase the carrying capacity of the wire mesh at the back wall of the Eastern Giant Buddha niche by additional steal wire ropes;*
4. *Note the efforts of the Afghan authorities to enhance site-security and stress the necessity of establishing a sustainable site-security plan;*
5. *Acknowledge the salvaging of plaster pieces, wooden pegs and strings from the surface of the Buddha statues (around 4000 pieces) which will be stored in 2008 in the newly built storage rooms at the Bamiyan Training Centre;*
6. *Recommend the conservation of the extraordinary relic and fragments of birch manuscript found in 2006 in collaboration with the relevant specialists. Establishment of a conservation laboratory at the Bamiyan Training Centre is encouraged in this context;*
7. *Note that the conservation of the back walls of the Western and Eastern Buddha niches has to take into account the specific qualities of the cliff material within each, as documented by the research of the geomagnetic and rock-mechanical analysis executed by the ICOMOS team and other international experts. We recognize that only in the Eastern Buddha niche are there larger parts of the original surface material of the statue that have to be urgently conserved by restorers. We acknowledge the necessity, therefore, of different approaches to the Eastern and Western Buddha niches;*
8. *Acknowledge the preparatory work for the reconstruction of the partition walls at the base of the Eastern Giant Buddha niche, destroyed by the explosion in 2001. This work should be completed using as much of the preserved material as possible;*
9. *Acknowledge the progress of the geological mapping combining the documentation of the backsides of both Buddha niches with the identification of the salvaged fragments. The documented and measured fragments will all be included in the 3D models of the Eastern and Western Buddhas. The 3D model of the Western Giant Buddha shall be completed with newly acquired 3D measurements after the removal of the remaining material in the niche;*
10. *Recommend for the long-term preservation of all fragments, a reversible step-by-step strategy reflecting the different location and the mass of existing material: the 'Big Buddha' has a large amount of massive fragments (up to 70 t), the 'Small Buddha' has original plaster surfaces and rock fragments in situ (right arm with robe, fragments of shoulders and head). The completed identification of all fragments can be considered as a first step. A second step would be the adequate storage of the documented material close to the Buddha niches, considering the possibilities of reassembling;*

Consider further proposals for the technical possibilities of an anastylosis (refer to Article 15 of the Venice Charter) as a method of reassembling the fragments of the Buddha statues. Different possibilities of reassembling individual fragments should be considered and be discussed by a Special Advisory Board as suggested in the recommendations of the Fifth UNESCO/ICOMOS Expert working group for the Preservation of the Bamiyan Site.

Recommendations of the Seventh Expert Working Group on the Preservation of the Cultural Landscape and Archaeological Remains of the Bamiyan Valley Munich, 12–13 June 2008[*]

[*] Abridged version without conservation of wall paintings, archaeological investigations, implementation of the cultural master plan and further preparation of the management plan, and training.

Consolidation and Conservation of the Giant Buddha Niches and Sculptures:

The Participants of the Working Group

1. *Appreciate the work of all international experts on the Giant Buddha niches and acknowledge the successful completion of emergency operations in consolidating both niches. In order to ensure the stability of the niches in the future, regular supervision of the existing manual crack gauge system and monitoring and regular cleaning of the existing drainage network on top of the cliffs of both Buddha niches is necessary;*
2. *Appreciate the successful installation of the Messerschmitt scaffold construction in the Eastern Giant Buddha niche and recommend its finalization to make the back walls accessible to restorers, engineers and geologists, and foresee a similar scaffold in the Western Giant Buddha niche after successful completion of the salvaging works;*
3. *Acknowledge the substantial progress made by ICOMOS experts in the salvaging of the fragments of the two Giant Buddha sculptures and endorse the finalization in 2008/09 for the Western Giant Buddha niche: for the protection of the material semi-permanent shelters are to be constructed;*
4. *Acknowledge the geological and rock magnetic documentation already applied on a test trench in the bottom part of the backside of the Western Giant Buddha*

niche and the almost completed documentation of the back wall of the Eastern Buddha niche made possible by the installation of the scaffold construction. The completion of this important work in both niches is further recommended. Also, the detailed rock mechanical damage assessment of the niches should be completed;

5. *Acknowledge the progress of the geological mapping combining the documentation of the backsides of both Buddha niches with the identification of the salvaged fragments. The documented and measured fragments will all be included in the 3D models of the Eastern and Western Buddhas. The 3D model of the Western Giant Buddha shall be completed with newly acquired 3D measurements after the removal of the remaining material in the niche;*

6. *Recommend as a priority the conservation of the original surface fragments in-situ at the back wall of the East Buddha niche by a restorer. The appropriate conservation strategy for the endangered parts of the backside (e.g. shoulders, head) has to be defined jointly using all the necessary technical expertise. Note that the conservation of the back walls of the Western and Eastern Buddha niches has to take into account the specific qualities of the cliff material within each layer, as documented by the research of the geological and rock-mechanical analysis executed by the ICOMOS team and other international experts. It is recognized that only in the Eastern Buddha niche there are larger parts of the original surface material of the sculpture that have to be urgently conserved by restorers. Therefore, the Eastern and Western Buddha niches require different conservation approaches;*

7. *Note the necessity to increase the carrying capacity of the wire mesh at the back wall of the Eastern Giant Buddha niche by additional steal wire ropes;*

8. *Acknowledge the preparatory work for the reconstruction of the partition walls at the base of the Eastern Giant Buddha niche (destroyed by the explosion in 2001) in order to increase the overall stability of the niche. This work should be completed in 2008/09;*

9. *Note that the monitoring results from the buttress of the Eastern Giant Buddha niche indicated no necessity of immediate action, however, monitoring should continue;*

10. *Recommend for the long-term preservation of all fragments, a reversible step-by-step strategy reflecting the different location and the mass of existing material: the 'Big Buddha' has a large amount of massive fragments (up to 70 t), the "Small Buddha" has original plaster surfaces and rock fragments in situ (right arm with robe, fragments of shoulders and head). The completed identification of all fragments can be considered as a first step. A second step would be the adequate semi-permanent storage of the documented material close to the Buddha niches, considering the possibilities of reassembling;*

11. *Consider further proposals for the technical possibilities of an anastylosis (refer to Article 15 of the Venice Charter) as a method of reassembling the fragments of the Buddha sculptures based on a re-evaluation of the specific, 'concrete' conditions. Different possibilities of reassembling individual fragments should be considered and be discussed by the Advisory Board at the appropriate time;*

12. *Acknowledge the salvaging of plaster pieces, wooden pegs and strings from the surface of the Buddha sculptures (around 8000 pieces) which will be stored in 2008 in the newly built storage rooms at the Bamiyan Training Centre. It is further recommended that the extraordinary relic and fragments of birch manuscript found in 2006 be conserved by appropriate specialists.*

Bert Praxenthaler
Report on Safeguarding the Remains of the Buddha Statues, 2008

Eastern Buddha

The clay surfaces of the Eastern Buddha that survived the blowing-up of the statue in 2001 had been spot-bonded to the back wall in 2004 as part of an emergency stabilisation measure.[1] These works could only be carried out by abseiling with a rope, because a scaffold had not yet been put up. In 2008, it was now possible to fix these original clay plaster surfaces. For this purpose the scaffold was extended with bracket-shaped cantilevers to get close enough to the clay plaster fragments. These two fragment areas can be found on the left side under the former arm of the Buddha, at a height of 9.6 m and measuring 15 square metres, and on the right side along a fold of the gown, slightly inside the other arm, at a height of 9.0 m and measuring six square metres.

Composition of the original clay plaster

The original clay plasters on the Eastern Buddha are all made up of three layers. The lowest layer immediately on the stone, the slush coat, contains chaff und was applied to the surface very wet and then spread with the fingers. These finger traces are still clearly visible today. To improve the adhesion clay lumps were pressed into previously mortised holes (diameters of 6–8 cm) with the help of a suitable stone. The actual plaster material was applied onto this layer, a clay mixture containing chaff and animal hair, c. 2–3 cm strong. Onto this second layer a fine layer of 2–3 cm was applied, which served as support for the colour coat. In several areas only the undercoating remains.

For the 2008 stabilisation work on the clay fragments tests with various mortars were carried out in advance. Upon the advice of Prof. Emmerling (Chair of Conservation Sciences at the Technical University Munich) Ledan was used as component.[2] After adhesion tests a mixture of Ledan TA 1, red clay and Dralon fibre seemed suitable for back wall bonding. For fixing the edges yellow clay, Ledan TB 1 and when required Scotchlite K1 as mortar were employed.[3] At appropriate spots where the mortar was particularly thick, for instance at elevations of folds, darts of V4A ribbed bars or sanded glass fibre beams were used.[4] These darts were bonded with a mortar of Ledan and yellow clay. Whenever possible, armature bores were carried out in areas of the clay plaster that already had surface damages or holes in order not to reduce the original substance unnecessarily. The spots where the darts were placed were marked with a small nail.

In order to be able to move those clay plasters, which were very detached from the rock face, back a little to their old position and thus to avoid the mortar for the bonding and the stabilisation of the edges becoming too thick, these loose plaster layers were carefully moistened on their reverse side to make the material a little bit more malleable. By means of a splaying apparatus, which we had made by metal craftsmen at the Bamiyan bazaar, the clay plaster fragments could be repositioned millimetre by millimetre and were battered afterwards.

At first, these works were carried out partly by Bert Praxenthaler and by stone restorer Mujtabah Mirzai, together with up to five Afghan workers. In the course of the works the reverse-side bonding and the fixing of the edges were mostly executed by the Afghan workers Qurban, Eshaq, Karim, Haidar and Abdul Ali. However, drilling and needling were only done by Praxenthaler and Mirzai.[5]

Relic find

During the works on the Eastern Buddha an object was found on 3 October 2008 in a cavity about 17 m above the ground level of the niche and above the clay plaster fragments on the left. This is most likely a Buddhist relic, which apparently was deposited while the statue was erected in a 10 cm-hole together with parts of plants and then closed with a stone. This cavity is the backmost base of the hole which used to hold the beam of the Buddha's right arm. It is located below the undestroyed rock parts of the Buddha's right shoulder. Effectively, the relic was hidden at the place of the Buddha's elbow joint.

The object consists of a cloth sack measuring 4 x 6 x 3.5 cm, tied with a thread and sealed with a clay seal. The base is circular with a diameter of 3 cm. The clay seal has two different oval stamps. Some of the dried plant parts could be identified as belonging to the local plant by the name of "esfand". The find was handed over to the Governor of Bamiyan, Dr Habiba Sorabi, on Friday, 3 October by Prof. Emmerling and Bert Praxenthaler and the relic is now in the care of the provincial government of Bamiyan.

Searching for mines

In 2008, the search for unexploded materials could be accomplished without any major problems. This was due to the fact that the de-mining company ATC was present

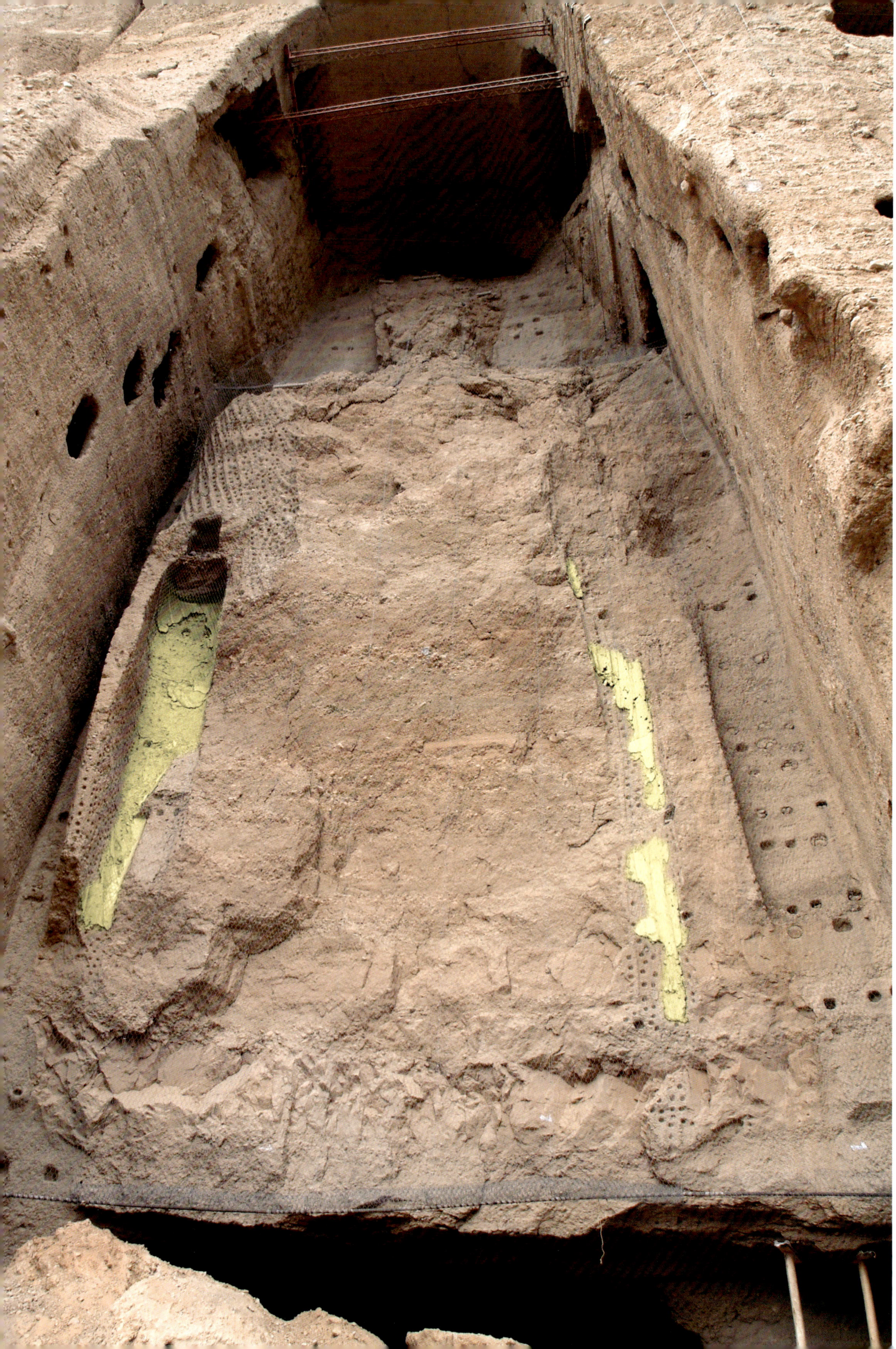

△△ Finger traces in the lowest clay plaster layer

▽▽ Clay lumps pressed into the holes with stones

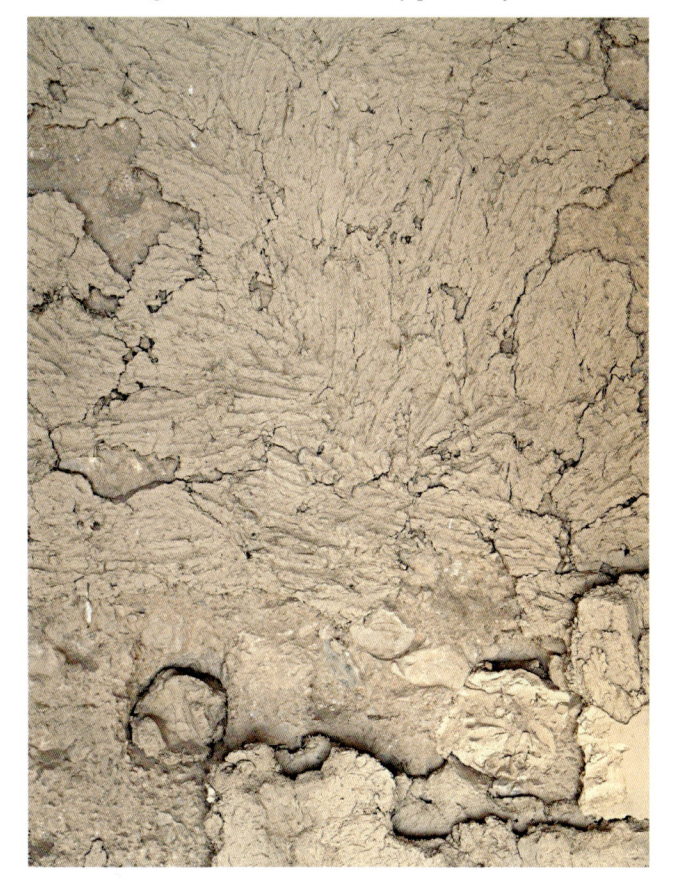

◁ Eastern Buddha, preserved original clay plaster areas (marked in yellow); in total about 21 square metres, secured in 2008 by gluing and needling

with a considerable number of staff at the castle hill of Shar-I-Golghola. If necessary, a search expert went to the Buddha during the salvage work to search for metal pieces with a detector and demine and remove explosives. Several unexploded explosives were removed; in the central cave between the feet of the Buddha considerable quantities of anti-aircraft ammunition was removed. This ammunition, which was still usable, was collected by the local police.

For the recovery work at the Western Buddha Afghan workers with certificates from the previous years were employed. Several of them were also repeatedly employed for work at the Eastern Buddha.

△ a　　　　　　　　　　　　　　▽ b

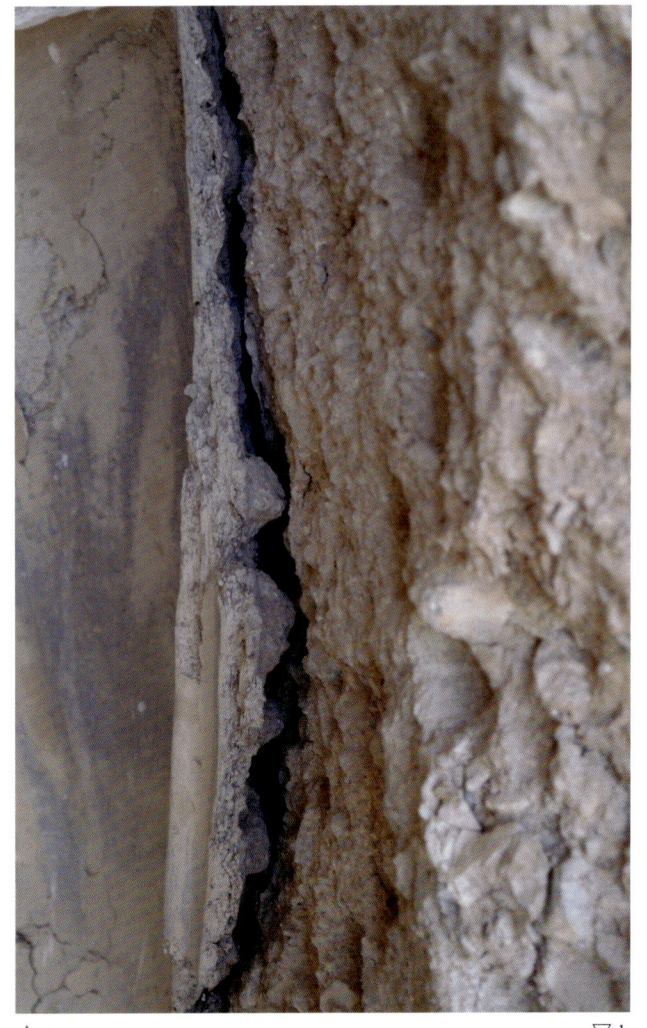

△ c　　　　　　　　　　　　　　▽ d

a, d Eastern Buddha: remains of clay plaster on the left, with lapis lazuli. Photo shows condition before treatment. All fragments are slightly detached from the rock face and are only kept together by being wedged on the left and right with the "clay-stone burling".

b Clay plaster with greyed lapis lazuli pigment, below in the centre the bond coat with bond holes; see also the stone used for pressing the moist clay into the holes.

c Three layers of clay plaster, partly detached from one another

1 In 2004, a mixture of ochre-coloured clay and gypsum was used, mix ratio 3:1. See report Praxenthaler 2004,
2 Ledan® TA 1 Leit 03, Ledan® TB 1, both are binding agents on the basis of lime with aggregates of Terra pozzuoli. Purchased from Fa. Dr. Kremer.
3 The mixture of the bonding mortar: 1 VT Ledan TA 1 and 3 VT red clay, c. 0.3 VT Dralon fibre. Due to its better bonding adhesive power the red clay was selected. For fixing the edges 1 VT Ledan TB 1 and 3 VT yellow clay were mixed, depending on layer thickness aggregates of Scotchlite K1. Yellow clay for colour adaptation. All materials purchased from Fa. Dr. Kremer.
4 Ribbed bars V4A 6mm from Kummetat Stahl, Frankfurt, glass fibre beams 5 mm from Fa. Fibrolux, Hofheim.
5 Particularly qualified workers were integrated into the works tep by step. They were not merely made familiar with the work techniques, but also with the basics of restoration.

Original clay plaster fragments (right side of the Eastern Buddha) are carefully pressed to the rock face by means of a splaying apparatus after bond mortar had been backfilled. In most cases this apparatus was hinged to the scaffold. The surface of this apparatus was adapted to the texture of the clay plaster and was made of small wooden boards. ▷▷

Original clay plaster fragments (right side of the Eastern Buddha), preparation for the setting of anchors: Mujtabah Mirzai drilling a hole into an existing bullet hole for an anchor. ▷▷▷

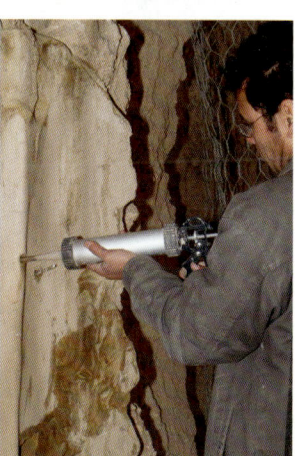

Bonding of clay plaster fragments; by means of a splaying apparatus pressure is carefully put on the clay plaster fragments; on the left underneath the arm hole. ▷▷

▽ Bonded and secured clay plaster fragment underneath the arm hole.

△ Eastern Buddha, Buddhist relic found on October 3, 2008

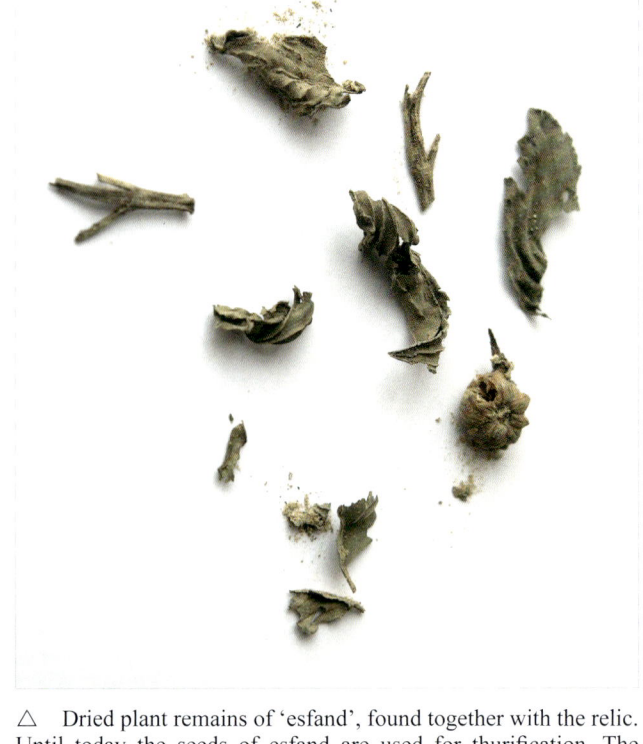

△ Dried plant remains of 'esfand', found together with the relic. Until today the seeds of esfand are used for thurification. The smoke is believed to keep away evil ghosts.

△ Eastern Buddha, Buddhist relic found on October 3, 2008

△ Eastern Buddha, Buddhist relic, view from below: circular diameter, inside a coin?

△△ Eastern Buddha, rock cavity with hole in the back wall where the relic was found. The hole is the remains of the beam hole for inserting the Buddha's right arm beam

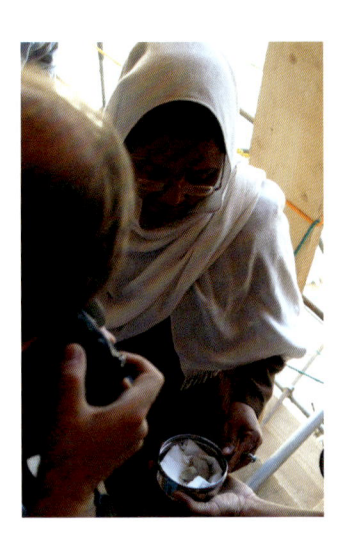

◁ Dr. Habiba Sorabi, the Governor of Bamiyan, accepting the relic

Erwin Emmerling, Bert Praxenthaler and Edwin Fecker on the scaffold of the Eastern Buddha ▷

Recovery of fragments at the Western Buddha

At the Western Buddha site the salvage work was continued by means of a wheel loader. Most of all, the cave entrances were exposed and all caves were cleared.

The rock fragments situated around the cave entrances were deposited on pallets in the back cave on the right. It was possible to let a very large rock fragment (c. 30–40 tons) lying to date on the stump of the Buddha's left foot, where it threatened to fall off, slide down between the Buddha's feet. From there, it will be possible to move it away with a crane sometime in the future.

Clay plaster finds

Once again, a great number of finds from the surface area (clay plaster, pegs, string, etc) was recovered. In the central, backmost cave many clay stucco ornaments were found. For the salvage and classification of these materials we were actively and competently supported by Mr Rasul Shojaei, an archaeologist from Yakaulang, Province of Bamiyan, who completed his archaeology studies in Iran.

◁ The team at the Western Buddha

▽ Recovery of fragments at the Western Buddha

△ Recovery of fragments at the Western Buddha

△ In front of the niche another small interim shelter for fragments, as the other storage halls in front of the niche are already full. The Buddha's feet are already recognizable.

△ Recovery of fragments at the Western Buddha

△ Careful examination of the Buddha rubble; finds are stored in zinc plate boxes

▽ View of the Western Buddha niche from above: Large, very heavy fragments weighing between 50 and 80 tons could not be moved without an adequate crane; they were wrapped up on site to protect them against moisture

▽ For the time being, the fragments are stored in a cave at the niche's entrance

Edwin Fecker

Report on Preservation Measures in the Eastern Buddha Niche, 2008

Thanks to the good cooperation with the Afghan engineers, craftsmen and helpers it was possible to realize the recommendations and assessments of the Sixth and Seventh Expert Working Groups (see pp. 134–136).

Fragments of the Eastern Buddha Niche

During the last years a lot of Buddha fragments have been removed from both niches and stored in roofed shelters. At the same time all fragments have been numbered and their dimensions, specifics and geological characteristics have been documented. According to a compilation by Georgios Toubekis the total number at the Eastern Buddha is several hundreds (Bamiyan Reports 2006–2007). These fragments are predominantly in both shelters to the west of the niche of the Eastern Buddha. A small number of fragments are still in the Buddha niche or in front of it. It is the matter of 16 very large fragments altogether. So far these fragments could not be transported to the shelters, because a bigger crane has not been available on-site. Thus the fragments were packed in alkathene sheets to protect them against deterioration. As the alkathene sheets had already embrittled by UV radiation, they cracked in some places due to high winds or were even frazzled. Thus the fragments were unpacked and the sheets replaced. On this occasion the already numbered fragments were photographed, their measures taken, their specifics recorded, and their geological characteristics documented.

Figure 1 shows the list of the fragments KBF001 to KBF016 with their measures and specifics. Figure 2 shows a site plan of the niche where the position of all fragments and the belonging number is drawn in. Figures 3 to 5 show photos of the particular fragments from different perspectives.

Reconstruction of the partition walls

It was in the middle cave behind the feet of the Small Buddha (cave no. I) where the explosive charge was initiated (see fig. 6). Hereby the partition walls to caves no. V and II as well as the front wall of all three caves were completely blasted out. Thus caves no. V, I and II have a common ceiling now which is crossed by a new formed gaping vertical joint (see fig. 7). This joint parallel to the slope extends only partially into cave no. V and is feathering in the west wall of cave no. V. In the east wall of cave no. II it is still some centimetres open.

There are several smaller rock plates which could fall down from the ceiling of the three caves. These rock parts, which are on the verge of falling from the ceiling of caves no. V, I and II, have been temporarily supported with wooden props. A major function of the reconstruction of the parti-

Fig. 1. Buddha fragments KBF 001–016

Buddha Fragments
Eastern Buddha - Small Buddha

ID-No.	Storage location	Pallet No.	plaster holes	plaster holes	Plaster remains	Silt	Conglomerate max. size in cm	surface area cm		Fragment size cm			Photo DSCN	year	notes	Name
	S=Shelf							width	length	width	length	depth				
	D=Depot		amount		√=yes	√=yes										
	BN=Buddha Niche							sum (m²)		sum (m²)						
	B=below BN															
KBF001	BN			no	na	no	0-12			190	170	100	DSCN 0646.jp	2008		
													DSCN 0647.jp	2008		
KBF002	BN			no	na	no	0-13			75	120	90	DSCN 0648.jp	2008		
KBF003	BN			1	na	no	0-19	10	10	190	170	130	DSCN 0649.jp	2008		
KBF004	BN			no	na	no	0-15			180	230	110	DSCN 0650.jp	2008		
KBF005	BN			no	na	no	0-10			120	190	105	DSCN 0651.jp	2008		
KBF006	BN			7	na	no	0-8	20	70	118	180	105	DSCN 0652.jp	2008		
													DSCN 0653.jp	2008		
KBF007	BN			no	na	no	0-21			85	100	60	DSCN 0654.jp	2008		
KBF008	BN			no	na	no	0-10			70	90	70	DSCN 0655.jp	2008		
KBF009	BN			no	na	no	0-9			85	110	70	DSCN 0656.jp	2008		
KBF010	BN			no	na	no	0-14			120	140	120	DSCN 0657.jp	2008		
KBF011	B			no	na	no	0-15			160	175	120	DSCN 0658.jp	2008		
KBF012	BN			no	na	√	0-11			220	245	125	DSCN 0659.jp	2008		
													DSCN 0660.jp	2008		
KBF013	BN			65	na	no	0-13	120	180	100	150	150	DSCN 0661.jp	2008	interesting piece	
								30	170				DSCN 0662.jp	2008		
								145	170				DSCN 0663.jp	2008		
KBF014	B			26	na	no	0-21	70	110	150	230	150	DSCN 0664.jp	2008		
													DSCN 0665.jp	2008		
KBF015	BN			47	na	no	0-7	110	200	200	230	180	DSCN 0666.jp	2008		
													DSCN 0667.jp	2008		
KBF016	BN			no	√	no	0-14	15	35	240	290	140	DSCN 0668.jp	2008		
													DSCN 0669.jp	2008		

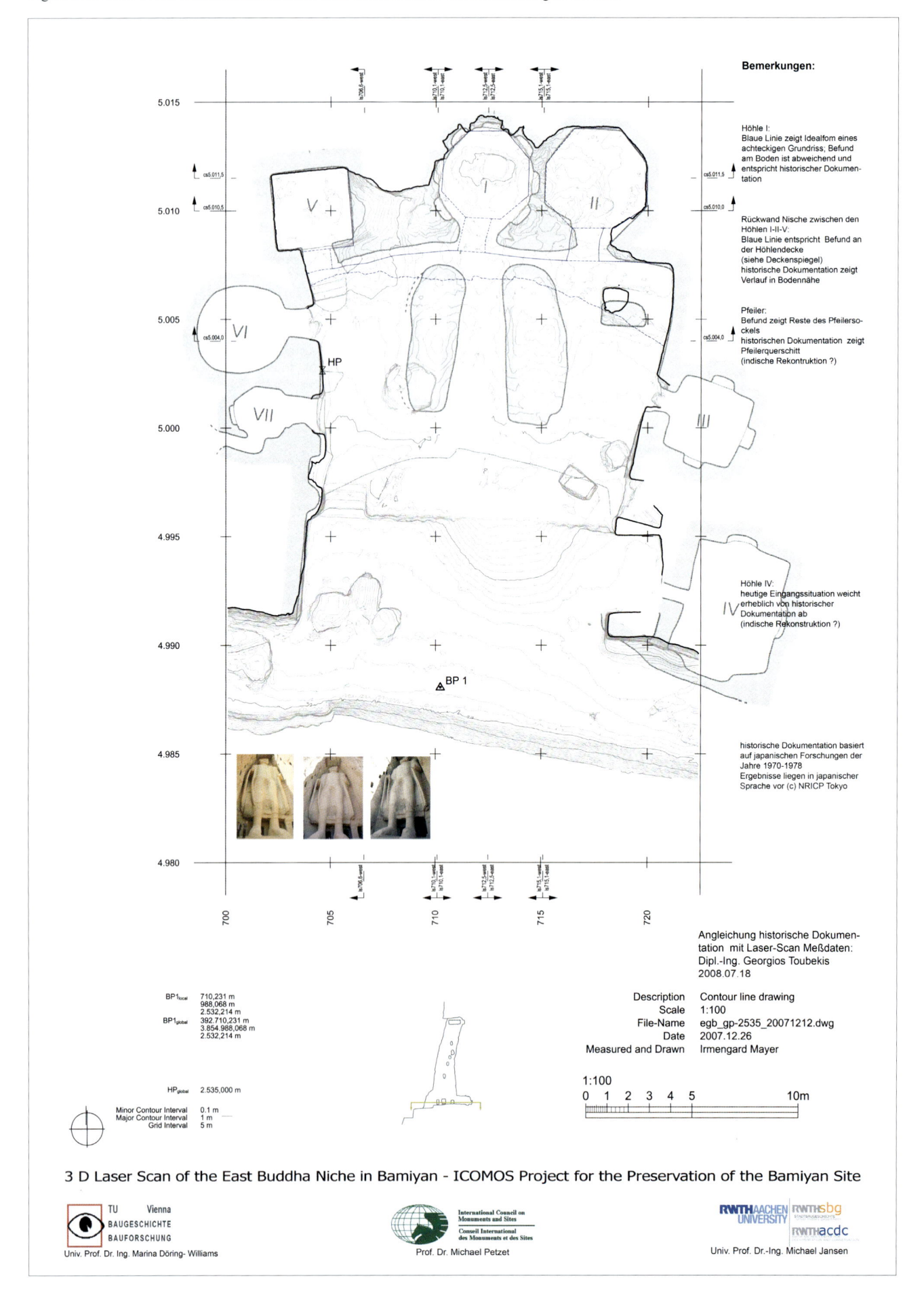

Fig. 2. Plan view of the Eastern Buddha niche with the location of the Buddha fragments KBF

tion walls is the stabilisation of the ceiling against local rock fall. Furthermore the reconstruction of the partition walls between caves no. V and I and caves no. I and II will guarantee an increase of the overall stability of the back wall of the Eastern Buddha niche.

To build the walls between the caves behind the ancient Buddha statue the smaller rock fragments, which were still in the niche and which did not show any treatment traces such as plaster remains or plaster holes, were used. Furthermore, fragments of approximately up to 0.1 m³ from a provisional deposit underneath the Buddha niche were transported upwards and also used to build the walls.

For the section of the partition walls between the three caves behind the ancient Buddha statue the site plan of the niche worked out by G. Toubekis was used, which is based on the 3D laser scan of the year 2006 (see pp. 117–121) and the historic documentation of Japanese research in the years 1970–1978 (see fig. 6).

The procedure when reconstructing the partition walls was as follows: The border margin of the walls was bricked up with quarry stones, afterwards the spaces between were filled with the fragments described above (see fig. 8). Thus the predominant part of the walls consists of fragments of siltstone and conglomerate.

Originally the walls of cave no. I had small niches which divided each wall of the cave and where statues were primarily standing. These niches have also been integrated into the reconstructed partition walls to approximate their original conformation. As a completion of the top of both partition walls a steel reinforced concrete beam was built where a connection to support further structural elements outwards is possible. At the same time it can fulfil the function of a compression strut if later a falsework for the fragments should be built, as I proposed in my report of 2006 (compare p. 109) After the hardening of the concrete beams the joint between beam and ceiling was filled with quarry stones and mortar, whereby all places at the ceiling are now protected against local rock fall. The supporting pillar under the eastern dress pleat, also blasted in 2001, has been reconstructed, too. Now it also supports a ledge that threatened to fall from the roof.

Upon completion of the partition walls they were plastered with a local loam mortar to adapt their appearance to the adjacent plaster of the undestroyed niche, a plaster used at the time of the restoration by ASI. This mortar for the partition walls was mixed in a hand barrow using predominantly loam with some water, straw chaff and burnt lime to get a smooth mash.

Documentation of fractures on the back wall

Due to the explosion in March 2001 rock sections which were partially loosened and are now on the verge of falling can be observed at the back wall of the niche of the Eastern Buddha.

Of the back wall of the niche a topographic record was made by a 3 D scan in October 2006. From this scan I. Mayer from Technical University Vienna and G. Toubekis from RWTH Aachen University created a front view rectified image of the back wall on a scale of 1:50 in order to record the discontinuities and partially loosened blocks. Based on these records the RWTH Aachen Center of Documentation and Conservation made a comprehensive description of the back wall of the niche and its specific features (see figs. 9–14).

The procedure at this description becomes apparent in the summary (fig. 11), where you can see that the back wall is divided into stripes resulting from the floors of the scaffold. Each stripe is two meters high, as the distance of the floors. The documentation begins with the stripe between floor 3 and 4 in the lowest part of the back wall and ends with the stripe between floors 12 und 13 where the scaffold ends.

Stripe 3/4 between floor 3 and 4 is characterized by a large number of small joints with a length of 0.5 to 1.5 m. These joints are only some millimetres open, which indicates that no rock fragments will fall down.

Underneath the right hand of the Eastern Buddha a dress pleat partially in good condition continues downwards, which is slightly loosened from the back wall at the lower east edge by some joints parallel to the wall between floor 4 and 6 (stripe 4/5, field b, c and d as well stripe 5/6, field c). The joints are scarcely open and end under the pleat. I consider the danger of falling of this section to be rather low. Safeguarding measures are not to be taken here, at best a fissurometer can be installed to make sure that the joints do not increase. The plaster made of clay, still residually present at the east side over these stripes has been secured by Bert Praxenthaler.

Upside stripe 6/7 up to stripe 10/11 the number of joints diminishes considerably. In this section the back wall of the Eastern Buddha is in such a condition that it is not necessary to be secured. Only at the west and east side where there are still rests of plaster made of clay Mr Praxenthaler has secured them.

The right shoulder is affected in many parts due to several new formed joints parallel to the wall and loosened from the back wall (stripe 12/13, field b, c and d). Some joints are open. In my opinion the danger that some parts may fall down and the total section may follow is high. As soon as the scaffold in this section is finished safeguarding measures should be taken with fibre glass anchors.

The left shoulder is also affected in many parts due to several new formed joints parallel to the slope and loosened from the back wall (stripe 11/12, field f and g as well as stripe 12/13, field e, f and g). Some joints are open up to about 10 cm. In these open joints decimetre large rock pieces can be seen which have been fallen into the open joint from the upper side of the shoulder. Only a rock gusset of about 1.5 m² avoids the falling of the section. The rock gusset is also showing disintegration. In my opinion the danger that the whole part will fall is very high.

The back wall of the Eastern Buddha is still showing in its highest part remains of the head of the Buddha. This is a large rock plate which is affected in joints parallel to the slope. The joints are slightly open. The whole part must be secured. I am considering the danger of larger rock falls in the near future to be low. The scaffold is not yet finished up to the level of the head.

Fig. 3. Buddha fragment KBF 001–016

△ KBF001 (DSCN 0646.jpg) △ KBF001 (DSCN 0647.jpg)

△ KBF002 (DSCN 0648.jpg) △ KBF003 (DSCN 0649.jpg)

△ KBF004 (DSCN 0650.jpg) ▽ KBF006 (DSCN 0652.jpg) △ KBF005 (DSCN 0651.jpg) ▽ KBF006 (DSCN 0653.jpg)

Fig. 4. Buddha fragments KBF 007–013

△ KBF007 (DSCN 0654.jpg)

△ KBF008 (DSCN 0655.jpg)

△ KBF009 (DSCN 0656.jpg)

△ KBF010 (DSCN 0657.jpg)

△ KBF011 (DSCN 0658.jpg)    ▽ KBF012 (DSCN 0660.jpg)

△ KBF012 (DSCN 0659.jpg)   ▽ KBF013 (DSCN 0661.jpg)

149

Fig. 5. Buddha fragments KBF 013–016

△ KBF013 (DSCN 0662.jpg)   △ KBF013 (DSCN 0663.jpg)

△ KBF014 (DSCN 0664.jpg)   △ KBF014 (DSCN 0665.jpg)

△ KBF015 (DSCN 0666.jpg)   ▽ KBF016 (DSCN 0668.jpg)   △ KBF015 (DSCN 0667.jpg)   ▽ KBF016 (DSCN 0669.jpg)

Conclusions

By completion of the partition walls the caves no. V, I and II can be entered without risk. Furthermore the reconstruction will guarantee an increase of the overall stability of the back wall of the Eastern Buddha niche.

As a permanent support of the loose rock formations at the left and right shoulder a fastening by anchors is necessary. As soon as the scaffold is finished and the shoulders will be accessible the works should start.

References

Fecker, E.: *Report on Rock Mechanics Aspects concerning the Small Buddha Niche in Bamiyan, Afghanistan*. Bamiyan Reports 2006–2007, pp. 153–179

Mayer, I.: *3D-Scanning for the Safeguarding of the Archaeological Remains of the Bamiyan Valley*. Technical University Vienna, 2007.10.29

Toubekis, G.: *3D Laser Scan of the East Buddha Niche in Bamiyan – ICOMOS project for the Preservation of the Bamiyan Site*. RWTH Aachen University, 2008.07.18

UNESCO/ICOMOS Sixth Expert Working Group on the Preservation of the Cultural Landscape and Archaeological Remains of the Bamiyan Valley. Tokyo, Japan, 19–20 January 2008

UNESCO/ICOMOS Seventh Expert Working Group on the Preservation of the Cultural Landscape and Archaeological Remains of the Bamiyan Valley. Munich, Germany, 12–13 June 2008

Fig. 6. Plan view of the Eastern Buddha niche with the contours of the destroyed caves and of the reconstructed partition walls

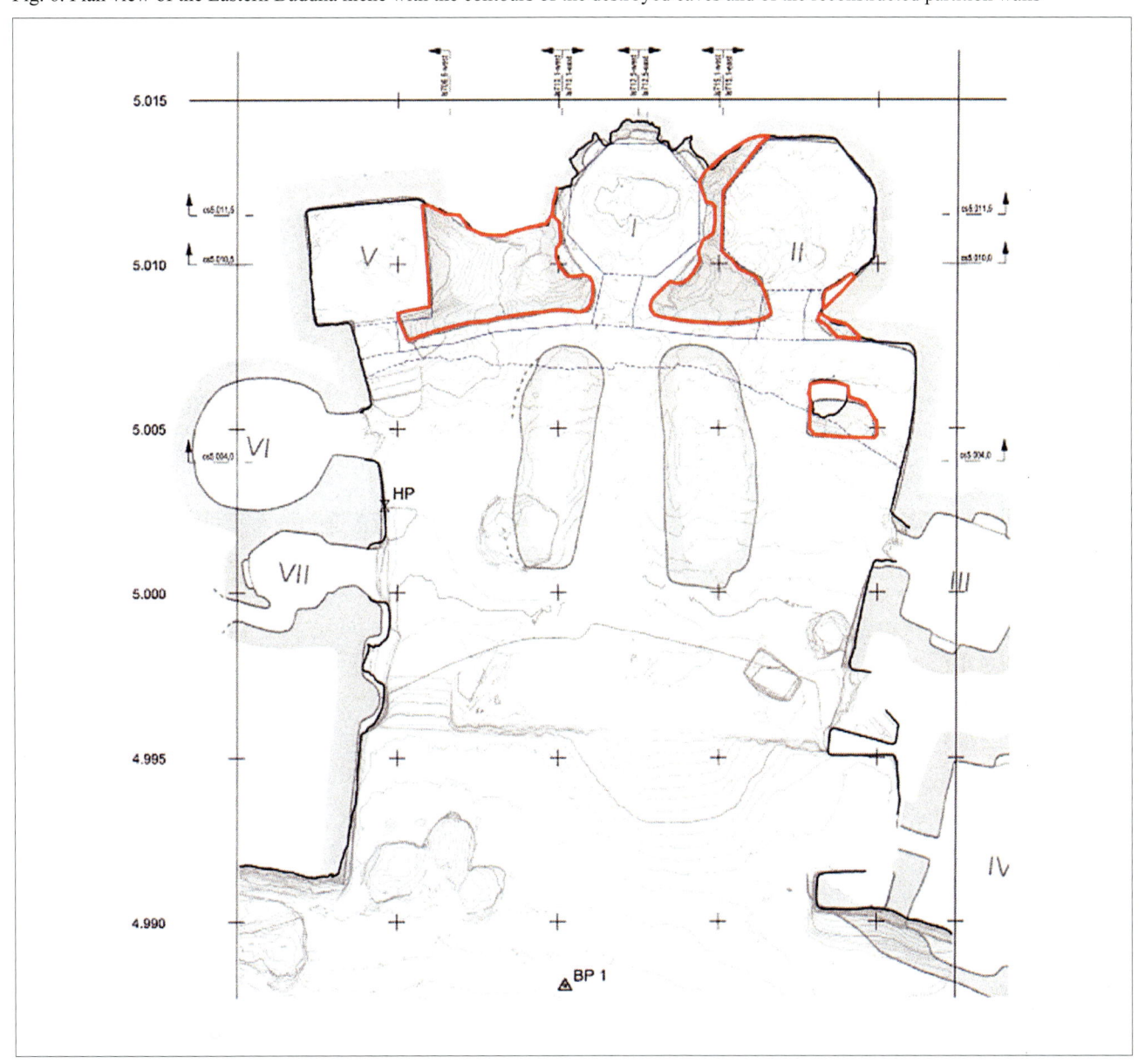

Figs. 7a, b, c. Destroyed caves at the base of the Eastern Buddha niche

152

Figs. 8a,b. Reconstruction of the partition wall between caverns no. I and II

Fig. 9. Eastern Buddha niche, damage assessment of the back wall

Fig. 10. Eastern Buddha niche, 3D laser scan, showing idealized reconstruction (blue line), original statue surface (green), back wall discontinuities (red)

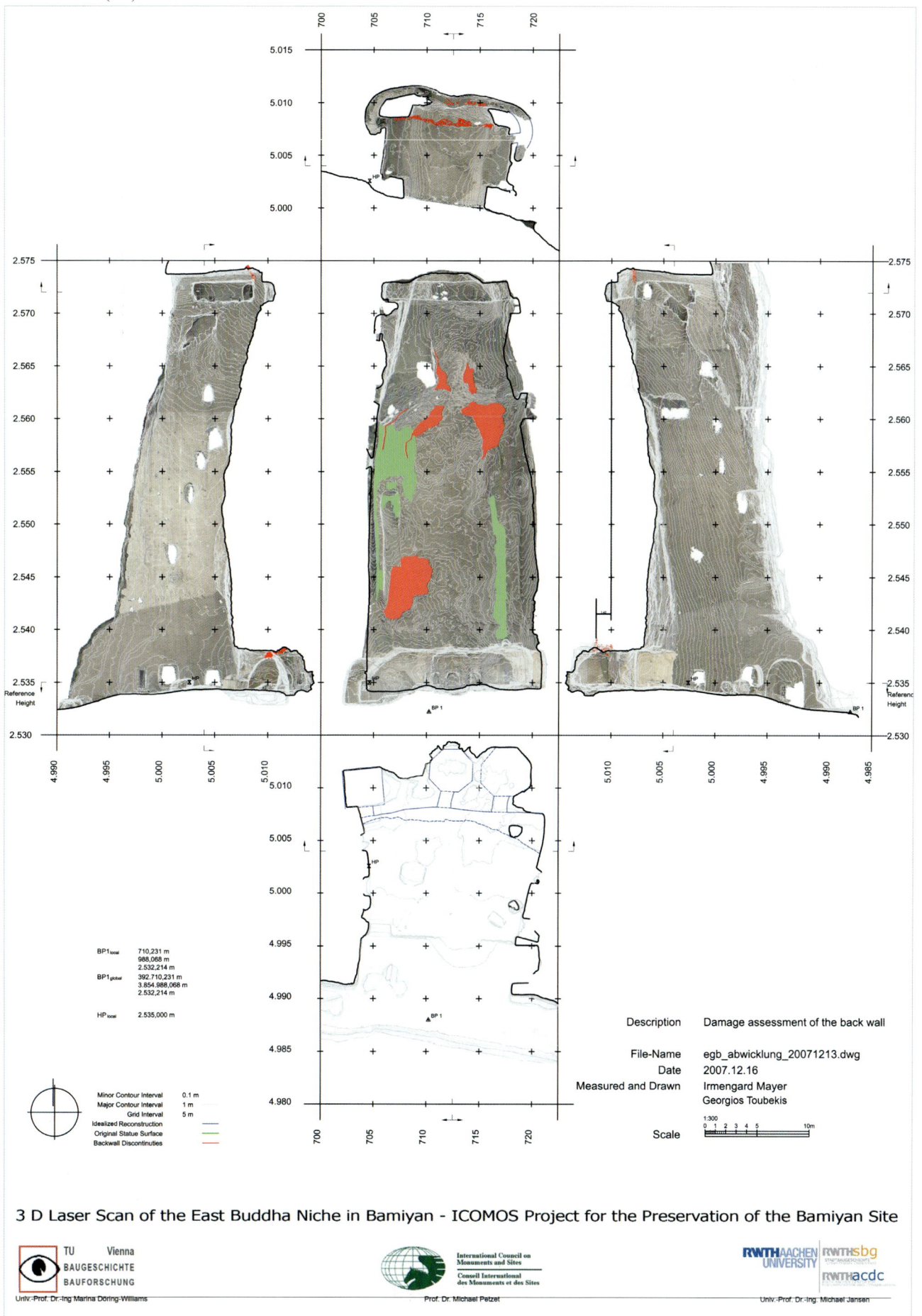

Fig. 11. 3D scanning, view east, with rectified image

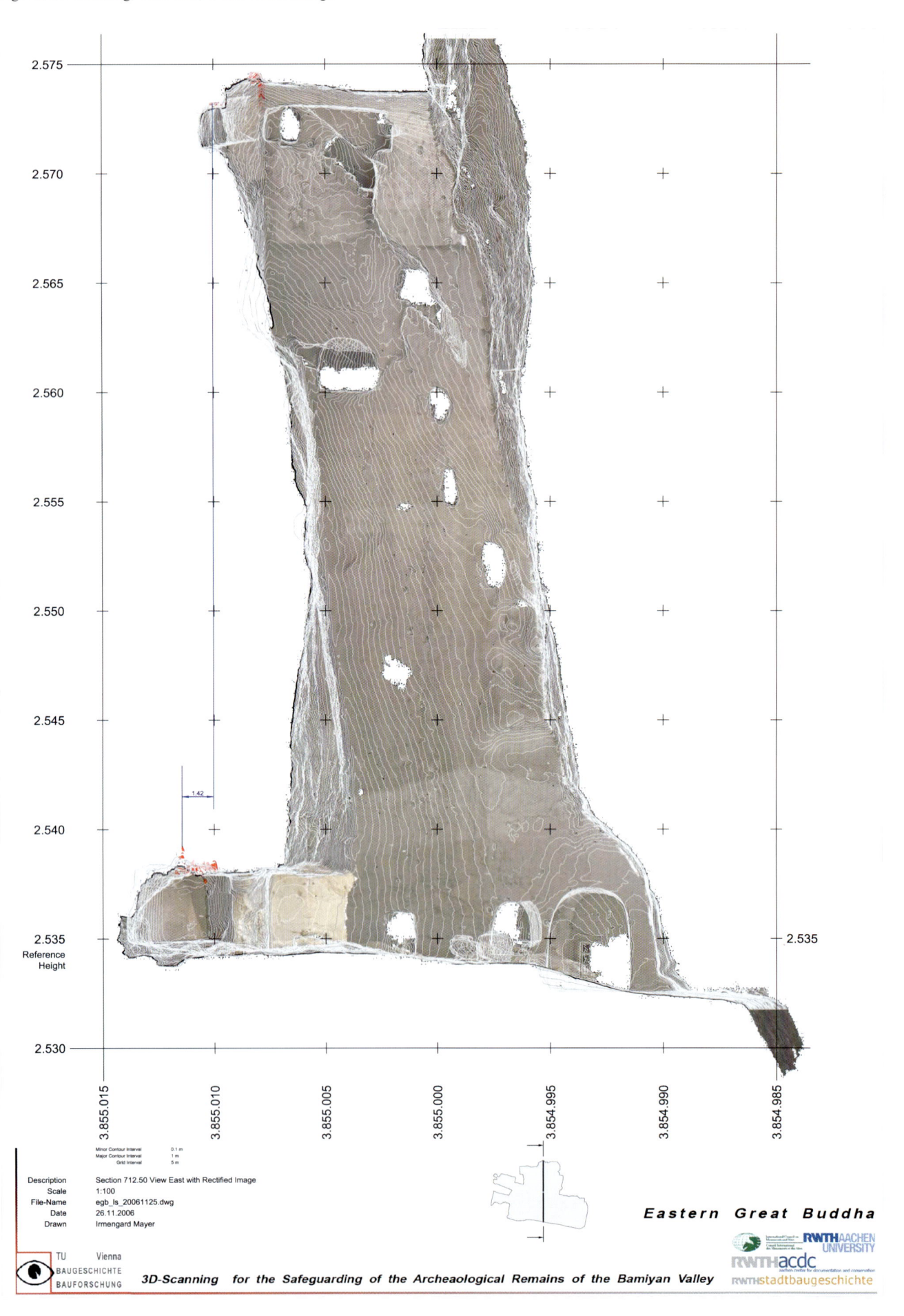

Fig. 12. 3D laser scan, damage assessment of the back wall with original statue surface (green), back wall discontinuities (red)

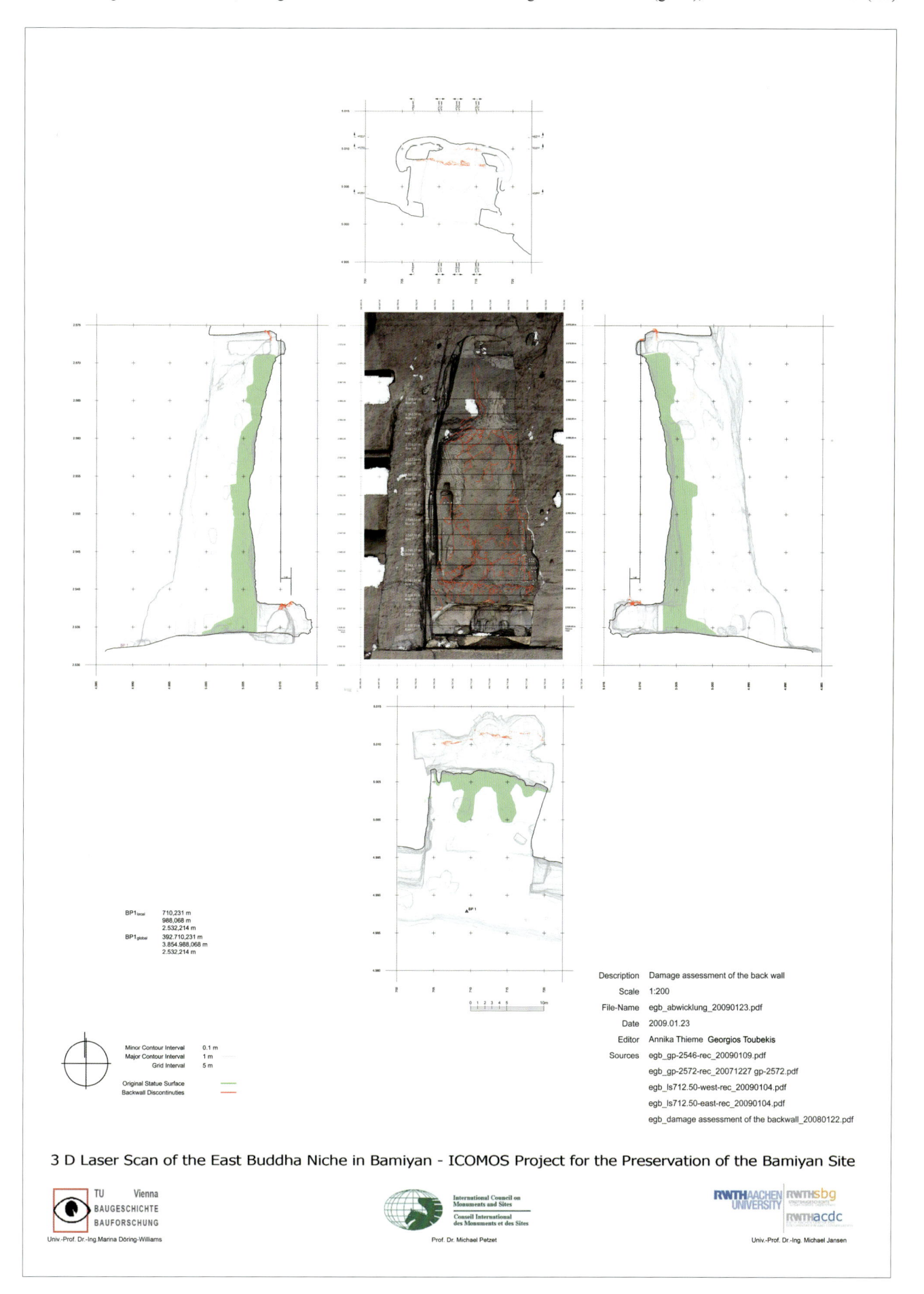

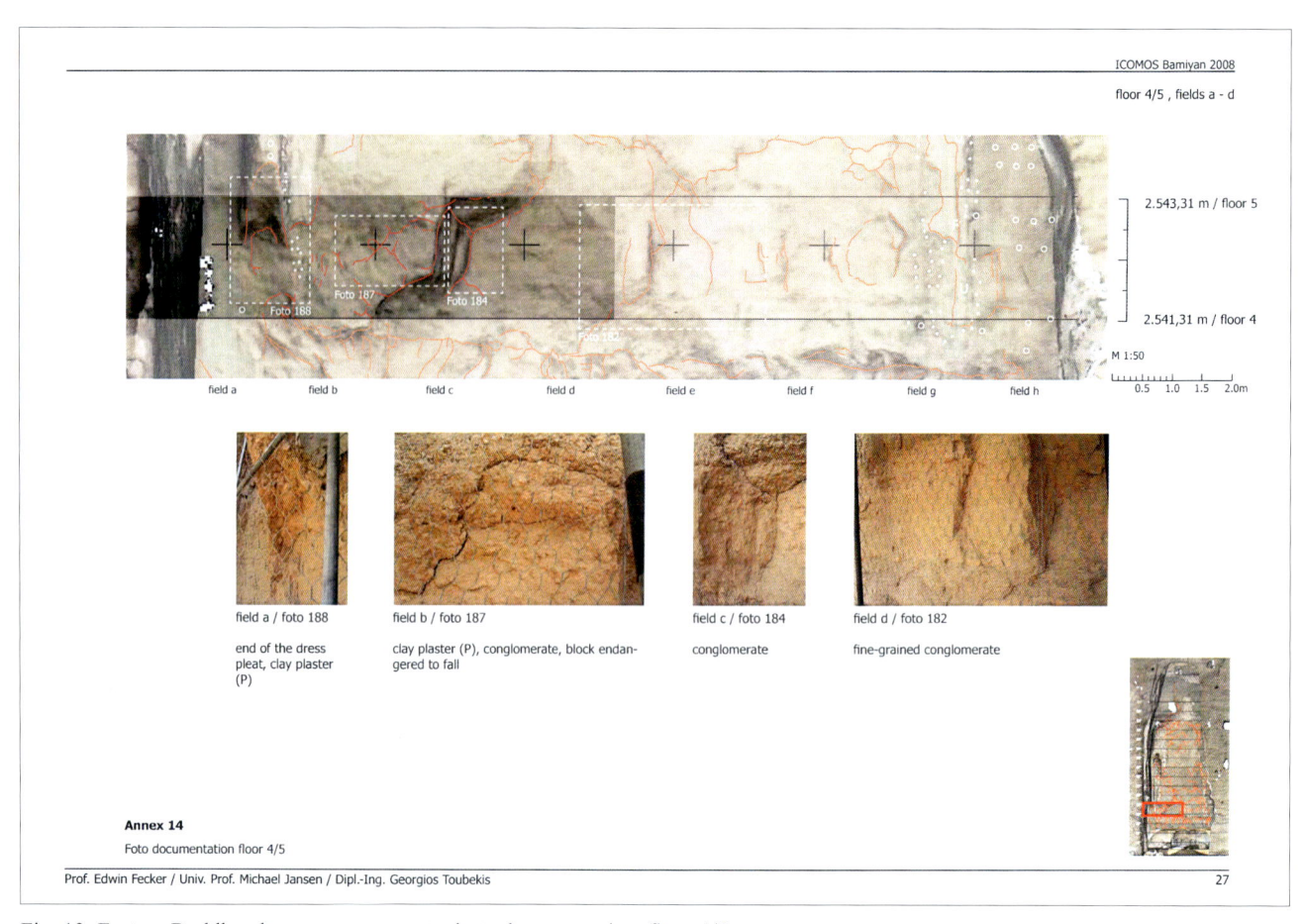

Fig. 13. Eastern Buddha, damage assessment, photo documentation, floor 4/5

Fig. 14. Eastern Buddha, damage assessment, photo documentation, floor 9/10

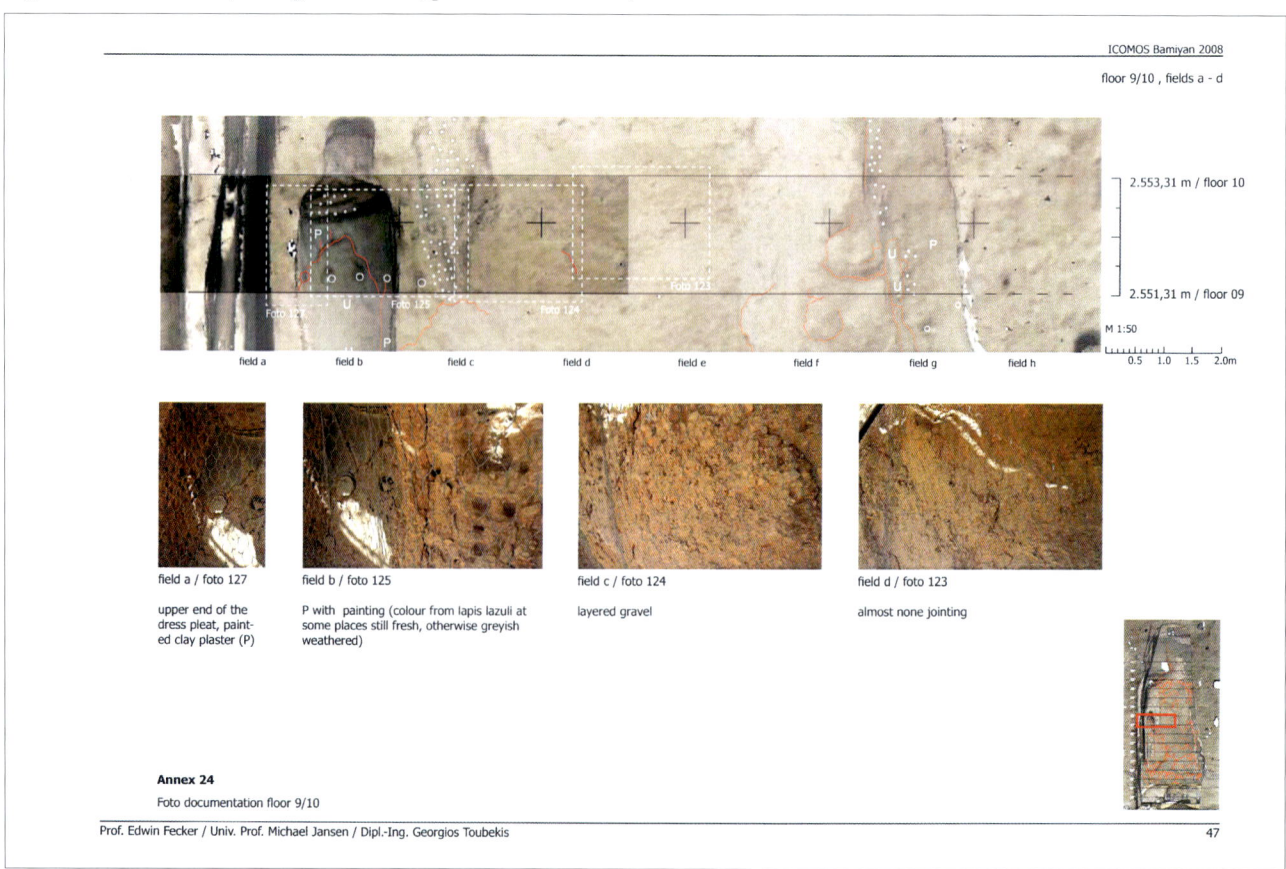

The scaffold provided by the Messerschmitt Foundation

2009

According to the plans of the ICOMOS project for 2009, once again supported by the German Foreign Office with 150.000 euros, the aim is to finally complete the salvage of all fragments at the Western Buddha site. Until now this had not been possible without a big crane to move fragments of up to 60 tons. In addition, our provisional shelters need to be extended as they are already very cramped. This extension is necessary as the fragments may have to be stored for a longer period. The intended improved storage of the fragments of the Western Buddha will also serve to document all objects more precisely and to present and explain them better to visitors. Moreover, the stock of plaster and stucco fragments recovered from the lower zone of the Western Buddha niche in 2008 needs to be integrated into the already inventoried stock of fragments.

For a start, at the Eastern Buddha site the plan is to more or less complete the stabilisation of the back wall. Once the upper part of the scaffold made available by the Messerschmitt Foundation has been completed, i.e. at the height of the shoulder and head of the giant statue, the back wall of the niche can finally be completely stabilised. Part of these measures is to secure an end-to-end crack behind the back wall by using grouted anchors and to fix several stone slabs threatening to fall down. These measures also include a more precise geological examination of those parts of the back wall that so far have not been accessible and of the roughly 400 fragments which may be suitable for a future anastylosis. Also a conservation method and detailed planning will be necessary, according to which the significant fragments, a number much smaller than at the Western Buddha, can be integrated into the overall, already in its present state clearly recognisable silhouette of the severely destroyed giant statue.

The following conservation concept for the back wall of the Eastern Buddha was developed by Prof. Emmerling in cooperation with Prof. Fecker and restorer Bert Praxenthaler and is based upon the experiences of 2008.

M. Pz.

Eastern Buddha niche, discussion about the safeguarding technology for the back wall

Conservation Concept for the Relief of the Eastern Giant Buddha and the Back Wall

The following conservation concept, in individual parts already successfully realised in 2008, should be continued in 2009 and completed until the end of the year.

The practical, on-site conservation work on the Eastern Buddha includes various tasks:
- Stabilization of the multi-layered clay plaster dating from the time of construction, with often surviving remnants of the original polychromy;
- Stabilization of Eastern rock slabs (c. 1–10 cm thick) which are sheering off parallel to the cliff surface;
- Stabilization of larger rock slabs with a thickness of more than 3 and up to c. 30 cm, sometimes a square meter or more in surface area;
- Stabilization of the large-format rock fragments salvaged from the rubble which have traces of workmanship from the time of construction ("dowel holes") or surviving remnants of the clay plaster.

The adhesion problems of the clay plaster, which is endangered almost everywhere, involve not only adhesion of the three plaster layers to one another but also adhesion of the plaster to the rock. Irrespective of the size and extent of damages, stabilization is only possible if suitable adhesives are used. In numerous cases additional mechanical stabilization measures must also be undertaken because of the substantial weight of the centimetre-thick plaster layers. Since all the plaster layers (as well as the stone!) react extremely quickly to moisture, optimal adhesives are those that can be applied using as little moisture as possible. The viscosity of the adhesive is adjusted to the size of the cavity between the individual plaster layers. The method of application (using tubes, syringes, spatulas or other suitable aids) is also determined by the size and/or geometry of the damaged site.

In order to further stabilize the original clay plaster layers (that is, the actual artistically formed surfaces) it is necessary to secure their edges by using sloping in-fills between the background stone and the consolidated surfaces; this is done with the same adhesive, which has to adhere not only to the stone but also to and on the plaster layers.

Depending on the size of the clay plaster surface, mechanical consolidation in the form of stabilizing dowels can also be necessary. Glass fibre dowels with a diameter of 1–3 or 5–30 mm or, for larger blocks, stainless steel dowels of appropriate length and thickness are used. To improve anchoring the glass fibre dowels are coated with sand using an acrylic adhesive.

The adhesive has to adhere to and between the clay plaster layers, and it also has to be possible to apply it to the stone. Following comprehensive testing, the product Ledan (developed in the heritage conservation field in Italy) was determined to be suitable; it can be modified as needed using properly prepared clay or sand from pits in the Bamiyan valley. Experience so far has proven that there is a sufficiently stable adhesion of all surfaces without the danger of saturating the clay plasters. All the other adhesives tested either lacked the appropriate properties or were unsuitable because of application problems on site. Adhesives of modified lime without additives are ruled out because of the working conditions at the site (high temperatures, low humidity, minimization of water content). The use of adhesives based on synthetic resins was rejected on principle.

The use of a considerable portion of clay or sand with the adhesive ensures compatibility and durability, and also means it is possible to work according to the principles of the Venice Charter. If necessary hair, straw or even synthetic fibres (Dralon) can be added to the adhesive.

Mechanical stabilization (stainless steel dowels) is also always necessary for the safeguarding of larger pieces of stone. Adhesion alone would be irresponsible because of the potential dangers of earthquakes.

All the necessary drilling for placement of the dowels is planned so that no historic surfaces will be damaged (drilling will be on surfaces that are already weathered). Nevertheless, drilling is problematic because the "cliff" is a sedimentary rock with inhomogeneous materials of differing strengths. Vibrations, also from hand-held drills, are extremely dangerous to the fragile surfaces. The stabilization work often has to proceed in stages: first consolidation of the endangered Eastern-scale remnants of clay plaster, followed by the necessary drilling work and finally consolidation of larger components.

This process also involves making the plaster layers plastic enough to be pressed back to their original position. They have to be supported while the adhesive sets.

This procedure can also be used to stabilize cracks, fissures and (depending on the thickness of the plaster remnants) stone slabs up to about 2–3 m² which are sheering off parallel to the rock surface. Suitable dowels can be installed up to a depth of c. 1 m. using hand-held drills.

More extensive mechanical stabilization measures which can only be carried out with suitable mounted drills are also necessary at quite a few locations.

Erwin Emmerling

Six Additional Tasks for 2009/2010

The programme of ICOMOS activities for 2009 was presented at a meeting in the World Heritage Centre in Paris on 29 January 2009. After another meeting with representatives of UNESCO on 16 April 2009 in Munich the programme was supplemented in June by a contract with ICOMOS Germany of 400,000 dollars within the framework of phase III of the Japan Fund-in-Trust project "Safeguarding the Cultural Landscape and Archaeological Remains of the Bamiyan Valley, Afghanistan". For the activity planning within the framework of Bamiyan Phase III not only the recommendations of the 7th Expert Working Group (see p. ##), largely already fulfilled during the ICOMOS campaign 2008, were relevant. Talks with the Afghan Ministry of Information and Culture (visit of Vice Minister Zia Afshar to Munich on 31 March 2009) were also very important.

In the following an abridged version of the planned activities, six additional tasks for the years 2009/2010, supplementing the above-described programme excellently:

Task 1: Stabilisation and conservation measures for the back wall of the Eastern Buddha niche

In the past years since 2004 when the back walls of the niches were secured with nets the work of the ICOMOS team, funded by the German Foreign Office, concentrated on salvaging the fragments from both Buddha niches. While due to the difficult outer circumstances it has not yet been possible to salvage all the fragments of the Western Buddha (work delayed because of finds of ammunition and bombs), work on the Eastern Buddha is already far advanced, following the recommendations of the 7th UNESCO/ICOMOS Expert Working Group: The completion of the missing upper part of the Messerschmitt scaffold in the Eastern Buddha niche will be the first step of this year's campaign (recommendations, point 2); the geological and rock-magnetic documentation and the 3D model of the niche are also far advanced (recommendations, points 4 and 5); the most important parts of the original plaster fragments in situ at the back wall were already conserved in 2008 (recommendations, point 6); the partition walls of the caves at the base of the niche have been reconstructed in order to increase the overall stability (recommendations, point 8). The detailed conservation concept for the back wall of the Eastern Buddha niche (see p. 160) developed from the experiences made last year was already discussed at the meeting on 16 April and welcomed by all participants. It is of course important that the work of the restorers is thoroughly coordinated with the experts in charge of safeguarding the rock structures. In correspondence with the cooperation arranged in Munich between Claudio Margottini and the ICOMOS team, the experiences made during the UNESCO emergency activities in 2003/04 and 2006 (see report by Margottini, pp. 175 ff.), funded by the UNESCO Japan Funds-in-Trust, will be integrated into the practical on-site conservation work. In some areas of the back wall of the Eastern Buddha niche, especially the zone of the shoulders, in addition to the mechanical consolidation with glass-fibre dowels and stainless steel dowels a more extensive mechanical stabilisation with strong anchors is necessary, involving considerable costs for a team with appropriate equipment working on site.

Task 2: Safety and stabilisation measures for the path leading up and down the Eastern Buddha niche

Although public access was never allowed this has not kept visitors from using the only provisionally secured corridors and steps in the cliff on both sides of the niche. The very urgent measure concerns not only the paths and steps on the sides but also the safeguarding of the rather dangerous upper crossing and the safeguarding of the accesses to the caves beneath the back wall in connection with the partition walls and the reconstructed pillar on the right.

Task 3: Conservation and documentation of rock fragments of both Buddha statues and equipment for stabilisation and conservation measures

For the preservation of all fragments the 7th UNESCO/ICOMOS Expert Working Group (point 10) recommended "a reversible step-by step strategy reflecting the different locations and the mass of existing material" and as first steps "the completed identification of all fragments" and "the adequate semi-permanent storage of the documented material close to the Buddha niches". In the meantime, all the cliff rocks from the Eastern Buddha and about two thirds of the cliff rocks of the Western Buddha that were broken off by the explosions have been salvaged in the last years and taken to provisional depots or protected with shelters. The stone demonstrates an extreme reaction to water. As soon as the stone blocks become wet (rain or snow) the sedimentary rock disintegrates into sand and all traces of the original surface treatment are lost. Besides, the stone blocks with traces of original treatments on their surfaces (drilling, dowel holes, recesses, etc.) are often so fragile and so traversed with cracks that they can hardly be moved.

There are various ways in which the numerous salvaged stone fragments can be classified:

The completely scaffolded Eastern Buddha niche

- Using procedures for geological prospection the layers of the sedimentary rock on the rear wall of the Buddha's niche and on the individual fragments can be detected. The results of these measurements make an approximate assignment of the stone blocks possible regarding the height of their original location.
- After records have been made of all traces of workmanship on the surface, these observations can be compared with historic photographs before the destruction.
- The analysis of the particle size on appropriate samples allows determination of a sequence of sedimentary layers which can then be used to assign the stone to a particular position in terms of height.
- Finally, as soon as the individual fragments are available as 3-D scans a computer-aided classification of the fragments will be possible at least for some pieces. At the same time this procedure will enable a virtual return and positioning of the fragments on the 3-D model.
- It is also possible to gain further information on the original location of the stone fragments using the polychromy of the surfaces and the imprints or outlines of clay plaster that has not survived.

Because of the fragility of the stone fragments even simple lifting presents dangers. In order to safeguard them, stabilization of the fragments is necessary regardless of their future use. Application of a consolidant up to a maximum depth of 1 cm is feasible using classic methods of stone consolidation. In view of the size of the fragments such a "crust formation" will not lead to fulfilment of the project goals. At this time the only appropriate procedure appears to be total impregnation using appropriate methods; these include the two alternatives: use of a vacuum sack or placement in a vacuum chamber (on site). Several means of impregnation are available: acrylic resin impregnation, silica acid ester (KSE) impregnation. All the procedures have advantages and disadvantages that must be weighed; in some cases they are also compatible with one another.

Continuing and improving the documentation on the rock fragments of both Buddhas, which also needs to be seen in connection with Task 4 (shelter for Western Buddha fragments), is an important precondition for future decisions on how to treat these fragments. It will be discussed at the appropriate time by the Advisory Board (see points 10, 11 of the minutes of the 7th UNESCO/ICOMOS Expert Working Group) and decided upon by the representatives of the Afghan Government. For the conservation of the fragile material, which cannot be solved with the usual methods of stone conservation, so far there are only the above-mentioned alternatives that will be tested by the ICOMOS team in 2009/2010.

Task 4: Semi-permanent shelter for Western Buddha fragments

In view of the substantial progress of the last years in the salvaging of the fragments of the two giant Buddha sculptures, the minutes of the 7th UNESCO/ICOMOS working group demand a replacement of the already overcrowded provisional shelter buildings by the construction of "semi-permanent" shelters for the protection of the material (point 3). Instead of a complex modern construction in combination with a kind of museum presentation of the Buddha fragments ICOMOS plans a solution in correspondence with the existing simple form, but more solid and functional. This will have the advantage that it does not interfere with the landscape and save money without anticipating future decisions about how to use the fragments. Apart from the costs a special factor speaks for a simple solution which can be carried out by local craftsmen: for conservation reasons the fragments already salvaged should be moved as little as possible, which means they should be kept at the site where they are now. Consequently, in view of the great amount of rock material the no longer sufficient shelter space of about 50 metres length will be stabilised under a new roof construction; then an additional new shelter should be erected. Individual and particularly big fragments will receive their own protective roofs near the Buddha niches. Through these constructions an enclosed courtyard will be created in front of the niche of the Western Buddha, consisting of the renewed shelters open towards the courtyard which could also be made accessible to visitors. The necessity to renovate and extend the existing shelters must also be seen in connection with the planned salvaging work in the Western Buddha niche meant to be completed in 2009.

Task 5: Permanent crane in the Eastern Buddha niche for maintenance/conservation access (planning)

A pre-condition for the installation of such a construction with trolley, engine and generator would be the dismantling of the Messerschmitt scaffold scheduled for the time after the consolidation and conservation of the back wall (according to present plans to be completed by end of October 2009). The scaffold could afterwards be used for future stabilisation work in the Western Buddha niche. As permanent crane such "hoisting equipment", a largely "invisible" construction at the top of the vault, could ensure that every part of the Eastern Buddha niche would be accessible for maintenance, control work etc by means of a movable cage. Such a "travelling trolley" would make the option of a future anastylosis possible, because the topographic conditions around the Eastern Buddha do not allow deployment of large equipment appropriate for moving heavy fragments. It is not yet possible to make a decision for such a construction, the advantage and costs of which have not yet been sufficiently tested.

Task 6: Kakrak Buddha niche and fragments stabilisation (concept and first steps for emergency measures)

Without in-depth examination the necessary funds for stabilisation measures at the Kakrak Buddha cannot even be roughly estimated. However, faced with the desperate situation of this monument difficult to access small funds could be used to at least make a start.

Munich, 6 May 2009, Michael Petzet

Bert Praxenthaler
Report on Safeguarding the Remains of the Buddha Statues, 2009

Eastern Buddha

After the remains of the clay surfaces of the Eastern Buddha still in situ had already been secured in 2008, during our first mission in June/July 2009 it was a matter of backfilling the cracks and needling the brittle back wall of the niche. In this context especially the areas of the statue that had survived the explosions had to be taken into consideration, such as the left shoulder and left fold of the cloak, parts of the head and smaller areas of the right fold of the cloak.

△ The protective net against rockfall had to be taken down

▽ Temporary covering of the brittle parts at the Eastern Buddha by means of heavy-duty tension belts as a first step of securing the back wall

Concept for rock stabilisation

Effectively, for the stabilisation of the back wall of the niche a plan of four stages was intended. Before the works the scaffold was adapted to the individual situation and the protective net against rockfall was taken down.

1. Stabilisation with heavy-duty tension belts

At first, on both sides of particularly brittle spots anchors with ring eyelets were inserted. At these anchors tension belts were attached, which together with timber wedges as interlayers could prevent rock pieces from falling down. These tension belts are only meant as an interim measure and can be removed once the stabilisation is complete.

2. Backfilling the cracks and fissures

For the backfilling of the cracks first of all the vertical crack grooves were sealed from outside with a mixture of yellow clay and Ledan. After this grouting the mortar mixture was filled in through an opening. Mortar mixture for fissures of up to 20 mm: Ledan TA 1 with washed and sifted river sand, for wider fissures: cement and river sand with Rheobuild 1000 as aggregate (after Tonoli/Crippa). This backfilling was carried out in several phases to avoid the unstable, moisture-sensitive stone of being partially dissolved and to reduce the danger of shearing. To enable the backfilled adhesive mortar to harden work was carried out at several places at the same time. Once a partial improvement of the consolidation was achieved, the grouting could continue at a higher level and then be backfilled.

3. Placing of steel anchors

After the hardening of the mortar the drilling could begin. The backfilling of the cracks led to some degree of stabilisation of the brittle parts; for an additional consolidation steel anchors of one metre length and 12 mm diameter (stainless V4A ribbed bars) were used. With conventional drilling apparatuses (Hilti T76) the drilling was carried out in several steps (8 mm, 12 mm, 16 mm). The holes were freed from dust with compressed air and afterwards the steel bars were fixed with cement mortar.

Salvage of fragments at the Western Buddha

At the Western Buddha the salvage was continued, at first only with shovels and wheel barrows. Later on, a 25 t crane was used for removing smaller fragments which were blocking the entrances to the caves.

Bracket-like cantilevers are added to the scaffold so that the niche's back wall can be reached

a   Temporary covering of the brittle parts
b   Sealing the cracks and backfilling step by step with mortar
c   Drilling of holes for the anchors (Ali Reza and Mujtaba Mirzai)
d   Removal of dust from the drilling holes with compressed air
e   Backfilling of mortar
f   Insertion of steel bars
g   The team at the Eastern Buddha
h   Exposing the Western Buddha's feet   ▷

△ a

△ b

△ c

▽ d

△ e

△ f

△ g

▽ h

165

Removal of rock fragments with a heavy-duty crane (left). The steps near the Buddha's shoulder are cleared of rubble so that a temporary base for the upper zone of the scaffold can be added (right).

Removal of rubble at the Western Buddha

△ The feet of the Western Buddha are exposed

Dinner after a day's work ▽

167

Removal of rock fragments with a heavy-duty crane

From above the Western Buddha's feet are now clearly visible

Edwin Fecker
Report on Stabilisation Measures in the Eastern Buddha Niche, 2009

The signatory was on site together with Bert Praxenthaler and Mujtabah Mirzai from 5–15 June, 2009, to make the above mentioned examinations.

The Sixth Expert Working Group in Tokyo, 19–20 January 2008 recommended *the conservation of the original surface fragments at the back wall of the East Buddha niche by a restorer. The appropriate conservation strategy for the endangered parts of the backside (e.g. shoulders, head) has to be defined jointly using all the necessary technical expertise (compare p. ##).*

On April 16, 2009 an expert meeting with representatives of UNESCO took place in Munich, where the further procedure in the stabilisation of the back wall was agreed.

Stabilisation works in the back wall

When the scaffold reached the shoulders the detritus was removed from them and temporary foundations for the further construction of the scaffold were made hereon (see fig. 1). The wire net fixed above the head was removed, then the loose rock fragments in the area of the cervix (see fig. 2). Afterwards the scaffold could be completed.

Before the stabilisation works at the back wall could start all rock fragments on the verge of falling were provisionally fixed with tension belts. The left and the right shoulders have been provisionally protected (see figs. 3 and 4), as well as the head and the wedge under the eastern gallery above the head (see fig. 5).

Afterwards all smaller rock parts which had been separated from the back wall by the explosion were secured. This concerns blocks of about 20 x 20 x 15 cm up to about 1.0 x 0.5 x 0.5 m. To secure these blocks high quality steel nails with a length of 50 cm resp. 100 cm were bought. To fill in the joint spaces Ledan was used, an injection mortar which is chemically-physically similar to hydraulic lime, and with which positive experience was made in restrengthening of paint layers on stonework underground.

To secure the blocks of the above-named dimensions it is necessary to fill the joint that separates the block from the back wall with injection mortar and to harden it. Then the rock can be drilled through, in the borehole filled with mortar a rock nail of the necessary length can be inserted (see figs. 6 and 7). If the joint were not filled in with mortar before, the rock could continue to loosen from the back wall by the vibrations of the drilling and eventually fall down.

The situation is different at the big blocks at both shoulders, at the head and under the eastern gallery, concerning blocks of several tons of weight, which cannot be secured with the above described measures. According to the agreements on April 16, 2009 in Munich these blocks have to be secured with rock anchors of several meters of length whose number and spatial arrangement will be decided by the experts together in situ in October 2009.

Documentation of the fractures in the back wall

Due to the explosion in March 2001 rock sections which have been partially loosened and are now on the verge of falling can be observed at the back wall of the niche of the Eastern Buddha.

From the back wall of the niche a topographic record was made by a 3D scan in October 2006. From this scan I. Mayer from the Technical University Vienna and G. Toubekis from RWTH Aachen University created a front view rectified image of the back wall in a scale of 1:50 in order to record the discontinuities and partially loosened blocks. Based on these records the RWTH Aachen Center of Documentation and Conservation has made a comprehensive description of the back wall of the niche and its specific features (see p. ##, figs. 11–15).

The procedure at this description becomes apparent in the summary (see p. ##, fig. 11), where the back wall is divided into stripes resulting from the floors of the scaffold. Each stripe is two meters high, as the distance of the floors. The documentation begins with the stripe between floors 3 and 4 in the lowest part of the back wall and ends with the stripe between floors 12 und 13 where the scaffold ended in the year 2008.

The completion of the scaffold in the year 2009 made it possible to document the higher areas of the back wall, starting at stripe 11/12 and ending at stripe 14/15. Stripe 11/12 between floors 11 and 12 is characterized by well-preserved parts of the Buddha at the western side, by a small number of joints in the middle part (field d and e), and by a rock gusset in field f which is no longer connected to the back wall. The right shoulder is affected in many parts due to several newly formed joints parallel to the wall and loosened from the back wall (see stripe 12/13, field c and d). Some joints are open for several centimetres. At the explosion a large number of rock pieces have been settled on the shoulder (field b), which all have been removed now that the in-situ rock is visible again.

△ Fig. 1a. Right shoulder after removal of the loose rock fragments

△ Fig. 1b. Left shoulder after removal of the loose rock fragments

△ Fig. 2a. Head of the Eastern Buddha before removing the loose rock fragments

△ Fig. 2b. Head of the Eastern Buddha after removing the loose rock fragments

△ Fig. 3a. Provisional stabilisation of left shoulder (upper part) with tension belts

△ Fig. 3b. Provisional stabilisation of left shoulder (lower part) with tension belts

▽ Fig. 4a. Provisional stabilisation of right shoulder

▽ Fig. 4b. Provisional stabilisation of right shoulder

△ Fig. 5a. Loose wedge under the Eastern gallery

△ Fig. 5b. Provisional stabilisation of the loose wedge

△ Fig. 6a. Drilling of anchor borehole

△ Fig. 6b. Removal of dust from the borehole

△ Fig. 7a. Preparations for refilling the borehole

△ Fig. 7b. Filling Ledan into the borehole

▽ Fig. 8a. Pushing anchor as far as possible into the borehole

▽ Fig. 8b. Driving anchor into the borehole with a hammer

Fig. 9. Trace of an open joint parallel to the back wall (red line)

The ICOMOS team in the Western Buddha niche, October 17, 2009

The left shoulder is also affected in many parts due to several new formed joints parallel to the slope and loosened from the back wall (see stripe 11/12, field f and g as well as stripe 12/13, field f, g and h). Some joints are open up to about 10 cm. In these open joints decimetre large rock pieces can be seen which fell into the open joint from the upper side of the shoulder. The left shoulder was also covered with a large number of rock pieces which settled there at the explosion. This detritus was removed so that the in-situ rock is now visible.

The back wall of the Eastern Buddha still shows in its highest part remains of the Buddha head (see stripe 13/14 fields d, e and stripe 14/15 fields b, c, d). The remains of the head are a large rock plate which is affected in joints parallel to the slope by newly formed ones. The joints are slightly open. The joint behind the remains of the head continues along the both shoulders. It is clearly visible as continuation in the corner of the back wall and both side walls of the niche (see fig. 9). It could not be found out how far this large joint continues upwards. But behind the shoulders is an opening of several centimetres which allows the conclusion that this joint must continue at least several meters vertically downwards.

This joint separates, at least in the area of shoulders and head, the remains of the Buddha body from the original back wall continuing above the shoulders and next to the head. In the shoulder area a 2 to 2.5 m thick rock part is separated from the in-situ rock by a dorsal open vertical joint.

Conclusions

The stabilisation of the smaller loose rock blocks in the back wall of the Eastern Buddha is largely finished. For this purpose the open joints have been filled with injection mortar and the particular blocks have been fixed with rock nails of 0.5 resp. 1.0 m length at the back wall.

Up to now the larger rock blocks at both shoulders, at the head and under the eastern gallery on the verge of falling are only provisionally secured. The final stabilisation with rock anchors still has to be accomplished. The steps in this process are:

1. Filling up the open joints with injection mortar;
2. Determination of the orientation and length of the rock anchors;
3. Drilling of the anchor boreholes (40 mm in diameter);
4. Setting of the rock anchors.

The documentation of the fractures in the back wall is finished and has been integrated in the topographic records of the back wall.

IV The Consolidation and Stabilization of the Buddha niches and the cliff in Bamiyan (2003/04; 2006)

Claudio Margottini

Abstract

The historical site of Bamiyan is affected by geomorphological deformation processes which were worsened by the blowing-up of the Buddhas in March 2001, when the statues, dating back to the 6th century AD, were destroyed. Not only was invaluable cultural heritage irremediably lost, but also the consequences of the explosions as well as the collapse of the giant statues added greatly to the geological instability of the area. Traces of rocks recently slid and fallen are relevant proofs of the deterioration of its stability conditions and most parts appear prone to collapse in the near future.

Under the coordination of UNESCO, a global project to assess the feasibility conditions for the site's restoration was developed; field data were collected and a mechanism for the potential cliff and niches' evolution was provided. In the meantime some consolidation works were carried out in the most critical rock fall-prone areas to avoid any further collapse in the coming winter season, but also to enable archaeologists the safe cataloguing and recovering of the Buddha statues' remains, still lying on the floor of the niches. The emergency activities started in October 2003 and included: the installation of a monitoring system, the realization of temporary supports for the unstable blocks, the stabilization of the upper-eastern and upper-western part of the Eastern Buddha niche, the minimization of the environmental impact of the actions taken. Consolidation works were mainly implemented by professional climbers, directly operating on the cliff.

Fig. 1. The Giant Buddha statues of Bamiyan in a depiction by Burnes, 1834

Fig. 2a. The Eastern Giant Buddha before the destruction

Fig. 2b. The Eastern Giant Buddha after the destruction

Fig. 3a. The Western Giant Buddha before the destruction

Fig. 3b. The Western Giant Buddha after the destruction

1 Introduction

In the great valley of Bamiyan, 200 km NW of Kabul, central Afghanistan, two big standing Buddha statues appear to visitors (fig. 1), carved out of the sedimentary rock of the region, at 2500 meters of altitude. Following the tradition, this remarkable work was probably done around the 6th century AD by some descendants of Greek artists who had gone to Afghanistan with Alexander the Great.

The two statues were destroyed in March 2001 by the Taliban, using mortars, dynamite, anti-aircraft weapons and rockets (figs. 2 and 3). The Buddhists as well as the world community, UN and UNESCO failed to convince the Taliban to refrain from destroying this unique cultural heritage. Nevertheless, since 2002 UNESCO has been coordinating a large international effort for the protection of the World Heritage site of Bamiyan and the future development of the area.

2 General features of the area

Extensive investigations were conducted on the site, in spite of the limitation of field investigation due to landmines. In detail the following activities were performed in the period 2002 until now. Most of the collected information is reported in Margottini (2003/b), Margottini (2004/a), Margottini (2007) and Margottini et alii (2005), and developed according to the standards and procedure described in Hoek and Bray (1994), and Turner and Schuster (1996). The developed activities include:

1. the inventory of geological and geomorphological features and existing mass movements;
2. the identification of predisposing factors to slope instability (climatology, petrology, mineralogy, sedimentology, seismology, geophysical properties of rocks, mechanical behaviour of both rock masses [in situ and laboratory] and discontinuities, discontinuities distribution);
3. the investigation of potential triggering mechanisms of landslides;
4. the kinematic analysis to identify potential failure mechanisms for cliff and niches;
5. the numerical stability analysis of cliff and niches, to identify the relationship between shear strength along the potential failure surface and conditions required to trigger the collapse;
6. experiences in previous restoration/consolidation works;
7. a manual crack gauge monitoring system was also installed showing no movement in the period September 2003 – March 2007;
8. automatic crack gauge monitoring system operating at the time of stabilization works (November – December 2003 and April – May 2004)

The investigations performed in the Buddha niches and the surrounding cliff in the Bamiyan valley highlight the following main features (Margottini, 2004/a; Margottini, 2007; Margottini et alii, 2005):

1. The area is located in mountainous central Afghanistan in a dry part of the world that experiences extremes of

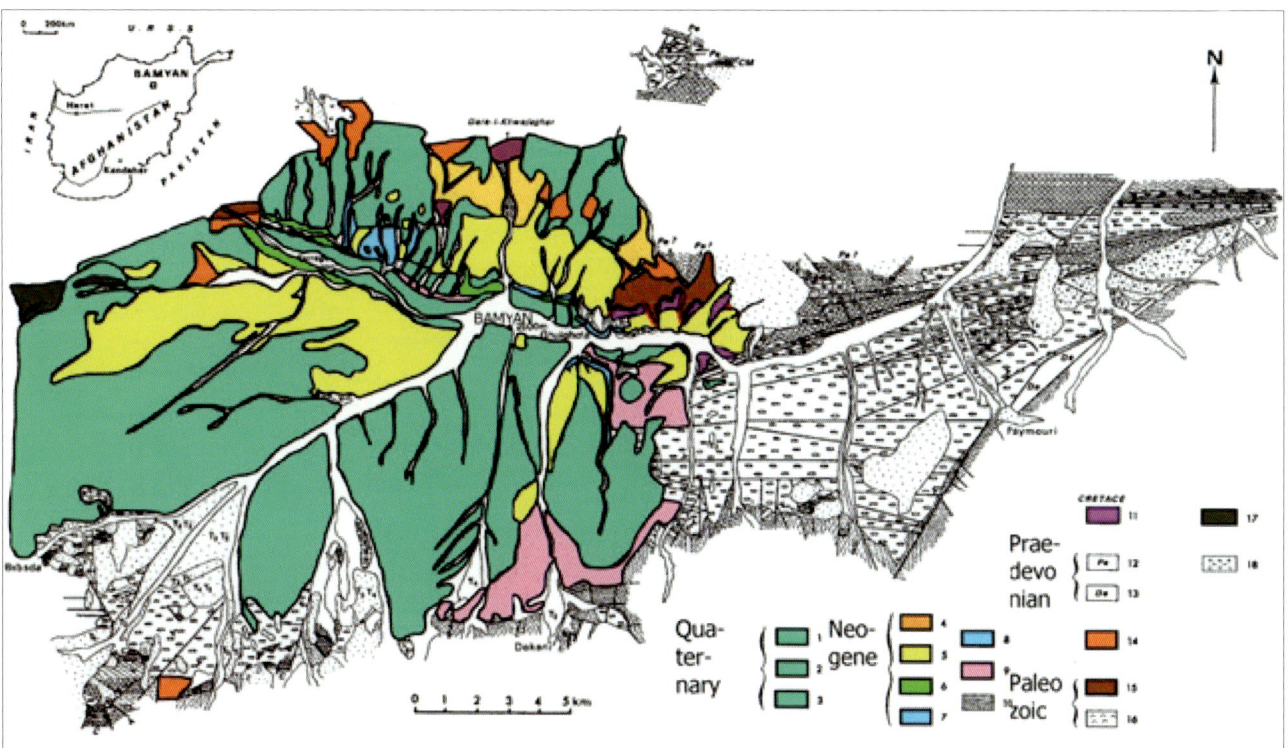

Fig. 4. Geological map of the Bamiyan region (Lang 1968, redrawn in Reineke 2006)

Fig. 5. The cliff with the Buddha niches and the rupestrial settlement

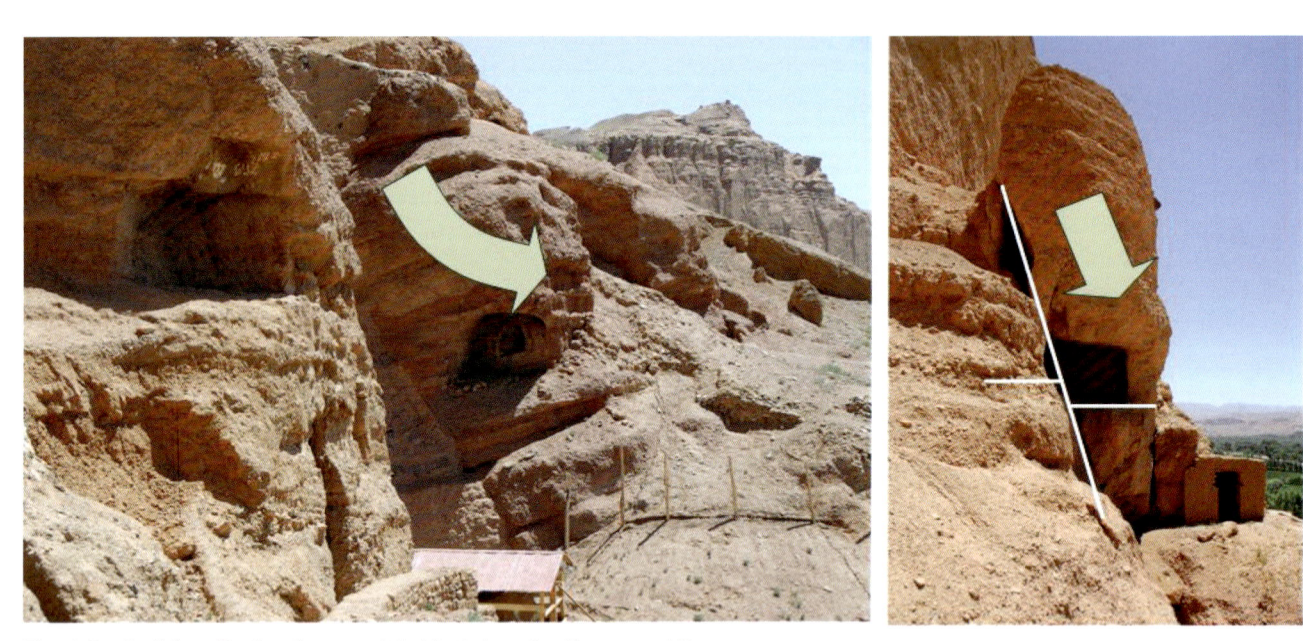

Fig. 6. Rock slides affecting the caves inhabited since the 6th century AD

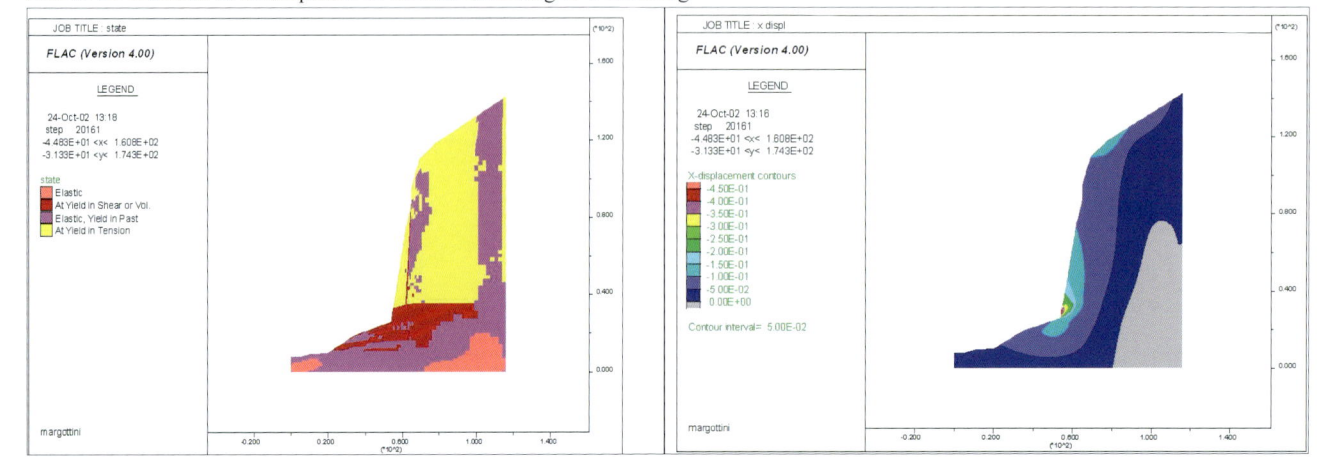

Fig. 7. State and displacement for the cliff of the Eastern Buddha with fracturing reaching the lower part of the cliff and the lower siltstone exhibit no cohesion as consequence of internal fracturing or weathering

climate and weather. Winters are cold and snowy, and summers hot and dry. Mean annual precipitation in Bamiyan is about 163 mm and mean annual temperature 7.4°C.

2. The area belongs geologically to an intramountainous basin, subsequently filled with debris originating from the surrounding mountain ranges (Lang, 1968 and 1971; Reineke, 2006). The neogenic, more or less horizontally bedded sediments can be distinguished into four strata, which are shown in figure 4. Starting with the Eocene Dokani-Formation (> 80 m sandy carbonates and anhydrite) and the Zohak-Formation (> 1000 m red conglomerates), the so called Buddha-Formation is deposited in the Oligocene and is built up by > 70 m yellow-brown pellites, sandstones, conglomerates and some volcanic material. At the top lie the miocenic Ghulghola Formation (> 200 m sandstone, clay and lacustrine carbonates) and the pliocenic Khwaja-Ghar Formation (approx. 200 m travertine, sandstone and conglomerate).

3. The rocks outcropping in the area are mainly conglomerates, with some strata of siltstone that largely slake when wet. The lower part of the cliff is predominantly siltstone, with two main sets of discontinuities spaced every 20–40 cm. The central part of the cliff is mainly conglomerate, well cemented and with a limited number of vertical discontinuities mainly paralleling the profile of the slope.

Figure 5 shows the general view of the site with the main morphological features and the rupestrial settlements. In such a light, the Bamiyan area is likely one of the most magnificent examples of cultural landscape worldwide. Major geomorphological processes include water infiltration, gully erosion, progressive opening of discontinuities in the outer parts of the cliff, weathering and slaking of siltstone levels, toppling of large external portions as well as isolated blocks along the cliff face, occurrence of mud flows probably when the siltstone is saturated, sliding of a large portion of the slope, accumulation of debris at the toe (Margottini, 2004/a).

Large rock slides were detected in the lower part of the cliff, now stabilized, covered by a large amount of debris; the occurrence of such a rock slide is kinematically conditioned by the presence of direct faults, not reaching the upper part of the cliff. With only two large rock slides it seems to affect the rupestrial caves and historical settlements.

3 Identification of the most unstable areas

The explosions of March 2001, apart from demolishing the statues, reduced the stability of the slope, mainly in the outer parts of the niches.

In the Eastern Giant Buddha niche, in addition to the collapse of the statue, there were three minor rock falls from the top of the niche. The blasting also degraded the upper eastern part of the niche where a stairway is located inside the cliff, and the wall between the stairs and the niche is quite thin (about 30–50 cm). This part was the most critically unstable site. The western side, as consequence of an existing buttress, suffered less damage. Nevertheless, a rock fall occurred and some instabilities are also evident in the eastern part.

Major effects in the Western Giant Buddha niche were the collapse of the statue and the consequent instability of the rear of the niche. Investigations of the possible long-term stability conditions of the cliff were computed using the explicit-difference-finite code, FLAC (Itasca Consulting Group, 2000). Considering the Hoek and Brown (1980) shear strength criteria for conglomerate and siltstone, and with a major discontinuity ranging from the middle of the cliff to the middle of the niche (only friction value for shear strength) the deformation of the cliff is relatively low and nowadays it seems to be in a stable condition. Since we consider the fracture in the conglomerate reaching the lower sandstone formation and decrease gradually the cohesion of siltstone due to fracturing/weathering, the cliff becomes unstable when the cohesion is near to nil. In such a situation maximum displacement and vector are at the base of the niche (fig. 7).

In general, the niche and the cliff need holistic stabilization work and not episodic and local intervention. Nevertheless, it must be recognized that one cannot propose a specific stabilization plan at the moment because any intervention has to be specified for the local conditions. At the present stage, it is convenient to set up a general master plan to be locally adapted according to further more specific investigations and data. The master plan includes mainly nails, anchors and grouting that will have a low environmental impact on the site.

Finally, the field data (Colombini & Margottini, 2003/a and 2003/b; Margottini, 2004/a), kinematic analysis, mathematical modeling, caves and crack distribution and detail inspection of the effect of the explosion allow the realization of figures 8 and 9 which show the most endangered sites for both niches. The explosions of March 2001, besides the demolition of the statues, reduced the stability of the shallower parts of the niches. In the Eastern Giant Buddha niche, in addition to the collapse of the statue, three minor rock falls occurred from the top of the niche. Blasting also degraded the strength of the rear of the highest right part of the niche, where a stairway is located inside the cliff and the wall between the stairs and the niche is quite thin (about 30–50 cm). This part presently has the most critical instability (A3 in fig. 8).

In the Western Giant Buddha niche, the major blast effects were the collapse of the statue and the consequent instability of the rear of the niche. A small rock fall occurred at the top of the niche (left side). Probably the greater thickness of the wall between the stairway going up into the cliff and the niche (about 1 m) inhibited the propagation of the blasting effects and resulted in less severe damage. A large crack, about 20-30 cm wide, is present in the corridor at the back of the head of the statue. Figure 9 shows the most critical areas found in the field inspection and/or identified by analyzing the different geological aspects investigated in this paper.

Fig. 8. Identification of the most critical instability areas in the Eastern Giant Buddha niche. The A3 block in the Eastern Giant Buddha niche exhibits the most acute instability

Fig. 9. Identification of the most critical instability areas in the Western Giant Buddha niche. The arrow points to a serious problem inside the niche. Other important areas to secure are A4 and the top of A6

4 Emergency measures taken from 2003–2006

4.1 Overall strategy in the Eastern Giant Buddha niche

After the general strategy for stabilization, a follow up of activities was performed in September 2003, aimed to identify the potential negative evolution of the cliff and niches during winter 2003–2004. The result of a field mission suggested an immediate response to the upper east side of the Eastern Giant Buddha niche where the existing large fissures were widening and the risk of an immediate rock fall was estimated to be very high. This collapse could involve a large part of the upper eastern part of the cliff and then totally destroy the niche (fig. 10).

Emergency consolidation works were immediately planned and carried out in these most critical rock fall-prone areas to avoid any further collapse in the coming winter season, but also to enable conservationists to catalogue and recover the remains of the Buddha statues, still lying on the floor of the niches. The stabilization activities started in October 2003 and continued until the beginning of December 2003 (eastern side). A second operational phase was implemented in the period April – June 2004 (eastern side) and the final one in the period September – November 2006 (western side and top). Figure 11 shows all the study areas and the sites for intervention. Without considering the study phases, the practical activities included four different steps:

1. The installation of a monitoring system, to evaluate in real time any possible deformation of the cliff. Sensors were designed to monitor the entire working area, connected with an alarm system, to do work in safe conditions.
2. The realization of temporary protection includes steel ropes, and two iron beams suitable to avoid lateral deformation inside the niche from unstable cliff and blocks. Among the temporary work, a wire net was installed on the rear side of both niches to allow conservationists to work on the ground floor in safe conditions, just after the consolidation of the niche's wall.
3. The final stabilization of the east side of the niche, west upper side and top. In these areas anchors, nails and grouting were executed in order to reduce the risk of rock fall and collapse; particular care was addressed to the problem of grouting material due to the very high slaking capability of siltstone. The anchors placed in 2003 were pre-grouted to avoid any oxidation and then percolation inside the niche. As from 2004 it was decided to use only stainless steel materials, even if not pre-grouted.
4. Minimization of intervention (anchor/nail head finishing). Anchor and nail heads were designed to be placed slightly inside the rock and then covered by a mortar allowing a total camouflage of the work. A number of tests on the better mixture between cement, local clay/silt and water, to be used for covering the anchor/bolt heads, were also designed and developed in 2003, in cooperation with ICOMOS experts. The results highlight the better chromatic stability and robustness of the mixture.

4.1.1 Implementation on the eastern wall

On the eastern side of the niche a large external block was prone to collapse (fig. 10), and many others in the inner part. A real time monitoring network was planned and realized to monitor the most remarkable cracks and discontinuities. 11 potentiometric crack gauges, 0–50 mm, 4–20 mA, fitted with couplings and connecting cable (total length 350 m) were supplied in the first phase in 2003, with acquisition system (data logger) and data management software. An alarm system to detect any deformation (movement) possibly induced by the works on the main cracks present in this part of the cliff was also installed. The accuracy of the gauges was requested in 0.01 mm, to allow an accurate measurement of even a small deformation. The position of sensors is reported in figure 12.

The temporary protection includes a network of 0.6"

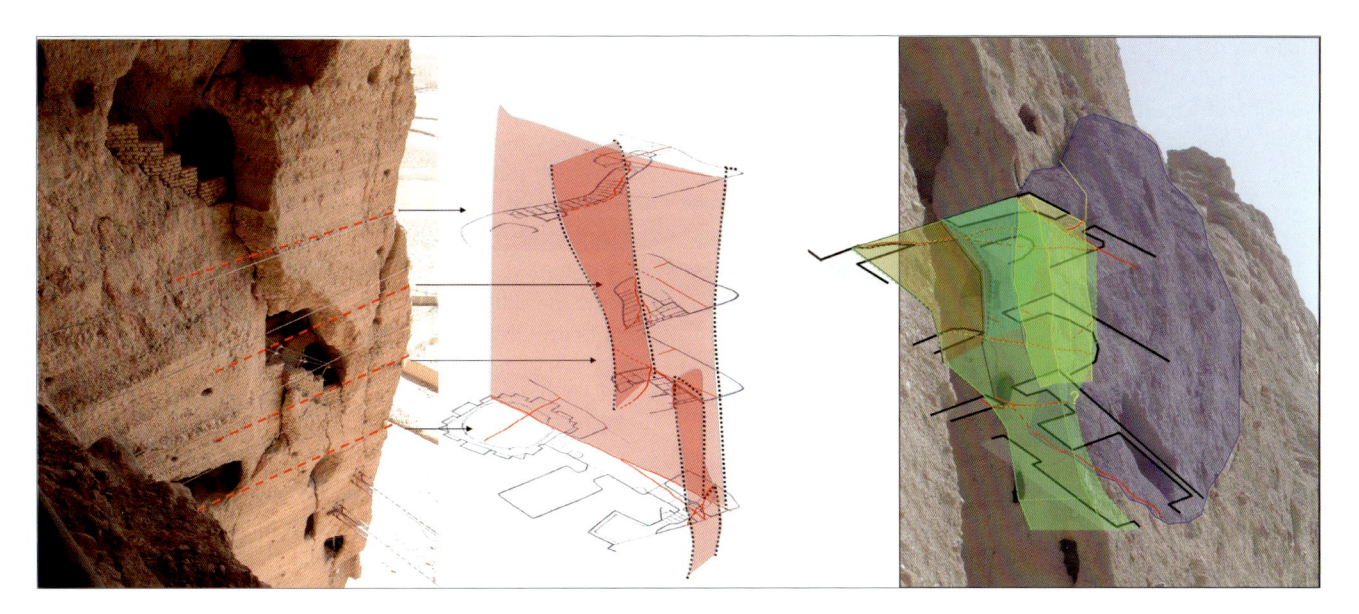

△ Fig. 10. Pattern of existing discontinuities at four different stories (left) and reconstructed unstable blocks in the upper east side of the Eastern Giant Buddha niche (right)

Fig. 11. Localization of the three areas of intervention in the Eastern Giant Buddha niche ▷

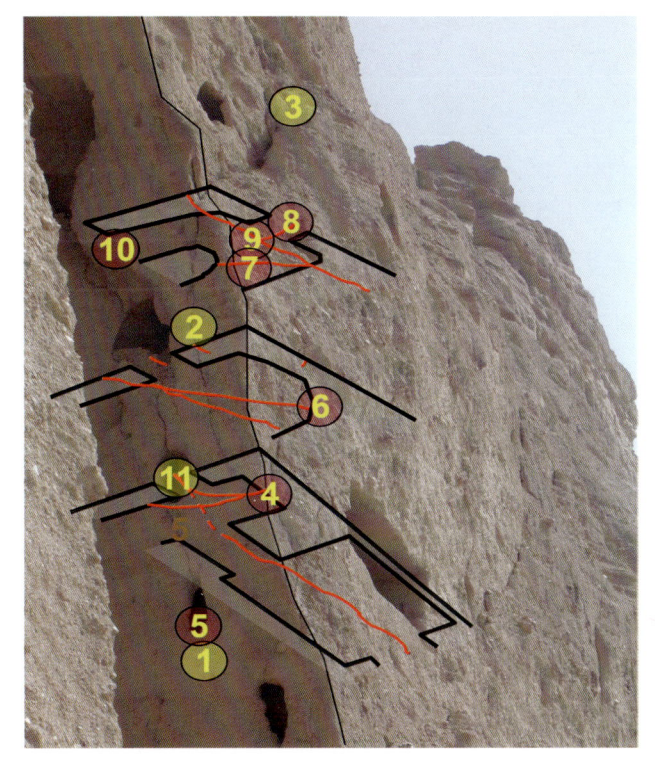

▽ Fig. 12. Distribution of the 11 sensors monitoring the crack's underlining of the most unstable block. On the left a detail of such sensors

diameter steel ropes with a light pre-tensioning, to sustain the most unstable block from possible collapse; steel ropes were fixed to short nails, irregularly placed to avoid any stress concentration in a given line or area. Two temporary beams, located laterally, to support the cliff deformation were designed and executed. Each beam was calculated to offer a resistance of about 40 tons, similar to two designed long anchors. Figure 13 shows the steel ropes and the two iron beams. The temporary protection elements were removed in 2006.

The consolidation was designed by means of passive anchors and nails, correctly grouted. Long anchors have a spacing of about 4 m since they exhibit in this configuration a factor of safety equal to 2, without considering the contribution of nails. Nails will not follow a precise configuration since they have to be designed on site to strengthen the shallower part of the block. Even anchors may have some not-homogeneous distribution, function of internal cavities. Details of calculation are reported in the following figure 14. There we have:

1. the geometrical distribution of load and the assumption for calculation, based on mechanic of rigid mass, and the related moment;
2. the assumption for moment calculation of anchors and the related factor of safety;
3. a comparison test about the possibility to generate toppling according to the static loads and the uniaxial compressive strength of material.

A major concern, at the very beginning, was certainly the understanding of adherence between grouting material and siltstone, a very slaking material. For this reason the choice was addressed to low water release grouting. This can be achieved by mixing water and cement with superplasticizer, a chemical additive suitable to maintain the water inside the mortar. The adopted composition was: $W/C = 1/2.0$ + superplasticizer.

A comparison between the standard strength for anchors and the possible mobilized one was investigated. Since anchors are designed to provide 20 tons each, the borehole shows a diameter of 9 cm and the active length was limited to only 5 m, we have: $2 \times 9 \times 4.5 \times 500 = 14131$ cm^2.

Without direct tests, the adherence between the mortar and the rock is generally calculated between 6 - 8 kg/cm2; assuming 5 Kg/cm2 we have about 70 tons. Then, the assumed strength of anchor is 20 tons that divided by 70 gives a result of about 28% of normal standards; alternatively, the real obtained adherence is about 1.41 kg/cm2, that is much less than the design one of 5 kg/cm2. The resulting factor of safety is about 5, suggesting a reasonable security with the designed loads. Anyway, due to the missing of information on detail geomechanical distribution of discontinuities on the deep, these feasibility assumptions were considered in favor of security.

The correctness of the adopted solution and also of the bounding capacity of grouting mortar is given from the anchor suitability tests, performed in 2004 to understand the bounding capacity of anchors in both siltstone and conglomerate. The design strength of passive anchors was assumed to be 20 tons; for a bounded length, after the major

Fig. 13. The temporary beam (left) and steel rope (right) for the temporary support of the upper eastern part of the Eastern Buddha

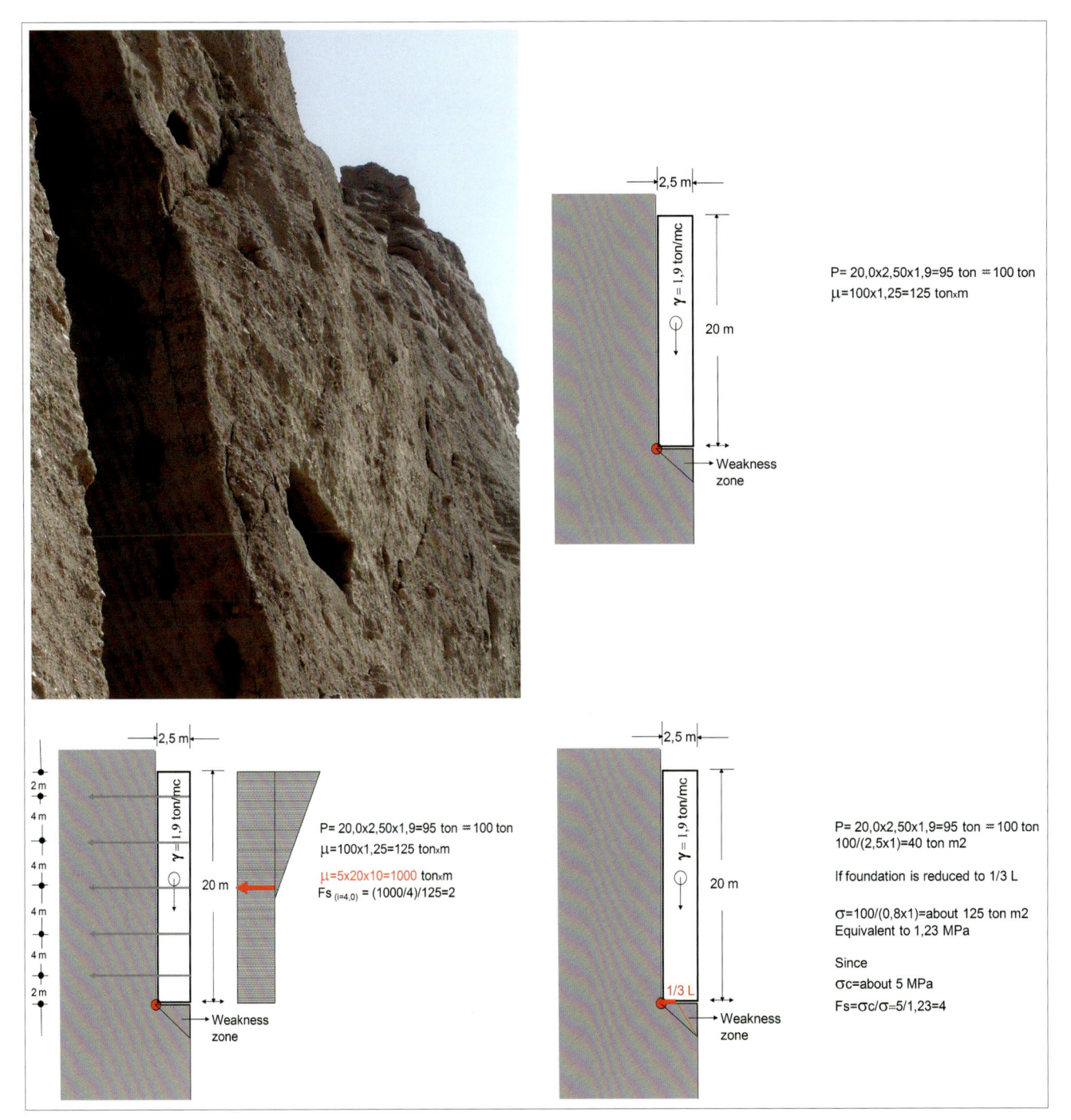

Fig. 14. The external block prone to collapse, the geometrical distribution of load and the assumption for calculation, moment calculation of anchors and the related factor of safety and an evaluation test about the possibility to generate toppling according to the static loads and the uniaxial compressive strength of material

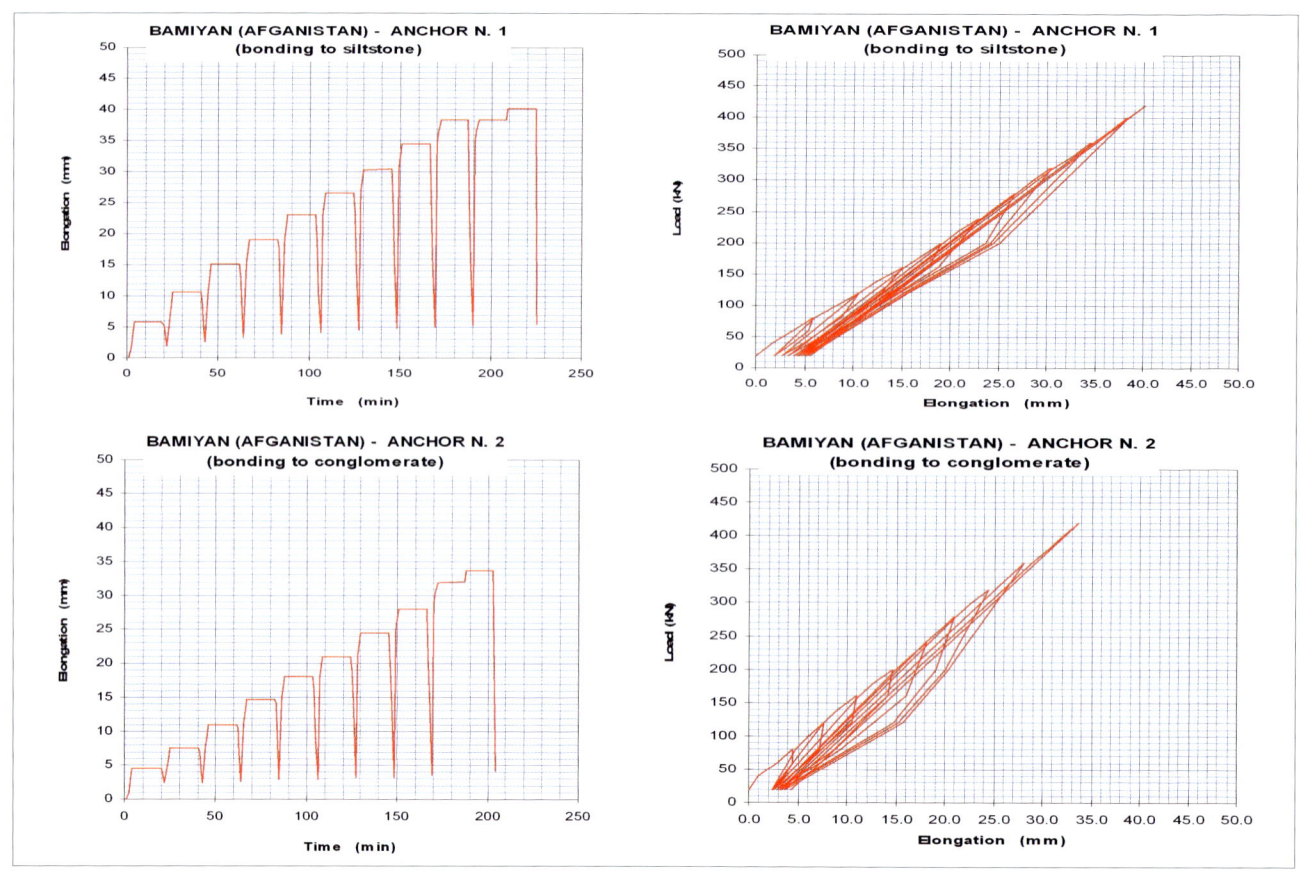

Fig. 15. Anchor suitability tests for siltstone and conglomerate, in 1 m length anchor. The load (kN) and respective time (min) and elongation (mm) are reported showing, up to 40 tons, the uphold of elastic domain and still the missing of any permanent deformation for the tested anchor

discontinuity, at least of 5 meters (about 4 tons per linear meter); the anchor suitability test was performed for 1 meter length, up to 40 tons, close to the yield capacity of steel. Up to this value no remarkable permanent elongation was detected, to demonstrate the correct bounding effect between siltstone and conglomerate and the anchors (fig. 15). These data confirm once more the appropriate choice of superplasticizer as an additive suitable to avoid any slaking phenomena in the siltstone.

In detail, in the eastern part of the niche have been placed:

1. 6 short passive anchors (steel nails, diameter 16 mm, FeB 44K, threaded, with couplers anchor plates and nut - single bar length L = 2.5 m) with diameter = 36 mm and length about 5 m, placed on the internal side of the niche (diamond head rotary machine);
2. 29 stainless steel passive anchors with diameter = 26 mm and a length of 5–10 m (in any case double of the last encountered fissure from the surface), 20 on the internal side and 9 on the external;
3. 17 passive anchors, pre-grouted to avoid oxidation, with diameter = 90 mm and length 15 m, for a total length of 200 m, placed on the external part of the cliff (Anchor bars VSL, diameter 26.5 mm, st 835/1030, pre-injected, with external corrugated sheathing, including plates and nuts).

Apart from the above-mentioned technical aspects, the main difficulty in this project was not only the typology of intervention and the used materials, but how to execute the work, also in a country like Afghanistan with low availability of equipment. Certainly, the first idea was the construction of a scaffolding but, due to the very high probability of rock fall and then the possibility of destroying it, with additional risk for the workers standing below hanging rocks, the economic cost of scaffolding itself, and the approaching winter season 2003–2004, the need to find an alternative solution came up. After a careful investigation and evaluation of possible alternatives for implementing the job, the choice fell on the use of professional climbers.

Climbers, also supported by ground staff, operated directly on the surface, abseiling from the top of the cliff, in a safe area, moving from top to bottom and then in safe condition with respect to any potential rock fall.

Another major difficulty was the calibration of drillings with respect to the existing cavities. In fact, a large number of caves (around 800) and tunnels are located in the cliff constituting a unique example of rupestrial settlement. The selection of drilling then required a detailed investigation of their orientation and inclination to avoid drilling and grouting in the archaeological caves.

As mentioned previously, great attention was paid to the methodology of consolidation. Short (16 mm) and medium (20 mm) length passive anchors (stainless steel) have been realized with a rotary drilling machine, with diamond head, to avoid any possible vibration. Cooling fluid faced the occurrence of slaking-prone siltstone in the presence of water: due to this the usage of water was limited when drilling the conglomerate and a mix of compressed air and water was adopted when discontinuities were detected and when a possible level of siltstone was encountered. Pre-grouted long passive anchors, used only in the first phase of 2003 (26 mm), were realized with a roto-percussion machine and the use of air as flushing medium. From a temporal point of view they were drilled only after the realization of shorter ones and from the further part of the unstable blocks, towards the most critical one. The purpose of small anchors is to sew all together the unstable masses and fix them to the nearby stable geological background. The long anchors have to homogenize this part to the most internal and stable geological material. Direction and inclination of anchors have been defined on site but, in any case, direction of deformation and perpendicularity to discontinuities have been taken into consideration. Temporal execution considered the principle to start from the most stable place to the most unstable. This is to start consolidation from the part where disturbance can better be sustained. In particular, with respect to the internal side of the niche, the lowermost unstable block was approached from the bottom of it to the top. In fact, at the top of the niche there is a hanging block that cannot be touched without having stabilized the lower part. Grouting was made with cement with added superplasticizer to avoid any water release capable of interfering with the slaking siltstone as well as to get the best possible adherence between bar and rock, namely composed as in table 1.

Table 1 Composition of grouting materials for both anchoring and crack filling

	Anchoring grout [kg/m³]	Crack filling motar [kg/m³]
Water	540	300
Cement	1360	610
Sand		1270
Additive Superplasticizer	7	7

In total, for grouting and filling in the eastern wall of the niche, approx. 17 m³ were injected, with 19,000 kg cement divided into:

1. short anchors grouting as 1,200 kg;
2. anchors grouting as 8,200 kg;
3. crack filling (from top) as 9,600 kg;

A minimization of impact was implemented by covering all the anchor steel plates with mortar of suitable color. In such a way it is now very difficult to identify the place where anchors and nails were settled. The composition and color of the mortar was established with the support of technicians from the International Council on Monuments and Sites (ICOMOS). A final arrangement should be provided by a conservator. The following figure presents the results of the activity.

The solution and the techniques adopted as well as the four-step improvement of activities proved to be quite satisfactory, since the monitoring system did not record any remarkable deformation in the unstable blocks throughout the working period (fig. 23).

4.1.2 Implementation on the western wall

The western side of the niche also suffers from the effect of the explosion. The existing buttress was probably constructed to reduce the risk of collapse of this flank which was considered extremely unstable to justify a very massive intervention by a French archaeological expedition in the late 1950s and early 1960s, finally strengthened and mitigated in the impact by the Archaeological Survey of India in the 1970s. Since the buttress seems to be connected to the cliff with bolts, it is possible that the sunk of this structure may produce a horizontal stress towards the external, inducing additional instability as testified by the intervention of ASI (fig. 24, courtesy Prof. Maeda, Kyoto University). Nowadays, there is some evidence (e.g. widening of small cracks) from which it is possible to hypothesize that the buttress hangs from the cliff, rather than sustaining it. This situation might increase the existing damage.

The effects of the March 2001 explosion are mainly evident at the top of the niche, probably where there is a maximum concentration of stress in consequence of the morphology of the niche (arch and pillar, as described in Colombini & Margottini, 2003/a). In particular (Margottini, 2004/b and Margottini, 2006) there is a small pillar (fig. 25) that needs immediate emergency intervention before collapse, possibly inducing large deformation processes to the whole western part of the niche. This part was also completely restored by the Archaeological Survey of India in the late 1970s.

Apart from the planned minor emergency intervention, any large intervention in this area should include geotechnical investigation on the present buttress foundation and, later on, the complete stabilization of the niche. Likely, the manual monitoring system installed in 2003 does not exhibit presently any further deformation of most severe cracks. The present emergency intervention, planned in the upper part of niche, was designed in order not to fix any part of the buttress to the cliff, since its possible evolution has not been investigated.

Also in this situation the general strategy of an emergency intervention was developed in four steps:

1. A monitoring system on the most relevant discontinuities. No. 6 potentiometric crack gauges were newly installed and tested on the west wall of the niche of the Eastern Giant Buddha to monitor the cracks identified as being the most dangerous in the area of the drilling and grouting works. The scheme of installation is reported also in figure 26.
2. A temporary support (fig. 27), by means of:
 a. the two existing long iron beams moved in the upper part of the niche, to provide some lateral support to the niche;
 b. two iron/wood beams capable of supporting any lateral deformation of the small pillar; the construction details of the beam were finally adapted with the materials actually available in Afghanistan;
 c. steel ropes bounding completely the pillar and cliff; 13

△   Fig. 16
Installation of temporary struts. During the installation the strut is fixed at the top of the cliff, in the safe zone

Fig. 19   △
Execution of nails at the roof of the niche

◁   Fig. 17
Final consolidation with the use of professional climbers and large rotary machine

Fig. 20   ▷
Execution of nails with rotary machine and diamond head

▽   Fig. 18
Execution of nails for the stabilization of unstable blocks

Fig. 21   ▽
Detail of execution of nails from inside the caves by means of a small rotary machine and a diamond head

Fig. 22. Covering anchor heads with proper mortar (test site)

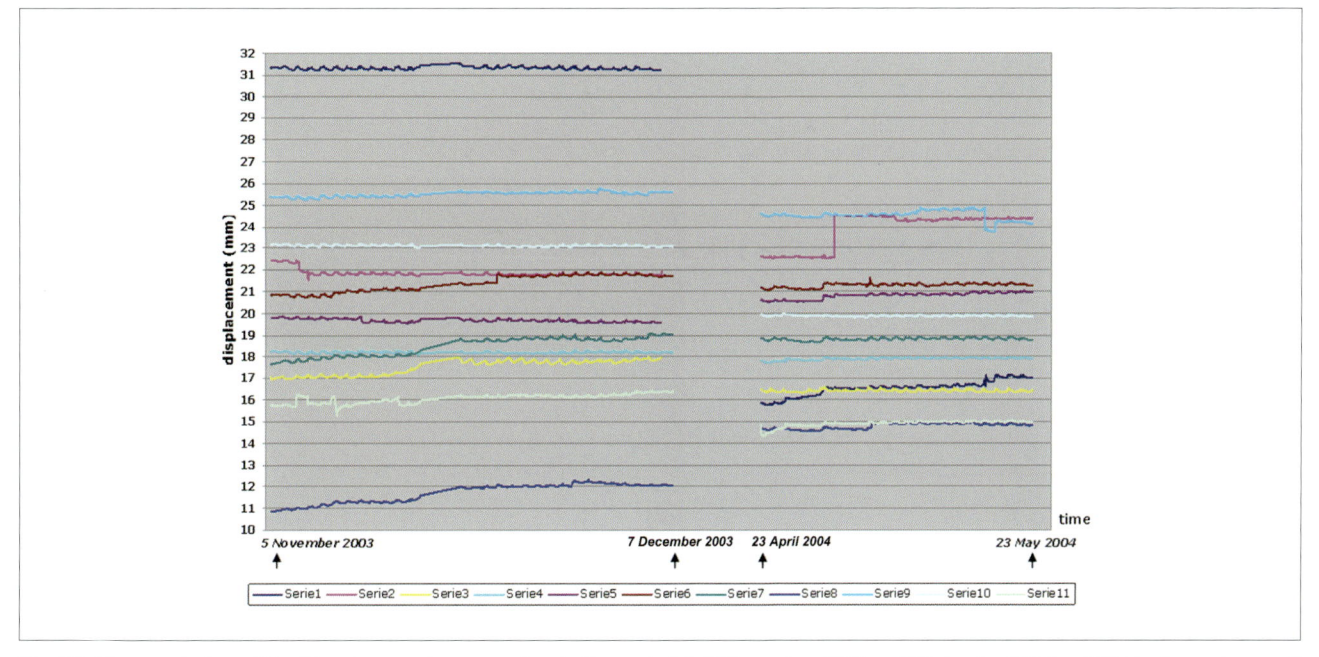

Fig. 23. Time evolution of the 11 extensometers operating in the period 5–7 December 2003 and 23 April – 23 May 2004 in the eastern wall of the niche, and showing no remarkable movements on the cliff. Some minor steps were caused by climbers, who hit the gauge placed on the cliff

Fig. 25. The most unstable element (pillar) on the western side of Eastern Giant Buddha niche ▷

▽ Fig. 24. Consolidation works done by the Archaeological Survey of India in 1969 (Courtesy of Prof. Maeda)

no. temporary steel cables have also been installed on the western side of the niche. Four of them were fixed through steel bolts on the inner/outer wall of the niche, whereas nine cables were circular cables embracing horizontally (6 no.), or vertically (3 no.), the rock pillar and the septum at elev. 2570.
3. Emergency intervention includes nails and grouting as follows:
a. Prior to starting the drilling works the large cracks in the area of the pillar at the left wall of the Eastern Giant Buddha were thoroughly filled in and grouted with cement. After the preliminary caulking, the main fissures were filled in using 0.96 m³ of low water-release cement grout, with some 1,200 kg of cement. Grout composition utilized was, as usual, C:W= 0.5 with superplasticizer.
b. For the drilling operations, a diamond rotary system, 50 mm diameter, has been adopted with the aim of limiting interferences as far as possible, produced by vibratory effects, to the limited stability of the structure in this area. A total of no. 12 stainless steel passive anchors, diameter 20.0 mm, have been installed, with a total drilled length of 52.4 m for these 12 anchors. In detail, nine of these nails connect the pillar internally, in both directions parallel to the face and perpendicular to it to create a robust net; two short passive nails located below and above the critical pillar, with depth less than the rear side plane, where a large crack was detected after the removal of fragments in the lower caves behind the feet of the statue. One passive anchor parallel to the surface aimed at stabilizing the upper gallery where a large fissure is present.

c. Low water release grouting in the boreholes, maintaining the composition of water and cement successfully adopted on the eastern side, which includes: W/C = 1/2.0 + superplasticizer. Approx. 2.0 m³ were grouted for the nail installation with 2,400 kg of cement.
4. A minimization of impact follows the same criteria established for the eastern side.

In the western wall of the niche, the total grout for grouting and filling was estimated at approx. 3 m³, with 3,600 kg cement (cracks and anchors). As mentioned before, the correctness of grouting was demonstrated by the suitability test for the anchors, that do not differentiate the anchor bounded to the conglomerate from the one bounded to siltstone, in which slaking is highly possible.

Figure 28 shows the distribution of the anchors as well as the chronological sequence of them. The latter is quite important to avoid disturbance to the most critical part of the cliff without having stabilized the boundary conditions. In addition, it provides further protection against water infiltration potentially slaking the siltstone as well as generating additional pore pressure.

4.1.3 *Implementation on the upper part*
In the upper part of the niche it was decided to install three permanent stainless steel passive anchors, 12 m long, sub-horizontal, with the following purposes:
1. to monitor the tensional state of the rock masses by means of 10 strain gauges placed in two of the anchors;

Fig. 26. The location or potentiometric crack gauges for discontinuity monitoring and alarm; in green are external sensors and red are internal to the cave

Fig. 27. The temporary support necessary for a secure execution of the work in the western wall: two long iron beams replaced in the upper part of the niche, the short iron resp. wood struts for local support and the steel ropes

Fig. 28. Distribution of the anchors and their chronological sequence ▷

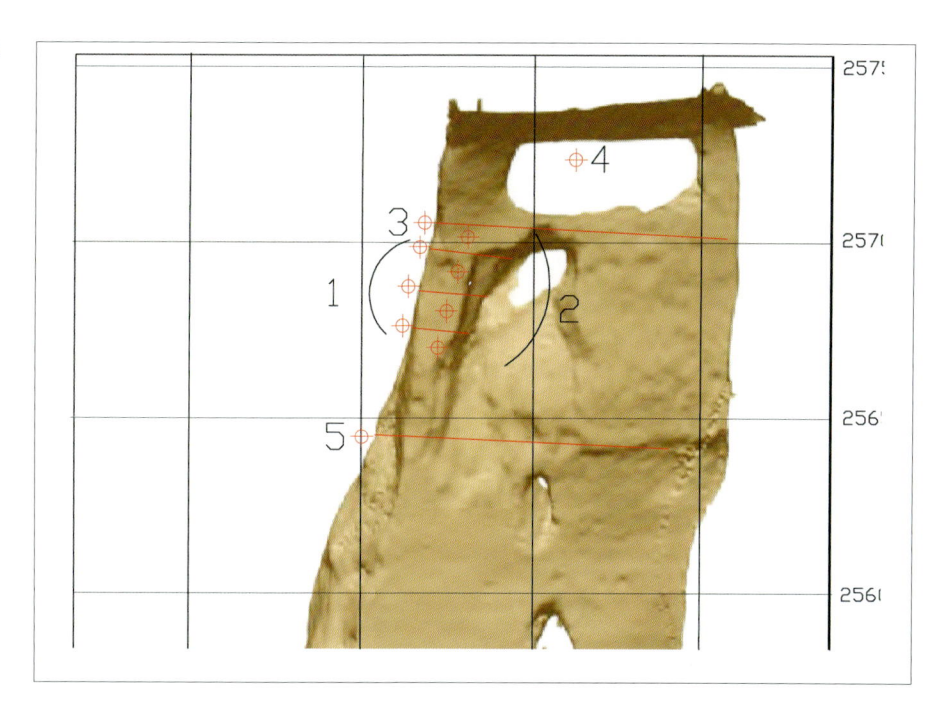

Table 2 Characteristics of the installed strain gauges

Transducer Type	Vibrating wire
Standard range	3.000 microstrain
Sensitivy	1.0 microstrain
Accuracy	0.1 % FS
Non linearity	Less than 0.5 % FS
Temperature range	-30°C
Gauge length	

Fig. 29. Drilling for the setting of nails ▷

◁ Fig. 30. Position of anchors on top of the niche. The yellow ones are monitored with 10 strain gauges

2. to grout the medium part of the cliff to avoid water infiltration within the niche during snowmelt or prolonged rainfall.

The position of these long anchors is shown in the following figure 30.

540 l of cement mix were utilized for the grouting of the anchors (600 kg of cement). Open vertical fissures, reaching downwards in the niche, were intercepted in the three boreholes at depths of up to 8 m (anchor no 39) and 9 m (anchor 41).

Anchors no. 39 and 41 were instrumented with the installation of a series of five spot weldable strain gauges (fig.31) in each anchor. The characteristics of these instruments are described below. The cables connecting the sensors were conveyed into small grooves to suitable steel boxes located in the niche, where readings can be taken utilizing the portable datalogger with LCD display.

3.1.4 Location and types of anchors and nails on the Eastern Giant Buddha Niche

In conclusion, in the Eastern Giant Buddha niche 64 passive anchors and nails were installed, for a total length of 443.5 m. The total amount of grouting was established in 19.7 m^3 of cement grout with 24,000 kg of cement.

The following figure 32 summarizes all the long passive anchors and nails and the related location.

The following table 3 reports type and length of each anchor and nail previously described.

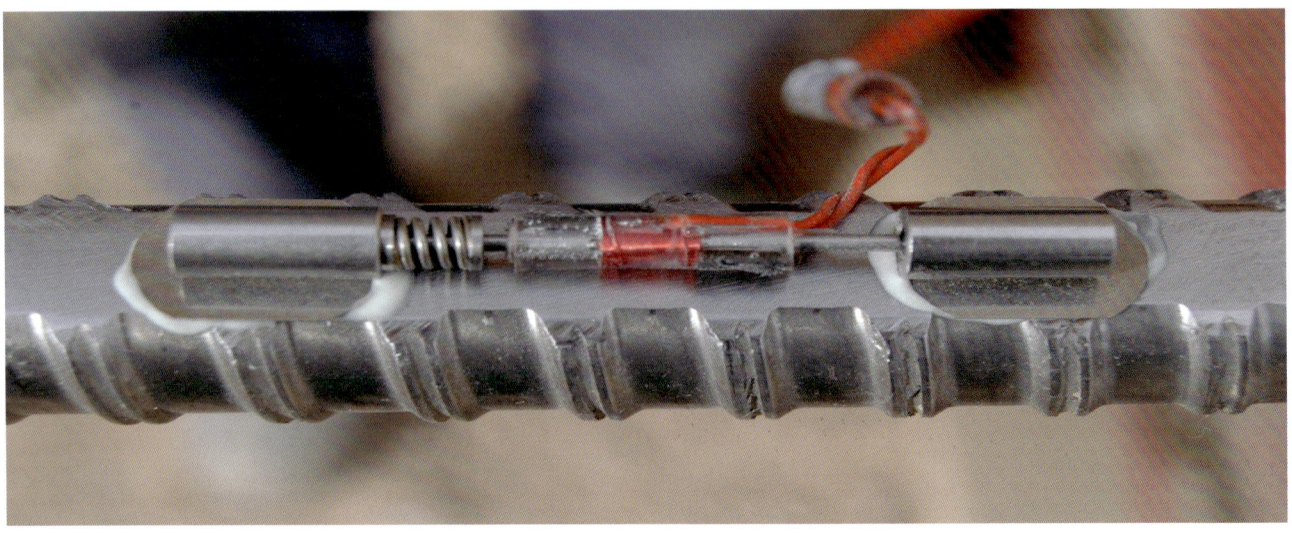

Fig. 31. Detail of a strain gauge

4.2 First interventions in the Western Giant Buddha niche
Despite the destruction of the statue, the Western Giant Buddha niche did not suffer extensively as a consequence of the explosion (Margottini, 2006). Emergency intervention includes (fig. 33):

a. grouting of the large fissure placed in the corridor, rear side of the niche,
b. other minor sites to consolidate.

The grouting of the large crack at the rear of the niche was carried out from the inside as well as from the outside (top of the cliff). Initially, the fissure was grouted and closed in the internal part of the niche, in order to protect the niche from cement infiltration and leaching from the top. Small pipes were required inside the cement to avoid internal overpressure. From the top of the cliff, inclined drills were performed and, when the fissure was encountered in the perforation, it was grouted with the same mixture of cement and superplasticizer described in Margottini (2003/a). Major attention was required for the execution of drillings on top of the cliff, due to the possible existence of land mines, even after a complete de-mining of the site as a result of rainfall run off.

Other minor interventions were required in two small sites, as reported in the design of figure 36. The possible risk of collapse, even for small pieces of rock, was completely avoided.

5 Conclusion

The present paper describes all the emergency interventions performed in Bamiyan for the consolidation of the niches and unstable blocks resulting from the explosions in March 2001, which were aimed at destroying the 6th-century giant Buddha statues.

The effect of the explosions was quite dramatic: the two statues totally collapsed and also some small parts of the niches fell down and mainly a large part of the Eastern

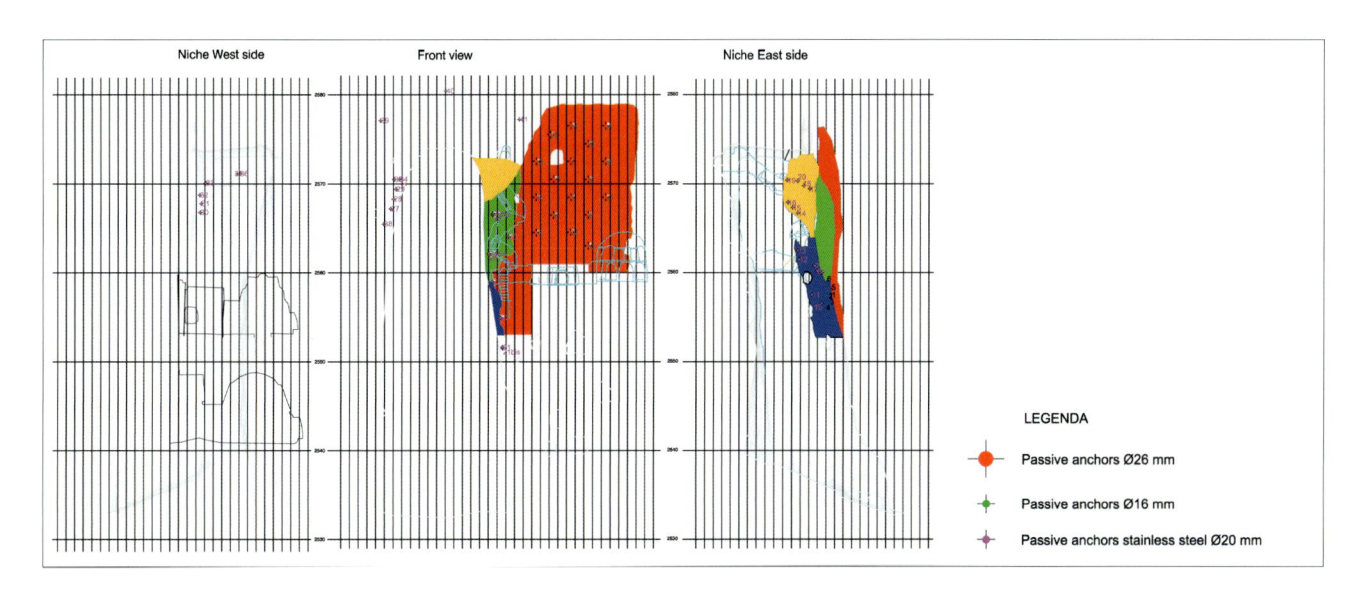

△ Fig. 32. Typology, position and length of executed anchors and nails (red is for passive anchors, pre-grouted, with diameter = 26 mm and length 15 m.; violet is for stainless steel passive anchors with diameter = 26 mm and a length 5–10 m.; green is for short passive anchors with diameter = 16 mm and length about 5 m, placed on the internal side of the niche (topographic data from Pasco, 2003)

Table 3 ▷
Type and length of each installed anchor and nail (for numbers refer to fig. 32)

anchor	"drill Ø 90mm Dywidag Ø 26/50mm"
n°	m
A	7.50
B	7.50
C	7.50
D	15.00
E	15.00
F	15.00
G	15.00
H	7.50
I	7.50
L	7.50
M	7.50
N	15.00
O	15.00
P	15.00
Q	7.50
R	7.50
S	7.50

anchor	"drill Ø 50mm Gewi Ø 16mm"
n°	m
1	4.20
2	5.15
3	5.20
4	5.30
5	4.85
6	4.50

anchor	"drill Ø 50mm stainless steel Ø 20mm"
n°	m
7	4.50
8	4.50
9	4.50
10	4.60
11	3.30
12	1.30 (Gewi Ø 16mm)
12 bis	5.00
13	5.00
14	7.00
15	7.50
16	7.50
17	7.50
18	7.50
19	7.50
20	7.50
21	3.00
21 bis	3.50
22	5.50
23	6.50
24	3.70
24 bis	5.00
25	4.50
26	2.50
26 bis	7.00

anchor	"drill Ø 50mm stainless steel Ø 20mm"
n°	m
27	1.50
28	1.60
29	2.10
30	4.00
31	4.30
32	4.60
33	5.00
34	6.00
35	8.30
36	5.00
37	2.00
38	8.00
39	12.00
40	12.00
41	12.00

Fig. 34a

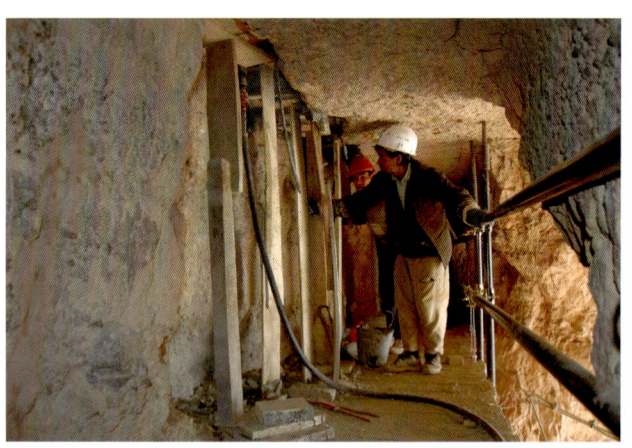

△ Fig. 33. Emergency intervention in the West Giant Buddha niche (topographic data from PASCO, 2003)

△ Fig. 34b ▽ Fig. 34c

◁ Fig. 34a
Large crack in the corridor at the rear of the niche before the grouting

◁ Fig. 34b
Large crack in the corridor at the rear of the niche during the grouting

◁ Fig. 34c
Large crack in the corridor at the rear of the niche after the grouting

Fig. 35. Detail of the grouting from the top of the cliff

Fig. 36. Drilling the lower part of the niche

193

Giant Buddha Niche was close to collapsing. UNESCO was prompt to undertake an emergency intervention to secure the remains of such an outstanding cultural heritage and, thanks to the generous financial support from the Government of Japan, work started in November 2003.

The activities were developed according to the following general scheme:

1. engineering geological study of the site, including laboratory testing and field work (the first were conducted in Europe in few samples and the latter conditioned in their execution by the presence of land mines);
2. installation of a high precision monitoring system;
3. realization of a temporary support infrastructure, to keep the blocks stable at limit equilibrium, also during the execution of works;
4. execution of the consolidation work, with professional climbers to avoid any activities below the hanging and unstable blocks, with a system of small and long passive anchors and grouting;
5. minimization of impact of anchor heads, with a mixture of special mortar, investigated in detail with the support of ICOMOS experts.

The result was quite satisfactory for an area that is slowly coming out from decades of war, and in which it was necessary to adopt the maximum of professional judgment in identifying weak points and limits in knowledge and, in the meantime, to adopt technologies capable of solving the problems in a very short time and in safe conditions.

After the investigations started in September 2002 and the practical intervention of October – December 2003, March 2004 and October – December 2006, the cliff and niche of the Eastern Giant Buddha (the most critical part) are now more stable and the risk of collapse has almost been prevented. The niche of the Western Giant Buddha has also been protected from water infiltration. Further work will be needed in the future, especially at the rear of both niches, but at least the major risk of collapse, including also the few remains not destroyed by the Taliban, has now been averted.

References

Burnes A.: *Travel into Bokhara*, London 1834

Colombini V., Margottini C. (2003/a): *Reducing the most critical rock fall-prone areas in the Buddhas niches in Bamiyan (Central Afghanistan)*, UNESCO Report July 2003

Colombini V., Margottini C. (2003/b): *Buddhas niches in Bamiyan valley: Emergency measures in autumn 2003, to permit future consolidation*, UNESCO Report Sept. 2003

Hoek E., Bray J.W.: *Rock slope engineering*, Institution of Mining and Metallurgy, Third edition revise 1981, Reprinted

Hoek E., Brown J.W.: *Empirical strength criterion for rock masses*, J. Geotechnical Engineering Div. A.S.C.E., Vol. 106, n. GT9 (1980), pp. 1013–1035

ITASCA Consulting Group: *Fast lagrangian analysis of continua*, vs. 4.0. Minneapolis, Minnesota, USA 2000

Lang, J.: *La serie neogene de Bamian (Afghanistan)*, C.R.Acad.Sci., 266, 26 p.2383–2384, Paris 1968

Lang, J.: *Bassins intramontagneux néogènes de l'Afghanistan,* Central- Rev. Geogr. Phys. Geol. Dynam., Paris, 1972 (2), 14, 4, pp. 415–427

Margottini C. (2003/a):*The geomorphological instability of the Buddha niches and surrounding cliff in Bamiyan valley (Central Afghanistan)*, UNESCO Report June 2003

Margottini C. (2003/b): *The Buddha niches in the Bamiyan valley (Central Afghanistan): instability problems and restoration plans in the UNESCO intervention*, Journal of the Japanese Landslide Society, Vol. 450, n. 3 (2003), pp. 246–249 (in Japanese)

Margottini C. (2004/a): *Instability and geotechnical problems of the Buddha niches and surrounding cliff in Bamiyan valley*, Central Afghanistan Landslides, no.1. January

Margottini C. (2004/b): *Definition of 2004 activities for implementing the emergency consolidation of Eastern Giant Buddha and for beginning the preservation of Western Giant Buddha from geological hazards*, UNESCO report March 2004

Margottini C. (2006): *Definition of 2006 activities for implementing the emergency consolidation of Large Eastern Buddha and for beginning the preservation of Large Western Buddha*, UNESCO Report August 2006

Margottini C. (2007): *Engineering geology and cultural heritages: the conservation of remaining Bamiyan Buddhas (Central Afghanistan)*, in: Sassa K, Fukuoka H. Wang F. and Wang G. (eds.): *Progress in Landslide Science*, Springer-Verlag Berlin Heidelberg 2007

Margottini C., Colombini V., Crippa C. Tonoli G. : *Emergency intervention for the Geo-Mechanical conservation of the Niches of Bamiyan Buddhas (Northern Afghanistan)*, in: Sassa K, Fukoka H., Wang F. Wang G. (editors): *Landslides – Risk analysis and sustainable disaster management*, Springer-Verlag Berlin-Heidelberg 2005

Reineke T.: *Environmental Assessment of the Bamiyan Valley in the Central Highlands of Afghanistan*, in: University of Aachen: *Bamiyan Masterplan Campaign 2005*, Aachen 2006

PASCO: *Buddhas laser scanner project*, 2006

Turner K, Schuster R: *Landslides, investigation and mitigation*, Special report, Transportation research board, National Research Council, 247, Washington 1996

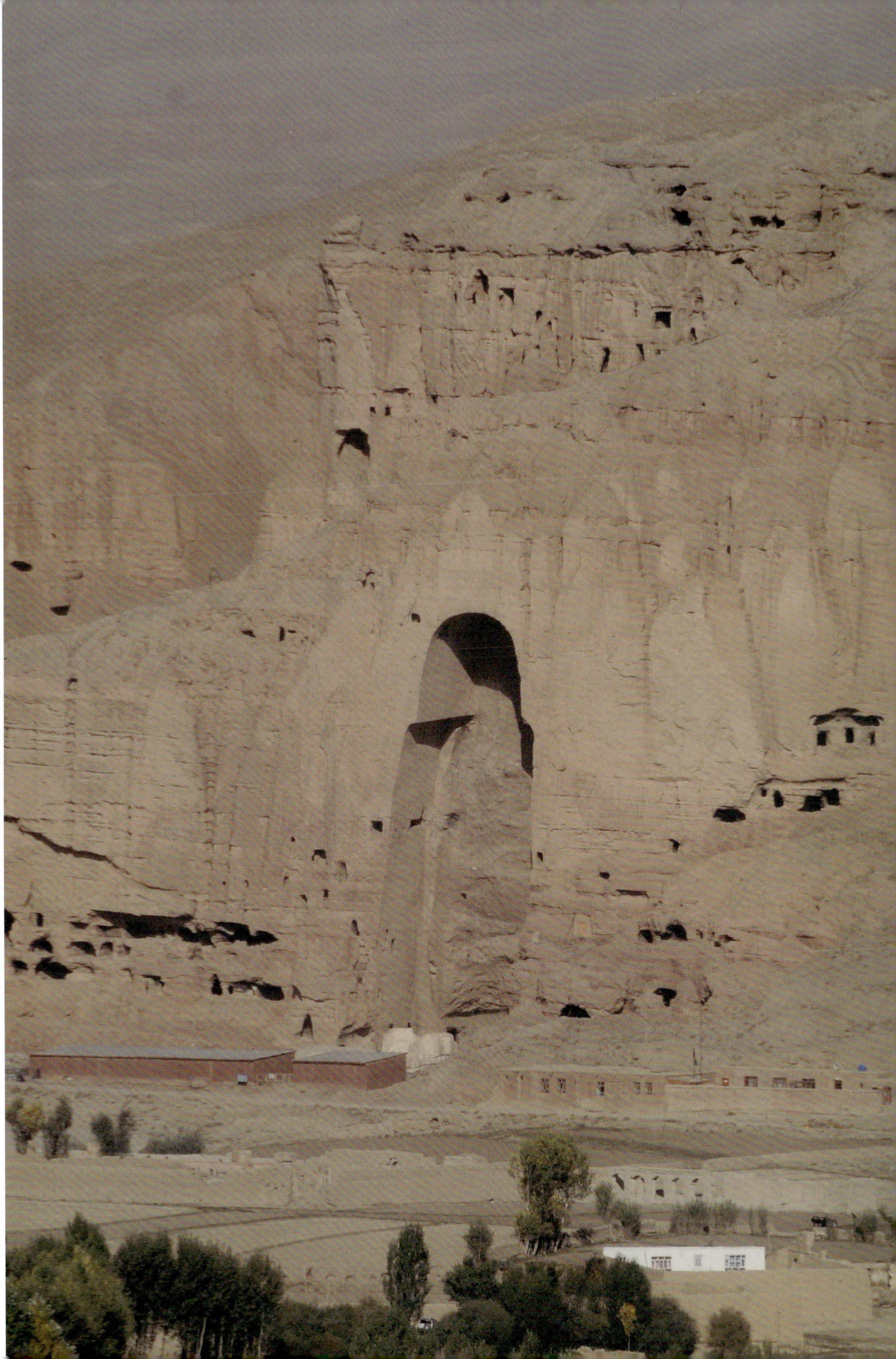

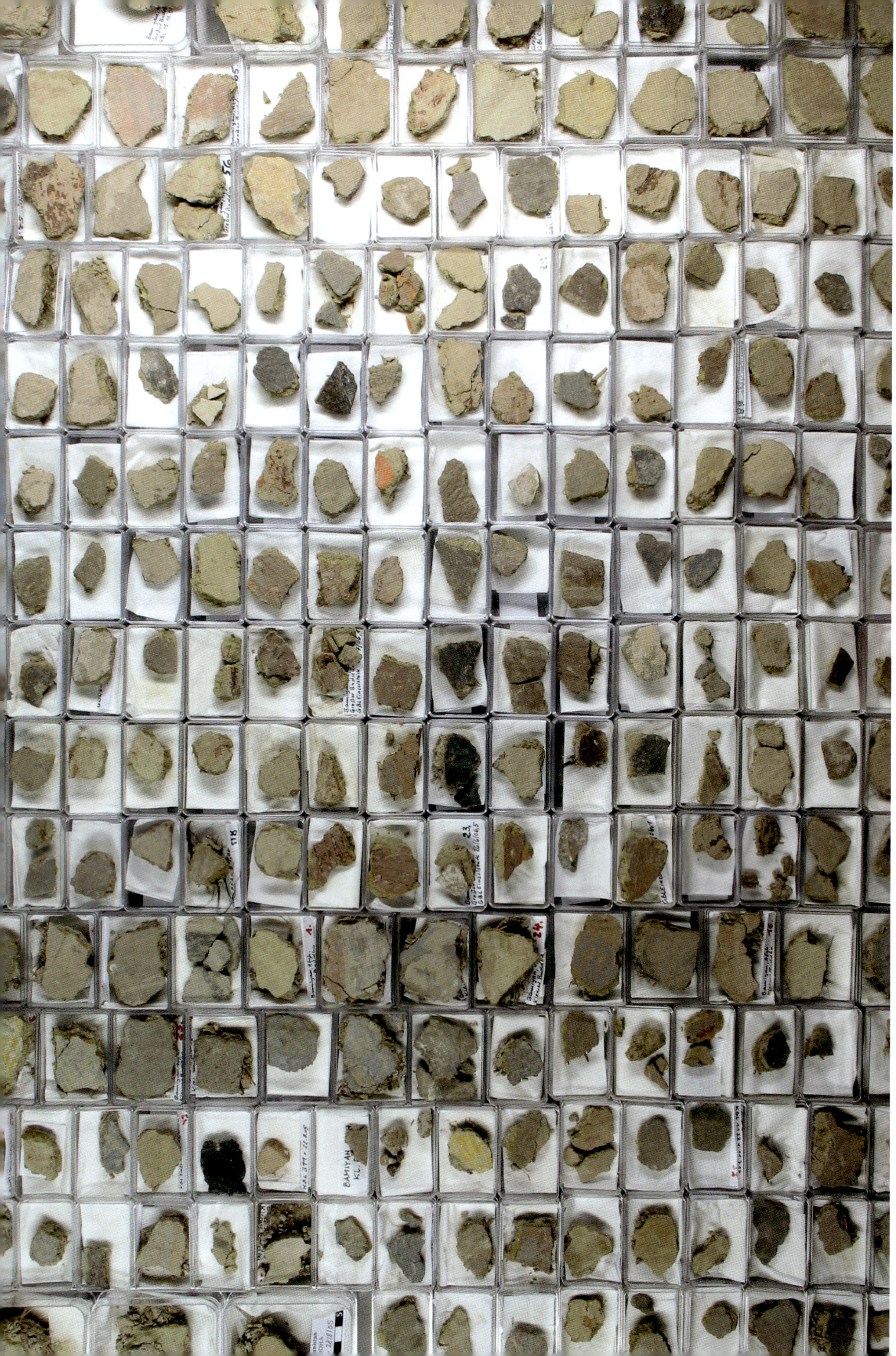

V THE TU MUNICH RESEARCH PROJECT ON FRAGMENTS OF THE GIANT BUDDHAS OF BAMIYAN (2007–2009)

Introduction

Although the Buddha statues of Bāmiyān have frequently been admired and discussed, their manufacturing techniques and their original appearance were never investigated in detail. Art historical observations only concerned their shape and style. Visitors with archaeological interest mentioned peculiar details, but even when a comprehensive restoration was executed by the Indo-Afghan co-operation in 1969–78, no systematic technical examination was carried out.

Between 2004 and 2008 about 10'000 fragments were recovered from the rubble at the feet of the statues. The fragments are the only clue to find out how the two statues were made, which materials were used and how their appearance changed over time. Therefore scientific analyses in-depth were carried out on the fragments.

From the large number of fragments, tiny pieces were selected by conservator Edmund Melzl for analytical purposes. Between autumn 2005 and autumn 2007, several hundreds of samples were brought to Munich allowing investigations on a large scale. A research team, financed by ICOMOS and the UNESCO, was established at the Technische Universität München (TUM), Lehrstuhl für Restaurierung, Kunsttechnologie und Konservierungswissenschaft (chair of restoration, art technology and conservation science).

The project team at the Technische Universität München and in Bāmiyān

The study group in Munich consisted of the conservators:
Erwin Emmerling – head of the project
Stephanie Pfeffer – supervision of examination, project organisation; examination of paint layers
Maruchi Yoshida – set up of a data base
Catharina Blänsdorf – examination of paint layers, identification of pigments; organisation
Additionally six students have contributed to the work with term papers concerning special questions:
Laura Thiemann and Eva Höfle – investigation on clay layers
Monica Reiserer and Nicole Wagner – investigation on paint layers
Maximilian Knidlberger – identification of pigments
Anna Rommel – translation of Russian texts on Central Asian painting techniques
The studies were supported by observations during the conservation work on-site. From the persons involved there, most important for the research project were:
Edmund Melzl – collecting of findings; fragment catalogue and photographic documentation
Bert Praxenthaler – observations on the Eastern Buddha in 2008, collecting of fragments
Between June 2007 and January 2009, examinations in various fields could be done. Besides the team at the TUM, external experts have been involved for special analyses.

Table 1 Overview of samples from the Giant Buddha statues

Material	Number of fragments from Eastern Buddha	Number of fragments from Western Buddha
clay with paint layers	102	173
clay without paint	2	2
pebbles from undercoat		1 box
chaff and hair from clay layers	46 samples	24 samples
wood from anchoring system	1 splinter	320 splinters 7 complete pegs
piece of rope		14
textile fragment		1
leather rags		2
leather pouch, small		1
stone fragment		1 (from junction of arm, blackened and partly molten by explosion)
white filling from Indian restoration		1

Table 2 Reference samples from Bāmiyān

Material	Origin	Amount
stone material	Buddha cliff face	2 boxes
clay layers	Kakrak Buddha	1 box
clay layers from the niches behind the Buddha statues	Eastern Buddha Western Buddha	3 samples 3 samples
loam from surrounding area	Keule kotschak Regischad Surch-kul Khami-Kalak	1 box 1 box 1 box 1 box
wooden pegs	niche I behind Western Buddha maybe from niche behind Western Buddha	3 pegs 1 wooden piece
wood samples (leaves, twigs)	Bāmiyān and surrounding	4 tree species
piece of rope	Bāmiyān bazaar	1 piece
hair of sheep, goats, donkey	Bāmiyān Valley	about 30 strands of hair

Table 3 Numbering system for fragments and samples

Numbering system by E. Melzl	GB – Western Buddha KB – Eastern Buddha	L – clay layers Ha – hair Hä – chaff F – rock
Numbering system TUM	ID	101 - 199 – PLM 201 - 299 – cross section 301 - 399 – XRD 401 - 499 – EDX 501 - 599 – quantitative XRD 601 - 699 – analysis of binders 701 - 799 – microscopic wood identification 801 - 899 – identification of hair 901 - 999 – ^{14}C radio carbon dating 1001 - 1099 – particle size measurements

Sample material

The samples brought to Munich are tiny pieces of the clay layers of the Buddha statues, comprising clay plasters with paint; plant parts, chaff, hair and pebbles from the undercoat and finish coat; splinters of wood and pieces of rope from the anchoring system of the clay layers on the Western Buddha. Stone samples were not collected. An overview is given in table 1.

Additionally, material from Bāmiyān and the surrounding area was collected by E. Melzl as reference samples. The samples are listed in table 2.

Investigations

The aim of the examination of the fragments was to identify the materials, to investigate the technique of manufacture and, as far as possible, to date the materials and to detect historical changes. The investigations comprised the following aspects:

- examination of the clay materials;
- identification of fibres from the ropes;
- identification of wood species on the wooden pegs;
- identification of corn species on the organic additives in the clay layers;
- identification of hair from the clay layers;
- AMS ^{14}C dating of organic materials;
- examination of paint layer sequence;
- identification of pigments;
- identification of binders.

Edmund Melzl has catalogued about 10.000 fragments of the Buddha statues found since 2004, using a numbering system (altogether 4757 entries until end of 2008). In this numbering system the first two letters indicate the statue, the following the type of material (see table 3).

Most of the fragments sent to Munich for examination are tiny pieces additionally retrieved from the rubble and not included in Melzl's catalogue. Thus a new numbering system was established in Munich using sample ID numbers and additional number codes to indicate the type of investigation carried out.

Analyses performed by external experts

Clay layers: Layer sequence and identification of materials
Two different methods have been used to characterise the clay materials of the clay layers: Quantitave XRD (x-ray diffraction) was performed by Albert Gilg, TUM, Chair of Engineering Technology, together with Eva Höfle. Laser scattering spectrometry was done by Laura Thiemann with support of Steffen Krause and Christina Schwarz at the University of the Federal Armed Forces, Institut für Wasserwesen, Munich. First measurements were carried out with the support of Retsch Technology GmbH, 42781 Haan, Germany.

Identification of wood species
The identification of wood species on the fragments was done by means of microscopic wood properties. First analyses were made by Dietger Grosser, Ludwig-Maximilians Universität München, in 2002. In 2008, twenty samples were analysed by Hans Georg Richter, Zentrum Holzwirtschaft at the University of Hamburg.

Reference material from Bāmiyān was identified using macroscopic phenomena (leaves, bark, wood) by Hans-Jürgen Tillich and D. Podlech, Ludwig-Maximilians Universität München, Faculty of Biology.

Identification of fibres and organic additives in the clay layers
The material of the ropes and the organic additives of the straw mud layer (plant parts, residues of threshing, grass) were analysed by Hans-Jürgen Tillich, Ludwig-Maximilians-Universität, Munich, Faculty of Biology, with the help of reference material from Bāmiyān (different corn species, *Dom-i-shutur* plant, modern ropes).

Identification of hair in the clay layers
The wisps of hair contained in abundance in the clay layers were analysed by Jan Grunwald, Landeskriminalamt, Munich, using reference samples from different animals (goat, sheep and donkey) in Bāmiyān, collected by Edmund Melzl.

AMS ^{14}C dating of organic materials
^{14}C AMS radio carbon dating was done in three parts. Georges Bonani from the ETH (Eidgenössische Technische Hochschule) Zurich, Institute for Particle Physics, analysed two samples in May 2004 and seven samples in January 2009. Pieter Grootes, Matthias Huels and Marie-Josée Nadeau from the Leibniz Laboratory for Radiometric Dating and Isotope Research, Christian Albrecht University Kiel analysed 13 samples in December 2004.

Pigments and binders
The layer sequences were analysed at the TUM. For pigment determination mainly polarised light microscopy (PLM) was used. For additional questions external experts were involved. Inorganic materials were analysed by Klaus Rapp, Munich (XRD, ESEM) and Vojislav Tucic, Bayerisches Landesamt für Denkmalpflege, Munich (XRD, XRF); Sonngard Hartmann, Susanne Greiff, Roman Germanic Central Museum Mainz (Micro XRF).

Ilaria Bonaduce and Maria Perla Colombini, University of Pisa, Dipartimento di Chimica e Chimica Industriale identified the binders in the different layers of 10 fragments.

Yoko Taniguchi, University of Tsukuba, worked on the investigation and conservation of the murals in the caves of Bāmiyān. She provided numerous historical photographs, many of them privately taken during a trip to India, and a lot of very valuable background information.

Catharina Blänsdorf

Catharina Blänsdorf, Edmund Melzl
Technique of Modelling the Buddha Statues

Introduction

The Giant Buddha statues have mostly been regarded as stone sculptures. Indeed, they were cut out of the rock of the cliff and the great bulk of them consists of stone. The visible surface, however, was made of clay. The clay layers were more than a thick 'priming layer', applied to obtain a smooth surface for the paint layers. They also served the purpose of perfecting the shape: The sculpting process reached its finish by a modelling with clay.

As there never had been a detailed investigation of the manufacturing technique of the two statues, nor analyses of the material before the statues were destroyed, the fragments rescued from the rubble provide a chance to understand how the Buddha statues had been made.

Moreover, the examination of the fragments offers a possibility to clear up a question discussed since the 19th century: whether the clay layers were part of the original design of the statues or a later addition in order to repair damaged stone parts. Therefore, the analyses were also aimed at the question if it is possible to date the clay layers or to distinguish between original and later phases.

Sculpting in stone and perfection with clay layers

The Buddha statues were cut out of the cliff face in the Bāmiyān valley. Inside deep niches they protruded as a high relief, their entire neck being attached to the back of the niche. The cliff in Bāmiyān consists of rocks with an uneven stratification containing horizontal layers of sand, pebbles, boulders, and fragments of materials, such as quartz, schist, sandstone, or limestone. In between there are more compact layers of clay and sandstone.[1] This porous and inhomogeneous material is not suited to sculpt fine shapes. Furthermore, it cannot be painted directly.

The technique of modelling in clay, which can be traced back in China to the Neolithic Age, is wide-spread in Central and East Asia. The combination of sculpting in stone and clay modelling is also frequent in Central and East Asian art. Buddhist cave sanctuaries which contain large sculptures often show transitional decoration ranging between small sculptures modelled in clay over a wooden support and wall decorations painted on thin clay plasters smoothening the walls. The large statues were often sculpted from the stone, but finished in clay, especially when the rock material was too inhomogeneous or coarse to cut out fine shapes. If thick layers of clay or protruding parts were applied, a substructure was required as a core of the shape and an anchorage to the support below.

Historical descriptions

Certain observations on the technique used for the production of the Buddha statues of Bāmiyān were already made between the 1830s and 1930s. Although the texts did not focus on the manufacturing technique, they nonetheless contain valuable information. They also include different considerations concerning the question if the clay layers were part of the original design or later additions.

Alexander Burnes who visited Bāmiyān and the two statues seems to have been the first to describe some technical aspects in his record on the Western Buddha of 1834:

The figure is covered by a mantle, which hangs over it in all parts, and has been formed of a kind of plaster; the image having been studded with wooden pins in various places, to assist in fixing it.[2]

With reference to Burnes, Carl Ritter who had not seen the statues himself wrote in 1838:

The body is not naked, but vested with a kind of cloak which covers all parts, but is made of an applied gypsum stucco. Numerous inserted pegs can still be noticed which incontestably served to reinforce this stucco.[3]

In 1843, Vincent Eyre gave a more detailed description and also touched on the question if the clay layers were part of the original design or the result of later repairs:

One circumstance struck me as remarkable, – which was, that in all those parts where the limbs are deficient, there are regular rows of small holes in which pieces of wood have been stuck, for the evident purpose of making the plaster adhere. From this it would appear either that an attempt had been made to restore the mutilated parts of these means, or that the figure was originally only partially sculptured on the rock, and the deficiencies made up with plaster in the way I have mentioned. From the apparent facility with which from the softness of the rock, the image might have been chiselled perfect at the first, I incline to the belief that an attempt has been since made to repair the work of destruction, during some temporary success of the heathen inhabitants against the Mahomedan invaders. The cliff is composed of that species of conglomerate known by the name of pudding-stone, consisting of very hard clay, thickly studded with various kinds of rounded pebbles.[4]

△ Fig. 1

△ Fig. 2

Fig. 1. Jean Carl standing on the right forearm of the Western Buddha [HACKIN/CARL 1933, detail from fig. 23]. The wooden substructure of the forearm is lost, but Carl is standing on the upper coating of the arm which Hackin described as made of bricks. In the *sangati* the holes for the pegs and the partly damaged fold ridges can be recognised.

Fig. 2. Western Buddha, holes of different sizes to insert wooden substructures. At the left arm, the part sculpted from the rock ends at the elbow. Forearm and hanging folds were modelled in clay over massive substructures. All fold ridges were applied in clay except for the deep ones between the legs. [ASI]

Fig. 3. Modelling system of the Eastern Buddha. Left: Right arm and right leg with holes in the stone visible in the lower part of the *sangati*. [NAMIKAWA 1999]
Right: Detail under the right arm with preserved blue paint layer. In the holes the pebbles for anchoring the clay are visible. [Praxenthaler]

▽ Fig. 4

▽ Fig. 5

Fig. 4. Left arm of Eastern Buddha in 1965: U-shaped part cut from the stone with holes visible at the hem of the sleeve cuff. The wooden support and clay cover of the top are already lost. [ASI]

Fig. 5. Below the right arm of the Western Buddha: The fold ridges are modelled in clay on the smooth stone surface. [Keith Worsley-Brown, June 1972]

The work published by Maitland, Talbot, and Simpson in 1886 presents the Buddha statues from a scientific point of view. Maitland, who made drawings of the statues, describes the clay layers and also discusses the question of their origination, coming to a result different from Eyre:

The idols themselves are rather clumsy figures, roughly hewn in the tough conglomerate of the rock, and afterwards thickly overlaid with stucco, in which all the details are executed. The whole arrangement shows that this was not done in later period, but is part of the original design of the figures.[5]

During the comprehensive expedition to the Bamiyan Buddha statues of the Délégation Archéologique Française en Afghanistan (DAFA) in the late 1920s, Joseph Hackin and Jean Carl explored the Western Buddha. Starting from the top of the head, Carl climbed down to the shoulders and went through a narrow corridor built with mud bricks connecting the shoulders. He used a rope to climb down from the right shoulder between the upper arm and the niche wall:

[…] and thus he arrived at the first section of the revetment made of bricks covering the piece of wood which formed the skeleton of the forearm and supported the hand raised in abhaya-mudra *(gesture of reassurance). On his climbing tour Mr. Carl discovered fragments of the surface 'skin' which was composed of a mixture of clay and chaff, covered with a very thin film of lime mortar. [This 'skin'] covered the rough modelling of the statue. We have collected fragments which imitated the drapery of the monk's robe. They still possessed their armature made of ropes and pegs, and coated with the red paint layer which originally had covered the entire robe (fig. 24).*[6]

The modelling of the surface – Eastern Buddha

All the cited descriptions concern the Western Buddha. The Eastern Buddha is only mentioned incidentally as being similar and – by Burnes – as being more perfect [in style], without indicating any technical details.[7]

Historical photographs allow drawing some conclusions about the stone sculpture. However, the stone was only visible in the damaged parts where the clay layers were already lost and assessment thus remains restricted to these areas.

Apparently, the statue was sculpted almost completely out of the stone. Details of the garment were elaborated or at least indicated. Fold ridges visible in the lower parts were distinctively sculpted. Here, the clay layers seem to repeat only what was laid out in the stone and to refine it slightly.

To reach a better adhesion between the stone and the clay, a multitude of conical holes was gouged into the stone. They seem to have been extended over the whole surface: They can be seen on the garment, the legs, in the face, and on the neck. The fold ridges were spared from holes which were concentrated in the recesses between the ridges.

Observations on the technique 2005–2008

The examination within our project showed that the holes are about 7 cm wide and of the same depth. They are positioned with a distance of 10 to 12 cm between each other. When the clay was applied, pebbles were pressed into the holes together with the clay, thus serving as mechanical interlocking between the stone and the clay layers. Some of the pebbles, together with remnants of the clay layer, have been found in-situ below the right arm (fig. 3).

The holes can also be seen on the edge of the sleeve cuff of the left arm, indicating that the whole forearm was worked in stone. The hands were already lost in the 19th century. In the historical photographs the forearms seem to be open on the upper side: It seems that the forearms were sculpted from the stone in a U-shaped form (fig. 4). At the end (i.e. the elbow) a deeper square hole was driven into the stone which can still be seen today. An anchoring construction was inserted into the U-shaped channel in the arm and pushed into the hole at its end where the stone stabilised it against tilting forward due to the weight of hand. The upper side of the arm was then closed, probably either with bricks or with clay. The anchoring construction was probably made of wood, either of a thick beam or of several beams put together.

Larger square holes in the small gap between the statue and the side walls could come from a scaffold which was necessary after the sculpting had been finished.

The modelling of the surface – Western Buddha

The technique of the Western Buddha differs from the one of the Eastern Buddha. While the Eastern Buddha is mainly worked out of the stone and the clay layers repeat the shape in the way of a thick priming layer, the clay layers of the Western Buddha have a more important part in the design of the statue.

At the Western Buddha, the fine details are not created in stone: The *sangati* is smooth except for the large and deep folds between the legs. The forearms seem to stick out of the rock as well as the hem of the *sangati* hanging down over the forearms in thin, far-protruding ridges (fig. 2).

Large square holes cut into the stone served to insert massive construction supports. The biggest were the ones in the forearms. In this connection it is interesting that in 1933 Hackin and Carl described the upper side of the forearm – on which Carl was standing during his climbing tour – as being made of *bricks* covering the lost timber which served as anchorage of the forearm (*revêtement de briques recouvrant la pièce de bois qui formait l'ossature de l'avant-bras*). Although a photograph gives the impression of solid clay rather than bricks, this description must have been based on close observation.

Rows of smaller square holes can be found along the protruding ridges of the *sangati* hanging down over the forearms and in the right lower leg. As the stone has broken away irregularly in these areas, the insertion of anchoring supports and the completion of the shape with other means than stone clearly appear as a method of repair. This repair

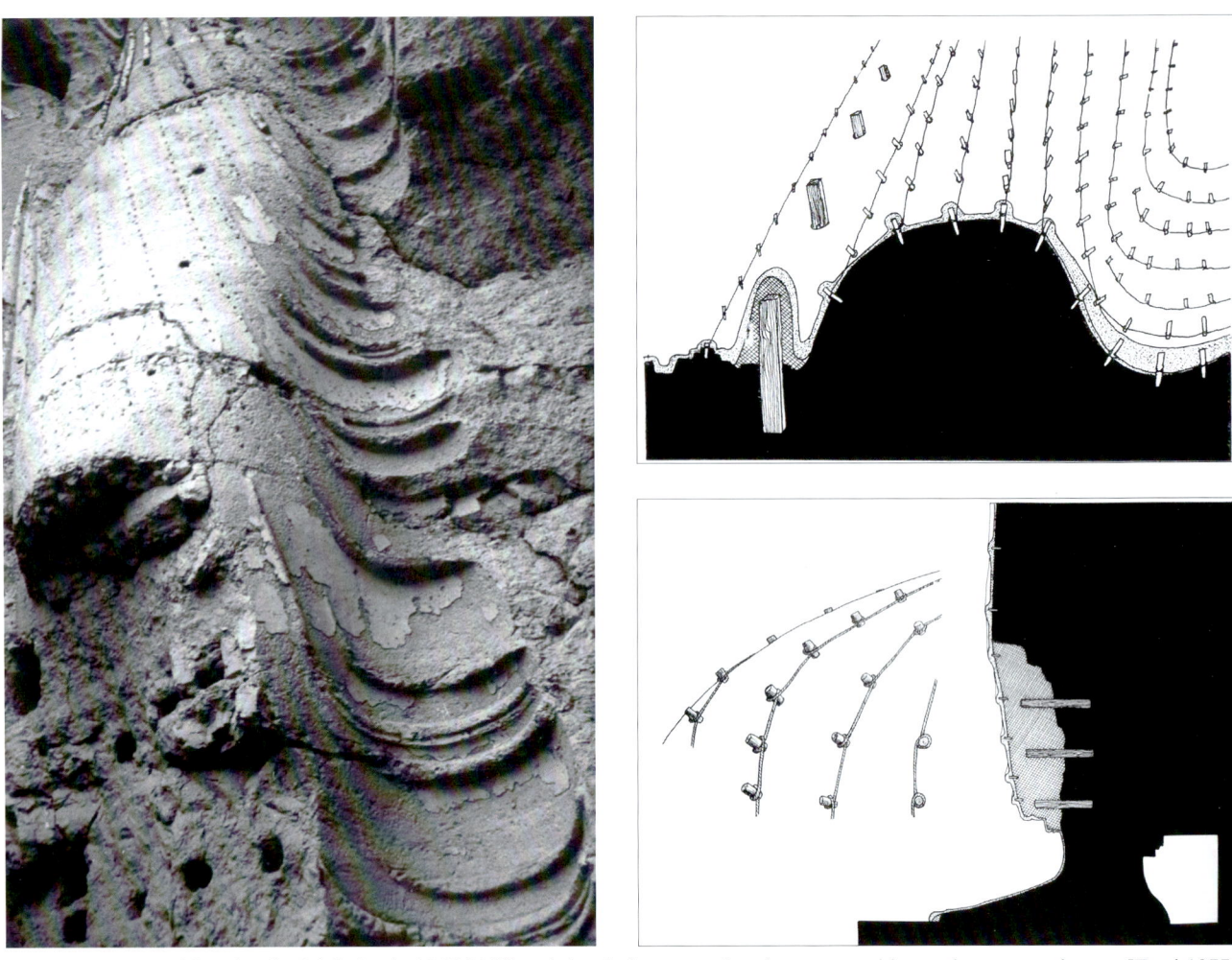

Fig. 6. Western Buddha, detail of right leg in 1965 [ASI] and sketch demonstrating the system with wooden pegs and ropes [Tarzi 1977, vol. 2. p. 117]

Fig. 7. Demonstration of system with fragments found in the rubble [Melzl]: Peg inserted into a hole in the stone (left) and peg inserted into a preserved eye in a rope (right).

can be the consequence of an early damage, as Vincent Eyre suggested, but it may also date back to the creation of the statue: Due to the soft rock with low stability, parts may have broken off during the sculpting, requiring a repair during the work process. In the case of the protruding ridges of the *sangati* hanging down over the forearms, the sculptors may even have considered from the beginning to add the most protruding part rather than attempting to cut these thin parts from the rock.

Fold ridges
The fold ridges are not indicated in the stone. This shows that at least for these parts the sculptors took the modelling with clay into consideration from the beginning.

The fold ridges possess a substructure of ropes affixed to wooden pegs. Square holes were driven into the stone to insert the pegs. The holes can only be found along the fold ridges, while the interspaces and recesses were spared. The holes are conical, with an edge length of 3.0 cm to 4.5 cm and a depth of about 7 cm. They were made using a pointed chisel. The distance between the holes measures 30.0 to 40.0 cm.

The ropes served as a mechanical stabilisation and core of the fold ridges. The pegs also increased the adhesion to the stone.

The system of ropes and pegs was a phenomenon that the authors of the 19th and early 20th centuries described as peculiar and amazing. In 1977, Z. Tarzi published sketches demonstrating the anchoring system of the fold ridges and of the larger broken-off parts part of the right leg (fig. 6).[8]

Observations on the technique 2005-08
Numerous fragments from the fold ridges have been found in the rubble, consisting of clay fragments with embedded ropes, hundreds of pegs and many pieces of ropes. Some clay fragments also show the imprint of a rope and a peg on the back[9]. The examination of these fragments revealed more details of this technique.

Pegs
The pegs are usually square or trapezoid in diameter and pointed. They measure between 12 and 20 cm in length, with an average of 16 cm (fig. 8). Many show traces of a saw at the cross section (fig. 9). The sides were hewn with an axe or a knife. Smaller pegs, sometimes wedge-shaped, of 8 to 12 cm length, apparently served to stabilise the peg inside the hole.

Very few wooden pieces found so far are round in cross section. It is not clear if they were really part of the Buddha or not.

Many pegs and also the reverse sides of some fragments show black dots, sometimes covering large parts of the wood (figs. 10–12). These black dots are of microbiological origin. Normally humidity is extremely low in Bāmiyān. Thus, this microbiological growth may date back to the creation of the statues when thick layers of clay provided enough moisture to allow microbiological growth.

Some pegs show traces of weathering at the end. This means that that they must have been exposed to the environment for a long time. It can be assumed that such traces come from weathered or damaged parts where the

Fig. 8. Selection of pegs, GBL 1371-75. Peg GBL 1375 shows weathering at the end [Melzl]

Fig. 9. Peg GBL 810 with cut of a saw (arrow) [Melzl]

Fig. 10. Peg no. 'a'. Black dots on the wood. Traces of pink slurry on the tip of the peg [Blänsdorf]

Fig. 11. Peg no. 'a'. Detail of black dots [Blänsdorf]

clay was reduced or lost (fig. 8, right).[10] Very few pegs show signs of wood pest or fungi attack.

Today many pegs are broken. Often the tip is broken off, others are reduced to splinters. This damage was caused by the destruction of the statues.

On a larger number of pegs soot or traces of fire have been found, but it is not clear if this dates back to the origination or to the destruction. Sengupta mentioned in 1984 that he found traces of charcoal in the large holes within the elbows of the Western Buddha. He assumed that the wooden anchoring system of the statues had been burnt at an earlier time.[11]

Fig. 12. Peg no. 'a'. Shell of dot opened to reveal white round material, indicating the microbiological origin of the dot [Blänsdorf]

Ropes

The ropes are rather thin, but show a durable quality. They vary in thickness, colour and manufacture technique.[12] The ropes were attached to the pegs in different ways (fig. 13). The simplest way was to take one rope and wind it around the peg once before continuing to the next peg (fig. 13, 1). Mostly two ropes had been plied together to form a double rope. To insert a peg, the twist was opened to form an eye (fig. 13, 2, 2a). Four ropes were plied together as well and used the same way (fig. 13, 2b; 14). Often one of the ropes or both (fig. 13, 3a and 3b; 15) are wound around the peg once, thus allowing to regulate the tension of the rope. In a rare case, a rope was split and the peg inserted between the strings (fig. 13, 4 and 16).

Generally pegs and ropes were separated during the destruction of the statue. Only very few pegs have been found that are still connected to pieces of the rope.[13] In one case two ropes were affixed to a round wooden armature with two knots (GBL 1773, fig. 17).

Large wooden anchoring beams

Several large beams were found in the rubble. They are square in diameter[14] and the end is blunt, not pointed. They were probably inserted in the large holes mentioned above. The holes seem to be driven up to 1 m deep into the stone.[15] The parts of beams found in the rubble are between 20 and 81 cm long. They were clearly broken off during the destruction of the statues. They were probably clamped in the holes using wedge-shaped planks which were about 7–8 cm shorter than the depth of the holes.

A large timber found at the Eastern Buddha proved to date from the same time as the clay layers (see: *Dating of the Buddha statues – AMS ^{14}C dating of organic materials*, in this publication). It was probably used as anchorage for larger protruding parts.

Fig. 13. Different ways of inserting pegs into the rope [Blaensdorf, Melzl]:

1 S-plied rope with simple loop

2 double rope with simple eye

2a Z-plied double rope with simple eye

2b two Z-plied double ropes with simple loop

3 double rope with loop

3a Z-plied double rope with loop in one rope

3b Z-plied double rope with loop in both ropes

4 Z-plied rope split to insert rope

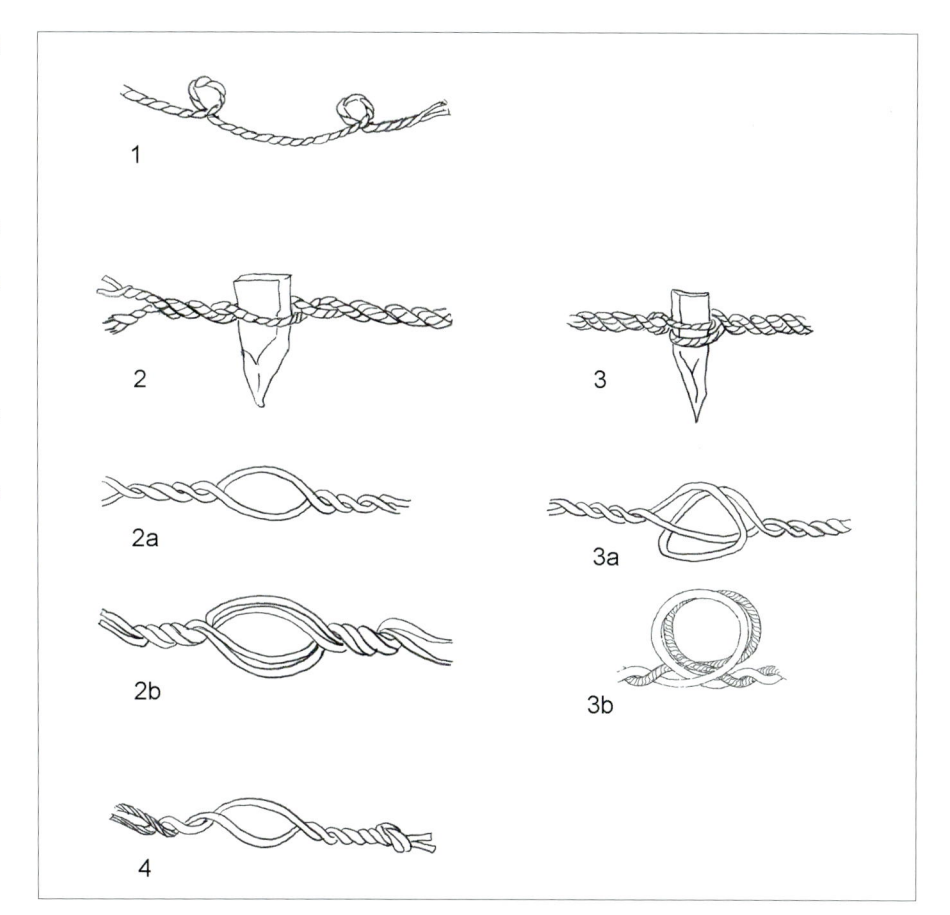

△ Fig. 14. GBL 1447: Double ply of four ropes with simple eye [Melzl]

▽ Fig. 15. GBL 1386: Plied double rope with loop in one rope [Melzl]

△ Fig. 16. GBL 662: Rope split to insert peg [Melzl]

▽ Fig. 17. Round peg GBL 1773 with two ropes [Melzl]

207

Clay layers

Before the destruction of the two Buddha statues, there was never a thorough examination of the clay layers covering both statues. The fragments examined in Munich are mostly too small or too damaged to allocate their original position. Our investigations therefore aimed at the question if it is possible to distingish between parts of the statues and the niches or cave murals, and between original parts and possible later completions.

The descriptions of the 19th and 20th centuries do not contain more than brief remarks concerning the clay layers. They all agree that these top layers served to model the details of the shape. BURNES 1834 even says that the folds hanging over the arms of the Western Buddha were modelled in *some kind of plaster*.[16] Burnes and Eyre called the layers *plaster*, Maitland used the term *stucco*. Both reports do not seem to refer to a specific material.[17]

In 1933, Hackin and Carl gave the first detailed description of the clay layers as '[...] *composed of a mixture of clay and chaff, covered with a very thin film of lime mortar.*'[18] We find a similar description in a report of 1934, written by Joseph and Ria Hackin, concerning the Western Buddha: '*The whole* [surface] *was then covered with a coarse mixture of earth and chaff and covered with a layer of lime mortar.*'[19]

The photographs taken at that time show that the clay layers did not only cover the statues, but continued on the sides of the niches. It is remarkable that these descriptions mention a lime mortar as top layer. No analyses were done, but it can be assumed that a lime mortar should be white or whitish.

The first scientific analyses were made by Gettens in 1937 on samples from murals of different caves. He describes that the support as clay reinforced with vegetable fibre, chiefly straw or grass, which is spread in a thickness of about 1 to 2.5 cm (half an inch to one inch) on the stone surface. On top a white ground was applied, which he identified as burnt gypsum (not calcite).[20]

The description of lime mortars might be inspired by the white ground layers visible on the murals, but it nevertheless appears strange as Carl and Hackin collected fragments from the hair and the fold ridges of the Western Buddha. None of the fragments from the statues collected in Bāmiyān since 2004 possesses a white plaster layer and most of them do not have any white layers at all.

type of layer	colour/properties	additive	thickness
finish coat ('intonacco')	more yellowish, hard, compact	sand, hair, charcoal	0.05–0.5 cm (often 0.2 to 0.3 cm)
under coat ('arriccio')	more greyish, less comapct, rather inhomogenous, inclusions of lime	threshing, residues, hair, pebbles	max. 15–19 cm (depending on shape)
clay-lime slurry	reddish pink, rarely grey or yellow		< 0.2 cm

△ Fig. 18. Schematic structure of clay layers

◁ Fig. 19. Traces of pink slurry on the back of a clay fragment. Plant material is visible in the undercoat. [Melzl]

From 1969 to 1978, the restorers of the Indo-Afghan co-operation repaired damaged parts of the two Buddha statues in Bamiyan. In the report on the restoration of the Eastern Buddha Sengupta describes the layers as being made of clay and adds an interesting detail concerning the Eastern Buddha, saying that it was '... *covered with plaster in three layers and painted.*'[21]

Observations on the technique 2005–08
Observations have been made during the collection of the fragments and on the sample material sent to Munich. On most of the fragments two layers can be distinguished, consisting of a thick undercoat ('arriccio') and a thin finish coat ('intonaco'). Underneath traces of a slurry have been found (fig. 19).

The combination of a coarse clay layer, usually straw mud, and a finer clay plaster, usually containing vegetable fibres or hair and sand, is a wide-spread procedure in Central Asia and China. Moistening and applications of clay suspensions improve the adhesion.

The back of the fragments prove that the stone surface showed traces of aging and fibrous dirt when the slurry was applied.[22] This seems to indicate that at least some months, perhaps a winter season, passed between sculpting and clay modelling. The clay layers of the Eastern and Western Buddha are very similar. The coarse layers, however, can be distinguished by their visual appearance:

The clay layers of the caves are thinner than those of the Buddha statues. They look different as the clay does not contain hair and the surfaces are mostly blackened by soot. So, the differentiation of the fragments between caves and statues was quite reliable.

It has to be kept in mind, however, that at the outline of the statues there has been a transition between sculpture and painted niche walls, so there might be some fragments belonging to both. As fragments of the niche's wall plaster could not be retrieved – or identified so far – a technical comparison was not possible yet.

Slurry
As many fragments of the Eastern Buddha are broken apart within the clay layers, the preparation of the stone support can only be reconstructed partially. Traces of reddish or grey slurry were found underneath the coarse clay layer of a certain number of fragments.

Many fragments of the Western Buddha show traces of a slurry. It has been observed on the stone surface, the back of clay fragments and on many of the pegs. As to the pegs, the slurry is often found only on the tip. This seems to indicate that the slurry was applied before the pegs were inserted. If it was intended to apply the clay as long as the slurry was still moist, this would mean an extremely expeditious procedure requiring a team working with divided tasks at high speed. Generally, the slurry is pink, but on some fragments yellow or grey slurry was found as well. Other fragments show a coating of a material that the Afghans identified as donkey dung. The preparation with animal dung can partly be attributed to the restoration of 1969–78,[23] but on some fragments it seems to be part of the original structure, for example on the wooden pegs GBL 1171–1180. The grey slurry definitely dates from antique times.

So far, only the pink slurry from the Western Buddha has been analysed. It is a mixture of clay, coloured reddish by hematite, and of ground limestone. Some samples contain a rather high amount of gypsum in different quantities. So it has to be assumed that gypsum was added deliberately.[24]

Undercoat
The layer is 15 to 19 cm thick. On the Eastern Buddha it is slightly thicker than that on the Western Buddha. The undercoat was often applied in several layers, which today partly detach from each other. The execution in several applications seems reasonable regarding the considerable thickness of the layer. In the surface often traces of fingers have been preserved (fig. 20), showing that the clay was applied with bare hands.[25] This technique is still practised in Asia today.[26]

As additives chaff, threshing residues and hair have been observed. On the Eastern Buddha the additives appear coarser and also contain straw. The material used here could be analysed. On the Western Buddha the plant parts are finer, but some fragments of stones and pebbles of about 1–3 cm length were imbedded, either as deliberate addition or by accident. Inside one fragment a small piece of leather was found, in another one a small piece of textile.[27] As leather and textile pieces obviously got into the clay accidentally, the stones, too, were probably not mixed in on purpose.

The added animal hair is white, brown, and black. At the Western Buddha it sometimes occurs in surprisingly big tufts (fig. 21). The addition of animal hair is an important peculiarity of the clay from the statues. Animal hair is not found in the plasters of the cave murals. In fragments from caves next to both statues, the coarse clay plaster contains straw and chaff and very few, very fine bast fibres (maybe jute). The fine clay layer does not contain any organic additives. Using these criteria, clay fragments from the statues can be distinguished from the ones of the caves. An additional criterion is that on fragments from the caves the surface usually is rather blackened by soot.

There is a number of fragments catalogued as parts of the Western Buddha which do not contain hair and also show a paint layer sequence quite unlike most of the other fragments, but their colours are bright, not darkened by soot. It is not clear yet if they belong to the Buddha statue or where they could come from.

One fragment from the Western Buddha shows a completely smooth and flat reverse side. It seems not to have been attached to the rock surface, but to another kind of support. So far, there is no hint what this could have been.[28]

Finish coat
On both statues, the finish coat is only 0.5 to 5 mm thick. Only in rare cases, the layer is thicker (up to 1 cm), obviously in connection with corrections in the modelling. It contains additions of sand, a very small amount of fine animal hair, and a considerable amount of charcoal. The surfaces are very smooth and obviously treated in order to perfect the shape and to compact the layer. Straight edges of c. 0.5 to

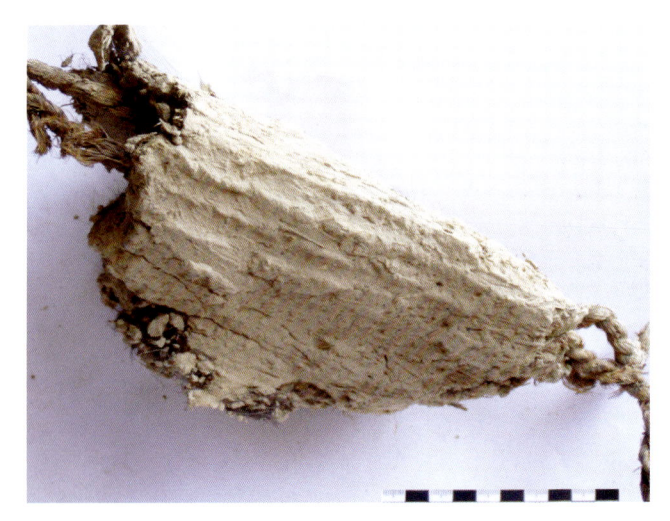

Fig. 20. Traces of fingers in the undercoat layers: Left: Fragment on-site. Right: Fold ridge of Western Buddha, fragment GBL 1088: Undercoat of a fold ridge of the Western Buddha [Melzl]

Fig. 21. Hair, sometimes in tufts, in the undercoat of the Western Buddha [Melzl]

◁ Fig. 22b. Fragments photographed in raking light showing 1 cm wide traces of modelling tools, ID 282 of GBL 775, size of sample 4 x 5 cm [Thiemann]

▽ Fig. 22a. Fragments photographed in raking light showing 2.5 cm wide traces of modelling tools, GBL 2425, length of fragment 7 cm [Melzl]

1 cm width indicate that flat modelling tools were used (fig. 22)[29]. Two pieces of leather detected in the rubble[30] can be interpreted as polishing tools.

Three-layer clay structures

In few areas of both statues, three instead of two clay layers have been observed.[31] A three-layered structure was already observed by the Indo-Afghan restoration team on the Eastern Buddha. In contrast to earlier assumptions, these parts do not seem to be a repair, but the result of changes for artistic or technical reasons during the modelling.[32]

Possible early repairs

Some fragments of the Eastern Buddha show the same type of yellowish coarse layer with finer additives, as they are characteristic for the Western Buddha. Assuming that the Western Buddha was made several decades later than the Eastern Buddha, this might be the result of an early repair or an added enrichment during the time when the Western Buddha was created.[33] ^{14}C-AMS dating proved that the work on the murals of the caves in the cliff continued until the late 9th century.[34] This means that craftsmen were around who could have repaired damages or changed some details.

Materials used in the Indo-Afghan restoration 1969–78

Several fragments clearly show traces of filling materials, plasters and overpaintings, which can be attributed to restoration interventions of the 20th century. Sengupta mentions that plaster of Paris was used for fillings in the murals in 1922-1923[35], but the French archaeologists probably did not carry out measurements on the statues themselves.[36] Thus the added materials found on fragments were brought in by the restoration of 1969–78:

Fragments of the repaired or reconstructed parts show that the restorers at that time partly worked with traditional techniques, but also used modern materials.

The clay plasters show very little additives; no hair was used. Animal dung was found as pre-treatment of the stone. Original pegs were re-used, visible on damages which occurred when they were driven into the wall again. Some missing pegs and larger anchoring beams were replaced by new ones.

For fillings sometimes on top of damaged original clay layers with 'gypsum' (dihydrate, semi-hydrate and anhydrite)[37] and cement[38] could be proved by analysis. A thin reddish clay plaster on top of a probably cement-containing plaster contained vegetable fibres.[39] According to oral information the Indian restorers added shredded strings as fibrous material to the gypsum.[40]

Most of the fragments show a thin light ochre layer or traces of it on top of the paint layer. The covering of still visible remnants of paint with this 'clay-wash' can be attributed to the Indo-Afghan restoration. It was identified as a clay suspension[41], sometimes containing larger quantities of gypsum and calcite.[42]

Faces

In the faces of the statues, the parts above the mouth were missing, in the case of Western Buddha even above the lower lip. The authors of the 19th century attributed this phenomenon to damage. Listing other damages including

Fig. 23. Earliest correct drawing by Maitland 1885 showing that the faces were cut-out and not weathered or mutilated [Talbot/Simpson 1886, p. 348]

△ (a)

▽ (b)

(c) ▷

Fig. 24. Faces: Photographs and drawings showing the cut-out faces and the trench at the bottom to insert a wooden substructure

(a) Head of Western Buddha [Namikawa 1999, Abb. 97]

(b) Head of Eastern Buddha, 1956 [ASI]

(c) Schematic drawing of the faces [Tarzi 1977, vol. 2, p. 115]

those by cannon shots, they presume that the faces were destroyed in a deliberate act of mutilation. Consequently, the drawing by Burnes shows the faces as if broken away. In the 1920s and 1930s, Godard and Hackin still followed this hypothesis.[43]

In 1885, Maitland sketched the two statues in a remarkably detailed way. His drawings show clearly that the faces were not broken off, but cut-out systematically, leaving a smooth vertical wall above the mouth. All later photographs corroborate the state indicated in his drawings (fig. 23). Cutting out the faces meticulously to leave a regular recess without damaging the surrounding parts does not look like the result of spontaneous violence – comparable to the shooting with cannons or hacking holes into the faces of deities painted on murals.

During the Indian restoration in 1969-78, the faces could be reached from a scaffold and examined in a much closer way than before. A trench was discovered between the horizontal and the vertical wall of the recess (fig. 24), suited to insert a support structure. Pieces of charred wood and charcoal were detected as well. This led to the conclusion that the faces were probably cut-out from the beginning and modelled over a rack of wooden poles which afterwards was covered with clay plaster.[44] The reasons why such an unusual and unique design for the faces was chosen cannot be explained yet.

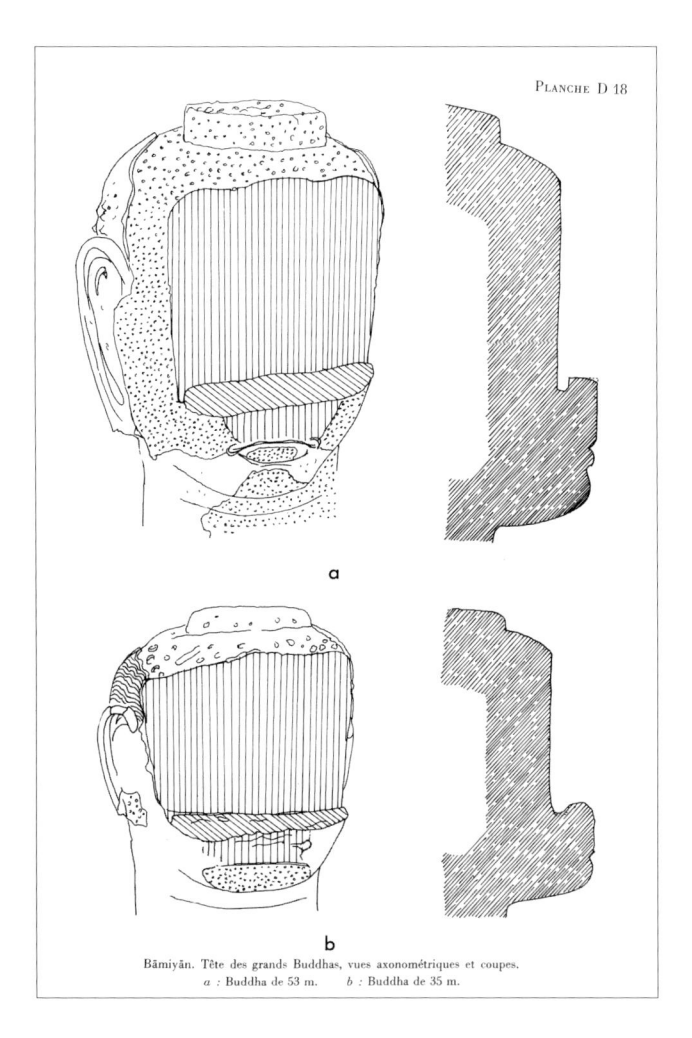

Bāmiyān. Tête des grands Buddhas, vues axonométriques et coupes.
a : Buddha de 53 m.   b : Buddha de 35 m.

References

Bauer-Bornemann, U., Melzl, E., Romstedt, H., Scherbaum, M.: *Überlegungen zum Umgang mit den Fragmenten der zerstörten Buddha-Statuen im Auftrag des deutschen Nationalkomitees von ICOMOS*, Dezember 2003 (unpublished report on the work in Bāmiyān 23.10.–3. 11. 2003)

Burnes, Sir Alexander, *Travels into Bokhara, together with a narrative of A voyage on the Indus*, London 1834, Reprint Oxford University Press 1973

Eyre, Vincent, *The Military Operations at Cabul (...): with a journal of imprisonment in Afghanistan,* London 1843, In: Godard et al. 1928, p. 87–88

Namikawa, Banri (Fotografie Stiftung e.V.): *Gandhara*, Präfektur Shimane 1999

Tarzi, Zemaryalai: *L'architecture et le décor rupestre des grottes de Bamiyan*, Paris 1977, 2 vols (vol. 1: Texts, vol. 2: Sketches, photographs)

Gettens, Rutherford: *The materials in the wall paintings of Bāmiyān, Afghanistan*, in: Technical Studies in the field of the Fine Arts, Volume VI, 1937–1938, p. 168–193

Godard, A., Godard, Y., Hackin, J.: *Les Antiquités Bouddhiques de Bāmiyān*, Mémoires de la délégation archéologique Française en Afghanistan, vol. II. Paris, Brussels 1928

National Research Institute for Cultural Properties Japan (ed.): *Radiocarbon Dating of the Bamiyan Mural Paintings*, in: *Recent Cultural Heritage Issues in Afghanistan*, vol. 2, Tokyo 2006

Ritter, Carl: Die Stupa's (Topes) oder die architectonischen Denkmale an der königlich Indo-Baktrischen Köngisstraße und die Colosse von Bāmiyān. Eine Abhandlung zur Althertumskunde des Orients, vorgetragen in der königl. Akademie der Wissenschaften, am 6. Februar 1837. Mit einer Karte und 8 lithographirten Tafeln. Berlin, Nicolaische Buchhandlung, 1838

Sengupta, R.: *The Restoration of the small Buddha at Bāmiyān*, in: ICOMOS (Ed.): *Momentum. 27.1*, York 1984, p. 31–46

Talbot, M. G. and Simpson, W.: *The rockcut caves and statues of Bamian*, in: *Journal of the Royal Asiatic Society*, Vol. XVIII, London 1886, pp. 303–350

Fig. 1. Metal trays with collected wooden beams, pegs and ropes [Melzl]

Fig. 2. Samples of wooden elements for analysis [Pfeffer/Blänsdorf]

Fig. 3. GBL 2368: Sculpted ornament with floral decoration, re-used as peg on the Western Buddha [Melzl]

214

Catharina Blänsdorf, Stephanie Pfeffer, Edmund Melzl
Identification of Wood Species

From the hundreds of wooden pieces found in the rubble of the Buddha statues 321 selected samples were sent to Munich for determination of wood species and ^{14}C-AMS dating (fig. 1 and 2). Most of these splinters come from the wooden pegs used on the Western Buddha (320 samples), one belongs to the anchoring system of the Eastern Buddha. Seven complete pegs were sent to Munich as well, but should not undergo invasive sampling. Additionally, samples of trees now growing in the valleys of Bamiyan, Fuladi and Kakrak were collected.

First analyses were made in 2002. The results were cedar and poplar.[45] In 2007 and 2008, the samples of wooden splinters were separated into groups according to macroscopic characteristics. From each group several samples were selected. Altogether 20 samples were analysed in the Zentrum für Holzwirtschaft at the University of Hamburg.[46] The samples GBL 5, 8, 39, 88, 126, 260, 261, 340, 367, 393, 1394, 1622, 1748, 1805 a, 1805b, 1805c, 1914, 2001a, 2011, 2098 were identified by means of characteristics of wood structures (microscopic analysis). Four different genera could be identified:
- *Populus* (poplar)
- *Sorbus* (rowan)
- *Cedrus* (cedar)
- *Quercus* (oak)

In 2007, the reference samples from the Bamiyan region were identified based on botanical characteristics.[47]

Interpretation of results

Different wood species were used for the pegs and anchoring timbers of the Western Buddha. Most of them were poplar, a tree which is still wide-spread in Bamiyan nowadays. It is still used as wood for construction like timbers and may have been used for the same purpose already in the time of the origination of Buddha statues. Cedar, rowan or oak trees, however, cannot be found in Bamiyan today.

Today trees and wood are very rare in Bamiyan. Maybe wood was a rather valuable good already during the time when the Buddha statues were made. The use of different wood species could mean that all available construction woods were used. This theory is supported by a small wooden element which came from a sculpted ornament and obviously was re-used as peg (fig. 3).

The analyses covered only a fracture of the wooden parts preserved in Bamiyan and also only a smaller part of the samples stored in Munich. Although groups were formed and samples were chosen carefully, a quantitative or statistic interpretation of the results is not possible. Several pegs found in Bamiyan were macroscopically identified as wood from fruit trees, but samples of these pegs could not be included in the analysis.

All identified species produce a durable wood, especially cedar. The state of preservation of most wooden elements is remarkably good.

Table 1 Identified wood genera and species endemic in Afghanistan

fragment numbers	identified genus	name	species endemic in Afghanistan
8, 88, 126, 340, 367, 393, 1394, 1748, 1805a, 1805c, 2098, 2011	*Populus*, family Salicea	popular Pappel	
5, 39, 1622, 1914	*Sorbus*, family Rosacea	haw, rowan Eberesche, Mehlbeere	*Sorbus cashmiriana* (Himalaya Eberesche/ cashmir rowan), *Sorbus lantana, S. microphylla, S. tianschanica, S. turkestanica*
260, 261, 2001a	*Cedrus*, family Pinaceae	true cedar/Echte Zeder	*Cedrus doedara* (Himalaya cedar)
1805b	*Quercus*, family Fagaceae	oak/immergrüne Eiche	*Quercus balood, Quercus floribunda, Quercus semecarpifolia*

Table 2 Species identified on samples of tress growing in Bamiyan valley

name used in Bamiyan	identified genus	name
tschinar	*Salix excelsa*	willow/hohe Weide
dschangali	*Salix cf. pycnostacya*	dichtjährige Weide
safeh-dal	*Populus spec.*	popular/Pappel
sabs-tschinar	*Populus caspica*	kaspische Pappel

Fig. 1. Ropes used for analysis of the plant species: ropes from the Western Buddha (on the left) and from the bazaar in Bāmiyān (long one on the right)

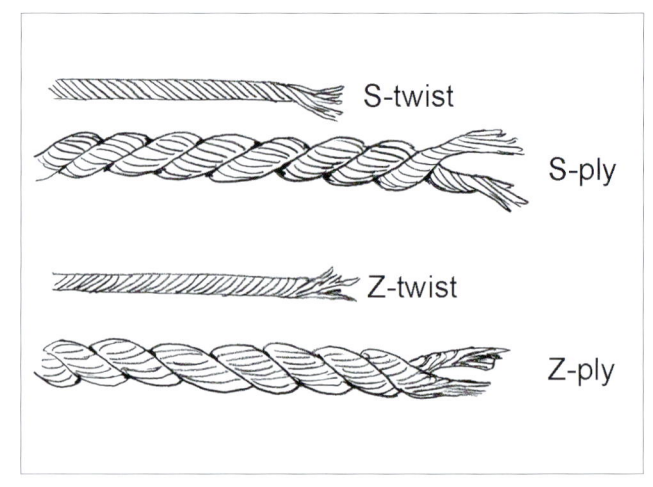

Fig. 2. Production technique of ropes. Most ropes show S-twist and Z-ply (above); one rope (GBL 662) is made in Z-twist and S-ply (below)

Fig. 3. *Astragalus cuneifolius* Bunge, in Farsi Dom-i-shutur

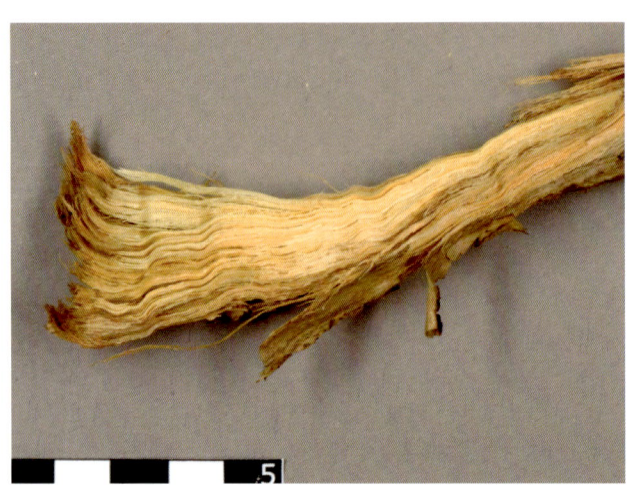

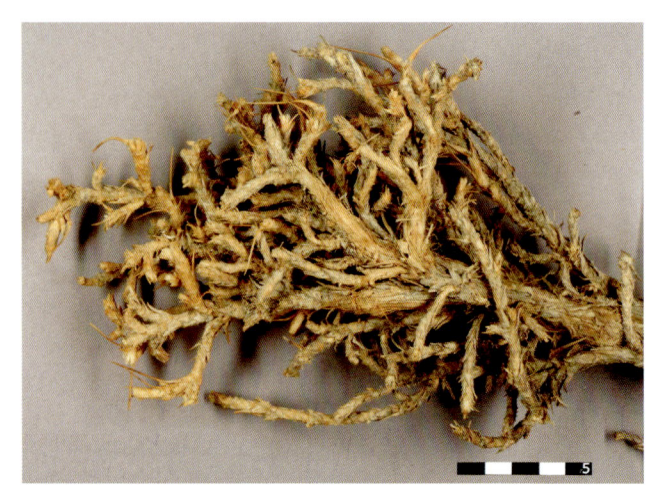

Stephanie Pfeffer, Catharina Blänsdorf
Materials Made of Plant Fibres: Ropes and Textile Fragment

Ropes and textile fragments, both from the Western Buddha, have been examined to understand their manufacturing technique and to identify the materials.

Ropes
Manufacturing
Ropes were used as core of the fold ridges of the Western Buddha. Hundreds of meters of these ropes have been found in the rubble. 14 small fragments have been brought to Munich for investigation (fig. 1).

The ropes are made of durable, long-fibrous material. The colour varies between light brown and dark brown. Many ropes are still smooth and flexible. The diameter varies considerably, measuring between 0.6 and 1.3 cm. In most of the cases the fibres were drilled in Z-twist to form a string. Two strings were then plied into an S-twist.[48] Only rarely a drilling in S-twist and Z-ply was observed (fig. 2).[49] These ropes probably were produced by another person.

Two ropes were plied together (in S-twist) to form a double rope. The rope with Z-twist, S-ply was used as a single rope. To connect it to the pegs, the rope was split and the peg inserted between the strings.

A rope bought at Bāmiyān bazaar as reference material (fig. 1, right side) looks similar, but differs from the ancient ones as it is a ply of three ends instead of two. This technique was not known in Antiquity.

Identification of material
Six samples of ropes, samples GBL 096, GBL 097, GBL 089 and three others without numbers have been analysed to identify the material. As the ropes produced and sold in the bazaar in Bāmiyān today looked very similar to the ones from the Western Buddha, a rope was bought as reference material. According to local people the ropes are produced from a plant called *Dom-i-shutur* in Bāmiyān. The plant does not grow in Bamiyan, but frequently in the mountains in the direction of Band-I-Amir. Of the plant the stem of about 50 cm length is used for making ropes.[50] A specimen of *Dom-i-shutur* could also be sent to Munich (fig. 3). All samples were selected by E. Melzl.

The analysis was made on the basis of botanical characteristics.[51] For this method leaves, parts of flowers or seeds are required.

The plant called *Dom-i-shutur* in Farsi could be identified as *Astragalus cuneifolius* Bunge. *Astragalus* is a genus with many species. The identified species, however, only grows

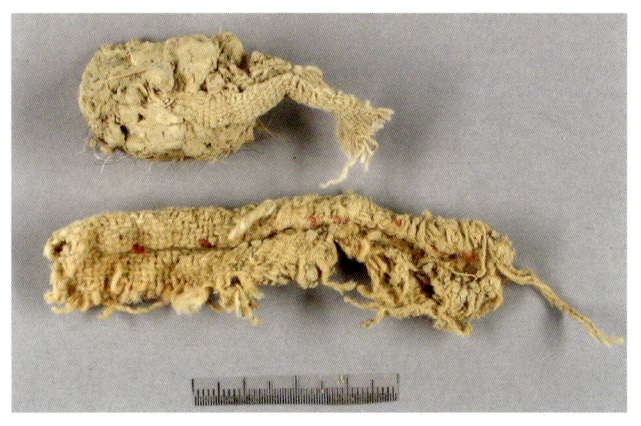

Fig. 4. Textile fragment and sample ID 36, front and reverse

Fig. 5. Comparison of the two textiles

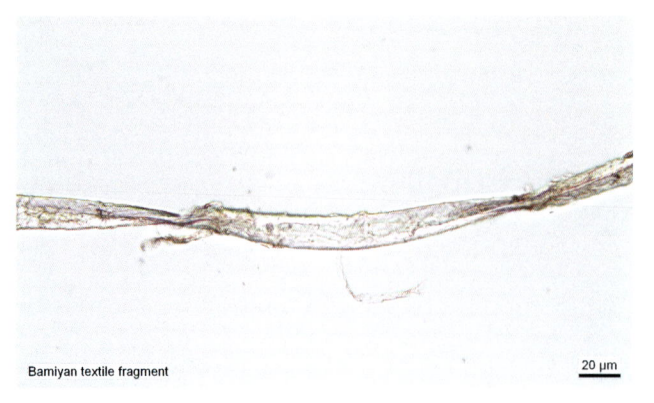

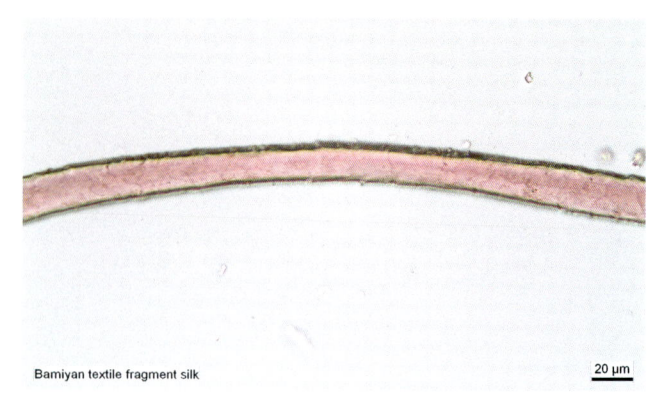

Fig. 6. Fibres of textile in transmitted light: cotton (left), red-dyed silk (right)

in a very small area. It is endemic in the area of Bāmiyān.[52] The plant is a shrub of up to 1.50 m in height.

A microscopic comparison between the plant fibres from the ropes of the Western Buddha and the *Dom-i-Shutur* specimen resulted in 100 percent consistency. The presence of the *Dom-i-Shutur* plant proved to be a lucky coincidence as the fibres microscopically are very similar to the type of hemp fibres which are very common and wide-spread in Central Asia.

Astragalus cuneifolius Bunge and a plant called Caragana have been described as material to make brooms and ropes in the area of Band-I-Amir (Central Afghanistan) today.[53] The identification of *Astragalus cuneifolius* Bunge is the first proof that this plant was already used in the past, as early as 550 AD.[54]

Textile fragment

A small textile fragment was found in the rubble of the Western Buddha. Its origin and use are unknown, but somehow it became part of the Buddha statue. Another small strip of textile was discovered imbedded in the coarse layer of sample ID 36, a clay fragment from the Western Buddha (fig. 4).

The textile fragment measures c. 9 cm x 1.8 cm. It is an undyed light brown textile, woven as a rather coarse tabby of quite thick threads (8 threads of warp and 9–10 threads of weft per cm^2). The threads show Z-twist. One edge is rolled in to form a hem which is stitched down with a red yarn, showing Z-twist and S-ply of two ends.

The textile strip inside sample ID 36 measures about 4 cm x 1.3 cm. It is light brown tabby as well, but it is finer than the other textile fragment. The warp is finer and denser than the weft (9–10 threads of warp and 17–20 threads of weft per cm^2). The threads show Z-twist.

The analysis of the fibres showed that both textiles are made of cotton. The red yarn is made of silk, probably wild silk (fig. 6).[55] The use of silk yarn indicates that this fragment originally was part of a garment or a decorative textile.

References

Dieterle, Alfred, *Vegetationskundliche Untersuchungen im Gebiet von Band-I-Amir (Zentralafghanistan)*, München 1973 (Dissertation thesis at the Ludwigs-Maximilians-Universität München)

H. Albert Gilg*, Catharina Blänsdorf**, Eva Höfle**, Laura Thiemann**

Mineralogical Investigations on Loam Plaster Fragments of the Destroyed Buddha Statues at Bāmiyān, Afghanistan

* Lehrstuhl für Ingenieurgeologie, Technische Universität München
** Lehrstuhl für Restaurierung, Technische Universität München

Introduction

No detailed investigations on the techniques and materials used as loam plaster and potential restoration existed before the destruction of the two Buddha figures at Bāmiyān. Many fragments of loam plaster were collected from the debris, however, without knowledge of their original position on the figures. Some undestroyed plastered areas exist only on the Eastern Buddha.

The aim of this study is a mineralogical characterization of individual loam coating layers and if possible, a reconstruction of various phases of renovation on the basis of material specific differences. A comparison with local loam samples from the Bāmiyān valley may help in determining the provenience of the raw materials at the time of construction. This contribution presents the results of a study in the interdisciplinary seminar at Lehrstuhl für Restaurierung, Technische Universität München (TUM), under the guidance of Prof. E. Emmerling und S. Pfeffer during the winter term 2007/2008 and summer term 2008.

Sample materials

We studied 175 fragments from the Western Buddha and 104 fragments from the Eastern Buddha. The internal structure of the loam plaster was investigated using a binocular microscope.

The plaster fragments mostly have a size of about 6 x 4 cm. The majority of fragments show two layers with an undercoat and an overlying finish coat (tab. 1). Few fragments consist only of one of the two layer types. Three fragments display three layers with an undercoat and two finishing coats. The additives in the loam plaster are straw, chaff or other plant fragments, and animal hair (goat, sheep). Often remnants of paint layers are preserved. Representative samples were chosen for more detailed examination and analysis (tab. 2).

The loam plaster fragments cannot easily be distinguished on the basis of their colour. The loam fragments of the Eastern Buddha are, however, often slightly more greyish, while that of the Western Buddha is more yellowish (fig. 1). The most common colour is 10YR 7/3 on the Munsell colour chart system.

The specific weight of the two loam plasters from the two Buddha statues is slightly different. Samples with a size of 7 x 4 x 3 cm³ from the Western Buddha weigh about 5 g more than samples of comparable size from the Eastern Buddha. The loam mixture of the Western Buddha is probably more compact. In all investigated fragments from the Western Buddha only grass has been added, while straw dominates as a plant additive in the Eastern Buddha.

In addition to the fragments of the Buddha statues, we investigated samples from several loam occurrences in the surroundings of Bāmiyān collected by E. Melzl. They derived from deposits that were most probably used in former times:

– **Khami-Kalak**: to the west in the Bāmiyān valley near Deh-e-Mullah-Golam in the alluvium of the Bāmiyān river
– **Surkh-kul**: first tributary valley to the west of the Western

Table 1 Differences between undercoat and finish coat

undercoat	finish coat
• thickness: up to 10 cm	• thichness: 0.5 to 5 mm
• often greyish, lighter	• often yellowish, darker, very compact and hard
• additives: straw, hair, sand	• additives: sand, hair
• uneven distribution of additives; partly in sheaves; hairs: light, dark, thin and thick	• hair: fine, light
• sand content: low	• sand content higher than in undercoat
• more inhomogenous and less compact	• black grains: inorganic as well as organic (charcoal)
• carbonate concretions	• mica

Table 2　Sample list

sample number	origin	selection criteria / description	layer type	grain size sample no.	XRD sample no.
1	Western Buddha		undercoat finish coat		1 – 301 1 – 302
11	Western Buddha	only finish coat	finish coat	11 – 1001	11 – 501
26	Western Buddha	reference fragment	undercoat finish coat	26 – 1001 26 – 1002	26 – 501 26 – 502
38	Western Buddha	finish coat similar to sample 55	undercoat finish coat	38 – 1001 38 – 1002	--- 38 – 502
43	Western Buddha	very light undercoat	undercoat finish coat	43 – 1001 43 – 1002	--- ---
55	Western Buddha	finish coat similar to sample 28	finish coat	55 – 1002	55 – 502
63	Western Buddha	exceptional sample: paint layer different from other fragments, finish coat darker, sand additives finer	undercoat finish coat	63 – 1001 63 – 1002	63 – 501 63 – 502
65	Western Buddha	very thin finish coat; reddish inclusion in undercoat	coarse loam plaster	65 – 1001	65 – 501
84	Western Buddha	coarse layer is not a loam plaster	undercoat finish coat	84 – 1001 84 – 1002	84 – 501 84 – 502
117	Western Buddha	colour different from other fragments	undercoat finish coat	117 – 1001 117 – 1002	117 – 501 117 – 502
159	Western Buddha	finish coat is not a loam plaster; rare colour coat type	undercoat thin dark brown layer	159 – 1001	159 – 501 159 – 502
174	Western Buddha	exceptional large schist fragment from the undercoat	undercoat finish coat		174 – 501
2	Eastern Buddha	reference fragment	undercoat finish coat	2 – 1001 2 – 1002	2 – 501/301 2 – 502/302
3	Eastern Buddha	three layers	undercoat finish coat (upper) finish coat (lower)	3 – 1001 3 – 1002 3 – 1003	3 – 301 3 – 302 3 – 303
200	Eastern Buddha	three layers	undercoat (brownish) finish coat undercoat (reddish)	200 – 1001 200 – 1002 200 – 1003	200 – 501 200 – 502 200 – 503
205	Eastern Buddha	colour different from other fragments	undercoat finish coat	205 – 1001 205 – 1002	--- ---
224	Eastern Buddha	probably not a loam plaster	undercoat (brownish) finish coat (reddish)	224 – 1001 224 – 1002	224 – 501 224 – 502
277	Eastern Buddha	reference fragment	undercoat	277 – 1001	---
278	Eastern Buddha	reference fragment	undercoat	278 – 1001	278 – 501
279	Eastern Buddha	reference fragment	undercoat	279 – 1001	279 – 501
280	Eastern Buddha	reference fragment	undercoat	280 – 1001	/
281	Kakrak Buddha	reference fragment for comparison with the two Buddha statues of Bamiyan	undercoat	281 – 1001	281 – 501
270	Keule Kochak	loam sample			270 – 301
271	Khami-Kalak	loam sample			271 – 301
272	Surkh-Kul	loam sample			272 – 301
273	Regishad	loam sample			273 – 301

Buddha, approx. 150 m from the Western Buddha
- **Keule Kochak**: between Surkh-kul and the Western Buddha
- **Regishad**: alluvium of the Bāmiyān river, approx. 1 to 2 km west of the Western Buddha

Analytical methods

In order to characterize the composition of the various loam plaster fragments, we analyzed their mineralogical composition, using powder X-ray diffraction analysis and grain size distribution as well as a laser diffraction analysis system. We examined 19 loam plaster fragments and their individual layers. The selection was based on optical differences, such as colour of the plaster, type and amount of additives and layer sequence. Six samples come from the Eastern Buddha, 13 from the Western Buddha. For comparison, a fragment of the Buddha in the Kakrak valley that consists exclusively of undercoat was included in the study. This fragment has a slightly different colour and coarser pebbles as compared to the undercoats of the Bāmiyān Buddha statues.

Particle size distribution
As the investigated loam plaster samples were generally too small and also too fine-grained for conventional sieve analysis, we chose a laser-based particle size analyzer to determine the particle size measurement. We used a HORIBA LA–950 particle sizer based on static light scattering that covers a particle size range from 0.01 µm to 2 mm and requires less than 1 g of material for analysis.

As the different loam plaster layers were inhomogeneous, we took several small samples from various parts of the fragments and mixed them thoroughly. The organic additives of hairs or plant material and rare coarse sand grains were removed using tweezers as they would infer with the measurement. The samples were disaggregated in sodium polyphosphate solution containing 3 g sodium polyphosphate in 15 ml deionized water using a ultrasonic bath. Every sample was measured three times and the results averaged. The results are presented as particle size distribution and the cumulative distribution.

X-ray diffraction analysis
The sample was gently disaggregated by hand using an agate mortar and sieved (< 0.25 mm) to separate organic additives, such as hairs or straw. If sample material was very limited, the sample was ground with an agate mortar by hand and the powder was fixed on a glass slide using acetone ('smear mount'). If enough sample material was available, two grams of the sample were ground for 8 minutes with 10 ml of isopropyl alcohol in a McCrone Micronising Mill using agate cylinder elements. The suspension was filtered, dried, and homogenized in an agate mortar ('powder mount').

The XRD analyses (2–70° 2θ) were performed on top-loaded powder mounts using a Philips-Panalytical PW 1800 X-ray diffractometer (CuKα, graphite monochromator, 10 mm automatic divergence slit, step-scan 0.02° 2θ increments per second, counting time 1 s per increment, 40 mA, 40 kV). For more detailed clay mineralogical investigations, a sample aliquot was dispersed using an ultrasonic bath in a 0.1 molar aqueous ammonium solution. The < 2 µm fraction was separated by sedimentation in Atterberg cylinders. The oriented clay mineral aggregates were prepared by sedimentation and air-drying of the aqueous suspension on glass slides ('oriented mount'). X-ray diffraction scans (2–20° 2θ) were performed on an air-dried, a glycolated (24 hours in saturated glycol vapor at 80 °C), and a heated sample (3 hours at 550 °C).

The identification of crystalline mineral phases was carried out using the characteristic diffraction lines and their d-values with the program IDENTIFY (Philips-Panalytical). Clay minerals were identified using the basal diffraction lines

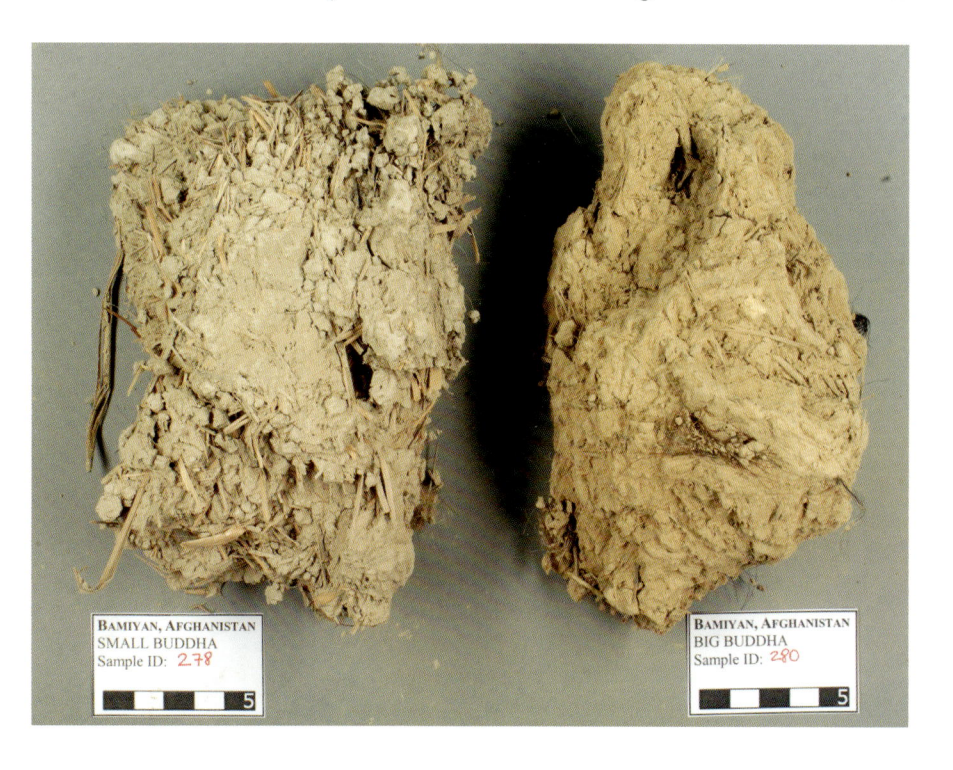

Fig. 1. Loam plaster fragments of the Eastern Buddha (sample 278, left) and the Western Buddha (sample 280, right) [Höfle, Thiemann]

on oriented mounts and their changes on glycolization.

Two different methods were conducted for quantification of crystalline phases. A small subset of 11 samples were analyzed using relative intensities of single mineral peaks at the Zentrallabor, Bayerisches Landesamt für Denkmalpflege, Munich, (Vojislav Tucic, analyst). This method yields, however, only semiquantitative results. The calcite content was determined for these samples by digestion of the carbonate in 10 wt. % acetic acid and weighing. The quantification of mineral content for most samples (23) was accomplished by the Rietveld method using the program BGMN (Bergmann et al. 1998).

Results

Particle size distribution

Four groups can be defined on the basis of the characteristic particle size distribution patterns shown in figure 2 and table 3. All groups have two characteristic peaks in the size distribution at 0.3 to 0.4 µm and 4 to 5 µm corresponding to the clay fraction and fine silt fraction, respectively. The four groups are distinguished on the variable contents of middle to coarse silt and fine sand fractions. Group 1 has a clearly visible shoulder at about 20 µm and a very small peak (0.2 to 1.2 %) at about 250 µm. In group 2, however, the shoulder at 20 µm is poorly visible and the 250 µm peak is well developed (2.4 to 3.4 %). Almost no particles are found in the 50 to 100 µm interval. Group 3 also has a large 250 µm peak (2.4 to 3.4 %), but an almost continuous distribution of particle sizes between 10 and 100 µm. Group 4 has a very broad peak between 250 and 700 µm that amounts to less than 1 %.

A few samples (84 and 224) cannot be attributed to any of the four groups. They are, as shown below, not original loam plasters, but restoration materials.

All group 1 samples are undercoats, while almost all group 2, 3 and 4 samples are finishing coats with the exception of sample 159. This indicates that in almost all finish coats a fine to medium-sized sand was added mostly to avoid shrinkage cracks. The group 3 and 4 patterns are relatively rare and can be attributed to optically unusual samples (ID 43, 63, 117, 159, 205). Group 4 pattern is only observed at the Western Buddha, while group 3 finish coats come from both Buddha statues.

X-ray diffraction analysis

The investigated loam plaster samples consist mainly of quartz, calcite, feldspars (orthoclase and albite), mica (muscovite), clay minerals, and trace amounts (<2 wt.%) of

Fig. 2. Particle size distribution (blue) and cumulative distribution (pink) curves of the four character groups of loam plaster fragments of the Bāmiyān Buddha statues

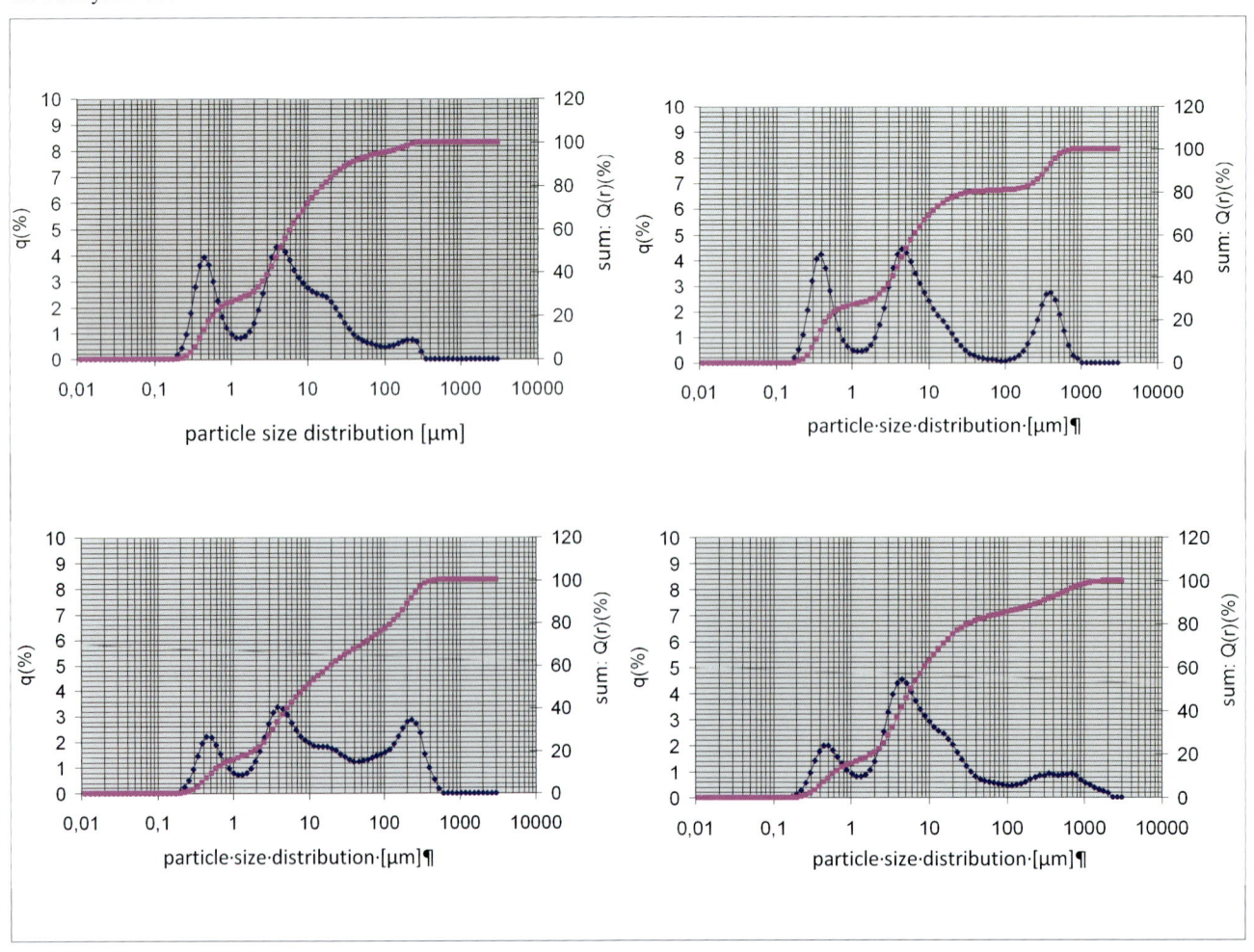

Table 3 Results of particle size distribution analyses

sample number	origin	layer type	analysis number	group
11	Western Buddha	finish coat	11 – 1001	2
26	Western Buddha	undercoat	26 – 1001	1
		finish coat	26 – 1002	2
38	Western Buddha	undercoat	38 – 1001	1
		finish coat	38 – 1002	2
43	Western Buddha	undercoat	43 – 1001	1
		finish coat	43 – 1002	4
55	Western Buddha	finish coat	55 – 1002	2
63	Western Buddha	undercoat	63 – 1001	1
		finish coat	63 – 1002	3
65	Western Buddha	undercoat	65 – 1001	1
84	Western Buddha	undercoat	84 – 1001	-
		finish coat	84 – 1002	-
117	Western Buddha	undercoat	117 – 1001	1
		finish coat	117 – 1002	4
159	Western Buddha	undercoat	159 – 1001	3
279	Western Buddha	undercoat	279 – 1001	1
280	Western Buddha	undercoat	280 – 1001	1
3	Eastern Buddha	undercoat	3 – 1001	1
		finish coat (upper)	3 – 1002	2
		finish coat (lower)	3 – 1003	2
200	Eastern Buddha	undercoat (reddish)	200 – 1001	1
		finish coat	200 – 1002	2
		undercoat (greyish)	200 – 1003	2
205	Eastern Buddha	undercoat	205 – 1001	1
		finish coat	205 – 1002	3
224	Eastern Buddha	undercoat (brownish)	224 – 1001	-
		finish coat (reddish)	224 – 1002	-
277	Eastern Buddha	undercoat	277 – 1001	1
278	Eastern Buddha	undercoat	278 – 1001	1
281	Kakrak Buddha	undercoat	281 – 1001	1

Table 4 Mineral composition of loam samples and plaster fragments based on semiquantitative XRD analysis

loam samples

sample number	quartz	calcite	mica	albite	chlorite	hornblende	gypsum	calcite*
270	50	25	11	6	8	-	-	28
271	62	14	8	9	7	-	-	13
272	66	11	10	9	4	-	-	14
273	51	22	10	10	7	-	-	24

loam plaster fragments

sample number	origin	quartz	calcite	mica	albite	chlorite	hornblende	gypsum	calcite*
undercoats									
1	WB	49	30	9	9	3	-	-	28
2	EB	51	27	9	9	3	1	-	25
3	EB	45	31	9	11	4	-	-	31
finishing coats									
1	WB	63	9	10	12	4	1	1	11
2	EB	68	6	10	14	2	-	-	8
3 lower	EB	56	19	11	11	3	-	-	22
3 upper	EB	61	13	9	15	2	-	-	16

* Calcite content determined by the acid digestion method
WB: Western Buddha; EB: Eastern Buddha

Table 5 Mineral composition of plaster fragments based on XRD analyses using the Rietveld method

sample number	origin	quartz	calcite	mica illite	feldspars (albite, orthoclase)	clay minerals (K, C, S)	hematite	gypsum	anhydrite
undercoats									
26	WB	49	14	14	14	8	1	-	-
63	WB	29	34	10	15	13	<1	-	-
65	WB	33	23	12	14	16	<1	-	-
117	WB	47	14	14	15	11	<1	-	-
279	WB	37	15	10	16	17	<1	-	-
2	EB	32	31	13	14	9	<1	-	-
200	EB	28	31	12	14	13	-	-	-
224	EB	15	6	7	22	2	-	25	21
278	EB	27	33	12	14	14	<1	-	-
281	KB	39	-	16	16	22	<1	-	-
finish coats									
11	WB	54	2	19	18	6	1	-	-
26	WB	55	4	17	17	8	<1	-	-
38	WB	52	3	13	21	12	1	-	-
55*	WB	49	3	14	19	14	1	-	-
63*	WB	44	11	9	21	12	1	-	-
84#	WB	24	11	9	22	13	-	19	1
117#	WB	30	4	15	36	14	1	-	-
2	EB	53	4	18	18	7	1	-	-
200	EB	38	5	15	18	12	<1	-	-
224	EB	18	4	10	4	-	-	39	26

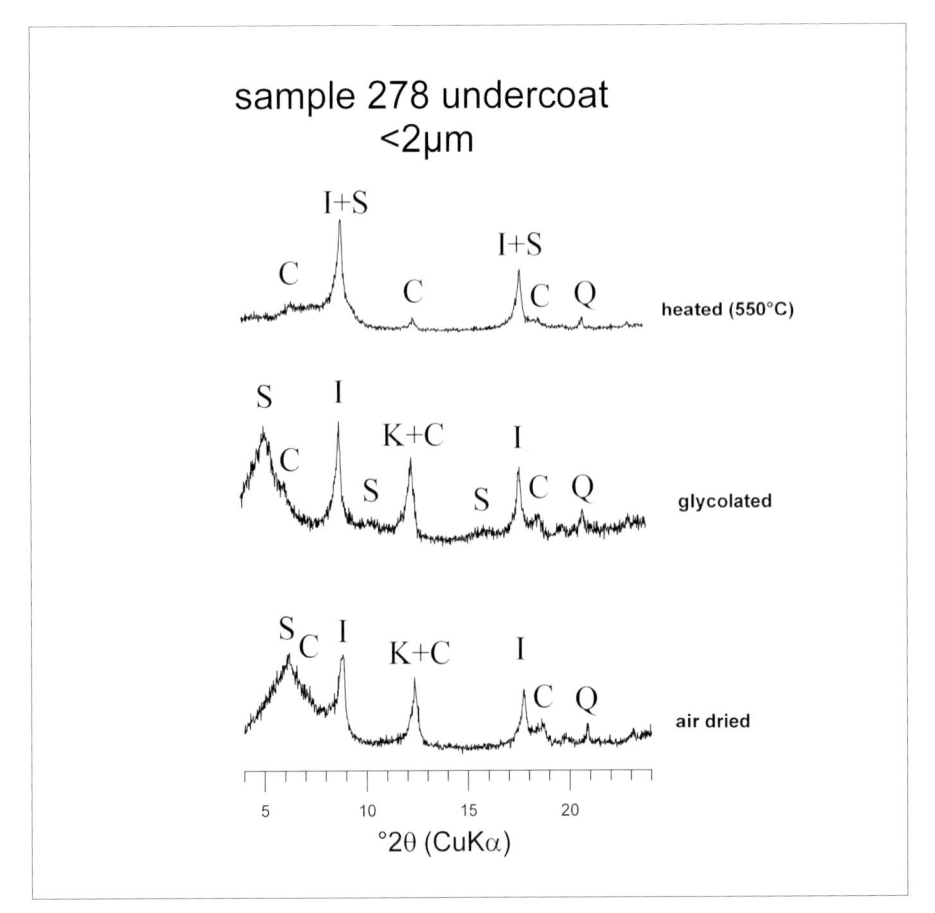

\# smear mount, large uncertainties   * conatains about 1% honrblende   K: kaolinite; c: chlorite; S: smectite
WB: Western Buddha; EB: Eastern Buddha; KB: Kakrak Buddha

Fig. 3. XRD patterns of air dried, glycolated, and heated oriented mounts (sample 278, undercoat) showing the presence of smectite (S), illite (I), chlorite (C), kaolinite (K) and traces of quartz (Q).

other phases such as hematite, amphibole (hornblende), and gypsum. Detailed investigation on two <2µm-fractions show that the dominant clay minerals are illite, chlorite, kaolinite and smectite (fig. 3). In a few samples (ID 84, 159 and 224), gypsum, anhydrite, and amorphous materials could be detected in major quantities suggesting that these fragments contain filling materials added during the Indo-Afghan restoration (1969-1978). The results of the semiquantitative analysis are presented in table 4, while the results of Rietveld approach are shown in table 5. The carbonate contents determined by the semiquantitative method are in good agreement with the independent measurements using the acetic acid digestion method. The two layers of sample ID 2 were analyzed by both quantification methods. The results are comparable considering the problems of sample aliquotation and heterogeneity, but clay mineral, mica, and feldspar contents were slightly underestimated by the semiquantitative method, and consequently the quartz contents were overestimated.

Nevertheless, the mineralogical composition of all investigated loam rendering fragments is very similar with major variations being detected mainly in the carbonate and quartz contents. The quartz contents of the finish coats (38 to 68 wt. %) are generally higher than those of the undercoats (15 to 51 wt. %). A sample with an unusual particle size distribution pattern of group 4 (low fine sand fraction) shows a relatively low quartz content (30 wt. %). The calcite content of the undercoats ranges from about 14 to 33 wt. %, while the finish coats have less than about 19 wt. % calcite. No significant differences were observed between the loam plasters of the Western and the Eastern Buddha. The higher quartz contents of the finish coats indicate the addition of quartz sand.

The local loam samples have very similar mineralogical compositions as the loam plaster fragments suggesting that the plaster material was locally sourced.

The single undercoat sample from the Kakrak Buddha, however, reveals no calcite and a high clay mineral content. This might indicate a different mud source for the coating of this Buddha; however, further investigations are warranted.

Conclusions

Microscopic, granulometric, and x-ray diffraction analyses of loam plaster fragments from the two Bāmiyān Buddha statues have shown that two distinct loam coatings exist. Both consist mainly of quartz, calcite, mica, feldspars (albite, orthoclase), clay minerals (illite, chlorite, kaolinite, smectite) and accessory hornblende, hematite and gypsum with additives of plant fragments (straw, chaff) and animal hairs. However, the undercoats clearly show lower quartz contents and lower proportions of fine to middle sand fractions as compared to the finishing coats. This suggests that fine quartz sand has been added to mud. Additionally, the finish coat appears more compacted and is devoid of coarse additives.

A few fragments contain major amounts of gypsum, anhydrite, and some amorphous substances that were probably added as filling materials during the Indo-Afghan restoration campaign (1969–1978).
Mineralogical analyses of neighbouring alluvial material show that the raw materials for preparation of the loam plasters of the two Bāmiyān Buddha statues were locally derived.

Acknowledgements

The investigations would not have been possible without the help of scientists of different institutions. Vojislav Tucic, Bavarian State Department for the Preservation of Monuments (Bayerisches Landesamt für Denkmalpflege), Munich, made the semiquantitative XRD analyses. Katharina Holzhäuser and Max Riehl, Lehrstuhl für Ingenieurgeologie, Technische Universität München, assisted to perform the procedure of quantitave XRD.

The particle size distribution was analysed firstly at Retsch Technology GmbH, 42781 Haan, Germany. Further analysis was performed at the University of the Federal Armed forces, Institut für Wasserwesen, Munich, with the support of Steffen Krause and Christina Schwarz.

Fig. 1. Grains and husks from the coarse clay of the Eastern Buddha

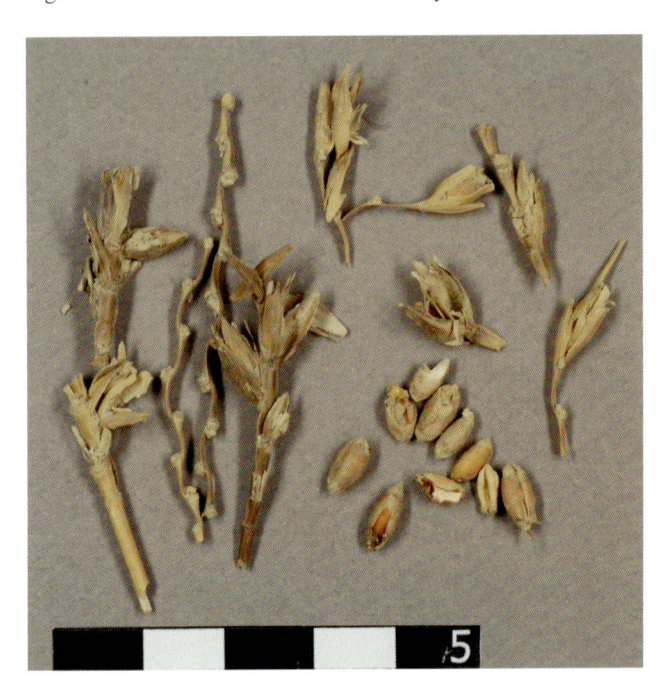

Fig. 2. Wheat (*Triticum aestivum*) from the Eastern Buddha

Fig. 3. Barley (*Hordeum vulgare*) from the Eastern Buddha

Stephanie Pfeffer, Catharina Blänsdorf
Organic Additives of the Clay Layers: Plant Materials

The organic additives of the clay layers consist of plant material and hairs. The undercoat contains chaff and hair, sometimes in tufts. The finish coat contains fine and mostly well distributed amounts of hair.

The organic additives found in the undercoat can be macroscopically identified as leaves and stems as well as parts of infructescences like husks and grains. At least the latter can be interpreted as residues of threshing.

The analysis was made on the base of botanical characteristics.[56] For this method leaves, parts of flowers or seeds are required. Fortunately, the materials imbedded in the clay plasters contained sufficient amounts of different parts of the plants. The samples selected for the analysis are listed in table 1.

Results

The analysis on the grains and husks resulted that the species of corn can be identified as common wheat (*triticum aestivum*, in German: Weichweizen, Nacktweizen) with more than 90 % of the analysed material. A low amount of common barley (*hordeum vulgare*, in German: zweizeilige Gerste) was found as well (figs. 1-3).

Table 1   Samples selected for identification of plant material

origin	number of samples	analysis
Eastern Buddha, undercoat	2	dec. 2006
Eastern Buddha, undercoat, collected in sept. 2006	1	not yet
tschaul, the main nourishment before introduction of potatoes	1	reference sample
corn species grown in Bāmiyān	3	not yet

Fig. 1. Fragments GBL 2377-2833 from the Western Buddha containing large amounts of hair [E. Melzl]

Fig. 2. Samples of hair taken from the clay fragments [S. Pfeffer]

Jan-Eric Grunwald
Organic Additives of the Clay Layers: Hair Identification

The clay layers of the Buddha statues contain animal hair. The hair was added as stabilisation of the clay. While the fine top clay layers only contain a low amount of fine hair, the undercoat contains more and thicker hair, often even in tufts or twisted strands (fig. 1). Samples of the hair were taken to Munich for analysis (fig. 2).

Several hair samples from the clay layers of the two Buddha statues (GBL 011; GBL 30/09/05,1; GBL 086; GBL 024; 25/09/06,2; KBL 004; KBL 084, KBL 208) were examined at the department for microtraces and biology at the Bayerisches Landeskriminalamt (Bavarian State Criminal Police Office) for identification.

Mammalian hairs are composed of three layers (from inside to outside): the medulla (core), the cortex, and the cuticle (scale layer). Species-specific characteristics of the entire hair and its layers, like (relative) size, shape, and structure, can be used to identify the former bearer of the hair.

For the present report, varying numbers of hairs from each sample were examined using low-power microscopy and then mounted on slides for high-power light microscopy. The sample hairs were compared to reference material collected from different common mammal species (goat, sheep, cow, and donkey[57]) in the valley of Bāmiyān by E. Melzl. Important diagnostic characteristics were e.g. structure and relative size of the medulla, cross-sectional shape and width of the hair, colour and pigmentation, and the hair profile.

The samples contained a variety of hair material, from small fragments of hairs (< 5 mm) to guard hairs approx. 150 mm long. Roots and tips are missing in most cases, a common feature of shorn hair or wool. The cross-sectional widths (at the widest part) often reach 100 μm (corresponding to a coarse human hair), the maximum width measured was 150 μm. Some samples contained balls of fine underhair (width approx. 10 to 30 μm). This underhair and other individual hairs lacking important diagnostic features could not be used for the discrimination of species, especially sheep and goat.

The hair colour varied between a yellowish white and brown to almost black. The cross-sections of the hairs and fragments were circular to oval, oblong, concavo-convex and dumb-bell shaped.

The majority of the examined hairs from the samples of both Buddha statues were identified as goat hair. They are consistent with the goat reference material in the most

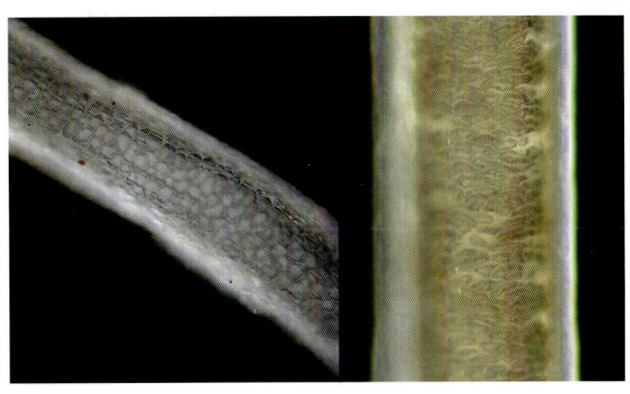

Fig. 3. Medulla structure of a sheep (left) and a goat hair (right; dark-field microscopy). Note the scalloped structure of the medulla lattice in the goat hair

Fig. 4. A hair from sample GBL 011 (Western Buddha, left) and from sample KBL 084 (Eastern Buddha, right, both brightfield microscopy). Note the goat-like medulla structure in both examples. The medulla on the left panel is still filled with air and therefore appears darker.

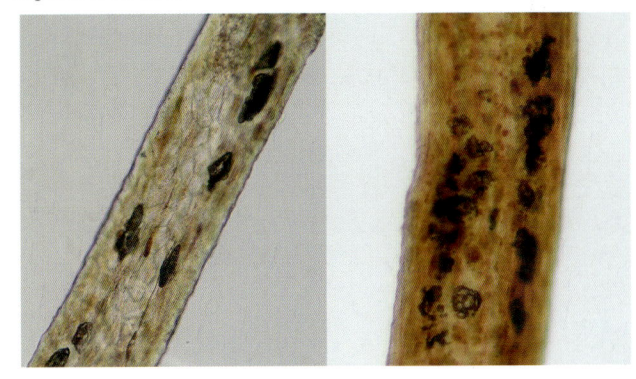

Fig. 5. Hair fragment from sample ID 55 (finish coat, left) and a sheep hair (right, both brightfield microscopy). Note the patchy, separated medulla

important diagnostic characters, especially in the structure of the medulla (figs. 3, 4).

Apart from fine underhair fragments, the two samples from the fine clay layers of the Western Buddha statue (ID 18 and ID 55) contained short hair fragments with dumb-bell shaped cross-sections and distinctive medulla structures and cuticle scale patterns, matching those of individual reference sheep hair (fig. 5). Especially the medulla structure could not be found in the goat reference material.

The sample from the finish coat of the Eastern Buddha statue (KBL 208) consisted only of two hair fragments that could not be assigned to a certain species, due to the lack of features.

To summarize, the examined samples of the undercoat from both statues consisted of goat hairs, mostly almost entire hairs or long fragments. In contrast, the samples from the top or finish coat contained only short fragments of hair, some of which were identified as sheep hair. Hairs of cow or donkey were not found in any of the examined samples.

Generally, domesticated animals including livestock are subject to selective breeding, which also affects the features of the hair, especially in mammals bred for wool like sheep or goat. This might over time result in major alterations or complete loss of important diagnostic features that are characteristic for the (wild) ancestor of a breed. Thus, hair of such animals can be hard to identify, especially without reference material from breeds common to the relevant area. In the present case, however, the guard hairs from the samples exhibit characteristic features and the reference material from the Bāmiyān valley provided the basis for a fairly reliable discrimination between sheep and goat hair.

Catharina Blänsdorf, Marie-Josée Nadeau, Pieter M. Grootes, Matthias Hüls, Stephanie Pfeffer, Laura Thiemann
Dating of the Buddha Statues – AMS ^{14}C Dating of Organic Materials

Introduction

Plant materials can be dated with radiocarbon dating. This method has improved greatly by the use of AMS (Accelerator Mass Spectrometry) regarding the sensitivity of the measurements and the amount of required sampling material. On the Buddha statues plant materials have been used in connection with the clay layers: the coarse clay layer contains straw and plant residues. The substructure of the fold ridges of the Western Buddha was made of wooden pegs and ropes. As many of these ropes have been found still imbedded in the clay, they provide short-lived plant material the date of which reflects the age of the Buddha. For larger protruding parts wooden beams have been used as anchoring elements. Most of the ones retrieved from the rubble come from the Western Buddha, but single ones could also be found on the Eastern Buddha.

As the attempts to date the statues until 2004 were based only on stylistic criteria, the hope was that the use of AMS ^{14}C would give exact dates und thus help to understand the origin and history of the statues.

It cannot be excluded that the clay layers are altogether younger than the sculpted stone and were applied in a phase of repair. There is no evidence for this assumption, but also no information definitely contradicting it. As the definite design was reached with the clay modelling, the stylistic criteria were also based on the clay rather than on the stone itself.

Dating based on historical and stylistic criteria

The beginning of Buddhist life in Bāmiyān and the building of a monastery are still unknown. Historical sources only tell that the first Buddhist period of Bāmiyān was interrupted in 770 AD by a hundred years of Muslim domination. In 870 AD, the region became Buddhist again until 977 AD when Islam irrevocably took over. The time span for the creation of Buddhist works of art can thus be restricted to the periods before 770 AD and between 870 AD and 977 AD. Furthermore, Xuanzang passed through the area around 630 AD and described Bamiyan as a flourishing Buddhist centre.[58]

Table 1 Overview of dating of the Buddha statues based on stylistic criteria

author	Eastern Buddha	Western Buddha	reason
Hackin 1922[3]	2nd to 3rd century	3th to 4th century	monastery linked to Kushan king Kanishka. It was built firstly around Eastern Buddha; Buddha shows Gandharan influence Western Buddha influenced by Gupta period or Mathura style Dating of caves (murals): executed East to West, dating from 3rd to 6th to 7th century
Yoshikawa 1939[4]			murals of niches around Western Buddha: 5th century
Rowland 1979, p. 87[5]	2nd to 3rd century or 4th to 8th century	5th to 7th century	Eastern Buddha: classical style of '*toga*'-like *sangati* or 'Neo-Gandhara' style between 4th and 8th century Western Buddha: influenced by Gupta period style of Mathura
Tarzi 1977[6]	580 to 630	6th century	
Kuwayama 1987[7]	middle of 6th century	middle of 6th century	change in trade routes between India and China; since middle of 6th century the Western route through the Hindukush passes through Bāmiyān
Klimburg-Salter 1989[8]	6th to 8th century, slightly older than Western Buddha	6th to 8th century	stylistic dating of murals in the niches and caves
Tanabe 2004[9]	635 to 645 or later		dating of murals around the Eastern Buddha; Xuanzang was either wrong or did not tell that the Buddha statues were not finished yet

Attempts to date the sculptures based on stylistic observations and historical sources have been made since the 1920s. A connection to the art of Gandhara is recognisable, but the estimation how fast or long-lasting this influence was on Bāmiyān varies considerably. For the Eastern Buddha dates between the 2nd and the 6th century were proposed, for the Western Buddha between the 3rd and the 8th century. The Eastern Buddha is mostly assumed to be slightly older than the Western Buddha.[59] More recent stylistic studies tend to date them to the 6th to 8th century and thus later than the authors of the first half of the 20th century. The most important attempts of dating are listed in table 1.

The National Research Institute of Cultural Properties, Japan and the Nagoya University used AMS ^{14}C dating on organic materials taken from the murals of the caves at the Buddha cliff in Bāmiyān and other cave sites.[67] The samples were not taken from the caves connected to the Buddha niches themselves. The investigation revealed that the clay plasters of the murals were made between 438 AD and 980 AD.[68] This means that work on the cliff of Bāmiyān continued until the very end of the Buddhist time.

Aim of the investigation with AMS ^{14}C dating

The aim of the analyses was to obtain a dating of the organic materials used on the Buddha statues to understand if they date back to the same age or to different ages. The latter would mean that at least parts could be attributed to repair phases.

As clay layers and ropes were found still connected to each other, it was obvious that they must stem from the same time. For the pegs, however, it was only clear that they belonged to the system of substructure using ropes, but they could have been replaced. For the larger wooden elements, consisting of beams or poles of 20 to 80 cm length, the assumption was that they were positioned in the larger square holes discernible at both statues, but had never been seen in situ. Thus they could have been originals as well as replacements or even not have belonged to the statues at all.

In some areas on both statues, three clay layers instead of the usual two layers were found, all of them below the paint layer. This raised the question if the top layer(s) – and consequently also the paint layers – had to be interpreted as later repairs. 22 fragments were selected for AMS ^{14}C dating (see examples in figure 1). The sample material comprised:

- 12 samples of straw and chaff from the clay plaster of both statues;
- 2 samples of wooden pegs and ropes of the Western Buddha;
- 2 samples of ropes;
- 4 samples of larger wooden beams of both statues;
- 1 sample of a wedge to adjust the larger wooden beam.

11 samples came from the Eastern Buddha and 10 from the Western Buddha. One additional sample was taken from niche I behind the Western Buddha to investigate if the niches were decorated at the same time as the clay modelling of the statues. The samples are listed in table 2.

The samples were analysed in three measuring phases, in May 2004, December 2004 and February 2009 and they were done at two institutions:

Dr. Georges Bonani, ETH (Eidgenössische Technische Hochschule) Zurich, Institute for Particle Physics	2 samples	May 2004
	7 samples	January 2009
Prof. Dr. Pieter Grootes, Dr. Matthias Hüls and Dr. Marie-Josée Nadeau, Leibnitz Laboratory for Radiometric Dating and Isotope Research, Christian-Albrechts-Universität zu Kiel	13 samples	December 2004

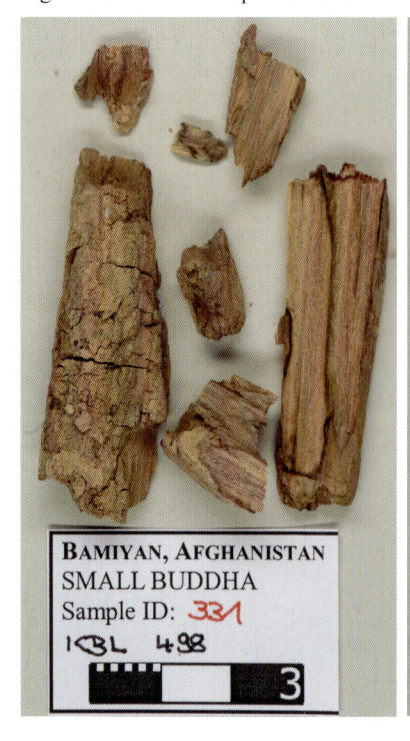

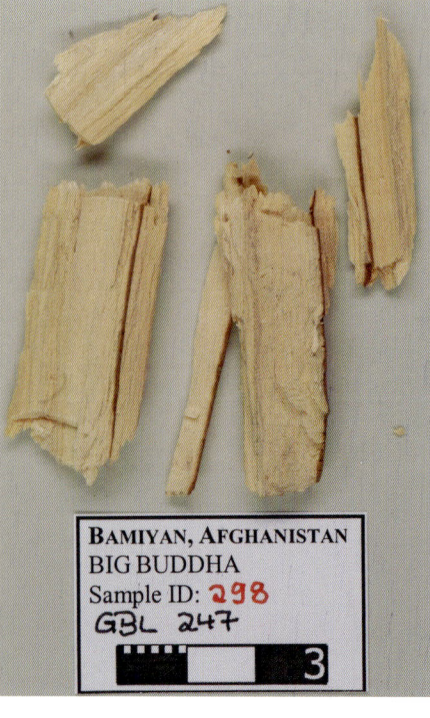

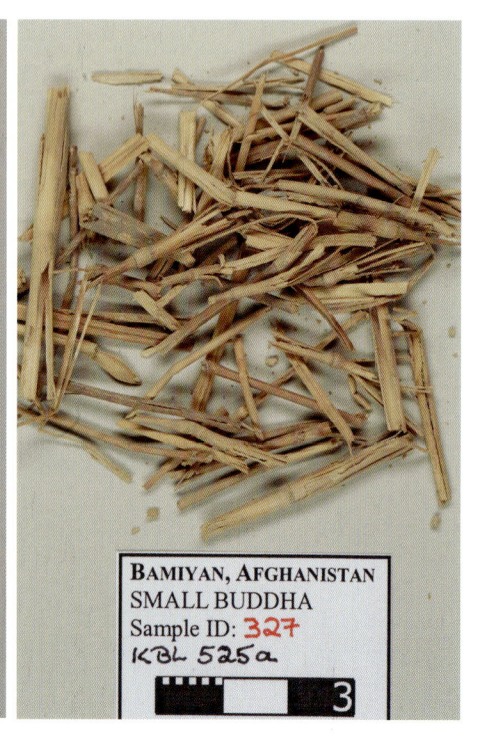

Fig. 1. Three of the samples selected for ^{14}C-AMS dating

Table 2 List of samples for ^{14}C-AMS dating

sample code	lab no.	statue	material/description	institution/year
Kleiner Buddha – 1	ETH-28498	Eastern Buddha	plant metrial from clay	ETH 2004
Kleine Buddha – 2	ETH-28499	Eastern Buddha	plant material from clay	ETH 2004
KBL 026	KIA 25567	Eastern Buddha	chaff from undercoat	Kiel 2004
KBL 037	KIA 25568	Eastern Buddha	chaff from undercoat	Kiel 2004
KBL 052	KIA 25569	Eastern Buddha	chaff from undercoat	Kiel 2004
KBL 085	KIA 25570	Eastern Buddha	chaff from undercoat	Kiel 2004
KBL 095	KIA 25571	Eastern Buddha	chaff from undercoat	Kiel 2004
KBL 172	KIA 25794	Eastern Buddha	chaff from undercoat	Kiel 2004
327-901 (KBL 525a)	ETH-36793	Eastern Buddha	chaff and straw from the two top layers of three-layered clay plaster	ETH 2009
328-901 (KBL 252b)	ETH-36794	Eastern Buddha	chaff and straw from the two top layers of three-layered clay plaster	ETH 2009
331-901 (KBL 498)	ETH-36788	Eastern Buddha	probably from a wedge for locking a larger wooden beam (from substructure)	ETH 2009
334-901 (KBL 530)	ETH-36789	Eastern Buddha	from 27 cm long round log, without bark (from substructure)	ETH 2009
GBL 106	KIA 25564	Western Buddha	chaff from undercoat	Kiel 2004
GBL 192	KIA 25565	Western Buddha	chaff from undercoat, relation to Great Buddha or cave wall not clear	Kiel 2004
GBL 016	KIA 25560	Western Buddha	rope	Kiel 2004
GBL 028	KIA 25561	Western Buddha	rope	Kiel 2004
GBL 033	KIA 25562	Western Buddha	wooden peg	Kiel 2004
GBL 091	KIA 25563	Western Buddha	wooden peg	Kiel 2004
298-901 (GBL 247)	ETH-36790	Western Buddha	from 51 cm long square beam, traces of saw, one side axed	ETH 2009
291-901 (GBL 248)	ETH-36791	Western Buddha	from 64 cm long beam, partly with bark, sawn and axed, covered with red slurry	ETH 2009
296-901 (GBL 254)	ETH-36792	Western Buddha	from 81 cm long square beam, one of the largest beams found so far, sawn and axed	ETH 2009
GBH 1	KIA 25566	Cave I, behind Western Buddha, back of niche, centre	wooden anchoring element	Kiel 2004

Procedure of AMS ^{14}C dating in Kiel

The excellent preservation of the sample material suggests little to no contamination and also allowed rigorous cleaning. The selected material was checked, mechanically cleaned under the microscope. It was then extracted with acid (HCl), base (NaOH) and again acid (HCl) to remove carbonates as well as acid and alkali soluble organic contaminants. The combustion to CO_2 was performed in closed quartz tubes together with CuO and silver wool at 900°C. The sample CO_2 was reduced with H_2 over Fe powder as catalyst, and the resulting carbon/iron mixture was pressed into a pellet in the larger holder. The sample material selected contained between 2.8 and 4.2 mg C.

The samples were measured at the Leibniz Laboratory in Kiel using the 3.0 MV HVEE tandetron-based AMS system equipped with a separator-recombinator. The final results are the averages of six-minute interval measurements. The number of interval measurements varied from 10 to 20, depending on the impact of the uncertainty on the calibrated 2 sigma ranges. The raw isotope ratios were compared to Oxalic Aced II (134.06 pMC) and background samples (coal) of similar sizes for process blank correction.

The final uncertainty of each measurement is the larger of either the counting statistics or the error on the mean (Standard Deviation / $\sqrt{n}$). Although this practice is sometimes contested, it has been adopted in Kiel because some samples vary more than others during measurement. The idea is that this instability (up to ~ 1.5 x counting statistics) should be included in the overall uncertainty of the final result. This instability is believed to be due to the impurities in the sample gas, producing graphite of a lesser quality. The uncertainty of our background correction is also included in the uncertainty of the final result.

The product of the probability distributions vs. calendar age of the 11 samples from the Eastern Buddha and eight samples from the Western Buddha were calculated using OxCal 4.0 (function combine), and the 1 σ and 2 σ probability ranges calculated from it by the program.

Interpretation of results

The results of the single samples are listed in table 3. All of the samples can be dated to the 5th to 7th century, except for one sample of a wooden beam which probably has to be dated after 1950. It can be interpreted as a replacement or support beam inserted by the Indian restorers.

Table 3 Results of ^{14}C-AMS dating

sample code/lab no.	material	^{14}C age	ages (probability)		institution/year
Eastern Buddha					
Kleiner Buddha-1, ETH-28498	chaff	1440 ± 40 BP	1 σ range: 585AD-650AD (68,2%)	2 σ range: 550AD-660AD (95,4%)	ETH 2004
Kleiner Buddha-2, ETH-28499	chaff	1460 ± 40 BP	1 σ range: 570AD-640AD (68,2%)	2 σ range: 530AD-660AD (95,4%)	ETH 2004
KBL 026, KIA 25567	chaff	1499 ± 19 BP	1 σ range: 550AD-600AD (68,3%)	2 σ range: 535AD-635AD (95,4%)	Kiel 2004
KBL 037, KIA 25568	chaff	1540 ± 23 BP	1 σ range: 430AD-490AD (35,6%) 530AD-570AD (32,6%)	2 σ range: 4300AD-580AD (95,4%)	Kiel 2004
KBL 052, KIA 25569	chaff	1499 ± 19 BP	1 σ range: 550AD-595AD (68,2%)	2 σ range: 535AD-615AD (95,4%)	Kiel 2004
KBL 085, KIA 25570	chaff	1503 ± 25 BP	1 σ range: 545AD-595AD (68,2%)	2 σ range: 440AD-490AD (4,0%) 530AD-640AD (91,4%)	Kiel 2004
KBL 095, KIA 25571	chaff	1532 ± 22 BP	1 σ range: 440AD-490AD (22,0%) 530AD-580AD (46,2%)	2 σ range: 430AD-600AD (95,4%)	Kiel 2004
KBL 172, KIA 25794	chaff	1510 ± 22 BP	1 σ range: 540AD-590AD (68,2%)	2 σ range: 440AD-490AD (6,9%) 530AD-610AD (88,5%)	Kiel 2004
327-901, ETH-36793 (KBL 525a)	chaff	1510 ± 30 BP	1 σ range: 535AD-600AD (68,2%)	2 σ range: 430AD-490AD (14,9%) 500AD-630AD (80,5%)	ETH 2009
328-901, ETH-36794 (KBL 252b)	chaff	1475 ± 30 BP	1 σ range: 560AD-620AD (68,2%)	2 σ range: 540AD-645AD (95,4%)	ETH 2009
331-901, ETH-36788	wooden beam	> 1954 AD			ETH 2009
334-901, ETH-36789	wooden beam	1515 ± 35 BP	1 σ range: 460AD-490AD (7,0%) 530AD-610AD (61,2%)	2 σ range: 430AD-620AD (95,4%)	ETH 2009
Western Buddha					
GBL 106, KIA 25564	chaff	1459 ± 21 BP	1 σ range: 585AD-640AD (68,2%)	2 σ range: 560AD-645AD (95,4%)	Kiel 2004
GBL 192, KIA 25565	chaff	1503 ± 15 BP	1 σ range: 545AD-585AD (68,2%)	2 σ range: 540AD-605AD (95,4%)	Kiel 2004
GBL 016, KIA 25560	rope	1448 ± 19 BP	1 σ range: 600AD-640AD (68,2%)	2 σ range: 575AD-650AD (95,4%)	Kiel 2004
GBL 028, KIA 25561	rope	1450 ± 16 BP	1 σ range: 600AD-640AD (68,2%)	2 σ range: 575AD-645AD (95,4%)	Kiel 2004
GBL 033, KIA 25562	wooden peg	1441 ± 24 BP	1 σ range: 600AD-645AD (68,2%)	2 σ range: 575AD-655AD (95,4%)	Kiel 2004
GBL 091, KIA 25563	wooden peg	1451 ± 22 BP	1 σ range: 595AD-640AD (68,2%)	2 σ range: 565AD-650AD (95,4%)	Kiel 2004
298-901, ETH-36790	wooden beam	1460 ± 30 BP	1 σ range: 580AD-640AD (68,2%)	2 σ range: 550AD-650AD (95,4%)	ETH 2009
291-901, ETH-36791	wooden beam	1425 ± 30 BP	1 σ range: 605AD-650AD (68,2%)	2 σ range: 575AD-660AD (95,4%)	ETH 2009
296-901, ETH-36792	wooden beam	1455 ± 35 BP	1 σ range: 580AD-645AD (68,2%)	2 σ range: 550AD-660AD (95,4%)	ETH 2009
GBH 1 (cave behind Buddha), KIA 25566	wooden beam	1461 ± 21 BP	1 σ range: 580AD-635AD (68,2%)	2 σ range: 560AD-645AD (95,4%)	Kiel 2004

Results of AMS ^{14}C dating in Kiel

The calibration of the average of the results for both statues shows that the Eastern Buddha was built about 50 years before the Western Buddha. The calibration of the age of the Eastern Buddha of (1513 ± 7 BP) leads to a 2 sigma probability range of 540 to 591 AD while that one of the Western Buddha ranges from 580 to 636 AD. The sample taken from cave I behind the Western Buddha (sample GBL 192 / KIA 25566) can be dated to exactly the same time as the samples from the Buddha itself.

The very good agreement between the samples of the Western Buddha (except for one sample) also shows that the period of the manufacturing did not take too long. The larger scatter in the ages of the Eastern Buddha could indicate that the coating of the Eastern Buddha took longer to make than the one of the Western Buddha (fig. 2).

The samples analysed in Zurich showed that the chaff taken from the three-layered clay plaster could be dated to the same time as the usual double layered plasters. The three-layered structure thus could be proved to belong to the same modelling period; it is not a later repair. The larger wooden beams could be dated to the same time as the chaff and the pegs. This proved that they are part of the substructure. Table 4 provides a summary of the combined calibration for the measured samples.

Conclusion

The plant material (wood, ropes, organic additives of the clay) of both statues could be dated with AMS ^{14}C. The results of the single samples correspond to each other what means that wooden substructures and clay layers date from the same time. The time periods for the statues are:

Eastern Buddha	544 to 595 AD (2 σ)
Western Buddha	591 to 644 AD (2 σ).

Three-layered structures of clay could be prooved not to be a result of a repair, but of a correction during modelling, as they come from the same time as the usual two-layered structures.

Larger wooden elements recovered from the rubble also belonged to the statues. This seems to support the assumption that the larger damages on the right leg of the Western Buddha already happened during modelling and were reconstructed using timbers and clay or brick material. An obviously modern beam also showed that beams were replaced, probably during the Indo-Afghan restoration in 1969-78.

The results of the AMS ^{14}C-dating of the plant material can be interpreted as a dating for the creation of the statues, based on the assumption that wooden substructures and clay layers aslready originally must have been integral parts of the statues. The stone itself, however, cannot be dated. Thus there still is the possibility that the sculpting in stone started earlier or that the clay layers have been replaced at an early stage of repair. The fact that the existing clay layers survived more than 1500 years, however, and that no traces of older modelling could be detected supports the assumption that wooden support elements and clay are part of the original design.

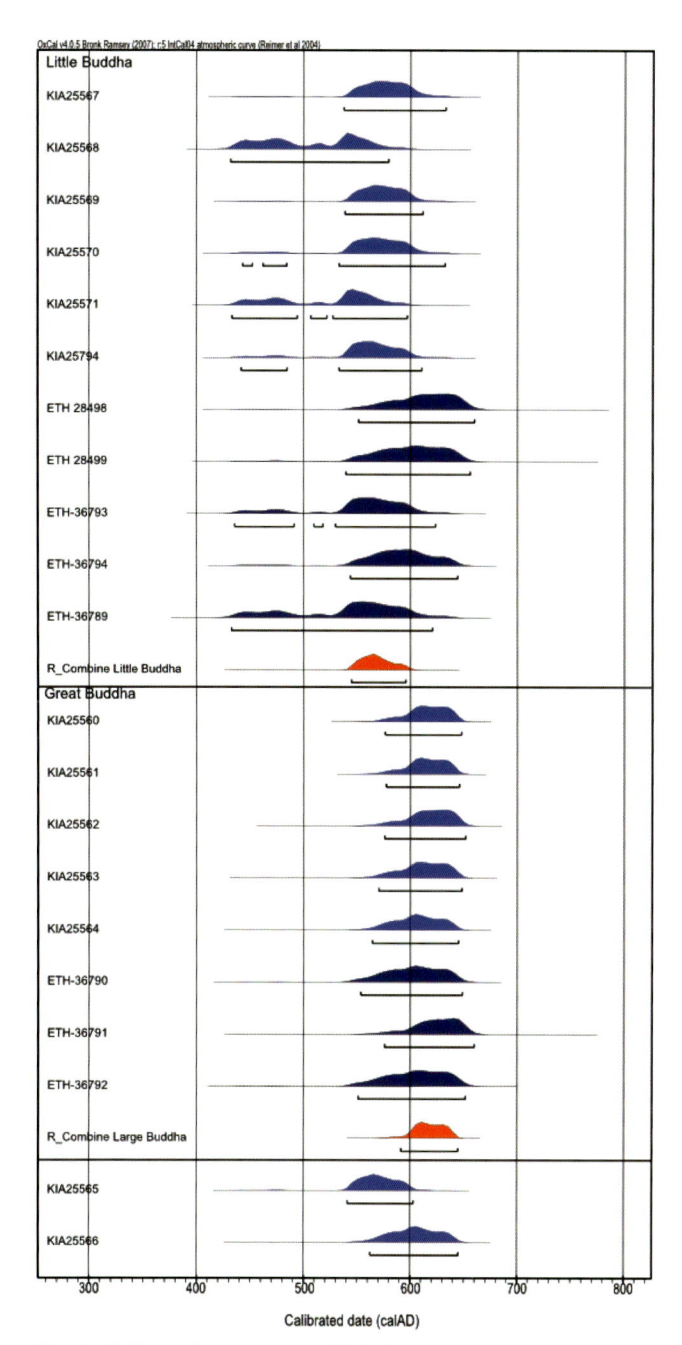

Fig. 2. Calibrated sample ages. Light blue colours refer to samples measured in the Leibniz Laboratory, Kiel, and dark blue colours to measurements done at ETH, Zürich. The red coloured field gives the product of the probability distributions vs. calendar age of the samples from the Eastern Buddha and the Western Buddha.

Table 4   Interpretation of ^{14}C-results. Overview of means

	Calendar years (probability)
Eastern Buddha	1 σ range: 549AD - 579AD (68.2%) 2 σ range: 544AD - 595AD (95.4%)
Western Buddha	1 σ range: 605AD - 633AD (68.2%) 2 σ range: 591AD - 644AD (95.4%)

References

Kuwayama, S., *Two Itineraries Concerning the Emergence of the Colossi in Bamiyan*, in: Gnoli/Lanciotti (ed.): *Orientalia: Iosephi Tucci Memoriae Dicata,* Rom 1987, cited in: NATIONAL RESEARCH INSTITUTE FOR CULTURAL PROPERTIES JAPAN 2006, pp. 136-138

Klimburg-Salter, Deborah, *The Kingdom of Bāmiyān: Buddhist Art and Culture of the Hindu Kush*, Naples and Rome, 1989

Nadeau, Marie-Josée; Grootes, Pieter M.; Hüls, Matthias; Melzl, Edmund; Petzet, Michael; Praxenthaler, Bert: *Dating of the Buddhas of Bamiyan*, Poster, 19th Radiocarbon conference, Oxford, 2006

National Research Institute for Cultural Properties Japan (ed.): *Radiocarbon Dating of the Bamiyan Mural Paintings*, in: *Recent Cultural Heritage Issues in Afghanistan*, vol. 2, Tokyo 2006

Rowland, Benjamin: *Die Kunst Zentralasiens*, Baden-Baden 1979

Tanabe. Katsumi: *Foundation for dating anew the 38 meter Buddha Image at Bāmiyān*, in: Silk Road Art *and Archaeology*, vol. 10, 2004, cited in: NATIONAL RESEARCH INSTITUTE FOR CULTURAL PROPERTIES JAPAN 2006, pp. 136–138

Tarzi, Zemaryalai: *L'architecture et le décor rupestre des grottes de Bamiyan*, Paris 1977, 2 vols (vol. 1: Texts, vol. 2: Sketches, photographs)

Wriggins, S.H., Xuanzang: *A Buddhist Pilgrim on the Silk Road*, Boulder, Westview Press, 1966

Catharina Blänsdorf, Stephanie Pfeffer, Edmund Melzl
The Polychromy of the Giant Buddha Statues in Bāmiyān

Introduction

Traces of paint have been observed and mentioned since the 19th century, but there has never been an examination.

When clay fragments of the Buddha statues were recovered from the rubble it became obvious that many of them showed remnants of paint layers. Although damaged and often hidden under clay-coloured layers, different colours could be distinguished.

Observed colours have been recorded in the fragment catalogue. In most cases, red, reddish ochre or greyish red are mentioned; in addition, brown, white, yellow ochre and blue are listed. However, there was no possibility for a thorough investigation on-site.

Though the material is abundant, there are grave deficiencies. The original position of almost all the fragments is unknown. A large number of pieces are missing as a result f the explosion. The surviving fragments were found scattered in the rubble at the feet of the Buddha statues. Most of them are too damaged or too small to be assigned to specific positions. They vary in shape and thickness, and the edges of the fragile clay are broken off, so they cannot be reassembled into larger areas. Conclusions can only be drawn on the basis of the surface shape or the structure of the clay support of larger fragments. Some fragments can be recognised as fold ridges in this way. The only distinction that can be made with some certainty is that between parts of the sculptures and fragments of the murals.

The identification of materials seemed to be appropriate as a base for all further considerations and interpretations. At the same time, literary sources and pictures were checked meticulously for hints on the colouration or on the remnants of paint layers. 276 tiny fragments of clay with paint layers were available for investigation, 173 coming from the Western Buddha, 103 from the Eastern Buddha. All fragments have been examined carefully. Microscopic examination, cross sections and pigment identification have been performed with support from Monica Reiserer, Nicole Wagner and Maximilian Knidlberger, students at the Technische Universität München, Chair of Restoration, under the supervision of Stephanie Pfeffer.

Historical records on paint layers

All preserved pictures, i.e. drawings and photographs, show the statues brown and monochrome. Nevertheless, written sources refer to colours and occasionally even mention paint layers. These records are the only chance to find some evidence on the distribution of colours and now and then even hint at changes of the visual impression over time. The earliest source to be mentioned dates back to the time of the creation of the statues. In the *Xi you ji*, describing his journey to India between c. 629–645, the Chinese monk Xuanzang writes about Bāmiyān:

'*To the north-east of the royal city there is [...] a stone figure of Buddha, erect, in height 140 or 150 feet. Its golden hues sparkle on every side, and its precious ornaments dazzle the eyes by their brightness*'. *[...] To the east of this spot there is a convent, which was built by a former king of the country. To the east of the convent there is a standing figure of Sâkya Buddha, made of metallic stone (teou-shih) in height 100 feet. It has been cast in different parts and joined together, and thus placed in a complete form as it stands.*[69]

The interpretation and the origin of the non-Chinese term *teou shih* is difficult. It seems to denote either a metallic, copper-containing stone or a metal. The indication that the statue was produced in parts led to the conclusion that a metal sculpture was meant which has been lost since then. However, the description mentions two giant Buddha statues, and the cited heights of 47 to 50 m and 33 m correspond fairly well to the two existing Buddha statues. If Xuanzang refers to the two existing statues, the first one, being made of stone, with sparkling golden hues and precious ornaments, would be the taller Western Buddha, and the other one would be the smaller Eastern Buddha appearing as if made of metal. As it is not proven that Xuanzang visited Bamiyan and saw the Buddha statues himself, interpretations must be cautious.

Another interesting description was written some centuries later and also by a man who may not have seen the Buddha statues himself. The geographer and biographer Yakut al Hamawi travelled in Afghanistan shortly before the invasion of the Mongols in 1221. He refers to the situation before the devastation of Bāmiyān by Genghis Khan's troops. He reports that the statues were called the '*red idol*' and the '*white idol*', and that they were standing in a building of an incredible height, carried by giant pillars: '*you see a building the summit of which is in incredible height; the summit is supported by giant pillars and is covered with paintings showing all the birds created by God. Inside are two huge idols cut into the rock and reaching from the bottom to the top of the mountain. One is called the red idol and the other one the white idol. You cannot find anything comparable to these two statues in the whole world.*'[70]

Although it is strange that the description sounds as if both statues were found inside *one* building, this mention of an edifice in front of the niches is interesting as it could mean that originally the niches were closed to the front or were sheltered behind a façade construction. These front buildings may have been built of wood and destroyed by the Mongols.[71]

The next description on colours dates from the late 18th century: '*these statues were visited at least ten or twelve times by a famous traveller, called Me'yan-Asod-Shah [...]. He informed me* [Francis Wilford] *lately that these statues are in two niches and about forty paces distant from each other. That the drapery is covered with embroidery and figured work; which formerly was painted of different colours; traces of which are still visible. That one seems to have been painted of a red colour; and the other, either retains the original colour of the stone, or was painted grey.*'[72]

There is some imprecision in this description – 40 (American) paces would correspond to 236 m, not to 800 m – and the description of the statues sounds like a compilation of Xuanzang and Yakut al Hamawi, but nevertheless it is possible that it was based on an eyewitness' account. Here the characterisation as 'red' and 'grey' is clearly connected to the dominating colours visible on the surfaces and not to names given by local people. Furthermore, it seems to be linked to the drapery as this is the largest and thus dominant part of both statues.[73]

Nevertheless, the paint layers were probably much reduced at that time and the overall impression obviously was not colourful. 19th-century sketches, drawn merely 30 years after Me'yan Asod Shah's visit, do not show any colours or painted decoration. The rather detailed description by Alexander Burnes of 1834 mentions the modelling, the damages, and the system of wooden pegs and plaster layers. Burnes also describes the murals preserved above the heads of the Buddha statues, but he does not mention any colours or traces of paint on the statues themselves.[74] The sketch he made shows some impreciseness in details and dimensions.[75] Nevertheless, he indicated the murals he had seen around the head of the Western Buddha, simplified as a

Fig. 1. Drawing by Alexander Burnes [BURNES 1834, next to p. 183]

THE COLOSSAL IDOLS AT BAMEEAN

spiral twine design.⁷⁶ The robes of the statues, however, are completely plain.

In the first scientific study on the statues, published by Maitland, Talbot, and Simpson in 1886, Maitland, who made the drawings of the statues (fig. 2), remarks: '*The idols themselves are [...] roughly hewn [...] and afterwards thickly overlaid with stucco [...]. The stucco appears to have been painted or at least paint was used in some places.*'⁷⁷

The sketches are quite precise regarding shape and dimensions: The proportions are realistic. Details of the drapery are depicted precisely. The cut-out faces can be recognised. Even technical details and damages like the losses on the legs and arms of the Western Buddha and the holes for the anchoring beams exposed in these areas are depicted. The drawings are black and white, however, and do not indicate any colouring.

In the later 1920s, J. Carl explored the Western Buddha during the DAFA campaign using a rope which helped him to climb down on the right forearm of the Buddha (fig. 3). He described what Hackin and he could see of the technology of the *sangati*: '*We have collected fragments which imitated the drapery of the monk's robe. They still possessed their armature made of ropes and pegs, and covered with a red paint layer which originally had covered the entire robe (fig. 24).*'⁷⁸

The German edition of the visitors' guide to the caves and statues of Bāmiyān of 1939, compiled by Joseph and Ria Hackin in 1934, mentioned traces of paint, but only for the Eastern Buddha: '*On the sleeve there are still some traces of red and blue paint and on the chin remnants of gold coating.*'⁷⁹

The Indian restorers of the Indo-Afghan co-operation in 1969-78 recognised remnants of paint, but did not record them. Sengupta briefly mentions the painted clay layers of the Eastern Buddha: '*Traces of pigments on the plaster show that the exposed parts of the body were painted in gold and the garment in blue.*'⁸⁰

At the end of their interventions, the restorers applied a suspension of clay and gypsum on all surfaces of the statues. This was done to unify and harmonise the overall impression, either because the restorers wanted to incorporate the newly reconstructed and repaired parts or because they were convinced that the statues were originally intended to appear

Fig. 2. Drawings by Maitland [TALBOT / SIMPSON 1886, p. 348]

Fig. 3. Hackin/Carl 1933, fig. 24: *sangati* of the Western Buddha

like unpainted stone. Thus, at least after 1978, the statues looked uniformly grey-brown.

Summarising the information about colours in historical sources, we can state that the earliest of them mentions ornaments and sparkling, and perhaps a metallic appearance. Since the 11th century the names of *Surkh-but* (Red Buddha) and *Khink-but* (White Buddha) can be found in descriptions of Islamic writers.[81] A relation to the dominating colours seems likely, although white is not a usual colour for Buddhist garments, since in Asian and Buddhist countries white is the colour of death and mourning.

The first precise mention of paint layers goes back to Maitland in 1885. The few, but nevertheless consistent statements in the literature are:

Western Buddha	*sangati*:	red
Eastern Buddha	garment:	red and blue; blue
	skin; chin:	gold

Possible colour distribution on the statues

For the interpretation of the different colours found, it is helpful to keep in mind how the statues are designed. With regard to the modelling, five main parts can be distinguished:
1. the outside of the *sangati* which is the largest part of the statue;
2. the lining of the *sangati* which might have been visible at the insides of the folds hanging over the arms;
3. the undergarment (*uttarasanga*), which has been visible underneath the *sangati* and perhaps at the forearms. At least at the Eastern Buddha it was visible at the lower parts of the legs, being longer than the *sangati*;
4. the skin, which after the loss of the hands and the severe damage of the feet was only preserved on the necks and faces;
5. the hair of which some strands near the ears were still preserved on both statues.

In addition, there may have been painted details such as patterns on the *sangati*, the lips or decorations in the hair. Due to earlier damages and losses, probably no traces of hair decorations or the lips were still existent before the destruction, but there could have been decorations on the *sangati*. The literary sources contain no evidence for colours or style, except the vague descriptions of "*golden hues*" and "*precious ornaments*", mentioned by Xuanzang, or the reference to "*embroidery and figure work*" reported by Me'yan Asod Shah.

The characterisations as a grey and a red Buddha can be interpreted as an overall impression and therefore related to the dominating colour of the garment. On the other hand, it can also refer to a more reddish or whitish clay surface.[82] Iconographic specifications regarding the colours of the clothes are not possible, as there is no consistent canon for Buddha's robes.

Examination of the paint layer sequences

The examined samples comprise 275 small pieces of painted clay, mostly between 1 and 4 cm in length (fig. 4). As most of them were not included in the list of findings set up in Bāmiyān, because they were too small, a new numbering system was set up.

The examination was mainly executed under the stereo microscope at 50 times magnification. In many cases this was sufficient to understand the layer sequence and had the advantage of being non-invasive. Groups of similar samples were formed. Some samples of each group were selected for cross sections to examine the layer sequences in detail. The pigments were identified for each group on significant fragments.

A very important result was that on most samples there is more than one paint layer. That means that the statues have been repainted. Several sequences of layers could be observed on a larger number of samples.

Underneath the paint layers, often a slightly reddish or brownish and sometimes transparent and slightly glossy layer can be observed which seems to have penetrated into the clay surface. This can be interpreted as a pre-treatment with an organic binder to obtain a dust-free surface, to reduce the danger of dissolving the clay and to homogenize the suction of the support. This kind of isolation layer on the clay plaster has been observed on the murals as well.[83]

Different from the murals, most of the samples do not show a white priming layer. If a white priming is found, it often is not a coherent layer, but consists of tiny remnants or partially present spots. This applies to all samples, independent of colour or layer sequences.

On top of the paint layers, almost all samples show a light ochre layer which can be attributed to the Indo-Afghan restoration. This layer mostly consists of a clay suspension, sometimes mixed with charcoal or gypsum, probably to adjust the colour. Some samples show a more compact clay layer which seems to be a completion and can contain the same type of plant fibres also found in the gypsum fillings. Additionally, splashes of white and brownish pink or bright ochre can be found on top of the paint layers or the clay suspension, probably from retouching completions.[84] Larger spots or streaks come from gypsum accidentally dropped on the surface. Some fragments are coated with a transparent, glossy, slightly elastic material which probably is a modern synthetic consolidant. On some fragments fibres stick to this layer, obviously from an attempt to wipe off the surplus of consolidant.[85] In the following the materials of the Indo-Afghan restoration are not mentioned further.

The samples have been classified into six different groups with several subcategories. Most of the groups can be found on both statues. All samples of one group show similar layer sequences which are described in the following.

Understanding the layer sequences and the relation between the samples was a difficult task due to the fact that the samples differ extremely in state of preservation and thus in their visual impression. Most fragments are partly or completely covered with the clay suspension and others are blackened by soot. On many fragments the paint layers are thinned or have partially flaked off. The confirmation if the idea about layer sequences obtained at the examination with the stereo microscope was correct could only be achieved by examining a larger number of cross sections. Although in the end most fragments could be assigned to the groups, a number of samples only show tiny traces of paint which were difficult to understand and could not be related to any layer or sequence.[86]

The samples which are darkened or blackened by soot sometimes do not show more than vague traces of paint layers, but some can be assigned to groups 1, 2, 3 and 5, which means that they came from different parts of the robes of the statues.[87] It can be assumed that they belonged to lower parts or areas next to the caves where the surfaces were blackened by the soot of fires.

Groups 1 and 2
Groups 1 and 2 comprise samples which on the whole appear reddish, resulting from layers of pink, orange and red. The two groups differ regarding one aspect: In group 1, the first layer is a white priming layer which seems not to be coherent, but only preserved in some spots. It is missing in the fragments of group 2.

Fig. 4. Most of the 275 painted clay layer fragments examined in Munich [Pfeffer / Blänsdorf]

Western Buddha

The first paint layer is pink. The layer is thin and of light colour. In one sample red was found instead of pink (sample ID 91). The second layer is minium-red. It is thick, soft and powdery and the surface has often discoloured to brown or even black. As minium can be found in lacunae of the pink, it obviously is a repainting. Four fragments obviously possess a double layer of orange (samples ID 59, 98, 54 from group 2 and sample ID 49 from group 2–4).

The third layer is a thin greyish-white layer which could be a priming layer rather than a paint layer. The forth layer is a red layer. It often is rather thick, and sometimes brush marks can be distinguished. The fifth layer is a thin, hard, and semitransparent white which does not seem to be a paint layer, but a crust or coating. On top there is the light ochre applied in the restoration of 1969/78.

As two samples were taken from a fragment which can be definitely recognised as part of a fold ridge (GBL 852, fig. 5), fragments of group 1 and 2 can be interpreted as part of the outside of the *sangati*.

Eastern Buddha

The first paint layer is pink, but mostly of darker pink than on the Western Buddha. Sometimes it even looks red. The pink seems to be applied in two layers.

In the only sample assigned to group 1, the pink is lighter than the one found on samples of group 2. If there was a minium layer at all, it can be only traced by single blackened particles. On top there is a thin layer containing some red particles.

In group 2, cross sections of the pink show some black or orange particles between the two layers. Underneath the pink a transparent, slightly reddish isolation layer is visible. The following layer is minium-red. It often is only preserved in traces or discernible as blackened crust. The layer seems to be thinner than that on the Western Buddha.

The third and last layer in both groups is white. In one example of group 2 there is grey on top of the white. Two samples show considerable blackening by soot.[88]

Fig. 5. GBL 852, part of a fold ridge, from which the samples ID 48 (group 2–4) and 169 (group 2) have been taken

Fig. 6. Layer sequence: Western Buddha, group 1 (left) and group 2 (right)

Group 1 – Western Buddha

Sample ID 165, length of picture 45 mm

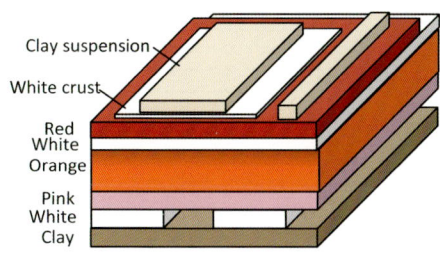

sample ID
all layers present: 14, 18
double layer of minimum: 59, 98, 54 (without pink), 49 (from group 2–4)
pink unclear, red in minimal traces: 112, 135

red missing: 7, 76, 81, 104, 118
red missing, covered with glassy brown: 47a

white an red missing: 102

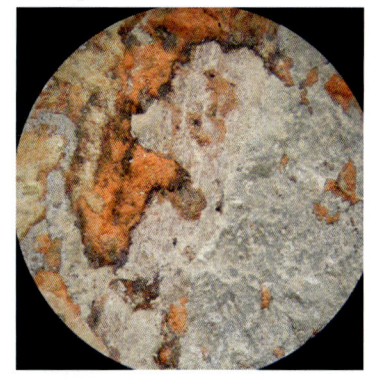

ID 165, diameter of picture 9.5 mm [Pfeffer]

ID 47, cross section of sample, 500 times magnified (white layer appears transparent due to saturation with imbedding resin; red layer missing) [Reiserer]

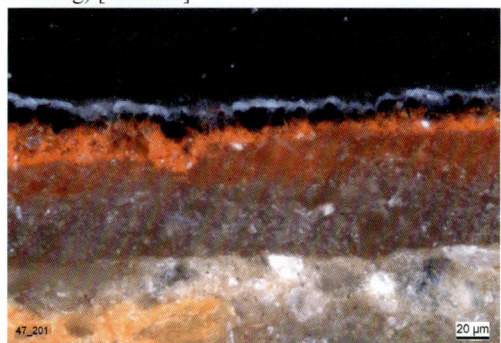

Group 2 – Western Buddha

Sample ID 100, length of picture 45 mm

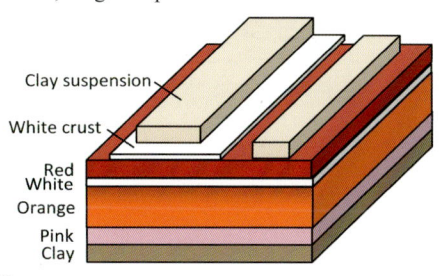

sample ID
all layers present: 4, 5, 8, 9, 16, 17, 22, 23, 26, 30, 35, 39, 52, 55, 56, 58, 64, 69, 72, 78, 79, 87, 91, 95, 97, 100, 107, 110, 115, 117, 125, 132, 134, 140, 146, 148, 153, 154, 161, 162, 165, 167, 168, 173
pink unclear or missing: 23, 30, 54, 153, 166
orange only in tiny traces: 32, 127
red missing: 21, 42, 109, 169; 142
red in tiny traces: 126, 144
red and white missing: 25, 282
pink, red and white missing: 43, 45

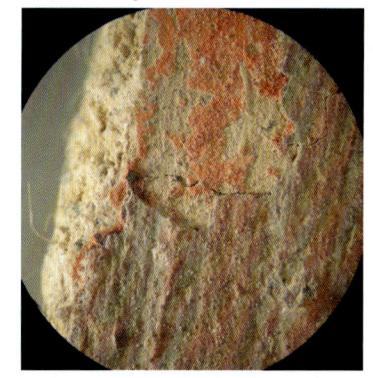

ID 97, diameter of picture 9.5 mm [Pfeffer]

ID 97, cross section of sample, 200 times magnified

Fig. 7. Layer sequence: Eastern Buddha, group 1 (left) and group 2 (right)

Group 1 – Eastern Buddha

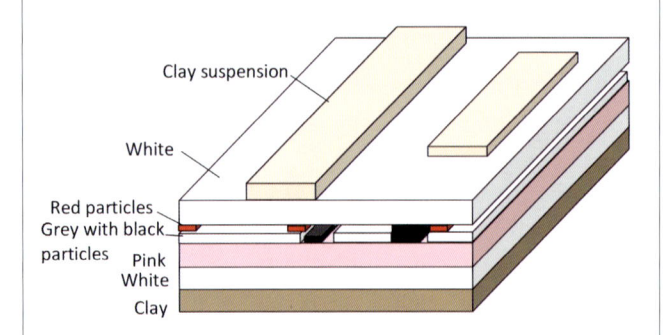

Clay suspension
White
Red particles
Grey with black particles
Pink
White
Clay

sample ID
all layers present: 241

Sample ID 241, thin sction in reflected light and transmitted light under crossed polar

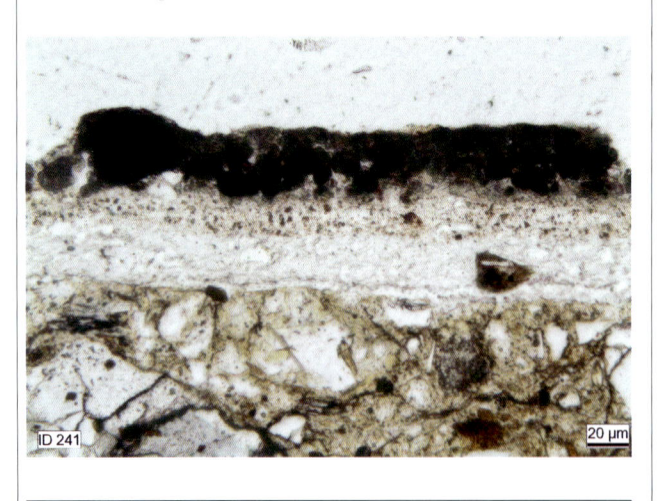

Group 2 – Eastern Buddha

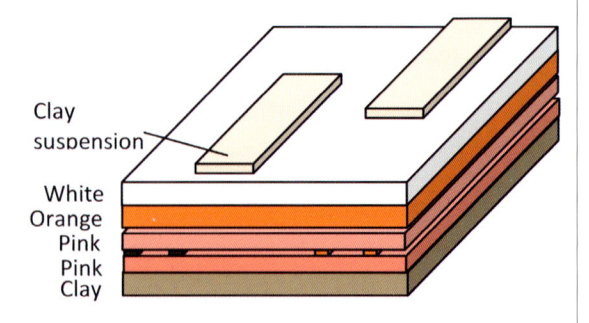

Clay suspension
White
Orange
Pink
Pink
Clay

sample ID
all layers present: 203. 204, 206, 208, 219, 220, 223, 230, 234, 245
grey on top of white: 238
gypsum on top of white: 243
orange and white in remnants: 190, 199, 201, 233
remnants of pink: 175, 232

Sample ID 245, cross section

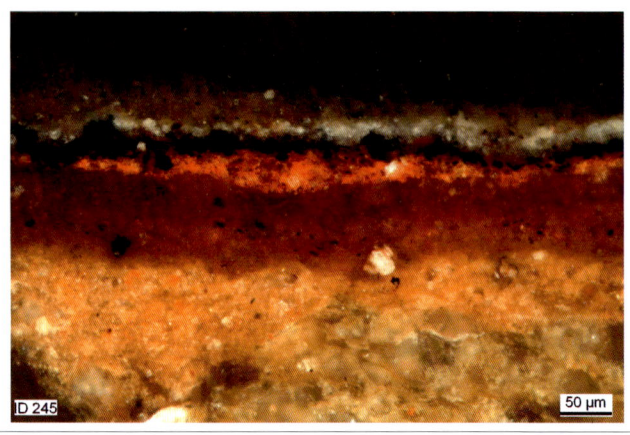

Groups 3 and 4
Groups 3 and 4 comprise all fragments with a brown paint layer as top layer. The visual appearance differs considerably from dark to light, reddish to greyish brown, from smooth to heavily structured or scaly, from matt to glossy. The separation into more than one group was made in the attempt to assemble fragments which look more similar on the overall impression into one group. The closer examination proved that this overall impression often does not correspond to the paint layer sequences. As a kind of compromise between the visual appearance and the layer sequence the separation was made by the number of brown layers: Group 3 contains fragments with two brown layers. Subgroups separate the peculiarly structured, glossy dark brown fragments (fig. 8 top row) from the scaly or smooth and rather matt fragments (fig. 8, lower row). Group 4 comprises fragments with only one brown layer. In both groups traces of red or orange can be found underneath the brown. On the Eastern Buddha the fragments only show one brown layer without red layers underneath.

Independently of the visual impression in colour, gloss and structure, all brown layers share an important property: They are very poor in pigmentation and seem to consist mostly of binding medium. The layers are always semi-transparent and show aging cracks. The degree of gloss, the development of a scaly or wizened surface and maybe even the colour seem to be linked rather to aging phenomena than to deliberate differences made by the craftsmen. Overall, the brown layers appear more like a coating or a glaze, not an application of paint.

Transition between groups: Group 2–3, 1/2–4, 5–4
The closer examination showed that on the samples of the Western Buddha there is a connection between groups 1 and 2 to groups 3 and 4, because the layer sequence of group 1 or 2 often is found underneath the brown layers. Considering this kind of transition two more groups were formed, named group 2-3 (= transition between group 2 and 3) and group 1/2-4 (transition between group 1 or 2 to group 4). Thin brown layers are also found on blue layers or just on a grey layer which seems to be soot. This connects group 4 also to group 5 (blue).

Group 5
Group 5 contains all samples with blue paint layers. The blue was underpainted with a dark layer. On the Western Buddha this is a dark grey, on the Eastern Buddha the layer is black and sometimes rather thick. In one sample instead of the blue layer there is a white layer containing single blue particles. Two samples of each Buddha show a white layer underneath the dark grey or black.

The blue is overpainted once, using the same system of dark underpainting and blue. The overpainting mostly appears lighter in colour. Several fragments only show the first or the second layer, indicating that the other one was lost.

Overlapping layers: Group 1–5
There is one sample from the Eastern Buddha, sample ID 256, on which a transition between a red area (group 1)

Fig. 8. Western Buddha, group 3: Samples with glossy, structured surface (top row), matt surface (middle row) and white below brown (lowest row)

Fig. 9. Layer sequence: Western Buddha, group 3 (left) and group 4 (right)

Group 3 – Western Buddha

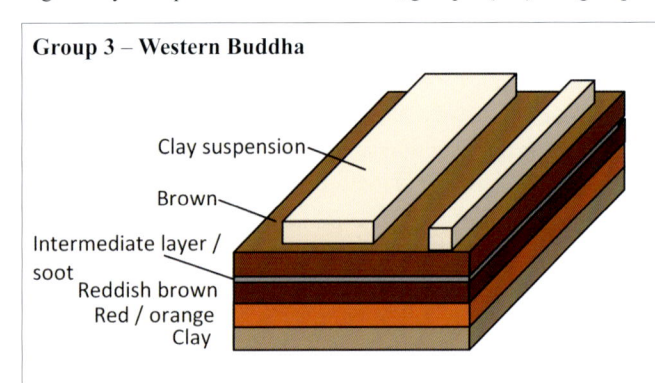

ID 6, diameter of picture 25 mm [Pfeffer]   ID 108, 50x [Reiserer]

Group 3 glossy
all layers present: 106
red/orange missing: 6, 51, 108, 128, 129, 133, 156, 158, GBL 2400+

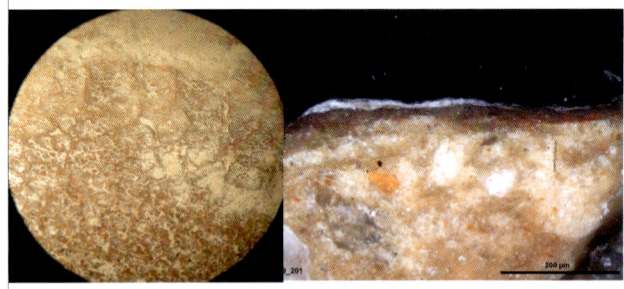

ID99, diameter of picture 25 mm [Pfeffer]   ID 99

Group 3 matt
red – brown – soot/whitish layer – brown: 10, 46, 99, 114
red – brown – brwon – brown: 94, 145, 170
pink/orange – reddish brown – brown: 36, 40, 163
orange – brown – grey – brown: 47c
very thik cly wash on top: 36, 46, 170

Group 3 – exemption
white – brown – interim layer – brown: 20

Group 4 – Western Buddha

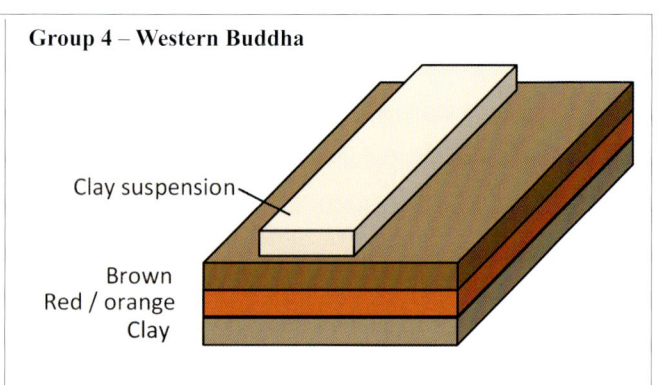

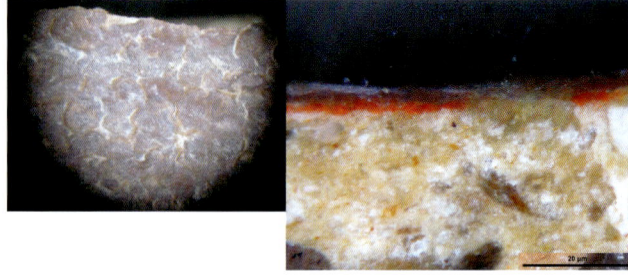

ID 172, diameter of picture 5 mm [Blänsdorf]   ID 172, 200x [Blänsdorf]

Group 4 with red
red – brown (scaly, smooth or wizened): 83, 96, 130, 143, 147, 172
red – light brown: 61, 68, 73, 85
reddish pink – greyish brown: 74

Group 4 without red
light brown: 77, 101, 120, 138, 152

Group 4 – exemption
white – streaky brown: 57

Fig. 10. Layer sequence: Eastern Buddha, group 3 (left) and group 4 (right)

Group 3 – Eastern Buddha	Group 4 – Eastern Buddha
sample ID glossy, structured surface: 210 rather matt, smooth surface: 215, 242, 267	**sample ID** smooth: 187, 197, 205, 207, 211, 268 wizened: 195, 275 thick clay wash on top: 3, 181
sample ID 267 [Thiemann]	sample ID 275 [Blänsdorf]
Sample ID 267, cross section, 200 times magnified [Blänsdorf]	Sample ID 275, diameter of picture 5 mm [Blänsdorf]

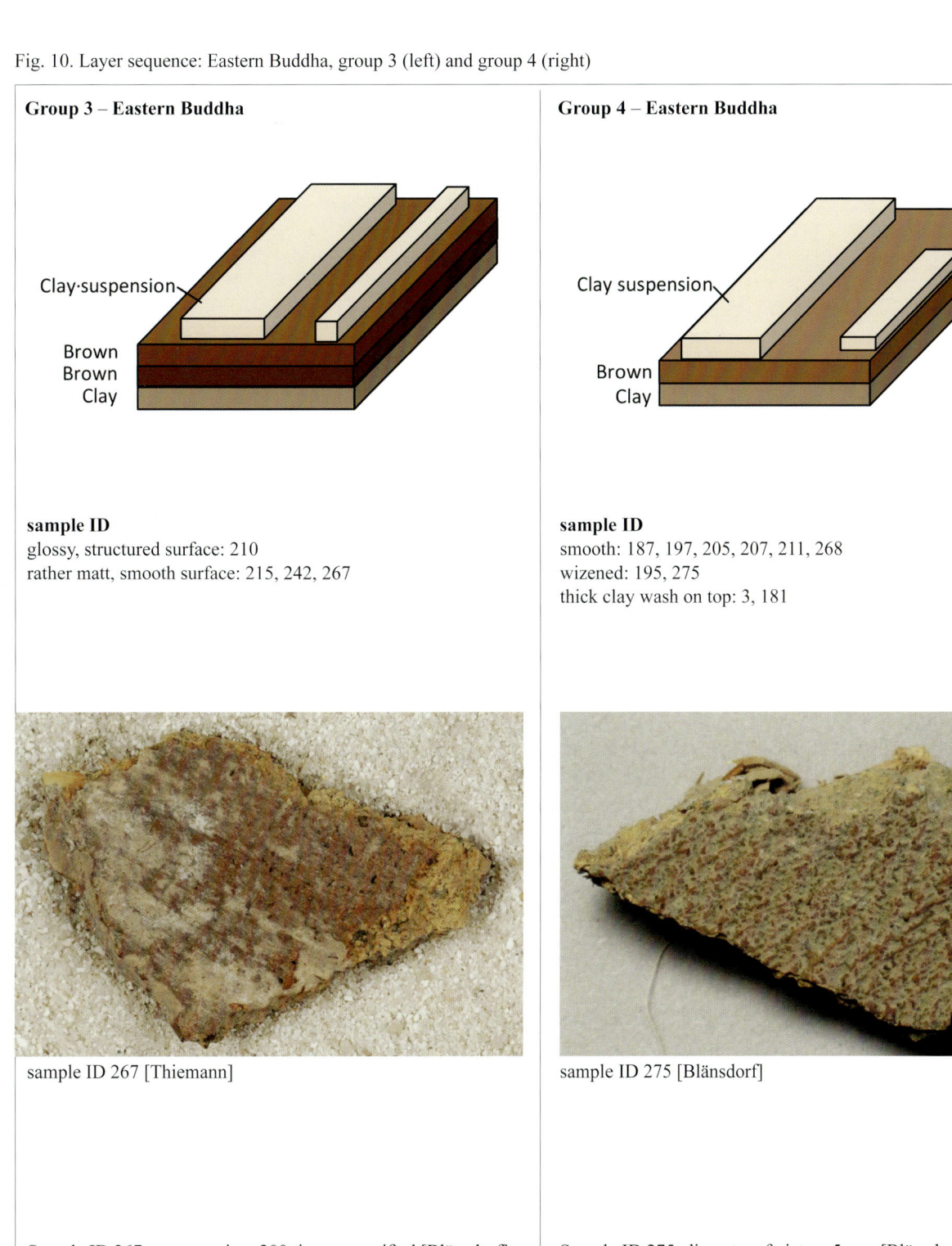

247

Fig. 11. Layer sequence: Transition of groups 1 or 2 to 3 or 4

Group 2–3 – Western Buddha

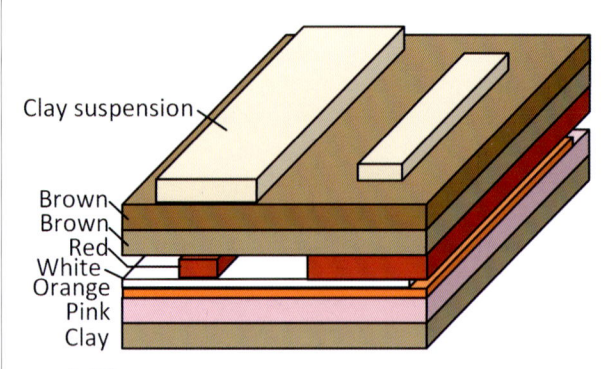

sample ID
white or pink – orange – brown – soot – brown: 19
orange – white – brown – brown: 37, edge 1
red – brown – brown: 37, edge 2
orange – red – brown – brown: 38b
pink – orange – brown – brown: 171

Group 1/2–4 – Western Buddha

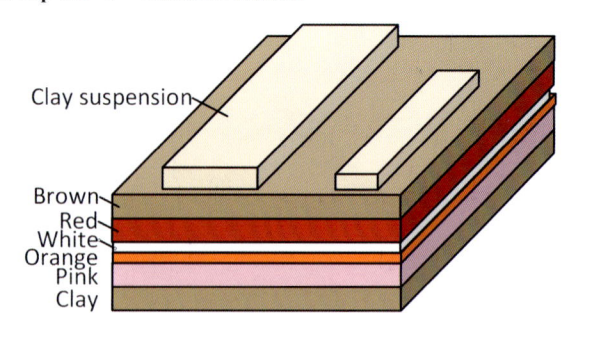

sample ID
group 1 without red – light brown: 47, 38a
group 2 – brown: 31
pink – orange – red – brwon: 48, 89, 92, 149, 105
(pink) – red – brown: 50, 60
pink – orange – orange – brwon: 49
pink – orange – brown: 33
orange – red – brown: 24, 28, 150
orange – dark red – brown: 53
orange – brown: 137, 157
pink – light brown transparent: 75

Group 1/2–4 – Eastern Buddha

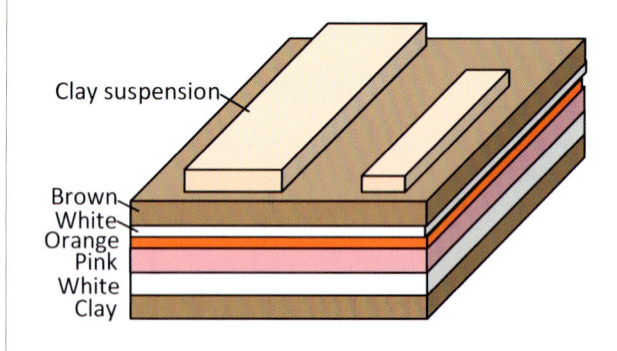

sample ID
249

Group 5 – 4

Western Buddha
white – light blue – soot – light brown: 103

Eastern Buddha
black – light blue – light brown: 193
black – brown: 266

Group ? – 4

Western Buddha
soot – light brown: 122, 131

Fig. 12. Layer sequence: group 5

Group 5 – Western Buddha

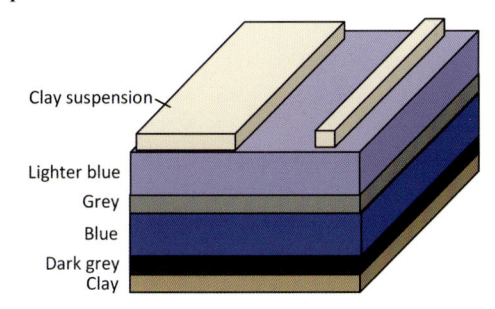

sample ID
all layers present: 164
only first grey-blue layer: 103

Group 5 – Western Buddha, first blue with white underneath

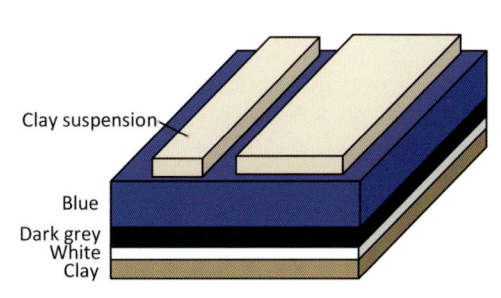

sample ID
all layers present: 121, 123

Group 5 – Eastern Buddha

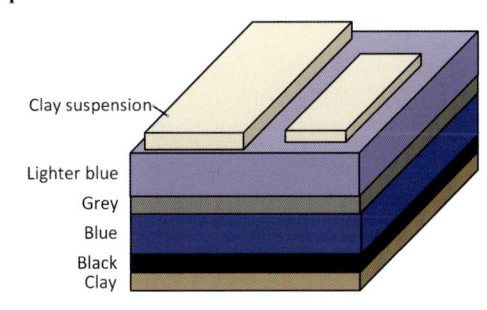

sample ID
all layers present: 184, 194, 202, 214, 235, 237, 247, 248, 269, 276, 285
black – blue – grey – (light blue in traces): 212, 221
black – blue particles – crust: 179, 227, 254, 274
black – blue: 216, KBL 497
traces of black and blue: 196, 250
black – grey crust: 176, 266
black – white with blue particles: 222
grey preserved: 217
grey – light blue: 185, 178, 186, 192, 209, 213, 226, 231, 254, 257, 259
black: 189, 198, 236

Group 5 – Eastern Buddha, first blue with white underneath

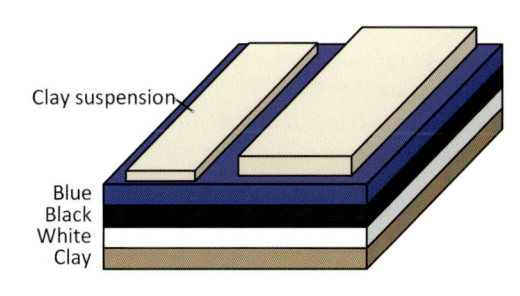

sample ID
all layers present: 239
white – black or grey – blue: 262
white – black – light blue: 196
white – grey – light blue: 264
white – light blue: 255

Western Buddha, sample ID 164, 200x [Blänsdorf]

Eastern Buddha, sample ID 235, 200x [Blänsdorf]

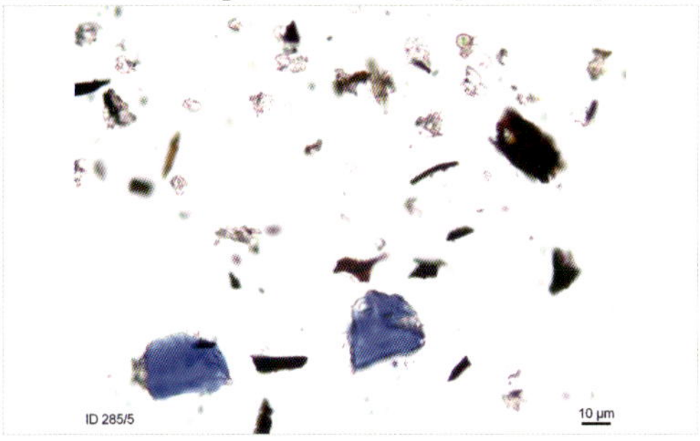

249

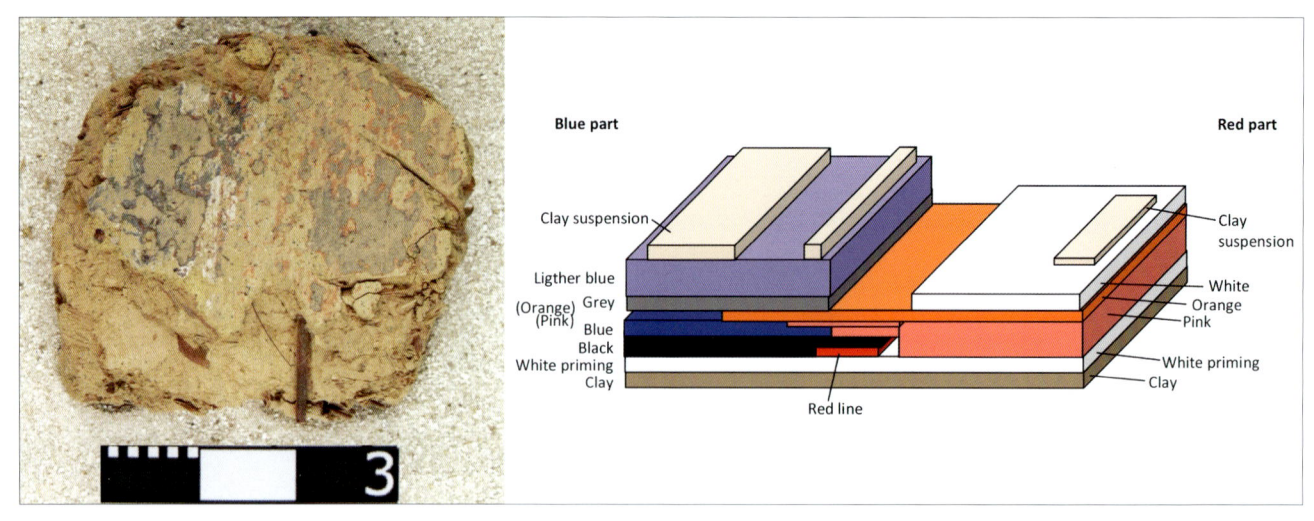

Fig. 13. Layer sequence: Eastern Buddha, transition of blue area (group 5) to red area (group 1)

and a blue area (group 5) is preserved. Different from the majority of samples it possesses a white priming layer which covers the whole surface. In the middle there are traces of bright red which seem to stem from a thin line. This line is overlapped from the blue part by the black underpainting and partly the blue. From the red part the pink overlaps the blue. Pink can also be found directly on the clay, where the white is missing. As no cross-section could be made it is not possible to say if there are one or two pink layers. The orange overpainting covers the pink and overlaps the blue. The blue overpainting partly covers the orange which had already discoloured at the surface. The white overpainting can be found on the orange.

This confusing sounding situation can be interpreted as follows: The red line marked the border between the red and the blue part. The blue part was black and then blue, subsequently the red part was painted pink. In a next phase the red part was overpainted with orange. In a last phase the red part was overpainted in white and the blue part with grey and light blue.

So far, this is the only sample showing this kind of transition. It is not clear if it represents the situation on the whole statue or even both statues. Nevertheless, it is the first and only possibility to understand in which sequence red

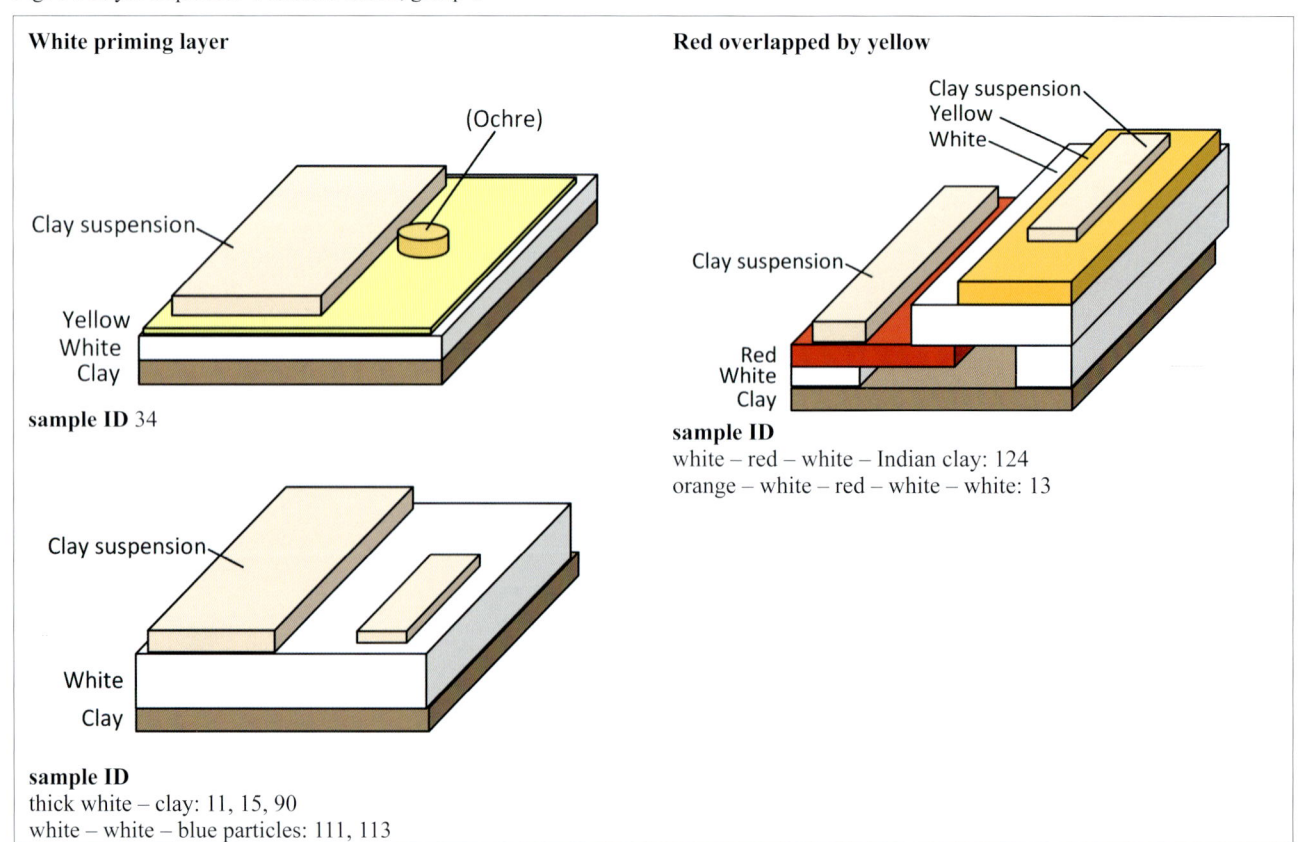

Fig. 14. Layer sequence: Western Buddha, group 6

White priming layer

sample ID 34

sample ID
thick white – clay: 11, 15, 90
white – white – blue particles: 111, 113

Red overlapped by yellow

sample ID
white – red – white – Indian clay: 124
orange – white – red – white – white: 13

250

and blue areas were repainted.

Group 6

Group 6 comprises different samples with a white priming layer. On top there are yellow or red layers or traces of blue.

These samples are unusual and differ from the other groups in some regards. Only fragments ID 11 and 15 possess animal hair as additive of the clay while in the other fragments there is remarkably little hair (ID 90) or no hair at all. The clay surface appears grey instead of yellowish. ID 11 and 15 possess a rough clay surface, while the others are completely smooth.

The white layer is thick and seems to be a priming layer. In two samples (ID 111 and 113) small circular pits from air bubbles can be seen as they are typical for gesso grounds. Sample ID 13 looks white under the stereo microscope, but the cross section revealed traces of orange, covered by white and traces of red below two thick white layers. Sample ID 124 seems to come from a part where a yellow on a white underpainting overlapped a red on a white priming layer. The thin yellow layer found in sample ID 34 looks rather like a glaze, sometimes even like a patina rather than a paint layer. It is not clear if these fragments belong to the statue of the Western Buddha or come from adjacent parts like the walls of the niche.

Samples ID 244, 251 and 260 look very similar. A streaky red, painted over traces of white, is overlapped by a bright ochre yellow. The ochre was applied on a thick white layer, which also overlaps the red, probably too achieve a brighter colour. Two samples show a similar bright yellow ochre on a white ground. Sample ID 261 shows an additional thick white layer on top of the yellow. The clay layers contain hair and thus correspond to the clay mixture used on the Eastern Buddha.

Sample ID 228 also shows a streaky red. The red overlaps an area of blue possessing a white priming layer and a black

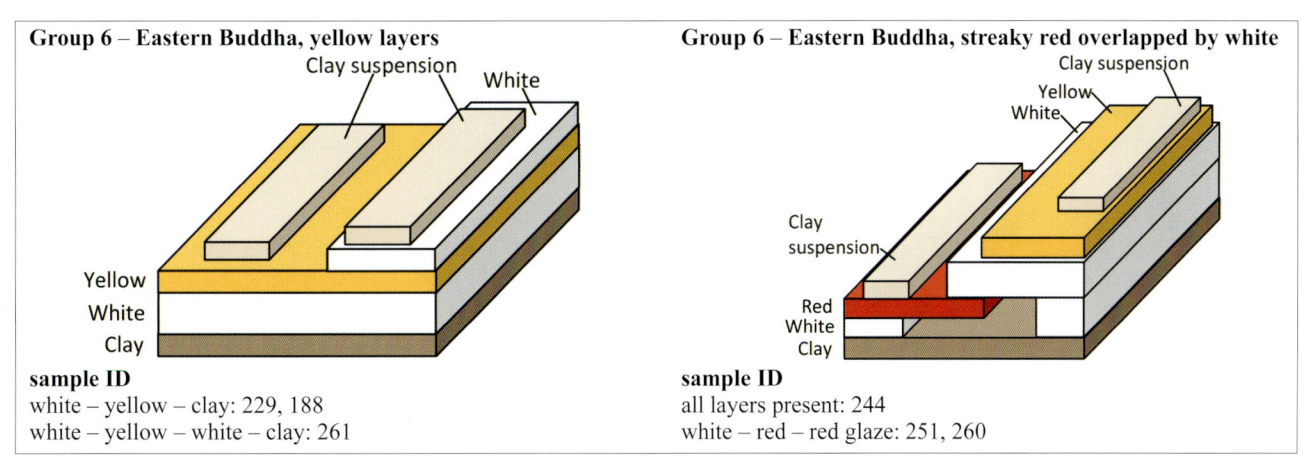

Fig. 15. Layer sequence: Eastern Buddha, group 6, samples with yellow ochre

Fig. 16. Fragments with yellow overlapping red. Sample ID 229, 261 (from KBL 977), 244 (from KBL 517) and 251 (from KBL 620), 260 (from KBL 709) and detail of ID 244 [Blänsdorf]

Fig. 17. Layer sequence: Eastern Buddha, group 6, fragments with red and blue

underpainting. The blue is overpainted with a second blue layer. The red is on the level of the second blue and thus has to be considered as an overpainting. The presence of white layers below and between the blue layers is an exceptional case and does not occur on other fragments.

The fragments were not found together and thus it is not clear if they come from the same area. Fragment KBL 620 from which sample ID 251 was taken was found together with a similar fragment. KBL 621 has a convex shape typical of the fold ridges.

Sample ID 246, from KBL 382, is interesting as it shows two layers different from all the other ones, but as third and fourth layer it possesses the same stratigraphy as the fragments of group 2. On a white ground layer two thin layers of rose red were applied on top of each other. The third layer shows traces of blackened minium, and the last one is the same white layer as in groups 1 and 2. The shape of fragment KBL 382 could indicate that it was part of a fold ridge.

The fact that samples ID 246 and 228 show overpaintings probably means that they were part of the Buddha statue as the murals in the niches apparently were never repainted.

Samples with several colours

Three samples from the Western Buddha show two or three colours next to each other (fig. 18). They do not resemble any other samples. Although the clay composition of sample ID 65 corresponds to other fragments of the Western Buddha, it is not entirely sure that the samples come from the statue itself, as the clay contains almost no hair. All samples possess a white priming layer.

Samples ID 65 and 66 show red, blue and white, but nevertheless they do not resemble each other. ID 65 shows a red on traces of a very thin layer of white. The red ends with a straight line and there it is overlapped by a light grey (white mixed with charcoal) and a dark grey (charcoal). Blue particles indicate that at least the dark grey was the underpainting of blue. ID 66 shows a more pinkish red. The blue is applied on top of the red in thin, dry strokes without a layer in between.

Sample ID 93 shows a light gold ochre. Reddish ochre is painted on top as a kind of glaze. The paint layer shows a distinct crack system.

Fig. 18. Fragments with several colours from Western Buddha, samples ID 65, 66 and 93 left to right [Blänsdorf]

Fig. 19. Sample ID 67 from Western Buddha; trace of a 15 mm wide line preserved in he isolation layer (paint layer missing), length of fragment 40 mm

Fig. 20. Fragment KBL 845 with 5 mm wide black line from Eastern Buddha [Melzl]

A sample from fragment KBL 845 of the Eastern Buddha shows a 5 mm wide black line on a light ochre background showing just the isolation layer (fig. 20).[89] A sample from the Western Buddha, ID 67, also shows a line (fig. 19). It is 15 mm wide and runs straight and with constant width. There is no paint layer preserved on this fragment. The reason why the line is still visible is either that it was drawn with a paint containing a higher amount of binding medium or a diluted ink which penetrated into the clay.

On both samples the clay contains animal hair. They seem to belong to the Buddha statue, but they are the only ones of this kind found so far.

Identification of pigments

The analyses were mainly performed by polarised light microscopy (PLM).[90] If required, x-ray diffraction (XRD), x-ray fluorescence (XRF) and scanning electron microscopy with element mapping (ESEM) have been used. The pigments identified on the fragments of the groups 1 to 5 are listed in table 2.

White
The white priming layers (first layer in groups 1, 5 and 6) consist of gypsum and white clay minerals. Mostly the content of gypsum is higher, but the ratios vary.

The white overpainting found on both statues in the samples of groups 1 and 2 consists of a white lead pigment, either lead white or another white lead composition. Anglesite (lead sulphate, laurionite (lead hydroxide chloride) and palmierite (potassium lead sulphate) have been analysed using XRD in a sample of the Eastern Buddha. The use of this with lead pigment is restricted to this second overpainting. One fragment, sample ID 15 has only one white layer which consists of lead white with quartz and therefore probably is a later repair.

Pink
Pink is mixed of rather fine iron oxides with the same white as that used for the priming layer (gypsum with white earth and calcite). The composition distinguishes the pink paint layer from the pink slurry used before the application of the clay layers, as the slurry contains fine yellow and red

253

iron oxides, quartz and clay minerals from a natural red earth and varying amounts of calcite, but no gypsum. This differentiation is helpful: Although the two materials differ slightly in colour (the paint layer being more orange, the slurry more greyish), confusion is possible as traces of both are found inside between the clay layers.

The pink layer of sample ID 243 contains grains of starch which could be barley and are probably related to the binder rather than to the pigments of the layer.

Red
The bright orange-red layers are painted with minium, containing some anglesite. The darker red overpainting in groups 1 and 2 consists of iron oxide. PLM preparations show a very pure, brownish red iron oxide, very fine, but often with some larger particles. The red layer underneath the brown (group 3 and 4, Western Buddha) contains very fine red iron oxides. Although some of these layers clearly correspond to the red overpainting of groups 1 and 2, one sample (ID 53) showed darker red particles. With PLM they appeared as fine, pure, bright red iron oxides, often in clusters and with almost no bigger particles.

White overpainting
The thin white layer overpainting the minium consists of a white lead material. Under polarised light the particles resemble lead white, although they are often more rounded than elongated. Few analyses with XRD revealed the presence of anglesite (lead sulphate), plattnerite (dark lead oxide), laureonite (lead hydroxide chloride) and palmierite (potassium lead sulphate), gypsum and clay minerals in the blackened top layer of the minium or the 'sinter crust' covering the blackened minium. The presence of a thin white layer was not recognized at that time. While the plattnerite clearly can be assigned to the blackened minium and the clay minerals and the gypsum to the thin white crust on top of the red overpainting, the other white lead compounds could come from the white layer itself.

Blue
The blue is natural ultramarine. The first blue layer contains many deep blue particles, while the blue overpainting shows a large amount of pale or partly coloured particles and thus probably was of a poorer quality.

The black underpainting contains charcoal black; grey underpaintings consist of charcoal mixed with gypsum. While the underpainting of the first layer is dark grey or even black, the one of the second layer is lighter grey and contains more gypsum and calcite.

Brown and 'sinter crust'
Brown layers contain fine particles of gypsum, few and fine particles of red iron oxides, calcite and white earth. There are only a few and small particles in the layers which seem very high in binding medium. It should be mentioned that the thin white semi-transparent 'sinter crust' which can be found on top of the red overpainting (Western Buddha, groups 1 and 2) contains the same mixture of pigments or fillers. There might be a connection between the brown and the white appearing layers.

Samples of group 6
The samples show the same pigments as were used on the other samples (red iron oxide, ultramarine), but the visible colour is different. The white ground layer contains fine gypsum with some calcite. For the bright pinkish red paint layers in ID 246 (Eastern Buddha) extremely fine dark red iron oxide (particle size mainly below 1µm) was mixed with very fine ground gypsum. The same fine iron oxide was used in sample ID 65 (Western Buddha), but here some fine minium was added, and there is no addition of white.

Bright yellow areas are only found on these special samples of group 6. They are painted with a very pure, fine and homogenous iron oxide hydroxide with varying ratios of calcite and few white clay minerals.

The overpainting of sample ID 246 consists of blackened minium (layer 3) and white lead pigments (layer 4) and thus is the same as in the corresponding layers of groups 1 and 2. The white on top of the yellow in sample ID 261 consists of gypsum.

Discoloration of minium
A striking phenomenon is the massive discoloration of minium. Almost all minium layers show a black crust. Thin or reduced layers of minium have transformed into black clusters, sometimes forming a crust (fig. 21, centre and bottom).[91] The discoloration seems to have happened only on the parts exposed to the environment, while minium which had penetrated into holes or shrinkage cracks of the clay is still bright orange. The discoloration is found on parts which seem never to have been repainted as well as on overpainted areas. On the few fragments with a double layer of minium, also the first layer has a black surface, which means that this was not a double layer application, but a later repair. Considering the possible time span of repair phases – altogether about 400 years – and the assumption that the blackening would be stopped or reduced when the surface is covered by another layer, the minium must have discoloured within some decades.

Surprisingly, there is also one sample which shows no problems of discoloration of minium (sample ID 62, fig. 21, top). As it seems not to have been repainted after the application of minium, it might have come from a hidden and thus well-protected area.

On cross sections it becomes visible that the orange layer is interspersed with clusters of black particles (fig. 22). An investigation with ESEM proved that the whole layer consists of lead compositions (fig. 23).[92] As components plattnerite PbO_2 (black), scrutinyite PbO_2 (greyish white or dark brown) were identified, next to the white anglesite $PbSO_4$ (white).[93]

The darkening of minium is a well-known phenomenon caused by the formation of black lead dioxide (PbO_2, plattnerite and scrutinyite). The conditions or initiating factors of this transformation are not entirely clear. The process can be accelerated by high humidity at high temperatures, but this does not occur in desert regions or dry regions like Bāmiyān. RIEDERER 1977 relates the formation of dark PbO_2 in minium layers from the murals in Kumtura and Kizil, Xinjiang, to the content of massicot in the paint layer, not to the minium itself[94], while ZOU et al. 1997 interpret lead dioxide as an

Table 2 Pigments identified on the fragments of groups 1 to 5 in Munich 2004–2009 (W. B. = Western Buddha, E. B. = Eastern Buddha)

group/analysed fragments	colour (in group)	Western Buddha	colour (in group)	Eastern Buddha	method
1 W. B. 14, 102, 47, 81, 165 E. B. 241	white crust	- gypsum, clay minerals - calcite, iron oxides	white + grey XRD	- anglesite (lead sulphate) - plattnerite (dark lead oxide) - laureonite (lead hydroxide chloride) - palmierite (potassium lead sulphate) - gypsum, clay minerals	XRD
	red (1 and 2)	- red iron oxide, containing maghemite and hematite - some white lead compound - sometimes: gypsum, mica			
	white (1 and 2)	- white lead compound - gypsum, calcite (- iron oxide)	white (1 and 2) PLM	- white lead compound - gypsum, calcite - dark iron oxides	PLM
2 W. B: 4, 52, 54 E. B. 245	black surface of orange (1 and 2)	- minium Pb_3O_4 (orange) - plattnerite PbO_2 (black) - anglesite $PbSO_4$ (white) - scrutinyite PbO_2 (greyish/brown) - quartz SiO_2 - kaolinite $Al_2Si_2O_5(OH)_4$ - dolomite $CaMg(CO_3)_2$	black surface of orange (2)	- minium Pb_3O_4 (orange) - darkened particles - white lead composition - calcite	XRD, SEM (W. B.) PLM
	orange (1 and 2)	- minium Pb_3O_4 - anglesite $PbSO_4$ and/or lanarkite $Pb_2(SO_4)O$ - sometimes: massicot PbO, gypsum $CaSO_4 \times 2H_2O$	orange (1 and 2)	- minium - white lead compound - calcite	XRD (W. B.) PLM (E. B.)
	pink (1 and 2)	- white clay, iron oxides - calcite	pink (1 and 2)	- white clay, iron oxides - gypsum, calcite	PLM
	white (1)	- white earth, gypsum - quartz, calcite	white (1)	- white earth, gypsum - calcite	PLM
3 W. B. glossy: 51 matt: 99, 163, 170	white/light brown	- gypsum, clay minerals - charcoal black, calcite, iron oxides	transparent browm	- gypsum, clay minerals, iron oxides, calcite - colonies of bacteria	PLM
	brownisch grey	- gypsum, clay minerals - charcoal black, calcite, iron oxides			
4 W. B. 164 E. B. 267, 268	red	- red iron oxide			
	orange	- minium - white lead compound			
	pink	- white clay, iron oxide - calcite			
5 W. B. 164 E. B. 235, 285	blue	- lasurite (particles small, not completely coloured) - calcite, white clay, mica	blue	- lasurite (particles small, not completely coloured) - calcite, white clay, mica	PLM
	grey	- charcoal black - calcite, diopside, iron oxides - colonies of bacteria	grey	- gypsum - charcoal black, calcite iron oxides	PLM XRD SEM
			white	- colonies of bacteria	SEM
	blue	- lasurite (particles small, not completely coloured) - calcite, white clay, mica	blue	- lasurite (particles small, not completely coloured) - iron oxides	PLM
	dark grey	- charcoal black - white clay, calcium sulphate	black	- charcoal black	PLM XRD
Indo-Afghan restoration	clay wash	- clay suspension - sometimes gypsum	Indo-Afghan restoration	- clay suspension - sometimes gypsum	PLM XRD

ID 62 of GBL 246

ID 62: Minium without discoloration

ID 59

ID 59: Minium with dark crust

ID 112

ID 112: Minium completely blackened

Fig. 21. Minium discoloured in different extent on three samples of the Western Buddha: The only sample without discoloration (ID 62), discoloured top layer (ID 59), minium completely blackened (ID 112)

oxidation product of minium.[95]

GETTENS 1937/38 remarks that the surface of minium layers on the wall paintings in the Bāmiyān caves has turned slightly brown, but not as brown as often observed in Chinese wall paintings.[96] Minium layers on the Buddha statues, however, often show an extreme blackening. It is possible that this was the reason for repainting these parts.

Bacteria
Another unusual finding was the presence of small spherical white particles found in white and blue layers (fig. 24, top). In some cases they intersperse the paint layers, but they can form rather coherent thick layers as well. They were also found on a sample from a filling probably made in 1969-78. With polarised light microscopy round particles with a diameter of 2 to 5 μm are visible with refractive index higher than 1.662 and strong interference colours (fig. 24, bottom). An examination with ESEM of a blue paint layer showed the absence of any heavy elements (fig. 24, centre). This led to the conclusion that these 'micro-spheres' are colonies of bacteria.[97] The same 'micro-spheres' have been detected microscopically in other blue samples from both Buddha statues. A thicker white layer on a sample of a reddish plaster completion from the Western Buddha (ID 84) microscopically showed the same spherical particles. Analyses with micro-XRF proved the presence of lead in the completion ID 84; a white layer between two blue layers (Eastern Buddha, ID 235) proved to contain a higher content of potassium, phosphor and calcium than the surrounding (fig. 25).[98]

Comparison to early Buddhist polychromies on clay support

A comparison to works of art of similar temporal and regional origin, of similar technique and purpose can help to understand the results obtained by the examination of the fragments of the Buddha statues in a larger context. Most important is the comparison to the murals of the caves in Bāmiyān, but a comparison to other Buddhist stone and clay sculptures and wall paintings on clay can be useful as well.

The comparison to pigments found in the murals of the caves in Bāmiyān reveals similarities, but also important differences (table 3). The caves, the construction of which extended over several centuries, show different techniques and materials. They also show yellow, green and black colours which were not present on the fragments in Munich. The blue paint layers in the caves were made with ultramarine underpainted with black. A black underpainting for green was also found in the Bāmiyān caves.[99] Cinnabar and orpiment were used for the murals, but not for the statues. The employment of special techniques may have been restricted to the interior of the caves. The application of oily and resinous binders in some of the caves must have influenced the choice of the colorants as well.[100]

Numerous sculptures from early Buddhist sanctuaries from the Middle East to Western China still exist, many of them made of clay or modelled over a clay core. Very few, however, have been examined carefully. Analyses of materials were not executed or have not been published in Western languages.[102] Investigations into the polychromy of large-size sculptures are missing completely. Descriptions and photographs of polychromy are limited to smaller

Fig. 22. Discoloration of minium: Cross section of fragment ID 166 from GBL 1510-15 (Western Buddha):
 (1) Minium interspersed with black particles
 (2) black layer on top of minium
 (3) overpainting containing iron oxide [Blänsdorf]

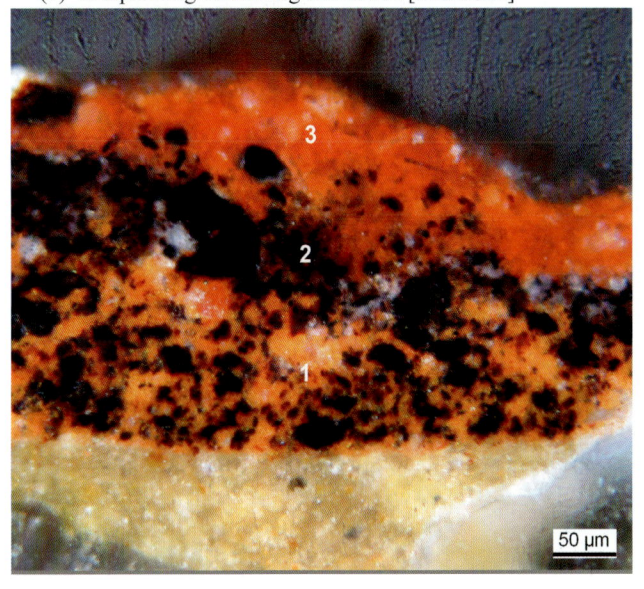

Fig. 23. SEM picture of the cross section with element mapping [K. Rapp]

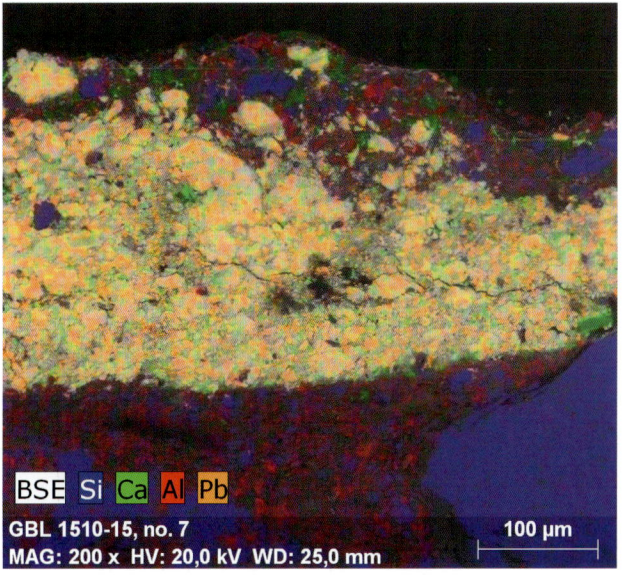

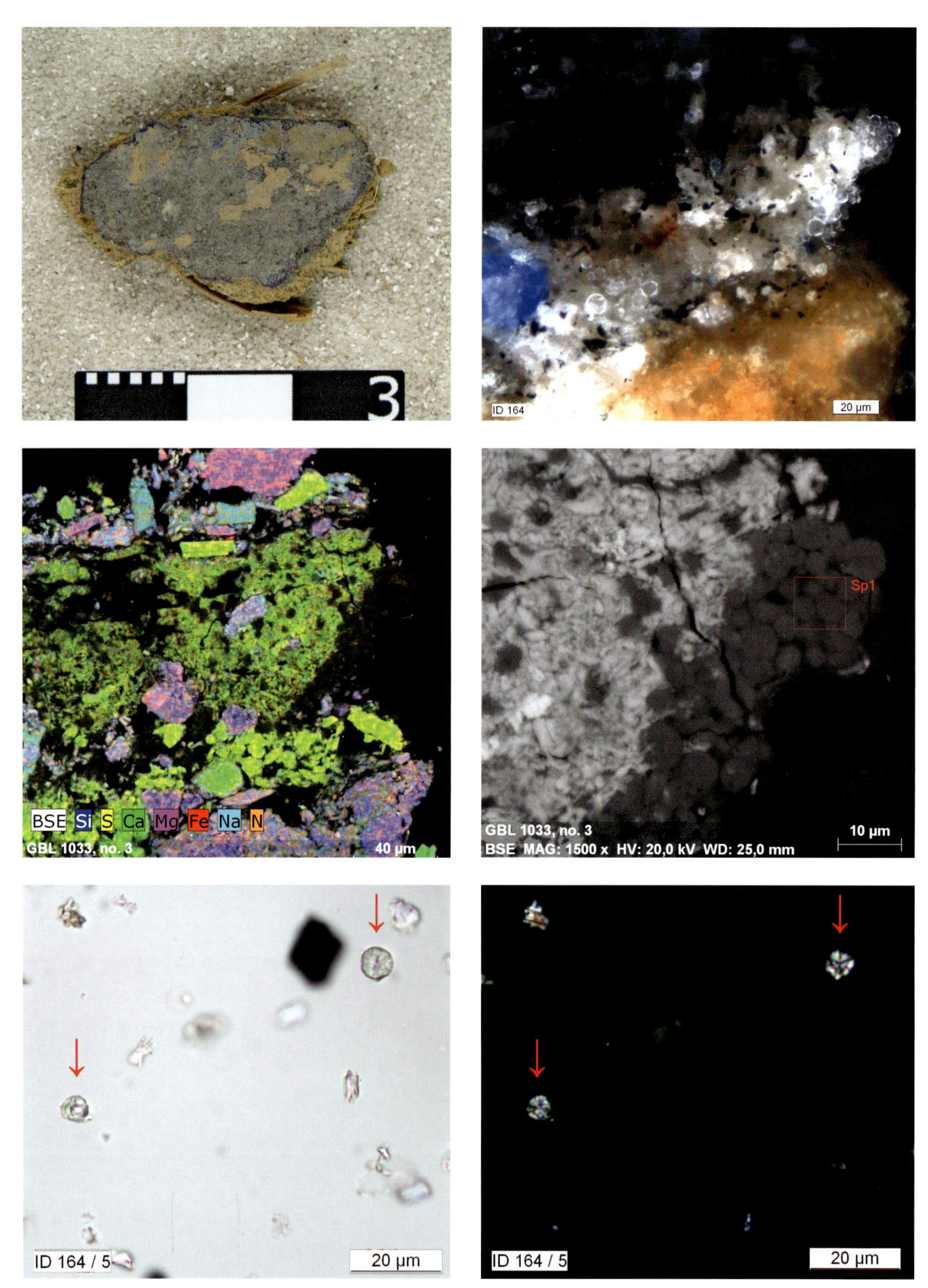

Fig. 24. Micro-organisms inside the first blue paint layer. From top left to bottom right: Sample ID 164 from GBL 1033 (Western Buddha); cross section of fragment; element mapping and SEM picture (BSE); PLM samples of blue layer in transmitted light and under crossed polar (arrows indicating the spherical particles)

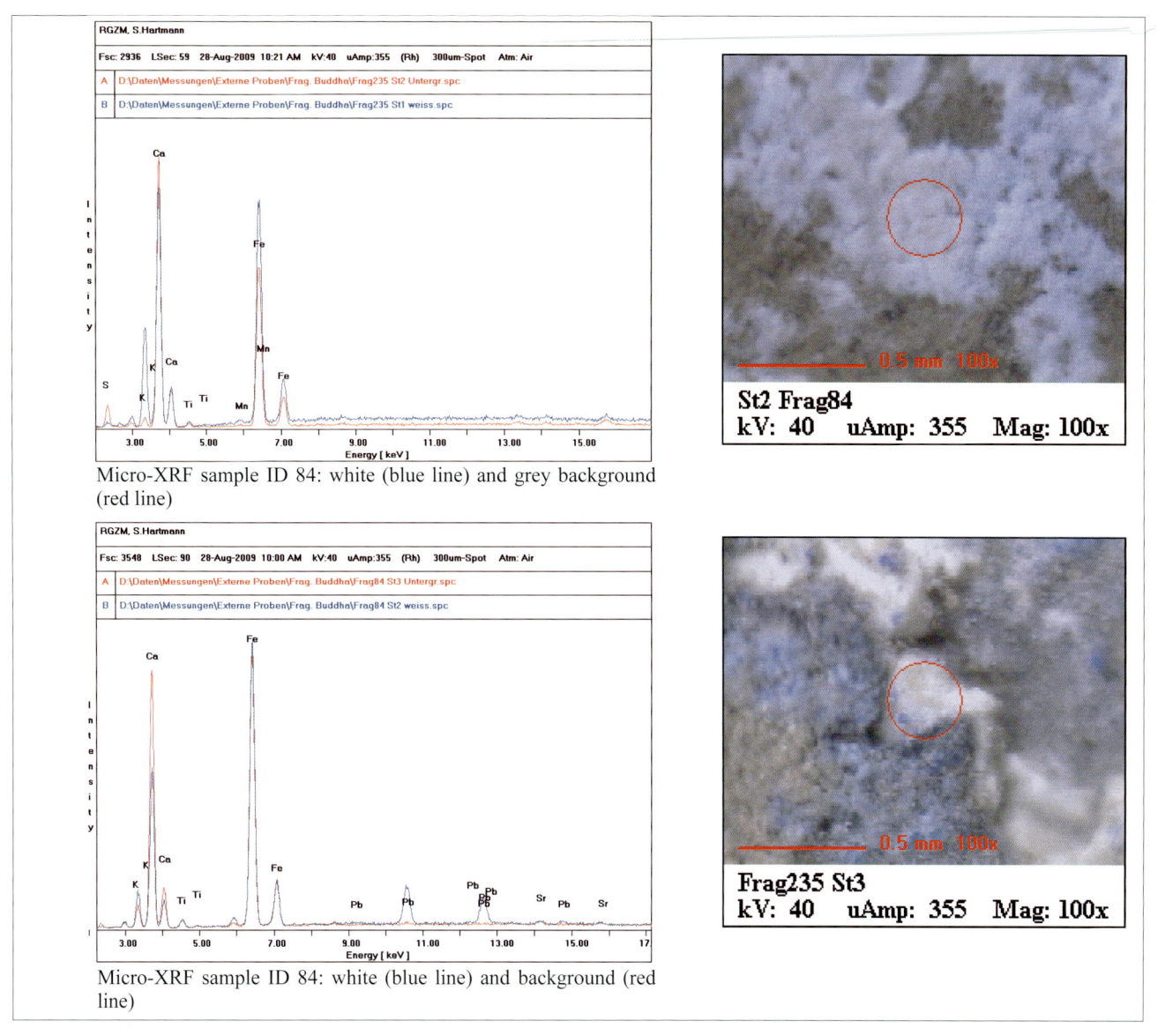

Micro-XRF sample ID 84: white (blue line) and grey background (red line)

Micro-XRF sample ID 84: white (blue line) and background (red line)

Fig. 25. Analyses of layers containing round white particles with micro-XRF [Hartmann, RGZM]

sculptures. These sculptures have always been indoors, and they required only low amounts of painting material. Both facts may have influenced the choice of the materials as well as the painting technique. The fragments from Nisa (Turkmenistan) are among the few sculptures that were carefully analysed. Their style and the choice of the colorants show a strong Hellenistic (i.e. European) influence, so it is disputable how far they can be regarded as typical of Central Asian sculptures, although they are made of clay. Here the paint layers were applied on a white preparation layer. There are no overpaintings.[103]

More information is available from scientific examinations carried out on wall paintings since the 1930's. Material analyses of Sogdian wall paintings exist for Penjikent (7th to 8th centuries, Tajikistan) and Afrasiab (6th to 7th centuries, Uzbekistan)[104]; for Western China as Kucha[105], of detached wall paintings from Kizil, Kumtura[106] and Miran (Xinjiang)[107], and the caves of Magao in Dunhuang[108] and Tiantishan in Liangzhou (both Gansu)[109]. Regarding Afghanistan itself, paintings from Sharistan and Kakrak have been examined.[110]

Some results from wall paintings in Ajanta[111] give an insight into the complex Indian techniques. In addition, there is one literal source from India, the *Visnudharmottara-Purana*, written between the 4th and 7th centuries[112], which gives some evidence on the painting practise of the early Buddhist paintings.

Preparation layers
KAKOULLI 2006 interprets the application of clay plasters as an Asian tradition unknown in Hellenistic murals.[113] Clay plasters are characteristic of Chinese wall paintings. Clay plasters and clay-lime plasters as preparation of the walls are described in the *Visnudharmottara-Purana* as well as in later Indian manuscripts. According to these manuscripts, the preparation of the support was finished by the application of a white ground always consisting of calcitic materials like lime or conches. It can be regarded either as the last plaster layer (a pure lime plaster on lime-containing clay plasters) or a white priming layer. It is not clear if the ground layer hardened by setting.[114]

Table 3   Comparison of analyses of the statues and the wall paintings in Bāmiyān

colour	Gettens 1937–1938	Momi/Seke 2006, p. 93–100	Analyses in Munich 2004–2009
	wall painting	wall paintings	statues
white priming layer	burnt white gypsum		
first white layer (priming layer?)			white earth, some gypsum and lead white
white	calcium sulphate	Fe, Ca white pearls: Pb, Ca, Cu	*no white*
orange	minium		minium
red	iron oxide of different colour, for dark shades addition of charcoal	Hg, Pb, (Fe) >> cinnabar, and minium or lead white	iron oxide, containing maghemite and hematite, some lead white
pink	iron oxide and white (calcium sulphate)		red iron oxides + calcite, lead white, sometimes gypsum
black	charcoal black		*black lines not analysed*
black below blue	charcoal black		charcoal black + gypsum
blue	ultramarine	ultramarine (?) and another pigment	ultramarine
yellow	ochre [1]	light yellow: As, Fe in Pb (realgar in hydrocerussite)	yellow ochre
brown			white clay minerals + iron oxides
green	- copper containing pigment, but no malachite or Cu-carbonate, maybe chrysocolla (Gettens) - atacamite (chrysocolla), paratacamite [1]	still green: Cu today black: Cu, Fe, Ca	*no greens*
greenish	mixture of carbon black and yellow ochre		*no greenish tinges*

[1] This result is reported only in Kossolapov/Kalinina 2006, p. 90.

Most Central Asian wall paintings possess a white ground. This holds also true for the caves and the Buddha niches in Bāmiyān.[115] As materials, gypsum or anhydrite have been identified in the wall paintings of Kizil and Kumtura, gypsum with chalk or magnesium containing chalk in Afrasiab.[116] The white priming on the sculptures of Nisa contains kaolin and gypsum.

Besides white preparation layers wall paintings of Western China also show coloured ones: A pink-coloured plaster layer containing gypsum and iron oxide as finishing on top of a clay layer is described for a wall painting of Miran. In the Mogao grottoes, the top layer over the straw clay plaster consists of a thin white lime wash or a red ochre ground.[117]

The Indian manuscripts also describe underpaintings (*imprimatura*) which were applied completely or partially after sketching the scenery in black or red on the white ground. They are mainly in yellow, but also in other light colours. Such underpaintings have been observed in the wall paintings of Ajanta, too. Black and red contour lines executed before the application of pigment layers could be detected there as well.[118]

Pigments

The colours of the examined wall paintings comprise white, orange and red, pink, yellow, brown, blue, green, and black. The palette in total is rather large. It includes (pigments used most often are underlined):

white:	gypsum, calcite, lime, kaolin[119]; lead white[120]; lead sulphate[121]
red:	iron oxide, minium, cinnabar[122]
yellow, brown:	ochres, lead pigments (litharge, orpiment), arsenic compositions (orpiment, realgar)[123], minium + laureonite[124]
blue:	ultramarine, azurite (China), Egyptian Blue, ultamarine (Nisa), indigo[125], unidentified blue [126]
green:	copper pigments (malachite, chrysocolla ?), man-made atacamite, paratacamite, verdigris[127]; green earth[128], mixture of orpiment + indigo[129]
black:	bone black, charcoal black, soot/lamp black/Chinese ink[130]
organic dyestuffs:	lilac lake[131], red lakes[132]; gamboge (yellow), indigo[133]

Regional influences can be especially detected in the choice of blue pigments. Ultramarine, available in Afghanistan in large deposits and excellent quality, is predominant in most Central Asian wall paintings. It was applied on a black underpainting. Additionally, in China azurite was found that is mined in China, and Egyptian blue on the sculptures of Nisa, which reflects Hellenistic influence. At the same time the presence of ultramarine in Nisa is among the earliest proved uses of lapis lazuli as pigment. This shows once more that the Central Asian painting techniques of the early Buddhist works of art have to be regarded as a fusion of traditions and influences from China in the East, the Roman-Hellenistic sphere in the West and an already well-developed Indian technique.

Decorations with precious metals were known in Central Asia and China. The application of gold leaves and gold powder with animal glue or plant extracts is described in the *Visnudharmottara*.[134] Gold applications such as gold foil and gold powder were found in Tiantishan.[135] A very special technique was discovered in the caves of Bāmiyān: Tin foil was cut in strips and applied as decoration. Coated with a yellow varnish, it gave the impression of gold.[136]

Interpretation of paint layer investigation

The samples investigated in Munich were selected with great care and meant to comprise the different types of paint layers discernible on the fragments found and stored in Bāmiyān. It is not sure, however, that all types of paint layers were included, inter alia because of the fact that so far the rubble heaps in the niches have not been completely excavated. Thus some types of fragments could still be buried in the rubble. It is clear that the samples do not represent the fragments found in Bāmiyān regarding the frequency of the single colours: At the Eastern Buddha, for example, many reddish fragments have been found which are statistically underrepresented in the samples. The strange brown colours of group 3 and 4, on contrary, are overrepresented regarding the number of fragments found.

There are only few colours: pink to red, blue, brown and ochre. Bright yellow, black and green were not present in the examined samples. White was only found as second overpainting. Compared to paint layers from the murals and works of art of Central Asia, the choice of pigments is rather limited and within the "normal" range. So far, there is no evidence of special decoration techniques as metal foils or gilding of any kind or painted ornaments.

Fortunately, many larger fragments still possess a convex or concave shape which can be attributed to the folds of the garment. As far as it was possible to investigate colours on-site, most of the fold ridges seem to be of reddish colour. As samples were taken from some of them, they can be linked to the samples of groups 1 and 2. The blue fragments of the Eastern Buddha can be assigned to the garment as well and there are two blue fragments of the Western Buddha which also have the shape of fold ridges.

Brown samples come from fragments with flat surfaces and cannot be assigned to any part of the statues yet. The character of the brown is very different from the other colours. While most paint layers are powdery, soft and show a smooth surface, the brown layers are hard and semi-transparent and either glossy with raised brush marks or scaly. The brown seems to be very rich in binder and poor in pigmentation and thus does not really look like a paint layer. As thin layers look light brown, the darker brown might be a result of ageing processes of the binding medium.

The examination showed that at least under most of the brown layers remnants of the red layers can be found. Mostly these remnants are merely tiny traces. This indicates that most of the paint had already flaked off when the brownish material was applied. Two samples were taken from the reddish fold ridge fragment GBL 852: While one sample belongs to group 2, the other is brown with traces of the red paint layers underneath. This proves that the brown was applied on parts of the *sangati* which had been red before.

At least in some parts the brown material was applied twice, with some time lag, as soot was found between the layers. As the brown was also found on top of surfaces completely blackened by soot, this can mean that the brown samples came from lower parts which were blackened by the fire lit in the caves and also more exposed to influences harmful to the paint layer. It should also be mentioned that even some of the Indo-Afghan clay layers possess some kind of brownish glossy patina which must have formed during the past 25 years. The reason or the intention behind the application of the brown layers remains unclear. It cannot even be assumed if the brown was intended to protect or to hide the colours or the surfaces or if it should be assigned to activities quite independent of any reasonable intervention on the statues.

A transition between the different coloured parts could only be found on a single sample (Eastern Buddha, ID 256), showing a red and blue area. As the sample possesses a coherent white priming layer it is not clear if it represents the usual situation of the statue.

All other samples showing more than one colour and an overlapping of different colours (group 6) are so different from all the others that it is not possible to connect them to any other group. It is completely unclear where they come from. The possibility that they were not integral parts of the statues themselves cannot be rejected, although they definitely do not belong to the murals in the caves.

In the end, there are two groups of samples, groups 1-2 and group 5, which can be interpreted as they clearly are part of the garment. In both cases some fragments have a white priming layer, while others do not possess it. In the case of groups 1 and 2 this led to a differentiation into two groups, although the remaining layers show the same sequence. These groups will be discussed in the following:

Priming layer
The white priming layer raises a problem which cannot be explained satisfyingly yet. The white is found in crevices which could be shrinkage cracks of the clay, and in small holes on the surface, but it rarely seems to be a coherent layer although it is partially applied quite thickly. The pink as the subsequent layer in groups 1-2 has penetrated into crevices and tiny holes of the clay surface indicating that there was no white priming present at that time. Two different explanations are possible:

1. The white priming was not meant to cover the Buddha statues completely. It could have dripped down when the walls of the niches were painted. As colour photographs of the 1970s suggest, they possessed a white priming. Another possibility is that the white priming was applied

only partially on the statues or so irregularly that larger parts were not covered. Compared to other works of art made of clay it seems unusual that there should have been *no* white priming layer, but on the other hand there is no information on comparable large-scale sculptures.

2. The white priming layer belonged to the first polychromy which, except for these tiny remnants, has completely been lost. As it does not seem plausible that the paint layer flaked off completely, this would mean that the paint layer was removed manually before repainting.

Pink
In the samples of groups 1 and 2, the pink paint layer is the first coherent layer we can find. As mentioned before, it often has penetrated into small cavities of the clay surface. This means that obviously it was often applied on the bare clay surface. The pink could be a paint layer, but also a coloured underpainting or priming layer. In China, for example, pale pink often is used as substitute or underpainting of gold on polychrome sculptures. If it was the support of another layer or of decoration, no trace of these seems to have survived.

At the Eastern Buddha there are two pink layers on top of each other, which can be interpreted as a double application or an early repainting with the same material. On sample ID 246, with two red layers on top of each other, it seems to be a repainting as the lower layer possesses a crack system which is filled up by the upper layer. But it is not clear if this sample can be integrated into groups 1 and 2.

Overpainting layers of groups 1 and 2
Both statues show the same layer sequence. The first overpainting was done with minium. Four fragments of the Western Buddha show two minium layers on top of each other. As the first layer is blackened, the second layer has to be interpreted as a repainting. As the second minium layer was found so rarely, it might also have come from a partial repair.

The second overpainting is a rather thin layer of lead white or a white lead compound. It can be assumed that this layer had the function to cover the discoloured minium layer and thus could be interpreted as a priming layer. On the Western Buddha, it was covered with iron oxide red, which seems to confirm the character of a priming layer. On the Eastern Buddha, however, the lead white layer remained the last and thus the visible layer.

Blue
Like the pink layers, the blue mostly does not possess a white priming layer. On the Eastern Buddha the blue is the colour of the lining of the *sangati* and may also be the colour of the undergarment (*uttarasanga*). Although small compared to the outside of the *sangati* (i.e. the largest part of the statues), the blue areas painted with ultramarine were of considerable size. It appears amazing that the precious ultramarine was used in such large areas and in rather thick layers. This is possibly due to the fact that ultramarine is mined in considerable quantities in Afghanistan. Compared to the good quality of the Afghan ultramarine, the pigment used on the Buddha statues, however, is rather impure and pale.

The blue areas were only repainted once, using ultramarine as well. It is easy to imagine that the blue was spared at one of the repainting phases either because of the price of the pigment or because the respective parts were less exposed and therefore less damaged, or because the damages were less prominent.

Conclusion of the examination – the garments of the Buddha statues

The reddish fragments and the samples of groups 1 and 2 can be assigned to the outside of the *sangati*. The blue was the colour of the lining of the *sangati* at the Eastern Buddha and may have had the same function on the Western Buddha. Starting from this premise, it is possible to get an idea of how the garments of the statues appeared over time. It is not clear if the overpainting was done on both statues at the same time, but it seems striking that exactly the same material was used on both statues. The findings of our investigations allow the reconstruction of different states of their appearance:

First situation
Both statues may have had a partial white priming or a polychromy that is completely lost.

Second situation
The outside of the *sangati* was painted pink, the inside blue. The pink could have been the support of another layer or decorations which are lost. The Eastern Buddha possesses two pink layers on top of each other, either as double application or as an early repair, maybe from the time when the Western Buddha was painted.

Third situation
The pink was overpainted with minium. The *sangati* of both statues now was bright orange. The lining of the *sangati* was still blue. The minium layer of the Western Buddha maybe was partially touched up after some time, as sometimes two minium layers on top of each other can be observed.

Fourth situation
The *sangati* was overpainted with a white lead pigment, maybe to cover the discoloured minium. On the Western Buddha this white layer was covered with a bright red iron oxide and thus was red again. On the Eastern Buddha, however, no additional layer seems to have been applied or it was lost without leaving any trace. The reasons for that are not clear.

The lining of the *sangati* was repainted with blue, using a poorer quality of ultramarine, mixed with more white. Thus the dark blue areas now appeared a lighter blue.

After this repair the largest part of the Western Buddha, i.e. the *sangati*, was red, while on the Eastern Buddha it was white. This strikingly corresponds to the names of *surkh-but* (Red Buddha) and *khink-but* (Moonwhite Buddha) which can be traced back at least to the 11th century.

Fifth situation

Some parts of the statues were covered with a brownish material, containing some soil and a high content of binding material. At that time the paint layers in the respective areas were already quite reduced. The parts overpainted with brown had mostly been red before, some also blue. Others had lost their polychromy completely, but were blackened by soot. At least in some areas the brownish material was applied again after enough time had passed for soot or other residues to settle on the surface.

It should be noted that these overpaintings were carried out in a remarkably short period in view of the effort necessary for repainting such huge statues. All paint layers have to be assigned to the periods of Buddhist predominance, that is

1. between their creation in 540 (Eastern Buddha) or in 580 (Western Buddha) and 770;
2. between 770 and 870 when Bāmiyān was a Buddhist region once more.

Concerning the reasons for the repeated overpainting, it should be pointed out that on many samples the older paint layers had been reduced to mere traces when the next paint layer was applied. This indicates that at least in more exposed parts the paint layers did not last very long. Additionally, the discoloration of the minium may have resulted in a very unpleasant change of the visual appearance.

For obvious reasons, at least the last overpainting (lead white/red iron oxide) should be attributed to the second Buddhist period, as damages must have occurred during one hundred years of neglect and perhaps also vandalism, and consequently may have been repaired. Showing this last version of colour distribution, the two statues became the 'Red idol' and the 'White idol' on account of their overall appearance.

References

Abdurazakov, A. A., Kambarov, M. K.: *Restaurierung der Wandmalereien von Afrasiab*, Taschkent, 1975

Barbier de Meynard, Charles: *Dictionnaire Géographique, Historique et Littéraire de la Perse et des contrées adjacentes: Extrait du* Mu´ǧam al-Buldān *de Yāqūt*. Paris 1861. Reprint : Sezegin, Fuat (ed.), Publications of the Institute for the History of Arabic-Islamic Science, Islamic Geography, Vol. 221. First Part Ābaǧ – Sirkān. Frankfurt am Main 1994

Beal, Samuel: *SI-YU-KI, Buddhist Records of the Western World, translated from the Chinese of Hsiuen-Tsiang*, London 1884

Bollati, Ariela: *Le sculture in argilla dipinta*, unpublished report 2008

Burnes, Sir Alexander: *Travels into Bokhara, together with a narrative of A voyage on the Indus*, London 1834, Reprint Oxford University Press 1973

Gettens, Rutherford: *The materials in the wall paintings of Bāmiyān, Afghanistan*, in: Technical Studies in the field of the Fine Arts, Volume VI, 1937–1938, pp. 168–193

Godard, A. Godard, Y., Hackin, J.: *Les Antiquités Bouddhiques de Bāmiyān, Mémoires de la délégation archéologique Française en Afghanistan*, vol. II. Paris, Brussels 1928

Gunasinghe, Siri. *La technique de la peinture Indienne, D'après les textes du Śilpa*, Paris 1957

Hackin, J. avec la collaboration de J. Carl: *Nouvelles recherches archéologiques à Bâmiyân*. Les Mémoires de la DAFA, vol. III, 1933

Hackin, Joseph and Hackin, Ria: *Bamian. Führer zu den buddhistischen Höhlenklöstern und Kolossalstatuen*, Alleinberechtigte deutsche Ausgabe, Paris, Les éditions d'art et d'histoire 1939. (Translation of the French edition: Hackin, J. & R.: *Le site archéologique de Bâmiyân. Guide du visiteur*. Paris 1934)

Kakoulli, Ioanna: *Intercultural links and trade of painting materials in the Greco-Roman period*, in: Yamauchi, K. et al.: *Mural Paintings of the Silk Road, Cultural Exchanges between East and West*. Tokyo /London 2006

Kossolapov, A. J./Marshak, B. I.: *Murals along the Silk Road, Formika*, St. Petersburg 1999

Kossolapov, Alexander, Kalinina, K.: *The scientific study of binding media and pigments of murals paintings from Central Asia*, in: Yamauchi, K., Taniguchi, Y., Uno, T (ed.): *Mural Paintings of the Silk Road,* Tokyo 2006

Melzl, Edmund; Petzet, Michael: *Small Samples from Giant Buddhas*, in: *Small Samples, Big Objects*, Proceedings of the Eu-ARTECH seminar, May 2007, pp. 65–79

Momii, Motomitsu and Seki, Hiromitsu: *Displaced cultural properties: non-invasive study on mural painting fragments from Bāmiyān*, in: Yamauchi, K. et al.: *Mural Paintings of the Silk Road, Cultural Exchanges between East and West*, Tokyo /London 2006

Namikawa, Banri (Fotografie Stiftung e.V.): *Gandhara*, Präfektur Shimane 1999

Rapp, Klaus: *Kurzbericht zu Pigmentuntersuchengen mittels Rasterelektronenmikroskopie / EDX für das Projekt Bāmiyān"*, 2009

Riederer, Josef: *Technik und Farbstoffe der frühmittelalterlichen Wandmalereien Ostturkistans*, in: *Beiträge zur Indienforschung*, Berlin 1977

Sengupta, R.: *The restoration of the small Buddha at Bamyian*, ICOMOS, York 1984 (Momentum 27.1), pp. 31–46

Sharma, R. K.: *Painting Techniques and Materials of Cave mural Paintings in India*, in: Yamauchi, K., Taniguchi, Y., Uno, T. (ed.): *Mural Paintings of the Silk Road*, Tokyo 2006

Taniguchi, Yoko and Otake, Hidemi: *The painting techniques, materials and conservation of Bāmiyān Buddhist mural paintings in Afghanistan*, in: *Mural paintings, mosaics and rock art*, vol. 1, ICOM Committee for Conservation, 2008

Taniguchi, Y., Cotte, M., Checroun, E. and Otake, H.: *Constituent Material Analysis of the Bāmiyān Buddhist mural paintings (II): a study of pseudo-gold leaf technique discovered at Cave N8a, using Synchroton-based μ-FTIR*, in: *Science for Conservation* (Journal and article in Japanese), No. 46, 2007

Talbot, M. G. and Simpson, W.: *The rockcut caves and statues of Bamian*, in: *Journal of the Royal Asiatic Society*, Vol. XVIII, London 1886, pp. 303–350

Wang Xudong/Fu Peng: *Summary of painting materials and techniques of the Mogao grottoes*, in: Yamauchi, K., Taniguchi, Y., Uno, T (ed.): *Mural Paintings of the Silk Road*, Tokyo 2006

Zhou Guoxin, Zhang Jianquan, Cheng Huaiwan: *Pigment analysis of polychrome statuary and wall paintings of the Tiantishan grottoes*, in: Agnew, N. (ed.), *Conservation of Ancient Sites on the Silk Road, Proceedings of an international conference on the conservation of Grotto sites 1993*, Los Angeles 1997

Wilford, Captain Francis (ed.): *Asiatick Researches, or Transaction of the Society Instituted in Bengal*, vol. 6, XII (On Mount Caucasus), London 1801

Ilaria Bonaduce, Marcello Cito, Maria Perla Colombini, Anna Lluveras[137]

The Characterisation of the Organic Binders

Paints are always made up of the same fundamental components: a pigment, which is most typically a fine powder of inorganic or organic coloured material, and, with the exception of frescoes, a fluid binder, which enables the pigment to be dispersed and applied with a brush. Historically, the binder could have been a proteinaceous material such as egg or casein, a vegetable gum, a drying oil, a natural wax or a synthetic polymer. After drying or curing, a solid paint film is produced. The surface on which the paint is applied generally needs to be prepared with a ground layer. Painters were not only artists but also "material scientists", since they had to able to select the best paint materials, process them and apply them in order to suit their needs and achieve the desired aesthetical results. They experimented with a wide range of natural materials[138] and used many layers of paint to produce particular effects. To our eyes the appearance of a painting is thus the final result of the interaction of this complex, highly heterogeneous, multi-material and multi-layered structure with light.

The chemical characterisation of organic components is of great interest because the different organic paint materials used help us to differentiate between the various painting techniques, and because the organic component of the paint layer is particularly subject to degradation. An analysis of organic paint materials is essential for their long-term preservation, to assess the best conservation conditions, to prevent and slow down the decay processes, and to plan the best kind of restoration. Macroscopic degradation phenomena, such as the loss of cohesion in the paint layers, are in most cases related to the chemical alterations of the organic media, such as depolymerisation, oxidation, hydrolysis, cross-linking, and biological attack. Chemical reactions between organic materials and pigments lead to discoloration or colour alteration.

For a complete understanding of the composition of paint layers, several techniques need to be used, including SEM-EDX, XRD, micro-FTIR, micro-Raman, SIMS and many others[139]. Nevertheless, at present, the coupling of gas chromatography with mass spectrometry (GC-MS) is the preferred analytical approach to characterise organic paint materials such as binders or varnishes. The versatility of GC in the investigation of a very broad set of natural organic materials that can be found in artworks was pioneered by Mills and White and confirmed by a number of successful applications and case studies.[140,141] The choice of GC is driven by the fact that natural organic substances are complex mixtures of many chemical species, which are very similar to each other: the resolution and determination of the molecular profile is essential in order to identify the materials present and the ageing pathways. Consequently, in this specific field, the coupling of GC with mass spectrometry is necessary due to the high number of compounds with similar retention times. In addition, because the most significant compounds are not available as commercial standards, identification cannot be based only on retention times, but requires the confirmation of mass spectra[142].

Experimental

GC-MS analytical procedure to characterise organic binders
The sample is subjected to ammonia extraction in an ultrasonic bath two times to extract proteinaceous binders. The sample is centrifuged, the supernatant ammonia solution is separated, and the extracted ammonia solutions are joined together. The residue containing insoluble organic (i.e. lipid and resinous materials) and inorganic species is kept apart. The extracted ammonia solution is evaporated to dryness, redissolved in trifluoroacetic acid solution, and subjected to extraction with diethyl ether (three times) to extract free acids (monocarboxylic, dicarboxylic and terpenoid) solubilised in the ammonia solution. The ethereal extracts are combined with the residue of the ammonia extraction. The residue of the ether extraction is subjected to purification on OMIX C4 tip. The purified solution, containing proteins and polypeptides, is evaporated to dryness and subjected to acidic hydrolysis assisted by microwave. The residue of the purification is discarded. After the hydrolysis, bidistilled water is added to the acidic hydrolysate constituting the *amino acid fraction*. An aliquot of the amino acid fraction is then analysed with GC-MS after derivatisation with *N*-methyl-*N*-(*tert*-butyldimethylsilyl)trifluoroacetamide) (MTBSTFA), using norleucine and hexadecane as internal standards, pyridine as solvent, and triethylamine as catalyst. The residue of the ammonia extraction, combined with the ethereal extract of the protein and polypeptide solution prior the OMIX C4 tip purification, is subjected to saponification / salification assisted by microwave with KOH in ethanol. After saponification, the alcoholic solution is diluted in bidistilled water, acidified with trifluoroacetic acid, and extracted with *n*-hexane (three times) and diethyl ether (three times). The organic extracts (containing fatty acids, dicarboxylic acids,

Table 1　Sample description

sample	provenance	layer	(built-up) description	sub-sample (analysed)	note
KBL 497*	Eastern Buddha	3	greyish blue	KBL 497	
		2	ochre		
		1	clay		
GBL 246*	Western Buddha			A 1+2	sample flake, containing all paint layers
				A 1	red layer, scraped by scalpel
				A 2	pink layer, scraped by scalpel
GBL 2400+*	Western Buddha			Bt	sample flake, containing all paint layers
				B 1	superficial whitish layer
				B 3	brown paint layer (probably two paint layers are contained
				B 2	yellow layer, probably clay
GBL Einzelstück (ID 172a)*	Western Buddha			Ct	sample flake, conatining all paint layers
				C 1	superficial whitish layer
				C 2	brown layer
				C 3	red layer, containing some clay from underneath
ID 277	Eastern Buddha	fragment	arriccio	277	fragment
ID 97	Western Buddha	7	red hard layer	97 – 7	scraped material, contains a bit of layer 6 as well
		6	grey hard layer	97 – 6	scraped material, might contain a bit of layer 7
		5	black powdery layer	97 – 5	scraped material, contains a bit of layer 6
		4	orange powdery layer	97 – 4	scraped material
		3	pink powdery layer	97 – 3	
		2	plaster	97 – 2	scraped material, might contain a bit of arriccio
		1	arriccio	analyses not required	
ID 172 (172b)	Western Buddha	4	brownish layer, semi-transparent	172	
		3	thin red layer (few residues)	analyses not required	
		2	plaster		
		1	arriccio		
ID 68	Western Buddha	4	residues of pigmented layers	analyses not required	
		3	transparent preparation layer	168 – 3	scraped material
		2	plaster	168 – 2	scraped material
		1	arriccio	analyses not required	
ID 188	Eastern Buddha	5	white layer (few residues)	analyses not required	
		4	yellow ochre layer	188 – 4	scraped material, containing some more of layer 4 than of layer 3
		3	white gypsum layer	188 – 3	sample flakes, containing more of layer 3 than 4
		2	plaster	analyses not required	
		1	arriccio		
ID 214	Eastern Buddha		brown material (restoration)	214 int	contains a bit of blue layer underneath
		6	blue layer	214 – 6	material scraped with scalpel
		5	black layer	214 – 5	material scraped with scalpel
		4	blue layer	214 – 4	material scraped with scalpel
		3	black layer	214 – 3	material scraped with scalpel
		2	plaster	analyses not required	
		1	arriccio		

* Saccharide materials have not been characterised in samples KBL and GBL

Table 1 Sample description (continuing)

sample	provenance	layer	(built-up) description	sub-sample (analysed)	note
ID 14	Western Buddha	8	Indian restoration (only one point)	analyses not required	
		7	grey layer	14 – 7 (5 – 4)	scraped material, containing also layers 5 and 4
		6	red layer (only one point)	14 – 6	scraped material
		5	orange layer	14 – 5	scraped material
		4	white layer	14 – 4	scraped material
		3	transparent layer	14 – 3	scraped material
		2	plaster	analyses not required	
		1	arriccio		
ID 108	Western Buddha	5	few residues of the Indian restoration	analyses not required	
		4	glossy brown layer	108 – 4	
		3	glossy brown layer	108 – 3	
		2	plaster	analyses not required	
		1	arriccio		

Table 2 Amino acid relative percentage content of sample KBL

sample	Ala	Gly	Val	Leu	Ile	Ser	Pro	Phe	Asp	Glu	Hyp
KBL	4.0	4.5	7.3	10.2	5.0	3.5	12.4	6.5	16.4	30.2	0.0

terpenoid acids, alcohols, phenols, hydrocarbons and other neutral and acidic substances arising form lipid and resinous fraction of the sample) constitute the *lipid-resinous fraction*. An aliquot of the lipid-resinous fraction is analysed with GC-MS after derivatisation with *N,O*-bistrimethylsilyltrifl uoroacetamide (BSTFA), using tridecanoic acid (C13) and hexadecane as internal standards, and isooctane as solvent. Experimental details are published elsewhere.[143]

GC-MS analytical procedure for the determination of saccharide materials
The sample is subjected to microwave assisted hydrolysis to free sugars from polysaccharide materials with high efficiency and reproducibility. Afterwards the hydrolysed solution is purified through a double-exchange resin to remove analytical interferences of inorganic cofactors. The resulting sugars are analysed by GC-MS after derivatisation. The derivatisation procedure is based on mercaptalation followed by silylation, in order to transform the aldoses and uronic acids into the corresponding diethyl-dithioacetals and diethyl-dithioacetal lactones. Using this method only one chromatographic peak for each analyte is obtained, providing simple and highly reproducible chromatograms. Experimental details are published elsewhere.[144]

Samples
In table 1, a description of the samples analysed is summarised. Samples, by means of a scalpel, have been eventually sub-sampled under the binocular microscope.

Results and Discussions

Sample KBL 497
The analysis of the proteinaceous content revealed the presence of proteins. The relative amino acid content is reported in table 2. In figure 1 the principal component analysis score plot is reported. The sample is perfectly located in the casein cluster, indicating that it (or milk) was the binder used to disperse the pigments.

The analysis of the acidic fraction revealed the occurrence of monocarboxyilic acid, palmitic being the most abundant, and small amounts of dicarboxylic acids, azelaic being the most abundant. The occurrence of fatty acids at a level higher than the quantitation limit, in addition to the occurrence of dicarboxylic acids, suggests that an oxidised lipid material is present. The profile is not in disagreement with that of milk fats. The proteinaceous content, together with the lipid profile might suggest that the binder is milk and not casein.

Since this sample is characterised by a superficial layer not adherent and, underneath, a quite compact layer, these two layers were sampled separately and analysed. In particular the following samples were collected: a sample from the superficial not adherent layer (KBL 1), one from the compact layer underneath (KBL 2) and another sample containing all layers (KBL 3). Sample KBL 1 showed an amino acid content at the blank level, while both samples KBL 2 and 3 showed a proteinaceous content above the quantitation limit level and the relative amino acid content

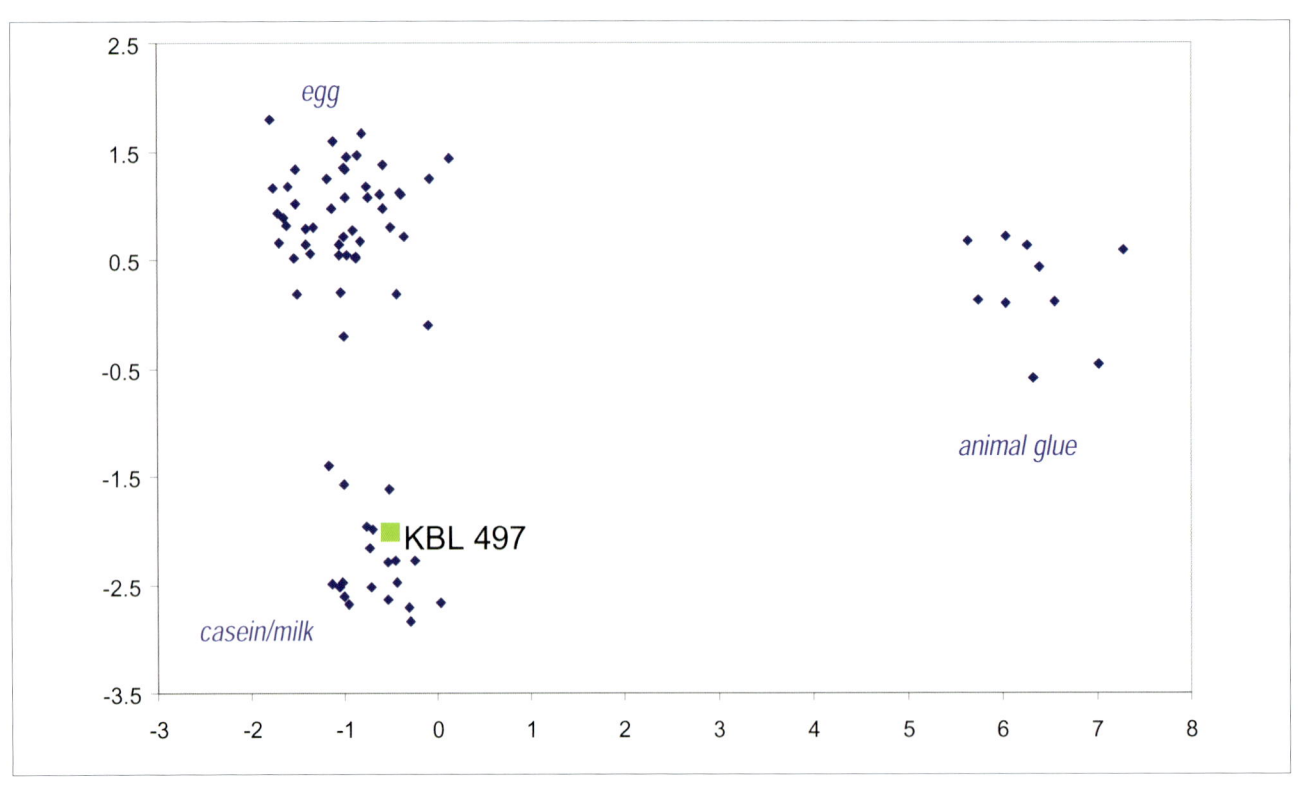

Fig. 1. PCA score plot of KBL497

Table 3 Amino acid relative percentage content of samples analysed

sample	Ala	Gly	Val	Leu	Ile	Ser	Pro	Phe	Asp	Glu	Hyp
KBL 2	5.4	8.0	12.2	14.9	8.0	5.9	7.7	4.8	10.8	22.4	0.0
KBL 3	5.5	7.2	10.5	11.9	6.5	5.3	9.7	5.8	12.1	25.5	0.0

Fig. 2. PCA score plot KBL497

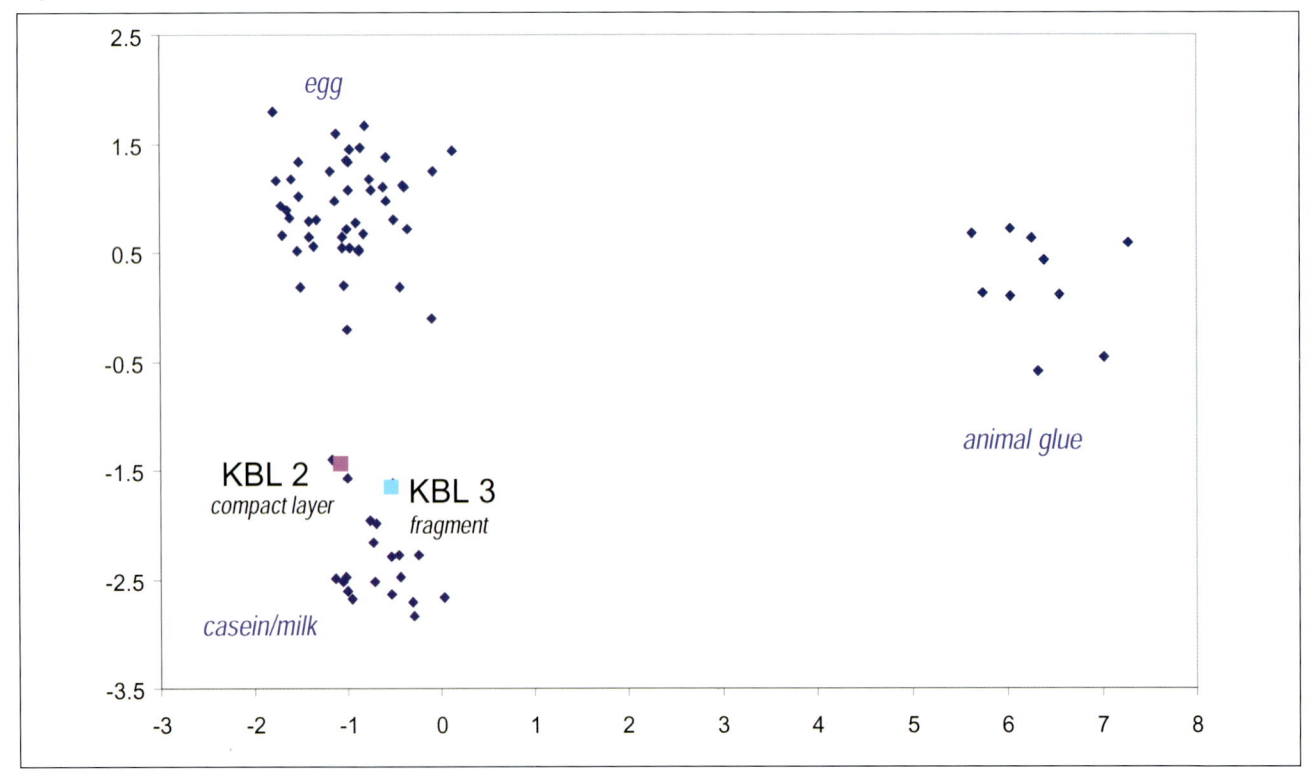

is reported in table 3. The samples were submitted to the PC analysis and the resulting score plot is reported in figure 2. Both samples are located in the casein cluster. Since the sample of the superficial non adherent layer showed a proteinaceous content at the blank level, it can be hypothesised that it has been realised using a binder, which was neither proteinaceous nor lipidic.

Samples GBL 246, GBL 2400+ and GBL Einzelstück (ID 172a)

All samples, with the exception of C1 showed the occurrence of proteinaceous material higher than the blank level. In table 4 the relative amino acid percentage content is reported together with the amount of proteinaceous material found (calculated as the sum of the eleven quantified amino acids).

The relative percentage amino acid contents were subjected to the principal component analysis (PCA) together with 104 reference samples containing egg, animal glue and casein (or milk) and the resulting score plots are shown in figure 3 (A, B, C).

The lipidic component has been analysed as well. All samples contained monocarboxylic acids with an even number of carbons, palmitic and stearic acid being the most abundant, and small amounts of dicarboxylic acids and monocarboxylic acids with an odd number of carbons. Cholesterol was identified in samples but sample A1+2. Beeswax was identified in small amounts in sample Bt and Ct.

GBL 246. All three sub-samples contain casein, as it can be inferred from the PCA score plot reported in Figure 1-A. The lipid fraction shows a fatty acid profile that is not ascribable to a drying oil in none of the sub-samples analysed. Moreover the high amount of stearic acid, together with the occurrence of cholesterol, odd number of carbon fatty acids and dicarboxylic acids ranging from eptandioic to hexadecandioic acid, point to the occurrence of a fat of animal origin (not egg lipids, since palmitic and stearic acid are in similar amounts). These results suggest that milk could have been used as painting medium for both paint layers.

GBL 2400+. The interpretation of the composition of this sample seems more complex and more investigation seems necessary to clarify the binding media composition layer by layer.

The lipid composition again point to the occurrence of a fat of animal origin, although not egg lipids, since palmitic and stearic acid are in similar amounts. Moreover very small amounts of beeswax have been identified in the sample flake: it might be ascribable to a restoration material, which was not identified in the B1 sub-sample because this was too small.

The sample flake (Bt) contains proteinaceous material, or, due o the position in the score plot, a mixture of proteinaceous materials. Animal glue is present due to the presence of hydroxyproline, its marker. Sample B1 contains both casein and animal glue. Sub-sample B3, representing the paint layers, and though in contact with B1 contain casein. Sub-sample B2, representing the clay in contact with the paint layer contains what seems a mixture of egg and animal glue. Since no fats were not present in the lipid fractions egg white must be hypothesised. Thus a possible interpretation of the sub-sample composition can be as follows: the superficial whitish layer (which is a restoration layer) was performed with animal glue; the brown paint layers have been applied with casein (probably milk, due to the occurrence of fats); and finally the clay was prepared with a mixture of egg white and animal glue.

GBL Einzelstück (ID 172a). The structure of this sample seems similar to the one from GBL 2400+. In fact the lipid fraction contains animal fats (not egg fats) as well as very small amounts of beeswax. The proteinaceous content reveals the occurrence of egg and animal glue in the sample flake, and the red sub-sample, containing some clay seems a mixture of the three paint proteinaceous binders. The brown paint layer seems to contain just casein. Thus also in this case it can be hypothesised that the paint has been applied with casein and the clay has been previously prepared with animal glue and egg white.

Samples ID 277, 97, 172, 168, 188, 214, 14, and 108

In all samples but sample ID 14 (sub-samples 14-3, 14-4/5/6 and 14-4/5/7) non drying fats, most likely from animal origin, were observed, being characterised by the presence of:

Table 4 Amino acid relative percentage content of samples analysed and amount of proteinaceus material found (µg)

sample	Ala	Gly	Val	Leu	Ile	Ser	Pro	Phe	Asp	Glu	Hyp	Proteinaceus material found
A 1+2	4.2	3.3	5.7	8.1	5.1	5.5	11.8	4.9	14.2	37.1	0.0	6.7
A 1	3.7	2.3	6.4	9.8	4.9	4.2	10.7	3.3	14.1	40.7	0.0	12.6
A 2	5.5	6.4	6.0	9.5	5.3	5.0	13.5	5.6	13.1	30.0	0.0	4.7
Bt	5.5	7.0	6.1	8.4	5.0	5.4	4.8	8.5	21.5	27.5	0.4	10.2
B 1	5.4	9.8	5.5	5.4	3.5	5.5	10.1	5.7	21.8	26.6	0.7	2.6
B 2	14.1	6.3	6.1	9.7	4.2	4.1	10.6	1.3	15.2	27.9	0.5	2.0
B 3	6.4	6.7	7.3	11.8	12.0	7.2	8.3	3.5	13.0	23.3	0.5	9.6
Ct	11.7	7.8	5.3	6.5	3.8	11.7	11.5	6.0	12.4	23.3	0.0	2.0
C 2	5.3	5.7	7.9	11.0	6.7	9.9	8.9	4.7	12.7	27.4	0.0	2.5
C 3	11.3	7.7	7.7	10.1	4.6	10.9	8.0	2.9	10.2	27.5	0.5	0.9

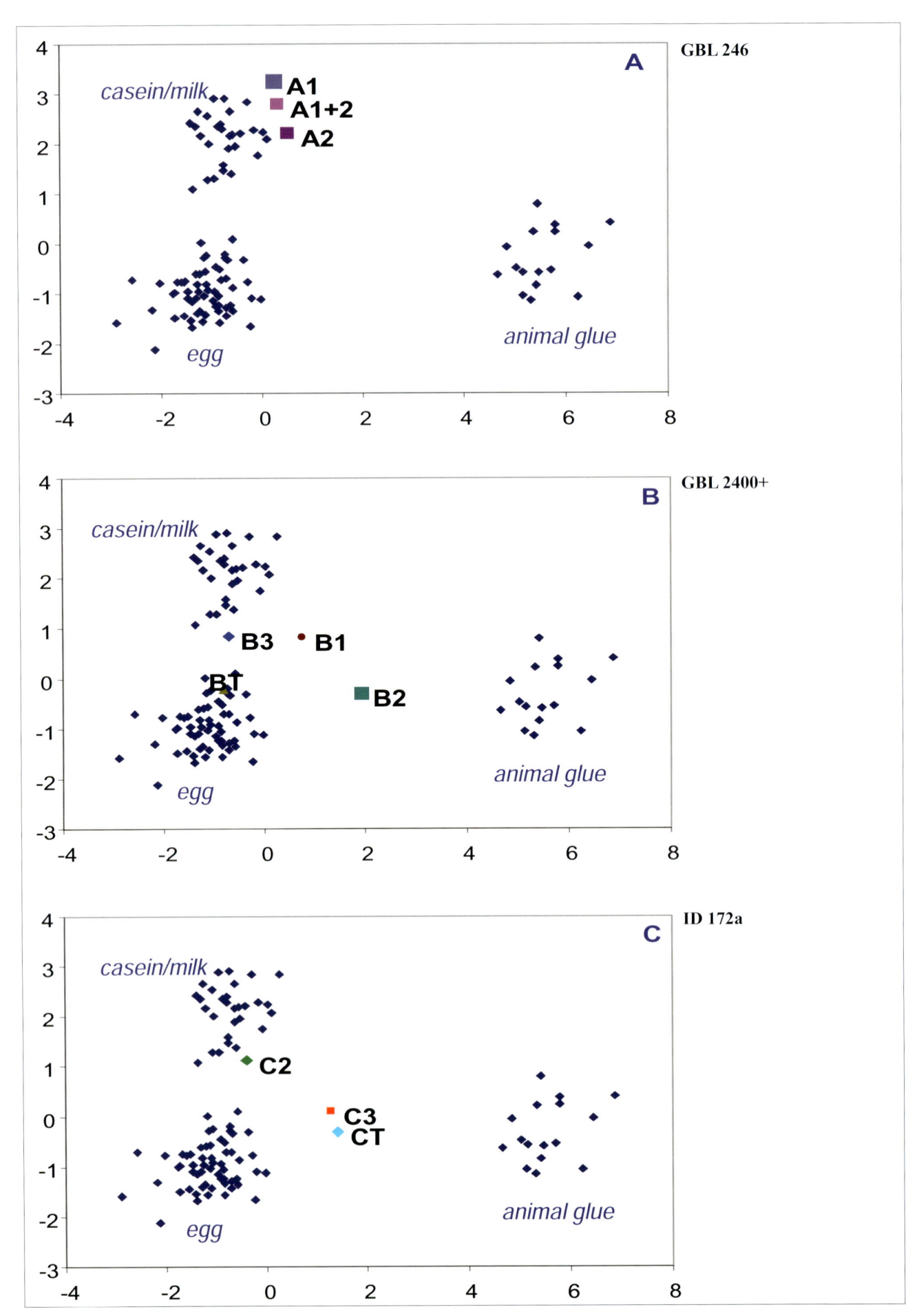

Fig. 3. PCA score plots (A, B, C) of GBL 246, GBL 2400+ and ID 172a

- monocarboxylic acids with even number of carbons (palmitic being the most abundant);
- small amounts of dicarboxylic acids (azelaic being the most abundant);
- small amounts of monocarboxylic acids with an odd number of carbons.

All samples showed the occurrence of proteinaceous material higher than the blank level, with the exception of the sub-sample 168-3, whose amino acidic content was between the detection and quantitation limit levels. In table 5 the relative amino acid content of the samples is reported together with the protein content, calculated as the sum of the eleven quantified amino acids. Any of the samples presented hydroxyproline in their composition indicating the absence of animal glue.

The quantitative percentage content of amino acids of the sub-samples determined from the amino acid fraction was subjected to a multivariate statistical analysis together to a data-set of 121 reference samples of animal glue, egg and casein, using the principal components analysis (PCA) method. Resulting score plots for each of the analysed samples are presented in figure 4.

Results indicate the use of egg in almost all sub-samples except for 97-5 and 97-2 (Western Buddha), where milk is the binding medium identified. The presence of non drying fats from animal origin identified in the lipid-resinous fraction (see above) indicated the use of egg yolk or whole egg. In sample 14 (sub-samples 14-6-5-4, 14-7-5-4 and 14-3) the absence of lipid materials suggests the use of the egg albumen (Western Buddha).

As far as the saccharide fraction is concerned, the glycoside profiles of the sub-samples are presented in table 6.
Three different kinds of sub-samples can be distinguished on the base of their polysaccharide content:
- polysaccharide content at the blank level of the procedure (97-7, 97-6, 97-5, 97-3-4, 168-3, 14-6-5-4, 14-3)
- polysaccharide content between the detection and quantitation limits (97-2, 168-2, 188-3, 14-7-6-5-4
- polysaccharide content higher than the quantitation limit (277, 172, 188-4, 214 int, 214-6-5, 214-4-3, 108-4, 108-3). Sample 188-4 contains also fructose.

The polysaccharide material could not be identified as one of the known plant gums, that is Arabic, tragacanth and fruit three gum. The presence of all sugars in samples 188-4, 172, 214-6-5, 108-4 and 108-3 suggests the use of a mixture of saccharide materials.

The sugar profiles observed are quite complex and the following remarks may be drawn:
- Sub-samples from the Western Buddha with a glycoside profile higher than the quantitation limit correspond to superficial layers and plaster ones.
- Sub-samples corresponding to plaster layers (97-2, 168-2) present a similar glycoside profile (xylose, arabinose and galactose). Galactose could be considered the result of the contribution of the saccharide content of the proteinaceous binder present in the samples.
- Sample 108-4, 108-3 and 172 consist in brownish layers on top of the sample build-up. However, quantitative profiles present some differences among them: all monosaccharides are present in sample 108 while in sample 172 glucose is absent and galacturonic acid

Table 5 Amino acid relative percentage content of samples 277, 97, 172, 168, 188, 214, 14, and 108

sample	Ala	Gly	Val	Leu	Ile	Ser	Pro	Phe	Asp	Glu	Hyp	Protein content [μg]
277	8.6	13.4	8.9	12.0	7.0	7.3	6.5	6.9	16.6	12.8	0.0	2.0
97 – 7	9.1	24.7	9.3	16.7	8.9	3.8	5.4	4.6	6.8	10.7	0.0	0.4
97 – 6	11.6	18.2	11.1	16.8	9.1	3.5	6.4	4.0	5.6	13.7	0.0	0.5
97 – 5	5.7	7.9	11.1	16.9	8.4	4.8	9.7	6.8	11.6	17.2	0.0	1.0
97 – 4 – 3	4.7	5.4	9.5	13.6	7.2	8.5	2.2	7.1	15.3	26.4	0.0	2.3
97 – 2	4.4	4.9	8.9	12.1	6.4	10.9	7.9	6.3	13.4	24.8	0.0	4.3
172	8.6	19.6	8.3	15.3	8.3	2.9	7.3	6.2	9.2	14.3	0.0	0.2
168 – 3	13.0	14.5	10.3	15.9	9.0	5.5	4.0	3.9	6.8	17.0	0.0	0.1
168 – 2	8.5	10.3	12.1	19.6	9.4	5.8	6.2	6.9	9.3	11.9	0.0	0.4
188 – 4	6.7	7.7	8.4	12.0	5.3	19.7	3.3	5.4	11.5	19.9	0.0	3.1
188 – 3	9.6	12.4	13.3	20.8	11.5	1.4	11.8	5.6	4.7	8.9	0.0	0.3
214 int	7.3	8.5	10.9	12.9	8.2	11.2	4.1	6.5	18.4	12.2	0.0	2.5
214 – 6 – 5	5.5	6.4	9.6	11.4	7.2	11.6	5.0	5.7	17.6	20.0	0.0	3.5
214 – 4 – 3	7.4	6.9	14.4	19.0	10.7	12.2	3.6	7.1	11.7	7.1	0.0	3.8
14 – 6 – 5 – 4	7.4	10.3	12.5	19.1	10.3	5.9	5.3	7.5	13.6	8.1	0.0	0.8
14 – 7 – 5 – 4	8.8	10.8	15.0	22.9	11.3	4.4	5.5	7.1	7.6	6.7	0.0	0.5
14 – 3	16.0	15.5	18.6	23.7	13.7	1.5	0.1	2.4	4.9	3.6	0.0	0.6
108 – 4	12.4	15.7	13.4	14.9	9.4	5.3	5.2	5.4	10.3	8.0	0.0	0.3
108 – 3	14.9	16.5	14.6	21.0	11.6	4.2	1.1	1.6	3.4	11.2	0.0	0.2

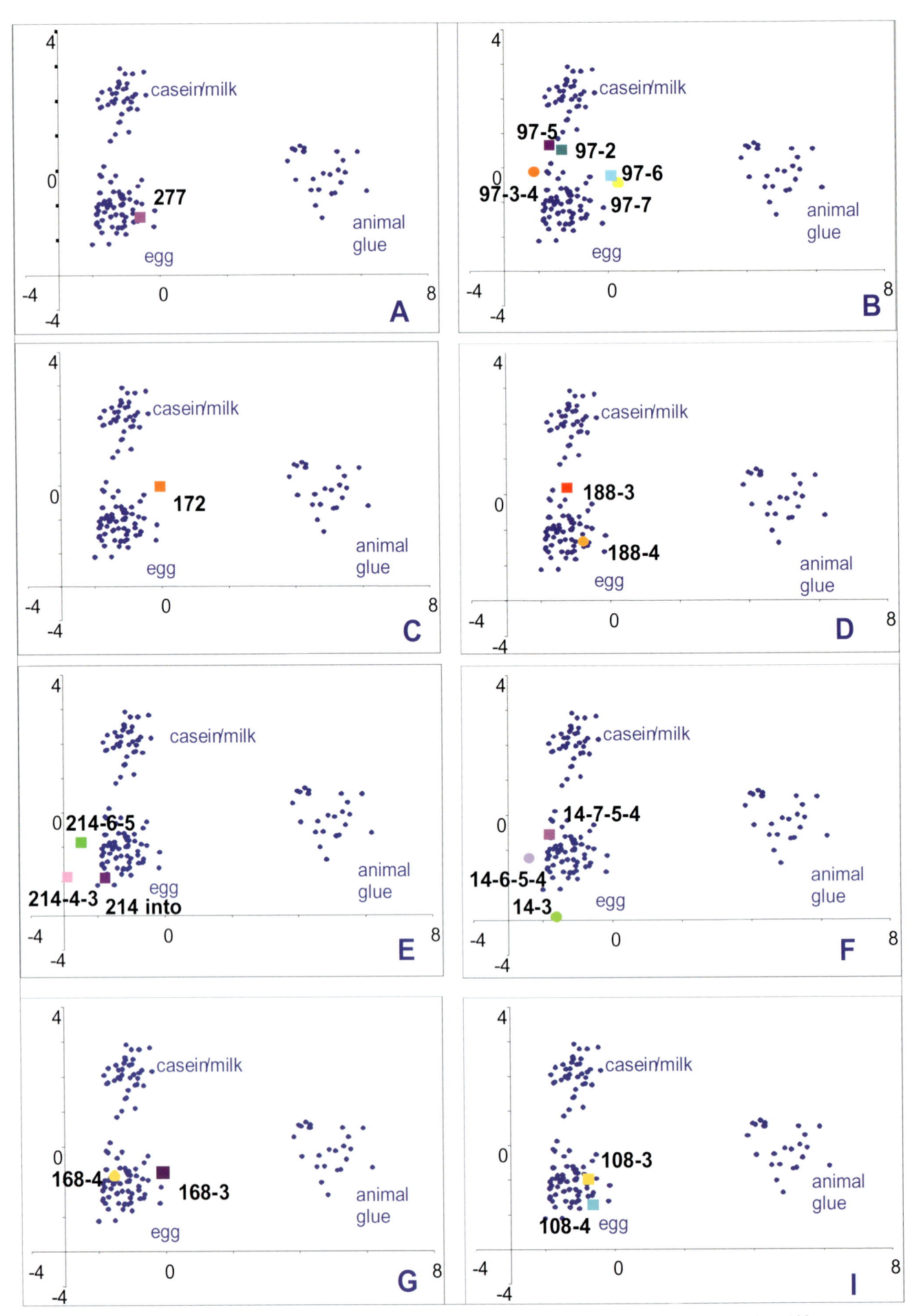

Fig. 4. PCA score plot of samples A) ID 277; B) ID 97; C) ID 172a; D) ID 188; E) ID 214; F) ID 14; G) ID 168; H) ID 108

content is higher than in sample 108. Sample 14-7-5–4 shows also a glycoside profile with all sugars but galacturonic acid.
- Samples from Eastern Buddha presenting a saccharide content higher than the quantitation limit correspond to the arricio (277) and to pigmented layers (188, 214). In particular:
- Sample 188-4 presents all the sugars and 5 peaks of fructose. The main sources of fructose are fruit, vegetable and honey.
- Sample 188-3 presents xylose, arabinose, glucose and galactose that are also present in higher amounts in sub-sample 188-4 suggesting a contamination from this layer.
- Sub-sample 214-int, corresponding to a restoration layer and 214-6-5 present a similar profile (though xylose relative amounts are very different). A penetration of the restoration material can be suggested by the data.
- The presence of all sugars in sample 277 suggests the use of a mixture of saccharide materials.

On the basis of the results obtained from the analysis of the polysaccharide, lipid and proteinaceous fractions it is possible to draw some conclusions on the sample and sub-sample compositions. In table 7 the organic materials identified in each sub-sample are reported.
On these bases it is possible to draw the conclusions summarised in table 8.

Interpretation and conclusions

The discussion of the painting technique is quite complex, and requires the support of conservators, to better understand the aesthetical effect of each paint layer, and their originality. Moreover, it can be assumed from the analysed materials that partly the binders of overpaintings have penetrated the lower layers, resulting in the presence of several materials inside a single layer. It is necessary to analyse more samples to assure the results, but it is possible to draw some conclusions as preliminary interpretation:

The *arriccio,* which is the undercoat underneath the finish clay coat, contains a saccharide material and small amounts of egg (sample ID 277). The addition of saccharide materials are known to have been used in Asian clay plasters to increase the viscosity and adhesiveness of (straw) mud modelling pastes: In China, water from cooking sticky rice (i.e. starch) or an extract of the *luo han guo* fruit have been used.

In the surface of the clay, egg has been found. Sample ID 168 contains egg, ID 14 egg white, ID 172a and GBL 2400+ a mixture of egg white and animal glue. It can be assumed that these materials have been used as isolation of the clay surface before applying the paint layers. In one sample (ID 97) milk was found in the surface of the clay. This can be interpreted as the traces of a lost priming layer although this can not be ascertained yet. All examined samples come from the Western Buddha. For a further interpretation more analyses are required.

Table 6 Glycoside profiles of ID 277, 97, 172a, 168, 188, 214, 14, and 108

sample	sugars									Saccharide content [μg]
	xylose	arabinose	ramnose	fucose	galacturonic acid	glucuroni acid	glucose	mannose	galactose	
277	44.5	22.9	2.3	1.0	0.0	1.4	17.6	3.1	7.0	129.0
97 – 7										-
97 – 6										-
97 – 5										-
97 – 4 – 3										-
97 – 2	y	y	-	-	-	-	-	-	y	-
172a	44.1	8.8	2.3	1.7	6.7	2.2	0.0	20.0	14.3	1.8
168 – 3										-
168 – 2	y	y	-	-	-	-	-	-	y	-
188 – 4	7.8	13.6	0.5	0.8	0.6	2.1	50.8	4.0	19.8	3.6
188 – 3	y	y					y		y	-
214 int	10.9	3.3	1.3	1.0	0.0	0.6	46.4	13.2	23.3	2.8
214 – 6 – 5	7.3	4.9	1.9	1.4	0.7	1.3	34.2	15.5	32.8	5.1
214 – 4 – 3	47.2	12.1	2.0	1.1	0.0	0.0	0.0	0.0	37.5	0.6
14 – 6 – 5 – 4	y	y	y	y	-	y	y	y	y	-
14 – 7 – 5 – 4										-
14 – 3										-
108 – 4	8.3	13.5	1.6	2.0	1.1	3.3	25.8	10.5	34.1	7.9
108 – 3	11.7	12.8	0.8	1.8	0.5	0.9	31.1	7.1	33.3	1.7

Table 7 Results of analyses of sub-samples

sub-sample	proteinaceous fraction	saccharide fraction	layer composition
277	egg	mixture of saccharide materials	saccharide materials (main component) and egg (whole-yolk)
97 – 7	egg	-	egg (whole-yolk)
97 – 6	egg	-	egg (whole-yolk)
97 – 5	milk	-	milk
97 – 3 – 4	egg	-	egg (whole-yolk)
97 – 2	milk	milk contribution	milk
172	egg	mixture of saccharide materials	saccharide materials (main component) and egg (whole-yolk)
168 – 3	egg	-	egg (whole-yolk)
168 – 2	egg	egg sugars	egg (whole-yolk)
188 – 4	egg	mixture of saccharide materials fructose detected	saccharide materials (including fruit juice of honey) and egg (whole-yolk)
188 – 3	milk	possible contamination from other layers	milk
214 int	egg	mixture of saccharide materials	saccharide materials and egg (whole-yolk)
214 – 6 – 5	egg	mixture of saccharide materials	saccharide materials and egg (whole-yolk)
214 – 4 – 3	egg	possible contamination from other layers	unidentified saccharide material and egg (whole-yolk)
14 – 7 – 5 – 4	egg	mixture of saccharide materials, possible contamination from the superficial layer	saccharide materials with egg white
14 – 6 – 5 – 4	egg	-	egg white
14 – 3	egg	-	egg white
108 – 4	egg	mixture of saccharide materials	saccharide materials (main component) and egg (whole-yolk)
108 – 3	egg	mixture of saccharide materials	saccharide materials (main component) and egg (whole-yolk)

Table 8 Sample composition, layer by layer

provenance	sample ID	layer	(built-up) description	organic material characterised
Eastern Buddha	277	-	arriccio (preparation layer underneath the plaster)	saccharide binder, with little egg (whole or yolk)
Western Buddha	97	7	red hard layer	egg
		6	grey hard layer	egg
		5	black powdery layer	milk
		4	orange powdery layer	egg
		3	pink powdery layer	egg
		2	plaster	milk
		1	arriccio	n.a.
Western Buddha	172	4	brownish layer, semi-transparent	saccharide binder and egg
		3	thin red layer (few residues)	n.a.
		2	plaster	n.a.
		1	arriccio	n.a.
Western Buddha	168	4	residues of pigmented layer	n.a.
		3	transparent preparation layer	egg (whole-yolk)
		2	plaster	egg
		1	arriccio	n.a.
Eastern Buddha	188	5	white layer (few residues)	n.a.
		4	yellow ochre layer	saccharide materials (including fruit juice or honey) and egg
		3	white gypsum layer	milk
		2	plaster	n.a.
		1	arriccio	n.a.
Eastern Buddha	214	7	brown material (restoration)	saccharide binder and egg
		6	blue layer	saccharide binder and egg
		5	black layer	saccharide binder and egg
		4	blue layer	egg
		3	black layer	egg
		2	plaster	n.a.
		1	arriccio	n.a.
Western Buddha	14	8	Indian restoration (only one point)	n.a.
		7	grey layer	saccharide material and egg
		6	red layer (only one point)	egg
		5	orange layer	egg
		4	white layer	egg
		3	transparent layer	egg
		2	plaster	white
		1	arriccio	n.a.
Western Buddha	108	5	Indian restoration residues	n.a.
		4	glossy brown layer	saccharide material and egg
		3	glossy brown layer	saccharide material and egg
		2	plaster	n.a.
		1	arriccio	n.a.

In samples from groups 1 and 2, i.e. the red parts of the *sangati*, all paint layers contain mainly egg. Milk was found in the orange layer of sample GBL 246 and the black layer of discoloured orange in sample ID 97. The use of milk or casein for this layer could also explain the massive discoloration of the minium as an aqueous binder would provide less protection for the pigment than an egg binder. In the preliminary interpretation we assume that the pink layer (= first preserved paint layer) was bound with egg, the overpainting with minium with milk or casein and the last overpainting with the white lead containing layer and, on the Western Buddha, iron oxide red, with egg.

The clay suspension from the Indo-Afghan restoration always contains polysaccharides. Traces of beeswax might be a contamination.

Blue layers (group 5) could not be interpreted satisfyingly yet. While in a sample from the Western Buddha (ID 214) both blue layers and their black underpaintings contain egg and polysaccharides, a sample from the Eastern Buddha (KBL 497) contains milk or casein. It is planned to do further analyses on other blue samples.

The brown overpainting layers (groups 3 and 4) provide a similar problem: while two samples (GBL 2400+ (group 3) and ID 172a (group 4) contain casein, two others (ID 108 (group 3) and ID 172b (group 4) contain egg and polysaccharides. While the polysaccharides may be interpreted as binder of the Indo-Afghan clay suspension, casein or egg should be the main components of the brown layers. As samples ID 172a and b in fact are two halves of the same fragment, they should contain the same binders. While on ID 172a the brown layers have been sampled, on ID 172b only a thin glossy layer on top of the brown was analysed.

This could mean that casein is the binder of the brown layer which possesses a thin coating containing egg and traces of the Indo-Afghan clay containing polysaccharides.

The identification of the saccharide materials cannot be performed since in all cases the sugar composition seems due to unknown saccharide binders. The use of honey or a fruit juice could be proven in one of the samples.

The white priming layer of sample ID 188 contains egg. The yellow ochre paint layer contains egg and polysaccharides, the latter may be a contamination of restoration materials of the Indo-Afghan intervention. ID 188 belongs to the samples of group 6 which cannot be assigned to the Buddha statues without doubt and thus could also show a different painting technique. The use of egg for the pigment layer however is comparable to paint layers which can be definitely assigned to the statues.

The interpretation of the analyses allows drawing a first, tentative conclusion on the painting technique: The undercoat of mud straw contains a saccharide material which probably was added to improve the plastic properties of the layer. The surface of the finished clay modelling was impregnated with a binding medium to obtain a dust-free support with homogenous absorption properties. Egg or egg white have been found in samples of the Western Buddha, in two samples a mixture of egg white and animal and in one sample milk. Further investigations are necessary, also including samples of the Eastern Buddha. Paint layers contain mainly egg, with exemption of the minium layer for which milk or casein seems to have been used. Brown and blue layer require more analyses to assure if egg with saccharides or casein/milk have to be regarded as the main component.

The clay suspension of the Indo-Afghan restoration contains an addition of saccharides which probably should increase the adhesion and the cohesion of the layer.

The analysed samples do not prove general differences between the painting technique of the Eastern and the Western Buddha, but more analyses are necessary to assure this fact.

Notes

1 BAUER-BORNEMANN ET AL. 2003, p. 3.
2 BURNES 1834, pp. 185-186.
3 RITTER 1838, p. 48. '*Der Körper ist nicht nackend, sondern mit einer Art Mantel überkleidet, der alle Theile bedeckt, aber aus einem aufgelegten Gypsstucco besteht. Noch bemerkt man viel eingetriebene Holzpflöcke, die unstreitig dazu dienten, diesem Stucco Halt zu geben.*'
4 EYRE 1843, p. 364, in GODARD et al. 1928, p. 88.
5 Maitland, P. J.: *Additional note on Bāmiyān*, in TALBOT/SIMPSON 1886, p. 348, cited in: GODARD ET AL. 1928, p. 93.
6 '[...] *il parvint ainsi jusqu'à l'amorce du revêtement de briques recouvrant la pièce de bois qui formait l'ossature de l'avant-bras et supportait la main levée en abahyapāni-mudra (geste qui rassure) (fig. 23). M. Carl découvrit, chemin faisant, des fragments de revêtement, composés d'un melange de terre et de paille hacheé recouvert d'une mince pellicule de mortier de chaux, qui garnissait le grossier épannelage de la statue; nous avouns recueilli des fragments simulant les plis du manteau monastique encore munis de leur armature de cordes et de piquets et revêtus de la couche de painture rouge qui couvrait primitivement le manteau tout entier.*' HACKIN/CARL 1933, p. 15. Fig. 23 shows Carl standing on the Western Buddha's right forearm; fig. 24 is a detail of the folds of the *sangati* (black and white).
7 BURNES 1834, pp. 185–186.
8 TARZI 1997, vol. 2. p. 117.
9 GBL 852: imprint of a peg; GBL 1445: imprint of a rope.
10 For example pegs no. GBL 826, 1367, 1733, 1734, 1737, 1825, 1911, 1923, 1937, 1939, 1950, 2009 and 2119.
11 SENGUPTA 1984, p. 41.
12 For a detailed description of the ropes see: *Materials made of plant fibres: ropes and textile fragment* in this publication.
13 For example fragment GBL 1651.
14 Few round timber were found as well, e. g. GBL 448l, but it is not clear if they belong to the Buddha statue or if they were parts of its original construction.
15 So far, there was no possibility to measure the depth exactly, because this can only be done on a scaffold.
16 BURNES 1834, pp. 185–186.
17 The *Gypsstucco* (gypsum stucco) mentioned by RITTER 1838 can be regarded as a misinterpretation of the word *plaster* (as plaster of Paris = in German Gips) used by Burnes to whom he explicitly refers.
18 HACKIN/CARL 1933, p. 15.
19 HACKIN 1939 (German translation of the French book of 1934), p. 38.
20 GETTENS 1937–38, p. 168.
21 SENGUPTA 1984, description on p. 41.
22 Visible for example on the fragments GBL 1025-27, GBL 1070, GBL 1088.
23 The preparation of rock surfaces with animal dung is regarded as a classical method in Indian wall paintings (personal information by Y. Taniguchi).
24 Analysis by XRD by V. Tucic in Nov. 2004, samples GBF 002 (on stone, sample 2) and KBL 073 (on clay, sample 3)) interpreted the results as clay–lime slurry (KBL 073) with a calcite content of 22 m% and about 1 m% of hematite as colouring material. GBF 002 contained 14 m% of gypsum and 8 m% of calcite and this is a gypsum clay or gypsum-lime-clay mixture. A content of 6 m% weddelite was detected. Quartz contents vary between 48-52 m%. – Analysis with PLM by C. Blänsdorf, peg from Western Buddha, no. a, found on July 7, 2007: Iron oxides, calcite, clay minerals, some gypsum and quartz, 1 particle lead oxide. The rather large calcite particles indicate the use ground limestone. Light pink areas contain more calcite than darker ones.
25 Visible for example on fragments GBL 1088 and 1205, both fold ridges of the Western Buddha.
26 In China, for example, clay mortars are traditionally spread on the walls with the hands. Wooden boards only serve to scoop up larger quantities from a bowl.
27 Leather piece in GBL 2026. Textile fragment: without number.
28 GBL 2090.
29 Visible on samples ID 28 and ID 53.
30 GBL 684.
31 Eastern Buddha: KBL 200, below the right arm: reddish undercoat, fine clay layer, greyish coarse layer; Western Buddha: GBL 1288–1292: undercoat, two finish coats.
32 KBL 285 from the Eastern Buddha could be dated by ^{14}C- AMS to the same time as the other clay fragments.
33 The paint layer on these parts is yellowish ochre.
34 NATIONAL RESEARCH INSTITUTE FOR CULTURAL PROPERTIES 2006, p. 121–124.
35 SENGUPTA 1989, p. 205
36 As they did not have a scaffold at that time, they probably could not reach the statues at all.
37 White filling with brown coating from the Western Buddha, sample 2 of July 2006. Analysis with PLM by C. Blaensdorf: yellowish white matrix calcium sulphate dihydrate and semi-hydrate, some calcite; white clusters: fibrous calcium sulphate semi-hydrate. Transparent particles: quartz (sand). – Sample ID 224, Eastern Buddha, analysis with XRD: anhydrite, dihydrate, amorphous substances, see: Mineralogical investigations on loam plaster fragments of the destroyed Buddha statues at Bāmiyān, Afghanistan, in this publication.
38 Sample ID 84, Western Buddha, analysis with XRD, see *Mineralogical investigations on loam plaster fragments of the destroyed Buddha statues at Bāmiyān, Afghanistan*, in this publication.
39 Western Buddha, sample ID 84.
40 Information by Mr. Ajan who worked in the restoration team. Fragment archive of E. Melzl, GBL 135.
41 Analysis by XRD, V. Tucic, September 2004 on sample GBL 001.
42 KBL 497, analysis with PLM, C. Blänsdorf, and XRD, V. Tucic. KBL 1524, 1, PLM by C. Blänsdorf.
43 Burnes says that the Western Buddha '*is mutilated; both legs having been fractured by cannon; and the countenance above the mouth is destroyed. [...] The hands [...] were both broken*'. BURNES 1834, p. 185. - Vincent Eyre 1843 describes the face of the Western Buddha as '*entirely destroyed*'. He also reports that the Eastern Buddha '*is greatly mutilated by cannon shot for which act of religious zeal credit is given to Nadir Shah*'. Godard explains the missing faces as a result of systematic mutilation. GODARD et al. 1928, p. 11 (Godard) and p. 88 (Eyre). – HACKIN 1939, p. 26, referring to the Eastern Buddha: '*Das Gesicht ist verstümmelt, die Hände fehlen ganz*' (englisch: The face is mutilated, the hands are missing entirely); p. 38,

regarding the Western Buddha: '*Das Gesicht ist eigenartig verstümmelt, vornehmlich Stirn, Augen, Wange, Nase*' (The face is mutilated in a strange way, especially the forehead, the eyes, the cheek, the nose).

44 SENGUPTA 1989, p. 205: '[…] *various theories were propounded as both of them have vertical cut from the forehead to the lower lip. Close observation, during the execution of restorations, revealed that the faces were modelled with wooden frames. A chase was cut in the depression of the rock behind the lower lip of each face, to receive the basal wooden beam on which were erected vertical posts for support of the horizontal stakes tied to them according to the required shape of the face. The other end of the horizontal stakes was made to rest on the rock for which rows of grooves in the vertical face are still visible. Pieces of charcoal and charred wood of the wooden frame of the face were recovered from the crevices where one could not reach without an elaborate scaffolding as was erected for the restoration work.*'

45 Dr. Dietger Grosser, Ludwig-Maximilians Universität München. The report was not available.

46 Analysis by Dr. Hans Georg Richter.

47 Prof. Dr. Tillich and Prof. Dr. D. Podlech, Ludwig-Maximilians Universität München, faculty of biology

48 Fragments GBL a, 506, 507, 612, 664, 708, 1139, 1368, 1447, 1773, 1832, 2458.

49 Z-twist, S-ply: GBL 662, 1 rope of GBL 708.

50 Information by Nasir Modabbir. According to Kabir, the plant can be found near the village of Schahidan in direction to Band-I-Amir. Fragment catalogue, GBL 283-288.

51 Analysis by Prof. Dr. Hans-Jürgen Tillich, faculty of biology, Ludwig-Maximilians University, Systematic Botany and Mycology, Munich.

52 Information by Prof. Tillich, also see: DIETERLE 1973, p. 13.

53 DIETERLE 1973, p.60.

54 Information by Prof. Tillich.

55 Analysis with transmitted light microscopy by C. Blänsdorf.

56 Analysis by Prof. Dr. Hans-Jürgen Tillich, faculty of biology, Ludwig-Maximilians University, Systematic Botany and Mycology, Munich, in December 2006.

57 According to photographs representatives of the species *Capra hircus*, *Ovis aries*, *Bos taurus*, and *Equus asinus*.

58 WRIGGINS 1966.

59 A comprehensive compilation of dating attempts since the early 20th century can be found in: Akira Miyaji, "The art-historical study on Bāmiyān and the radiocarbon dating", in: NATIONAL RESEARCH INSTITUTE FOR CULTURAL PROPERTIES JAPAN 2006, pp. 133. Although it focuses on the murals, information on the sculptures can be found here as well.

60 NATIONAL RESEARCH INSTITUTE FOR CULTURAL PROPERTIES 2006, p. 133 with reference to: HACKIN, JOSEPH: *L'Œuvre de la Délégation Archéologique Francaise en Afghanistan (1922-1933)*, Tokyo: Maison Franco-Japonaise, p. 19–57 : '*Hackin linked the ‚monastery built by a former king' mentioned in the Da Tang Xiyu Ji, to the Kushan King Kanishka. He was of the opinion that this monastery might have been built near the East Giant Buddha and concluded that the date for the beginning of the Bamiyan sites was around the second century A. D. He dated the East Giant Buddha which shows the influence of the Gandharan Buddhas in its weavy hair and the expression of the drapery to around the second and third century. In contrast, the West Giant Buddha, which has schematic, formalized drapery, he dated to around the third to fourth century, and he suggested that it might have influenced the Buddha images of Mathura in the Gupta period.*'

61 NATIONAL RESEARCH INSTITUTE FOR CULTURAL PROPERTIES 2006, p. 134: Itsuji Yoshikawa from the University of Tokyo made researches about Bamiyan in 1939.

62 '*Der Typ der römischen Toga, wie wir sie aus Bildnissen der Kaiserzeit kennen, ist hier in dem Mantel oder ‚sang-hati' des [kleinen] Buddha wiederzuerkennen. Nach dem noch streng klassischen Stil der Kleidung zu urteilen, könnte diese Statue etwa im 2. oder 3. Jh. entstanden sein […] oder daß wir es mit einem Beispiel für das Überleben oder Wiederaufleben des frühen Gandhara-Stils zu tun haben, wie wir es oft zwischen dem 4. und 8. Jh. in östlicher gelegenen Fundstellen Zentralasiens beobachten.*' - '*Die Statue selbst* [Großer Buddha] *ist stilistisch eine gigantische Vergrösserung der typisch indischen Buddha-Figuren aus der Gupta-Periode-Mathuras (ca. 320–600) […] eine Datierung zwischen dem 5. und 7. Jh. scheint für den gesamten Komplex des 53 Meter hohen Buddha angemessen.*'

63 NATIONAL RESEARCH INSTITUTE FOR CULTURAL PROPERTIES 2006, p. 136 with reference to: TARZI 1977.

64 NATIONAL RESEARCH INSTITUTE FOR CULTURAL PROPERTIES 2006, p. 137 with reference to: KUWAYAMA 1987.

65 NATIONAL RESEARCH INSTITUTE FOR CULTURAL PROPERTIES 2006, p. 137 with reference to: KLIMBURG-SALTER 1989.

66 NATIONAL RESEARCH INSTITUTE FOR CULTURAL PROPERTIES 2006, S. 138 with reference to: TANABE 2004.

67 NATIONAL RESEARCH INSTITUTE FOR CULTURAL PROPERTIES 2006. 43 samples of chaff and straw from the lower clay layer and one splinter of an anchoring beam for clay sculptures were taken for analysis. The samples come from the caves at Bamiyan, cave Nr. 43 and 44 in Kakrak (2 samples), cave no. 2, 4, 5 and 6 in Fuladi (6 samples), Da'uti caves (2 samples).

68 NATIONAL RESEARCH INSTITUTE FOR CULTURAL PROPERTIES JAPAN 2006, p. 121 and p. 147.

69 BEAL 1884, p. 50.

70 BARBIER DE MEYNARD 1861, p. 80: '*Cette ville est petite; mais elle est le cheflieu d'un territoire étendu. Dix jours de marche la séparent de Balkh, et huit de Ghaznah. On y voit un édifice dont le sommet est d'une élévation prodigieuse; il est soutenu par des piliers gigantesques et couvert de peintures représentant tous les oiseaux créés par Dieu. Dans l'intérieur sont deux idoles immenses creusées dans le roc et allant du pied de la montagne au sommet. L'une est appelée l'idole rouge, et l'autre, l'idole blanche. On ne peut rien voir de comparable à ces statues dans le monde entier.*'
Yakut or Yaqut ibn 'Abdallah ar-Rumi or Yakut al Hamawi, 1179–1229, was born in Greece and became a slave of an Arab merchant. The surname ar-rumi (the Roman) refers to his Greek parentage, the name al-Hamawi to his later hometown Hamah. From about 1212 to 1222 he travelled in Persia, Syria, Egypt, and Afghanistan. In 1221, he fled from the invasion of Genghis Khan's troops, settled in Mosul and started to write down a famous and extensive geographical dictionary. He spent his last two years in Aleppo. His dictionary *Mu'jam ul-Bulddn* includes all the places mentioned in Arab literature, listed in alphabetic order, reporting their geographical position, history, government, important monuments, and renowned citizens. A translation of the entries concerning the ancient Persian Empire

was published by Charles Barbier de Meynard in 1861.
71 Burnes reports an anecdote from the 'History of Timourlane by Sherif o deen' according to which the Buddha statues were so tall that no archer could strike their head (BURNES 1834, p. 188). This indicates that as early as in the 14th century (Tamerlane lived from 1336 to 1405) there were no edifices in front of the statues (anymore), because it is difficult to imagine that the archers aimed at their heads through an existing building, even if it was a half-open pavilion-like construction.
72 Sir Francis Wilford (1750 or 1760–1822) on the accounts of Me'yan Asod Shah, in: WILFORD 1801, pp. 464–466. If Me'yan Asod Shah really visited Bāmiyān ten or twelve times, he may have made these travels in the last two decades of the 18th century.
73 Another possibility to explain Me'yan Asod Shah's reference to 'embroidery' could be that he took the ridges of the folds and the partly exposed anchoring holes in the stone surfaces for remnants of decorations.
74 BURNES 1834, pp. 185–186. The description on p. 185 mainly deals with the Western Buddha: '*The figure is covered by a mantle, which hangs over it in all parts, and has been formed of a kind of plaster; the image having been studded with wooden pins in various places, to assist in fixing it*'. About the Eastern Buddha he only says that it is '*more perfect*' […] "*and has been dressed in the same way*'.
75 There are, for example, wrong details of the drapery, and a reduction of the real distance between the sculptures which, however, can be explained as an artistic trick to get both statues into one picture and still show them as very big.
76 Burnes reduced the design, just giving an idea of the paintings, but the text states clearly that he had recognised the figurative decoration: '*The niches of both have been at one time plastered, and ornamented with paintings of human figures, which have now disappeared from all parts but that immediately over the heads of the idols. Here the colours are vivid, and the paintings as distinct, as in the Egyptian tombs.*' BURNES 1834, p. 186.
77 Maitland, P. J.: *Additional note on Bāmiyān*, in TALBOT/SIMPSON 1886, p. 348, cited in GODARD ET AL. 1928, p. 93.
78 '*nous avons recueilli des fragments simulant les plis du manteau monastique encore munis de leur armature de cordes et de piquets et revêtus de la couche de peinture rouge qui couvrait primitivement le manteau tout entier.*' HACKIN/CARL 1933, p. 15. Fig. 23 shows J. Carl standing on the Western Buddha's right forearm; fig. 24 is a detail of the folds of the *sangati* (black and white).
79 HACKIN 1939, p. 26.
80 SENGUPTA 1984, p. 41.
81 For example the names are mentioned in the texts by two Iranian travellers, Mohamad b. Ahmad al Biruni (died 1048) and Khwaja Abdallah Ansari (died 1089). MELZL/PETZET 2007, p. 69.
82 The undercoat of the Eastern Buddha is slightly more greyish than the one of the Western Buddha which appears more yellowish ochre.
83 MOMII/SEKI 2006, p. 94: A yellowish transparent organic layer was observed on the murals.
84 White and brownish pink spots: for example on samples ID 38, 53 and 74; ochre spots on ID 46.
85 Consolidant on the surface: for example sample ID 118, 135 or 54 (partially). Fibres sticking to the consolidant: ID 77.

86 Eastern Buddha: No surface: 200, 278, completion: ID 224. No or only traces of paint layer: ID 177, 182 (traces of red), 191 (traces of red), 225, 240, 258. Samples ID 177. Western Buddha: No surface: Samples ID 27, 44, 88, 151, 160; no paint layer: 1, 86 (yellow clay layer); not fitting into the group scheme: 71 (covered by clay slurry), 82 (traces of red); 136 (traces of white?), 174 (red); 63; sample ID 84, 159 filling materials from 1969-78.
87 Fragments blackened by soot: Western Buddha, group 1: ID 81, group 2: ID 63, 122, 131, 136; group 5, ID 103; soot with brown coating: ID 122 and 131.
88 Sample ID 239 and 241.
89 Sample present in Munich: Sample ID 180.
90 PLM: Catharina Blänsdorf, Maximilian Knidlberger, Stephanie Pfeffer, Technische Universität München, Chair of Restoration.
91 Visible for example on samples ID 47, 58, 59, 102 and 112.
92 RAPP 2009, p.2: Analysis of sample ID 166.
93 XRD of fragments ID 165 and ID 166.
94 RIEDERER 1977, p. 369.
95 ZOU ET AL. 1997, pp. 362–368.
96 GETTENS 1937/38, p. 189.
97 RAPP 2009, p.2.
98 Micro XRF with vacuum: Sonngard Hartmann, Roman Germanic Central Museum, Mainz.
99 TANIGUCHI/OTAKE 2008, p. 398, description of the *Laternendecken* with oily bound paint layers.
100 TANIGUCHI/OTAKE 2008, pp. 397–404: oily layers, white: lead white; green: lead white, chrysocolla (?).
101 This result is reported only in: KOSSOLAPOV/KALININA, 2006, p. 90.
102 Some analyses of sculptures from Dunhuang have been performed, but the results are available only in Chinese.
103 BOLLATI 2008, p. 196.
104 For Penjikent and Afrasiab see: KOSSOLAPOV/KALININA 2006, p. 90. Analyses by Kossolapov, A./Viazmenskia, L, in: KOSSOLAPOV/MARSHAK 1999; ABDURAZAKOV/KAMBAROV 1975. Translation and summary of results by Anna Rommel, Technische Universität München, Chair of Restoration, 2008.
105 KOSSOLAPOV/KALININA 2006, p. 90.
106 RIEDERER 1977, vol. 4, p. 353–423, identification of 17 different pigments in murals from Xinjiang ('Eastern Turkistan'), namely Kizil and Kumtura, survey in table on p. 386.
107 The antique oasis of Miran is located on the Southern Route of the Silk Road between Qarqan and Dunhuang in the Autonomous Region of Xinjiang. The paintings evidently show a strong 'Western' influence, characterised by Kakoulli as 'Greco-Buddhism with Asiatic influences'. KAKOULLI 2006, p. 82.
108 WANG/FU 2006, p. 114: compilation of pigment analyses of wall paintings from *c.* 430 to 780.
109 The wall paintings in the Tiantishan grottoes in Liangzhou in Gansu Province date from the Northern Wei to the Ming Dynasty. Examination of paint layers from the Northern Liang (397–439) to the Tang Dynasty (618–906): ZHOU ET AL. 1997, pp. 362–368.
110 KOSSOLAPOV/KALININA 2006, p. 90.
111 SHARMA 2006, p. 102.
112 Interpretation in: GUNASINGHE 1957.
113 KAKOULLI 2006, p. 82.
114 GUNASINGHE 1957, p. 15. Though he writes about quicklime, he

also refers to binders. Smoothing or burnishing of the surface is also mentioned.

115 GETTENS 1937/1938, pp. 186–193. – MOMII/SEKI 2006, p. 94.
116 Kumtura and Kizil: RIEDERER 1977. – Afrasiab: ABDURAZAKOV/ KAMBAROV 1975. Translation and summary of results by Anna Rommel, Technische Universität München, Chair of Restoration, 2008.
117 Miran: KAKOULLI 2006, p. 82. – Mogao: WANG/FU 2006, p. 117.
118 Underpaintings: GUNASINGHE 1957, pp. 57–60. Ajanta is located in the north-eastern part of the Indian state of Maharashtra, 100 km north of the city of Aurangabad. – Black and red contour lines: SHARMA 2006, p. 102.
119 Analyses for white: Afrasiab: gypsum, kaolin; Penjikent: calcite, gypsum; Sharistan: gypsum; Kucha: gypsum, calcite (KOSSOLAPOV/KALININA 2006). Kumtura, Kizil: Gypsum (dihydrate), anhydrite (RIEDERER 1977). Tiantishan: gypsum, anhydrite, chalk and kaolin (ZHOU ET AL. 1997), Mogao: chalk, kaolin, talc, gypsum mica (WANG/FU. 2006), Ajanta: lime/gypsum/kaolin (SHARMA 2006), Indian manuscripts (GUNASINGHE 1957, p. 43).
120 Lead white was found in the Bāmiyān caves, Afrasiab, Kucha, Kizil and Kumtura, and the Mogao grottoes.
121 ZHOU ET AL. 1997, pp. 362–368.
122 Orange and Red: Nisa, bright red: cinnabar, brownish red: red ochre, also mixed with kaolin for pale pink (BOLLATI). Afrasiab: red ochre; vermillion (ABDURAZAKOV/KAMBAROV 1975). Penjikent, red: ochre, orange: red ochre; Sharistan, red: ochre; Kakrak, orange: minium; Kucha: vermilion, minium (KOSSOLAPOV/KALININA 2006, p. 90). Kizil/Kumtura: minium, cinnabar, red ochre (RIEDERER 1977). Miran: iron oxides (?; KAKOULLI 2006), Mogao: vermilion, red ochre, minium (WANG/FU. 2006). Tiantishan: cinnabar, on Tang sculptures (?) also minium and cinnabar (ZHOU ET AL. 1997); Ajanta: red ochre (SHARMA 2006); *Visnudharmottara*: GUNASINGHE 1957, p. 45.
123 Yellow: Nisa: yellow ochre (BOLLATI); Penjikent: litharge, orpiment; Afrasiab: orpiment; Sharistan: litharge; Kucha: orpiment (KOSSOLAPOV/KALININA 2006, p. 90). Kumtura, Kizil: yellow ochre, orpiment (minimally used), massicot (RIEDERER 1977, p. 386). Miran: impure yellow and brown earths (KAKOULLI 2006, p. 83). Mogao: realgar (WANG/FU 2006). Tiantishan: very few yellow (ZHOU ET AL. 1997). Ajanta: yellow ochres (SHARMA 2006). Indian manuscripts: GUNASINGHE 1957, p. 44 (*Visnudharmottara*, pp. 48–49).
124 Brown: Penjikent magnetite, red; Sharistan: ochre brown; Kakrak: minium + laureonite ochre (KOSSOLAPOV/KALININA 2006, p. 90.
125 Blue: Nisa: Egyptian blue and ultramarine (BOLLATI). Afrasiab: ultramarine (ABDURAZAKOV/KAMBAROV 1975; KOSSOLAPOV/KALININA 2006, p. 90). Penjikent: ultramarine; Kakrak: ultramarine; Sharistan: ultramarine; Kucha: ultramarine (KOSSOLAPOV/KALININA 2006, p. 90). Kumtura, Kizil: ultramarine, azurite, indigo (RIEDERER 1977, p. 386). Mogao: azurite, ultramarine (Wang et al. 2006). Tiantishan: azurite (ZHOU ET AL. 1997). Ajanta: ultramarine (SHARMA 2006). Indian manuscripts: GUNASINGHE 1957, pp. 47–48 (description does not clearly indicate which pigments are mentioned in the *Visnudharmottara*).
126 Next to ultramarine in Bāmiyān caves: MOMII / SEKI 2006, p. 93–100.
127 Green: Nisa (BOLLATI 2006); Penjikent: no green; Sharistan: malachite, black: tenorite; Kakrak: paratacamite; Kucha: atacamite (KOSSOLAPOV/KALININA 2006, p. 90). Kumtura and Kizil: chrysocolla (RIEDERER 1977). Miran: malachite (KAKOULLI 2006). Mogao: malachite, verdigris (WANG/FU 2006). Tiantishan: malachite, in Tang dynasty paint layers: atacamite and paratacamite (ZHOU ET AL. 1997).
128 Ajanta: SHARMA 2006.
129 Afrasiab/Penjikent: natural orpiment with indigo. Indian manuscripts: GUNASINGHE 1957, pp. 45–46.
130 Black: Nisa: charcoal (BOLLATI); Kakrak: burnt bone; Kucha: burnt bone, gypsum, (KOSSOLAPOV/KALININA 2006, p. 90). Kumtura, Kizil: soot, carbon black (RIEDERER 1977, p. 386). Miran: carbon black, from Chinese ink (KAKOULLI 2006). Tiantishan: soot (ZHOU ET AL. 1997). Ajanta: lamp black (SHARMA 2006).
131 Nisa (BOLLATI 2006).
132 Dunhuang: Analysis by Xia Yin, C. Blänsdorf with PLM 2005. An early investigation resulting in madder: Gray, B.: *Buddhist Cave Paintings at Tun-Huang*, London 1952, cited in: RIEDERER 1977, p. 358. Analyses of red lakes in Bāmiyān caves and Kizil: personal information by Yoko Taniguchi.
133 Kumtura and Kizil: RIEDERER 1977, p. 385.
134 GUNASINGHE 1957, pp. 53–54.
135 ZHOU ET AL. 1997, pp. 364–365.
136 TANIGUCHI ET AL. 2007, pp. 181–188.
137 Laboratory for Chemical Science for the Safeguard of the Cultural Heritage, Department of Chemistry and Industrial Chemistry, University of Pisa, Via Risorgimento 35, 56126, Pisa. Italy, e-mail: ilariab@dcci.unipi.it.
138 Mills, J. S., White, R.: *The Organic Chemistry of Museum Objects*, Butterworth Heinemann, 1994.
139 *Scientific Examination for the Investigation of Paintings. A Handbook for Conservator-restorers*; Pinna, D.; Galeotti, M.; Mazzeo, R., Eds.; Centro Di della Edifimi srl: Firenze 2009.
140 *Organic Mass Spectrometry in Art and Archaeology*, Colombini, M.P.; Modugno; F., Eds.; John Wiley & Sons, in press, 2009.
141 Andreotti, A.; Bonaduce, I.; Colombini, M.P.; Modugno, F.; Ribechini, E.: *Organic paint materials and their characterization by GC-MS analytical procedures*. In *New Trends in Analytical, Environmental and Cultural Heritage Chemistry*; Tassi, L.; Colombini, M.P. Transworld Research Network: Kerala, 2008, Chapter 15.
142 Colombini, M.P.; Andreotti, A.; Bonaduce, I.; Modugno, F.; Ribechini, E. *Analytical strategies for characterising organic paint media using GC-MS, submitted for publication*.
143 Bonaduce, I.; Cito, M.; Colombini, M.P. *The development of a GC-MS analytical procedure for the determination of lipids, proteins and resins in the same paint micro-sample avoiding interferences from inorganic media*, Journal of Chromatography A, 1216 (2009) 5931–5939.
144 Bonaduce, I.; Breculaki, H.; Colombini, M.P.; Lluveras, A.; Restivo, V.; Ribechini, E., *Gas Chromatographic-Mass Spectrometric Characterisation of Plant Gums in Samples from Painted works of Art*, Journal of Chromatography A 1157 (2007) 275–282.

MONUMENTS AND SITES/MONUMENTS ET SITES/MONUMENTOS Y SITIOS

Published so far/publiés jusqu'à present/publicados hasta el momento: Australia, Bolivia, Bulgaria, Canada, Cuba, Cyprus, Czech Republic, Dominican Republic, Egypt, Hungary, India, Israel, Jamaica, Japan, Russia, Sri Lanka, South Africa, Zimbabwe (18 vols.), Colombo 1996 (out of print/épuisés / agotados)

Monumentos y Sitios de Chile, Santiago de Chile 1999
Monuments and Sites: Finland, Helsinki 1999
Monuments and Sites: Indonesia, West Java 1999

NEW SERIES/NOUVELLE SÉRIE/NUEVA SERIE:

I	International Charters for Conservation and Restoration/Chartes Internationales sur la Conservation et la Restauration/Cartas Internacionales sobre la Conservación y la Restauración, Munich 2001, second edition Munich 2004
II	Catharina Blänsdorf/Erwin Emmerling/Michael Petzet (eds.), The Terracotta Army of the First Chinese Emperor Qin Shihuang, Munich 2001
III	Wu Yongqi/Zhang Tinghao/Michael Petzet/Erwin Emmerling/Catharina Blänsdorf (eds.), The Polychromy of Antique Sculptures and the Terracotta Army of the First Chinese Emperor, Munich 2001
IV	Dirk Bühler, Puebla – Patrimonio de Arquitectura Civil del Virreinato, Munich 2001
V	ICOMOS-CIAV, Vernacular Architecture/Architecture Vernaculaire/Arquitectura Vernácula, Munich 2002
VI	Helmut Becker/Jörg W. E. Fassbinder, Magnetic Prospecting in Archaeological Sites, Munich 2001
VII	Manfred Schuller, Building Archaeology, Munich 2002
VIII	Susan Barr/Paul Chaplin (eds.), Cultural Heritage in the Arctic and the Antarctic Regions, Lørenskog 2004
IX	La Representatividad en la Lista del Patrimonio Mundial – El Patrimonio Cultural y Natural de Iberoamérica, Canadá y Estados Unidos, Santiago de Querétaro 2004
X	ICOMOS-CIIC, Encuentro Científico Internacional sobre Itinerarios Culturales, Ferrol 2005
XI	The Venice Charter/La Charte de Venise 1964 – 2004 – 2044?, Budapest 2005
XII	The World Heritage List: Filling the Gaps – an Action Plan for the Future / La Liste du Patrimoine Mondial: Combler les lacunes – un plan d'action pour le futur, compiled by Jukka Jokilehto, with contributions from Henry Cleere, Susan Denyer and Michael Petzet, Munich 2005
XIII	Francisco J. López Morales (ed.), Nuevas Miradas sobre la Autenticidad e Integridad en el Patrimonio Mundial de las Américas/New Views on Authenticity and Integrity in the World Heritage of the Americas, San Miguel de Allende 2005
XIV	Encuentro Científico Internacional sobre Ciudades Históricas Iberoamericanas, Cuenca 2005
XV	ICOMOS-ISCS, Illustrated Glossary on Stone Deterioration Patterns/Glossaire illustré sur les formes d'altération de la pierre, compiled by Véronique Vergès-Belmin, with contributions from Tamara Anson Cartwright, Elsa Bourguignon, Philippe Bromblet et al., Paris 2008
XVI	The World Heritage List: What is OUV? Defining the Outstanding Universal Value of Cultural World Heritage Properties, compiled by Jukka Jokilehto, with contributions from Christina Cameron, Michel Parent and Michael Petzet, Berlin 2008
XVII	Susan Barr/Paul Chaplin (eds.), Historical Polar Bases – Preservation and Management, Lørenskog 2008
XVIII	Gudrun Wolfschmidt (ed.), Cultural Heritage of Astronomical Observatories – From Classical Astronomy to Modern Astrophysics, Berlin 2009
XIX	Michael Petzet (ed.), The Giant Buddhas of Bamiyan – Safeguarding the Remains, Berlin 2009
XX	Michael Petzet, International Principles of Preservation, Berlin 2009